Ma, it's a cold aul night an i'm lookin for a bed

Ma, it's a cold aul night an i'm lookin for a bed

Martha Long

SEVEN STORIES PRESS

NEW YORK

First published in 2009 Great Britain by Mainstream Publishing Company, Edinburgh

First Seven Stories Press paperback edition January 2017.

This book is a work of non-fiction based on the life, experiences and recollections of the author. In some cases, names of people, places, dates, sequences or the details of events have been changed to protect the privacy of others. The author has stated to the publishers that, except in such respects, not affecting the substantial accuracy of the work, the contents of this book are true.

Seven Stories Press
140 Watts Street
New York, NY 10013
www.sevenstories.com

College professors may order examination copies of Seven Stories Press titles for free. To order, visit http://www.sevenstories.com/textbook or send a fax on school letterhead to (212) 226-1411.

Library of Congress Cataloging-in-Publication Data

Long, Martha (Irish Author)
 Ma, it's a cold aul night an I'm looking for a bed / Martha Long. -- First Seven Stories Press edition.
      page cm
 "First published in Great Britain in 2009 by Mainstream Publishing Company, Edinburgh"--Title page verso.
 ISBN 978-1-60980-598-2 (hardback)
 ISBN 978-1-60980-696-5 (paperback)
 1. Long, Martha (Irish author)--Childhood and youth. 2. Poor teenagers--Ireland--Dublin--Bi-ography. 3. Teenage girls--Ireland--Dublin--Biography. 4. Homeless Youth--Ireland--Dublin--Bi-ography. 5. Dublin (Ireland)--Social conditions--20th century. 6. Dublin (Ireland)--Biography. I. Title. II. Title: Ma, it's a cold old night and I'm looking for a bed
 DA995.D8L665 2015
 941.8'350823092--dc23
 [B]

                                                    2014038385

Printed in the United States

9 8 7 6 5 4 3 2 1

To my life's blood, my children. Family is all that matters.

To my readers. I do it now for you . . . (certainly not for the money!
It wouldn't pay my bus fare into town!! Sniff!)

Especially for those of you who have carried a lifetime of pain.

Walk with me through the days of my life. These are the early days.
It did get worse. There were many times when life was too terrifying
to live . . . and too terrifying to die.

But here I am, telling you all about it. Who would have thought
I would open my mouth and let go of all the secrets I had kept
hidden. Right into my middle years.

I want you to know you are not alone.
Take comfort, it does get better.

People are all the same under the fur coats and the Gucci sunglasses.
They have just managed to find an expensive way of hiding
the same kind of pain you and I carry!

This is my way of dealing with it. Sharing it with you.

To Bill, my long suffering publisher. (I have his heart broken!)
Ahh! Where would I be without you, Bill? You're one in a million!

To Aidan Roddy (Blackrock). A gentleman and a scholar.
A busy man who will share his precious time with me. Just to stand
and stare. Share a joke, exchange a tale, letting the march of time
float on. That short time of laughter and ease makes the shackles
of duty in a busy life all the lighter. Thanks, Aidan.

To Viv, a very brilliant and lovely girl. A great gift to us all,
and a credit to your mammy.

To Caoimhe and David, two of the nicest people who ever walked God's earth. (In spite of my daftness!) You saved my life. Was I not the lucky one, to have two rare special people like you around when I nearly copped it! Truly, I won't forget your kindness. Especially for looking after the children. May all your dreams for both of you come true. Thank you for caring.

To my two dear friends, with whom I am lucky to have met through the book, Susan and her gorgeous daughter, little princess Shayléigh, for indeed she is one. Thank you, Shayléigh, for your lovely present. It is very precious to me. It is also a constant reminder of a wonderful little girl.

IN MEMORY

To the forgotten children who suffered in a harsh uncaring world.

To all the men, women and children, some gone to their rest, others, tragically, went before their time.

As tender little children, you did not gaze into the warmth of a loving pair of eyes. There were no loving arms to wrap you, and drive away your fears.

For some of you, your destiny was the harshness of a cold walled prison, manned by cold hard people, crippled by their lack of warmth.

They were ideally placed, to deal with the unwanted sins, the bastards, the poor, in a hypocritical world paying lip service to a God-less Church who wielded a mighty and frightening power.

Leaving the horror and loneliness of an institution did not free you. The mark of pain and rejection was written all over your face. The world recognised you. You were nobody's child. Therefore, easy prey for those who wished to eat you alive.

It was too much. Some of you, I remember, ended it all with a watery grave. Others endured, until it ended in a laneway, being found as a bundle of rags, lying next to the rubbish bins. You were overcome by cold, hunger, and the ravages of alcohol. There was nobody to claim you.

As in life, now you lie in death, in a unmarked grave. Just, nobody! You lost even your name. Your suffering was in vain.

Thomas! Maryann! John! Alfred! I remember you!

You will always be alive in me. My story is your story.
I speak for you all.

May you now rest in peace.

I

I woke from my doze glancing out the window as the car slowed
down. Ah great! Dublin. I looked back behind me, seeing the
huge wall of the Phoenix Park and the narrow roads, ditches and
fields of the countryside fading into the distance as we hit the city.
Lovely! Dirty Aul Dublin. Where I left my heart. Now I can feel
home again. Ye can keep the country for the culchies. Gawd, even
the memory of being locked up down there makes me feel sick. I
shivered, just thinking about that home for little children. No! If
that's what nursing is all about, it is definitely not for me.

I hoisted meself up in the front seat and looked out the window,
seeing the sight of Euston Station as we flew past in the car.
That's where the country people take the train home. I looked
over at Miss Boddington. 'Eh, I think you can let me out here,
Miss, I can take the bus back to the convent' Thinking I have
no intention of going back there! I've had enough of being locked
up and want me bleedin freedom.

'Good gracious, no!' she said. Flicking her head with the mass of
lovely brown bouncy hair swinging around her neck, and landing
in a wave, sitting back to nestle on her shoulders. I looked at her
with the lovely pink powdered face and the light-pink lipstick on
her lips, with the little bit of blue eyeshadow setting off her lovely
grey eyes. I could smell her perfume and stared in admiration as
her legs pumped away at the pedals on the floor of the car, and
her lovely tweed skirt sat just above her knees showing off her
lovely legs. Gawd! I wished I was her with the lovely hair and
the lovely clothes and the lovely cream car with the cream leather

seats. It looks a bit like a sports car. I breathed in a sigh, smelling her delicious perfume. Gawd! What wouldn't I do to be meself in her clobber driving her car and I actually own it! Yeah! I will one day, and I'm making no mistake about that!

'Until we hand you over,' she said, slamming down the pedal and raising her knees, flicking her eye at the truck with the load of cattle screaming in the back with the canvas cover on top to keep the rain off the cows. They looked through the wooden bars at us with their tongues hanging out, screaming and moaning. Reminding me of babies when they are trying to have a good cry, but not managing to squeeze out many tears. 'You are still our responsibility!' I heard her say, tuning in to what she was talking about. 'You are only a young girl of sixteen!'

'But, Miss! I am my own person! I'm left the convent. It was me who wrote to you in the home to do the children's nursing. That was my idea! The nuns had nothing to do with it. If I hadn't gone to you, I would be out in the world by myself with nobody having any responsibility for me! I'd be working and on me own,' I said. Trying to talk her around to letting me out of the car.

'No! No, dear,' she said, waving her head. 'I must hand you back. It is up to the nuns then. Someone must take responsibility for you.'

Ah, fuck! She's a Protesdant. The Catholics don't work the same way. No one is responsible for me. The nuns get rid of you when they stop getting the money from the state when you reach sixteen, unless you are still going to school.

Sister Eleanor will kill me! I lasted no end of time in that home for the little children. Stuck out in the arsehole of nowhere, and living in a big old dark mansion with loads of girls who crept around like nuns, no life in them at all. It must be something to do with them all being Protestant. They are very different from the young ones in the convent. Quieter, and more respectable. Then there was all that getting up at five in the morning and looking after poor little sick children that looked like they were on death's door, and nothing for them but bed sleep eat get washed, sick vomit diarrhoea, and they all looked so pale and sickly. There was nothing there for them or us the students. Just more bloody slave labour! And you even had to learn to sew the children's clothes! Because that's what you have to do when you are a nurse or a governess, or whatever kind of job you get. I can't sew! I hate it!

Then it was after three years of being stuck there, sitting exams and then going to the children's hospital for another year and a half! Sure I would never be able for the exams. I never went to school! How would I be able for exams? You have to start in the babies' class like everyone else if you want to start sitting exams at the end of your school days. That is no good for me. You can't go back to school in this life. The system is, you start school and learning as a baby, and work your way through the classes, that's it. So I have to find another way to make me mark in this life. Anyway, I will educate meself with books.

I blinked, coming out of my doze, and looked, seeing we were flying through the village near the convent. I burst out laughing suddenly, at the thought of seeing the look on Sister Eleanor's face when she sees me back already. How long was I gone? Not long!

'Are you all right?' Miss said, giving me a queer look. My face went bright red letting her see me laughing out loud to meself. She'll think I'm a bit queer laughing at nothing.

'Eh, I was just thinking of something funny,' I said, not thinking that any more as the car turned in the gates and headed up the avenue, landing me back in the convent. Jaysus! What will I say? She's going to kill me! Ah, maybe she will be delighted to see me. I missed her! Then I laughed again. No, she wants to get rid of us. Not have us trailing after her for ever! Oh, Jaysus! I'm really for it.

'Come along, dear, take your suitcase,' Miss said, holding open the boot of her car and waiting for me to make a move. I lifted the suitcase and stood waiting while she slammed the boot down and bounced up the steps to ring the doorbell. I trailed up, not in any hurry to face being back here. The door opened and Natalie Fleming from the middle group stood staring at me while I took her in. Jaysus! She has my job now, and she's wearing my working smock! Gawd! She must be fourteen and left school.

'Hello, Natalie,' I said, moving in and pushing her out of the way with me suitcase. I was feeling a bit jealous, thinking she has my job now, and it didn't take the nuns long to replace me. She stopped staring at me, after taking in the style of me from head to toe, and blinked, looking up at Miss, then lifted her jaw off the ground and clamped her mouth shut to get on with her business.

'I will go and get Sister fur you,' she said, trying to make herself sound grand. Then whipped off, making my smock twirl around her, because it was fitted around the waist and flared out. I was raging! She picked up the little gong and went off looking very important with herself, and started banging it, before she even hit the institution. Ma Pius will kill her! Serves her right! The little upstart, thinking she could do my job. She didn't even invite us to go into the parlour. Just left us standing here in the bloody entrance hall. She probably forgot how to treat the visitors because I was here and I'm only one of them. Fucking eejit! I hope Ma Pius comes along and sees us stuck here. She will eat the head off that young one and then realise she won't get anyone as good as me!

I was feeling a bit lonely and like I didn't belong here any more. Even though I know I don't belong. I'm supposed to be left. But I would love to stay for just a little while and be part of things again. Have Sister Eleanor fussing and shouting at me, but knowing she has to put up with me because I live here. Now I don't know what's going to happen, or where I am going to go. I had it all worked out. Do the children's nursing and get a good job travelling as a children's nurse with a very rich family. Or work in a hospital. But that was only a dream. I would never pass them exams. But I might have made it to the rich family as a nanny! Jaysus! Now I belong nowhere or to no one! Sister Eleanor doesn't have to bother about me any more.

'Ah, Miss Boddington!' Sister Eleanor said, rushing in the door all smiles and gums and bowing to the Miss then smiling at me.

'I will leave you, Martha,' Miss said, taking her eyes off Sister and smiling at me. 'Good luck for the future,' she said, then smiled at Sister.

'Thank you ever so much,' Sister said, smiling and bowing, taking my arm, saying, 'You wait in there, Martha.' She nodded to the parlour. My heart gladdened at the sight of Sister Eleanor, I had been a bit lost without her, and not knowing anyone and hating the food and the strange place.

Natalie stood at the gong hanging it up, and keeping her eye on what was going on, and giving me a suspicious look, like she might lose her job because I was back.

The door slammed shut and Sister came flying in roaring. 'Martha Long. What is the meaning of this? Why did you leave the home?' She bent herself in two, with that crucified look on her face, not one bit pleased to see me. I felt a thump in my chest and a pain flit across me, then I started to go cold. 'You are not coming back here!' she snorted, warning me, shaking her head and waving her finger, looking like mustard and mortal sin. I felt me heart sinking with the pain of her not wanting me and felt a hardness hit me.

'I didn't ask to come back!' I shouted. Picking up me suitcase and making for the door. Feeling foolish and stupid because me heart was breaking and I wasn't wanted any more.

'Wait! I have a job for you. A call came in two days ago, and when the home rang here yesterday to say they were bringing you back, I telephoned the family to say I would be sending you.'

'What is it?' I asked, dropping me suitcase, feeling happy at knowing where I was going and having somewhere to go.

'It's only for five weeks. They don't want you to do much, Martha. It is a young couple with two little boys and the mammy has just had a new baby girl. They will be flying to Brazil for three weeks. So you will be helping her mother to take care of the children. Meanwhile, it is lucky for you. Because they want you to start straight away and settle in before they go away in two weeks. So! After that, you can arrange to get yourself fixed up in a new more permanent job. In the meantime, it will give you the time to organise yourself, Martha!' Sister Eleanor said, bending down to me, her voice softening.

'All right, Sister,' I said, happy she wasn't looking at me like I was a nuisance and delighted to get a job. 'When do I start?'

'Oh, right away,' she laughed. 'I already telephoned the lady to say you were on your way. So hurry! Here is the address. You take the bus from the Quays. It is out towards Howth. You get the bus . . . Here! Everything is written down on that,' she said, handing me a piece of paper. 'Goodbye now!' she said, rushing to open the front door for me. I picked up the suitcase and smiled at her, seeing her eyes flit on me then empty. The life in her draining out through her face, letting her mind fill up with nothing but worry. Fretting and thinking of all she had to do as she headed me out the door and down the steps.

I looked back to wave, but she was already gone with the door slammed shut. I got a feeling of being empty hitting me again. But then I lifted. OK, at least she's happy with me. She was nice to me! I can always ring her to say hello. Yeah! I'm not really on me own. I stopped and took the address out of my pocket and checked it. Right! Here we go! I picked up the suitcase and headed off down the avenue for the second time. This time it's for good. She would have my guts for garters if I showed up here again. I rushed off to take the bus into the city centre, dying to get into town and see what's happening.

2

I sat staring out the window as the bus heaved and bullied its way through the traffic, then groaned to a stop as we made our way up Dame Street. We crawled along behind a row of bicycles, and the driver sat on his horn, wanting them to give him a gap in the traffic and let him get on with trying to cross over the Liffey. Only the bigwigs live on this side. The real Dubliners live on the other side, north of the Liffey.

I enjoyed myself no end, looking out at the latest fashions all the people were wearing. I stared at a girl wearing a Chinese-looking pin-stripe frock with the stand-up collar and the zip up the front and the hem ending just below her arse, hugging the young one's fat, wobbly thighs. It was a lot shorter than my frock. Gawd! That's very daring. I stared at her rushing along through the crowds, watching her hem swing around her arse, waiting to see if you could see her knickers. Jaysus, yeah! I got a glimpse of white cotton knickers. Gawd! I definitely wouldn't wear mine that length, and end up making a show of meself, letting everyone see the colour of me knickers. Still, she looks lovely. Pity about the legs, they look like tree trunks.

I admired her page-boy hairstyle, cut short like a little elf, making her look like a boy. I wonder if I should get me hair cut like that? No! Definitely not. It took me long enough to get it to shoulder length, I was bald long enough.

Then me eyes peeled over to the two young ones standing at the bus stop on the other side of the road. Gawd! The state of her. Me eyes were on stalks staring over. One of them was a lovely blonde with a page-boy hairstyle, but she was wearing a flared pink-dotted white frock right up to her arse, and she was so pregnant she looked like she was about to have it any minute. All the cars were slowing down and honking their horns at her, and she lifted her chin and looked away like she was Lady Muck. Then she said something to the other one with a big mop of red frizzy hair that stood up like she got an electric shock, and huge goggle eyes staring out through milk-bottle glasses. The two of them turned their backs and stared in at the shop window. Totally ignoring the people staring and the aul fellas going mad whistling and honking and waving out the windows of the cars. She's definitely not Irish, she's probably American and most certainly not married. And she stands there in broad daylight showing what she had for her dinner. Jaysus! She's showing everything she's got.

I stared like mad as the bus moved slowly through the traffic. Yeah! Definitely foreign, yeh can tell by the expensive look of her. She's well fed and has lovely brown legs. I wonder how she came to get herself in that state? And she doesn't seem to care! That's judging by the way she's carrying on. Gawd! Imagine going out looking like her in that condition. She sure has a nerve, that one. I could read her lips when she said something to the friend. It looked to me like she said, laughing at the same time, 'Come! Let us turn our back, they are so rude.' What I can't understand is, what did she expect, looking like that in a short baby-doll dress? It's very peculiar, but still, I wouldn't mind being a bit like her, without the pregnant bit.

Hmm! I wonder about that, foreigners are so different. They're better dressed and more easy-going than us. Not tight-faced and haggard-looking, like the rest of the people. All rushing home to get things done, and worrying their life away. I wonder how the foreigners manage that. They seem to know more then we do about what's happening in the world. Yeah! They're more educated than us as well. What I can't understand is, we send missionaries to Africa, and send them good money as well. But then they come here and go to the College of Surgeons and learn to be doctors! When they are supposed to be poor! That means we are supposed to be rich! When, as a matter of fact, most people haven't got two half-pennies to rub together, and a lot of people here can't even read and write. I just can't work that one out at all.

The bus fought inch by inch through the traffic then spotted a gap and the engine roared, while he tried to climb up the little hump on the bridge over the Liffey and get the speed. But it was all noise and puffs of blue smoke and the tearing of gears, while the engine screamed and we still crept along like an aul nun of ninety out on a mission.

The bus gasped, puffing its way over the bridge, then picked up speed as we went down the little hill, swerving madly to avoid an aul fella pulling across in front of us on his bicycle, nearly landing the lot of us in the Liffey – and I can't even swim. Then nearly hitting a pony, coming up on the inside. The pony was doing grand up until then. Happily rushing home, dragging the empty coal cart behind him, and minding his own business with nothing on his mind but the bag of oats waiting for him back at the stables, and probably dying to get snuggled down into the lovely bit of nice warm, dry hay after a long aul hard day's work. The coal man rocked on his feet, nearly losing his balance while he tried to steady his left leg dangling in the air and threw his balance, getting him standing again, and pulled tight on the reins, holding them high in the air with his hands together and the whip held grasped in his right hand. The horse danced to the right, showing the whites of his eyes and his ears pinned back, snorting air out through his nostrils, sending a fine spray of water and steam billowing around his head. 'Whoa, there! Easy now!' The horse steadied, still stamping his hoofs, rolling his eyes at the bus and wondering if the danger was over or should he make a run for it. 'Easy, easy!' shouted the coal man, pulling tighter and higher on the reins. All the time keeping his eye on the horse and getting ready to give a mouthful of curses. The horse gave one final dance and settled to a slow trot.

'Yeh blind fuckin bastard!' roared the coal man, giving all his attention to the bus driver. 'Yeh shouldn't be left in charge of a babby's pram. Never mind a fuckin bus!'

The driver whipped open his little window. 'Who're you callin a blind bastard? You! Yeh fuckin eejit! Yeh eejit!'

'Yeh nearly landed me and the horse inta the next world!'

'It wasn't my doin! It was tha thick bastard there on the other side a ya! Him there on the fuckin High Nelly!'

'I'll give him High Nelly!' roared the coal man, whipping the cap off his head showing a snow-white forehead, while the rest of his face was black as the ace of spades. He slapped the cap back on his head and slid it over his forehead, pulling it tight around his head, then set his sights on the aul fella pedalling away like he hadn't a care in the world as he turned right down Eden Quays, making straight out in front of a bread van, forcing the driver to sit on his brakes and nearly swerve into two cyclists pedalling side by side. The coal man whipped up the horse, making to go after the cyclist, screaming, 'Yeh whore's fuckin melt! The curse a Jaysus on yeh, yeh four-eyed fucker! I'll do time for you if I get me hands on yeh!'

The bus driver blasted his horn and waved at the aul fella, who kept pedalling away down the middle of the road with not a bother on him. No bus or bread van was going to get in his way, as he headed himself off down the quay leaving a lot of aul fellas cursing him to hell.

'Jesus Christ almighty! Did yeh see tha? And did yeh ever hear the like a the language outa them!' roared an aul one sitting in front of me, as I sat with me back to the driver, sitting on the long seat where I could see everything going on, making sure I'd miss nothing. 'Did yeh?' she roared at me, leaning over and tapping me knee.

'No, never,' I said, whipping me head back from the coal man and looking at her! 'An not one a them has even had a drop a drink on them! No, cold sober,' I said, looking very shocked, keeping the roars of laughing inside meself.

'Ah, Jaysus. Tha was a good one,' an aul fella shouted to the bus, laughing and coughing on his Woodbine.

'Well! You may be laughin! I'm not the better of it! Yeh wouldn't be laughin for much longer if we all upended, the lot of us, swimming for our lives in the Liffey without a life jacket!' snorted the aul one, shaking herself and staring over at him.

'Ah, sure, there's no harm in them. Sure, isn't it only aul guff!' he said, tryin to placate her.

'Guff, is it? Is tha wha yeh said? Guff, me arse! Between the pair a them we coulda ended up lying on a slab and everyone bein told we were lovely-lookin corpses! You may want tha, Mister, but I'll thank yeh teh keep yer comments to yerself, if yeh don't be mindin.'

'Ruckie up! Ruckie up!' shouted a pair of young fellas, making a laugh out of the aul ones. 'Go on, Missus! You tell him!' a skinny one shouted, trying to start a fight between the aul ones.

'Cut tha out!' shouted the aul fella, turning his vengeance on the skinny, pale-faced young fella with the mop of red carroty hair standing up on top of his head with a mind of its own. The young fella went red in the face, matching the colour of his hair, and turned with a shifty look to the fella sitting next to him, hoping for a bit of back-up. The other fella stared out the window, pretending it was nothing to do with him, feeling the heat from the dozen pair of eyes boring into them, with everyone on the bus staring over at them. 'Or I'll come down there and put manners on yeh with a boot up the arse,' said the aul fella, shaking his head slowly and resting his hands on his thighs, meaning business. He waited to see if there was any response, then snorted, throwing his eye out the window and cocking it around the bus, seeing the people shaking their head in agreement at the bloody cheek a them young ones speaking to their elders like that. Then he nodded his head, feeling satisfied now he had put them in their place and he could pick on someone that wouldn't give him lip. Unlike the aul one making him look like a real eejit for only defending the men.

I jumped up, grabbing me handbag and suitcase, rushing to get off the bus before it took off leaving me stranded up on Parnell Square and having to walk all the way back down again. The conductor banged the bell, getting the bus to stop, and said, 'Are yeh goin somewhere nice wit the suitcase, darlin?' Then he shook himself, lifting his neck, trying to make himself look taller then me, but only managing about half an inch.

'Yeah! I'm heading off up to the Phoenix Park to start me new job as secretary to President de Valera,' I said, laughing and trying to be smart.

'Yeah! If that's the case, my Aunt Biddy just won the pools and we're all off teh the Canary Islands.'

'Mind yeh don't go gettin yerself eatin by one a them canaries,' I said, curling me mouth down into a U-shape. And flicking me head away then back, flapping me eyelashes at him, trying to look beautiful and mysterious in me new hat and coat.

'I love yer hat,' he said, bending his head sideways, wanting to look at it from a different angle. 'Yeh know! That's style, tha is! Yeh look like something tha just stepped out of a fillum . . . wha was it called? Yeah! *The Spy Who Came in from the Cold.* Tha's it!' he snapped his fingers, delighted at remembering, hoping I'd think he was very intelligent.

I hopped off the bus, dragging me suitcase after me, and landed on the footpath outside the Metropole picture house. The bus took off with him hanging off the platform. 'I'll meet yeh outside there!' he shouted, with one hand covering his mouth and the other one stabbing at the entrance to the Metropole. 'Tonight! At half-past seven. We'll go to the pictures! Huh! Are we on?'

'Bye-bye!' I laughed, delighted he thought I looked lovely. The heat warming up me chest, making me want to stretch me neck and walk like the world belonged to me, because I was so lovely-looking. Jaysus! He really does mean a date! Imagine! Me getting a date! The young ones back in the convent would be raging if they knew. Mad with jealousy! Pity I can't meet him. But I'm starting that new job and God knows when I'll see the light of day again. I don't even know when I'll be getting me day off.

I stood at the edge of the footpath, looking up and down, judging my chances of getting across through the heavy traffic flying up and down O'Connell Street. I got a foot on the road and an aul one on a bicycle swerved in front of me, nearly taking the nose off me. 'Look out! Yeh eejit!' she shouted.

'Fuck you! Yeh blind cow!' I screamed in rage, as she knocked me suitcase, swiping the leg off me and knocking herself off the saddle, sliding down and hurting her arse. Her legs danced around the road trying to steady the bike and get her arse on the saddle and take off wobbling next to the footpath. She can't handle that bike, I thought, staring after her, me chest heaving up and down with the rage. Then she stopped and dropped her foot on the footpath and had the cheek to look back at me.

'Go home to yer mammy and tell her I said to lock you up, yeh dangerous bitch. Yer not fit teh cross the road. You've no sense!' she screamed back at me, rubbing her arse and thinking she was a safe distance away from me. Then she hopped back up again and went on pedalling up O'Connell Street.

I stared after her, with me mouth hanging open. Then it hit me. 'At least I don't have teh show me knickers teh get a man, yeh aul whore!' I screamed. Looking at her big fat culchie legs pumping up and down, the skirt blown up inta the air. She's fuckin lucky I'm practising to be a lady, because I'd a loving to give her a smack in the chops! 'The cheek a her! An she in the wrong!' I snorted, grabbing a hold of me suitcase and steadying meself to have another go, catching the eye of an aul fella.

'That's right, young one! You tell her,' puffed the aul fella, giving me a wink as he moseyed past, sucking on his Woodbine.

Ah, fuck, I'll never make it across from this end, not dragging this suitcase anyway. It will be the death a me, I thought, choking on the smelly black fumes. As cars, buses, trucks, delivery vans, and even horses and carts – and especially bleedin bicycles! – all peeled past me, flying up and down, me head going backwards and forwards with them, making me dizzy. They moved so fast, they made it look like it was the last one outa here puts out the lights. Before the world ends. What's their hurry? Jaysus! I forgot what it was like after being locked away in that convent for three years. I will have to walk up a bit and cross at the Pillar.

'Is that yerself!' screamed a woman inta me face, smiling and laughing. I stared at the woman standing in front of me with the thin grey hair and the bony tired aul face after too much living.

'Missus Redmond!' I shouted, me heart gladdening at the sight of me old neighbour from the Corporation buildings. Her and me ma, and me and her daughter were great friends.

'Jesus! Yer a sight for sore eyes,' she said, whipping me around to look at me. 'Looka the style a you! Here! Stand back, and let me get a good look at yeh!' I stood up straight and smiled, seeing her look at me from side to side then tighten the shawl around her shoulders and move in close to me. 'Gawd almighty, yer lookin lovely! Yeh turned out grand. I wouldn't a known yeh, only I recognised the face straight away. You were away. Weren't yeh!' she shouted. 'They sent yeh away! I know tha because I saw mention of it in the newspaper when it happened.'

'I was in the newspaper?' I said with a fright.

'Yeah! The evenin paper. Everyone was very sorry. You were very unfortunate and didn't deserve tha. Was it a convent they sent yeh to?'

'Yeah!'

'Was it hard?' she whispered, staring inta me face, seeing her eyes soften with the pity.

'Ah, it coulda been worse,' I said, thinking of the other places I could have ended up in.

'Did they make yeh work hard?'

'Yeah! Course they did,' I laughed. 'Yeh know what the nuns are like.'

'Oh, indeed I do! Only too well,' she said, nodding her head and twisting her mouth with disgust. 'Well, yer out now, aren't yeh? When did yeh get out? Are yeh just getting out now?' she roared, looking down at the suitcase.

'Yeah!'

'How is the poor mammy? Gawd! She'll lose her mind wit the excitement of having yeh back. Is tha where yer off ta now? Is she still out in Finglas? Gawd! I coulda got a house out there years ago. But I could never move from the city. I have everything here around me tha I need. I'd be lost out in a place like tha.'

'How have you been keeping?' I asked, looking at her poor tired face.

'Ah, I keep goin, I keep goin wit the help of God. Wha else can I do, Martha!'

'Yeah,' I whispered, me heart going out to her, seeing all the pain and hardship she's been through showing in her tired faded blue eyes. 'How is Emmy?' I shouted, thinking it would be lovely to see her again.

'Ah, God, Martha love! She's gone! Gone from me these last five months and two weeks and one day! I have it all off by heart,' she whispered, her eyes filling up with tears.

'Why! What happened?' I asked, hoping she wouldn't tell me the worst.

'She's dead, Martha. She was killed by a bus crossin the road, Martha,' she whispered. 'Killed stone dead tryin teh cross the road in London. At Trafalgar Square,' she whispered, with tears pouring down her cheeks. 'Me eldest daughter. Only just turned sixteen. It was two days after she turned sixteen he threw her out on the streets, and she went off to London. Tha's the last I ever saw of her. She was only less then two weeks there when it happened. It was all his fault,' she cried, looking back to that time, her voice trailing away. Getting lost back in time, remembering seeing her daughter's face for that one last time. I stared at her, feeling her pain. Waiting for her to come back to me. 'She's buried in England, Martha. But wha really breaks me heart is tha I can't afford teh bring her home! She's buried over there, and I never even saw the grave! They have her buried in a pauper's grave,' she muttered, staring into the distance. Then she dropped her head, burying her face in a handful of shawl, and wiped her nose looking up at me. 'Seein you has brought her back to me. I can still see the two of you so clearly, playin together, like it was only happenin now,' she laughed. Showing the tears and snots and saliva bubbling on the corners of her mouth. Her eyes lighting up with the memory. 'How will I ever get over tha, Martha? She went away because he threw her out! If he had left her alone, she would still be alive today.'

I stared at her, me eyes filling up with sadness at her terrible loss. I had the picture of me telling Emmy I'm going on a holiday to the Sunshine Home and worrying when she told me I had to have me head examined for lice and disease. And she checking me head for me and telling me I would pass no problem because I only had a few lice. God! Was that only yesterday? Or was it really years ago!

'She worshipped the ground you walked on, Missus Redmond, she wouldn't want to hurt you for the world. I'm very sorry for your trouble,' I whispered, taking her arm and rubbing her back. 'I'm going to light a penny candle for Emmy when I pass the first church I come to. And I'll light one for you, too. She's watching out for you from heaven. At least her worries are over, Missus Redmond,' I murmured.

'Yeah, it's true, there is tha teh be grateful for. Poor Emmy will never know another day's sufferin. I suppose I should be grateful for small mercies. Thank God for tha. Tha aul bastard gave her an awful life. Now he's sufferin for it. He drinks himself stupid tryin teh forget. But I will never forgive him, Martha. No, she won't have to suffer,' she said, thinking about it, and making up her mind it was one good thing. Then she shook herself and blinked and looked at me, and reached over to take me arm. 'Are yeh goin my way? I'm rushin up teh Moore Street teh get a few potatoes and a bit a meat for the dinner. Will yeh come wit me? Maybe yeh might like teh come home wit me and have yourself a bit a dinner. Would tha be OK?' she said, wantin me to stay wit her a bit longer, not wanting to let go of the bit of comfort of having someone Emmy was close to.

'Yeah! Course I will,' I heard myself saying, knowing full well the people were waiting for me and would probably ring the convent. To hell with it! I am me own person now, and I can do what I like. There's more good to be had by spending a few hours with poor Missus Redmond than them people will ever need. Anyway, Missus Redmond was very good to me in the past when I needed it, giving me the odd bit a bread and sugar when I could get the time to escape Jackser and go out on the street to play. So fuck them all! This is more important.

'Yeah! Come on!' I said happily, diving for me suitcase and taking off, holding onto her arm with me free hand, dying to see Moore Street again.

'Oh, tha's better,' Missus Redmond sighed, sitting down opposite me at the other side of the fire. 'We managed to get the lot of them down for the night. Do you hear?' she whispered, cocking her head to listen. 'Not a sound from them next door,' she breathed. 'They're gone out like a light.'

I looked down at the little one with her eyes closing, sitting cosily on me lap, her little fingers wrapped around the ends of me hair, twirling it and sucking quietly on her soother. Missus stood up and reached for the five-packet Woodbines sitting on the mantelpiece and took one out, lighting it with a rolled-up piece of paper she stuck in the fire and sucked on the cigarette, inhaling deeply, then sat down, stretching out her slippers to the fire.

'She's nearly ready to go down any minute,' mouthed missus, whispering and nodding to me. Letting the smoke pour out of her mouth and smiling down at the baby. 'Tha's me last babby,' she murmured, looking at little Joyce, conking out now with her head thrown back and the soother slipping out of her mouth. 'She's seventeen months, can yeh believe the time runs so fast! It was like only yesterday I was bringin her back from the Rotunda, only a bran new babby! Still an all! Thank God tha's all behind me. Sure, there's no work in her now. She's just on her feet. So tha's definitely the last a them. Nine a them I had, Martha love. Sixteen, if yeh include the ones I lost!' she said, her face dropping in sadness, staring into the fire, remembering all the children she lost.

'Come on!' she said quietly, standing up and taking the baby from me. 'I'll put her down, she's out for the count. I won't hear another word out of her till the morning. She's a grand sleeper, never any bother. I haven't had a day's trouble with her since the day she was born. She's a lovely quiet, content babby, God bless her. She sleeps in the cot next tch my bed in the third room. You put the kettle on, love, an I'll be back in a minute, we'll have a grand sup a tea an enjoy the peace an quiet while it lasts,' she laughed, flying out the door with the baby in her arms. I poured the tea, putting a drop of milk and one sugar in the mug and taking the cup for myself.

'Tha's it. Another day over and we can take it easy,' missus said, coming in and sitting down by the fire with the mug of tea. I went over to me bag sitting on top of me suitcase with the hat and coat thrown on top sitting behind the door, and took out me ten-pack Carroll cigarettes and handed one to missus. 'Ah, no, love. I only smoke these. They're not strong enough for me,' she said, lighting up another Woodbine.

'That was a lovely bit a dinner,' I said, still tasting the stew behind the back of me throat.

'Did yeh like it!' she said happily. Delighted I enjoyed the food she had to stretch teh give me.

'Yeah! I love a bit of coddle!' I said.

'The sausages an rashers do give it a lovely bit a flavour,' she said.

'Yeah! It was gorgeous. Do you know, the first and last time I ate anything like that was when Missus Dunne, who lived in the room opposite us, made it for me an the rest of us. That time me ma went into hospi . . .' I trailed off, not wanting to remember back that far.

She shook her head, understanding, saying nothing. 'Some things are better left unsaid, love. Them times are gone for you now. Don't look back. Just make sure you don't make the same mistakes as yer poor mammy and the rest of us did,' she said, staring at the fire. 'By the way,' she said slowly, thinking, 'you wouldn't a heard. But poor aul Missus Dunne is gone!' I lifted me head, looking straight at her with the fright. 'Yeah!' she said, staring at me face. 'These last eighteen months gone past. Cancer in the stomach, it was. Riddled with it, the poor woman, an she never knew a thing till the last. It was so sudden. She went inta St Kevin's Hospital, and they opened up her stomach and she was gone in no time. Never came back home. Her relations, one sister she had, came back from England and took the kids, Jimmy and Ellie, back with her. So tha's where they are now. Living in England. Poor Missus Dunne, God rest her, was well missed. She would do anything for anyone. We'll never see the like a her again.' Missus nodded, shaking her head up and down, staring into the fire with terrible regret at the loss of poor aul Missus Dunne.

I felt the tears well up inside me. God rest you, Missus Dunne. I won't ever forget you for all your goodness to me. Please, God, I pray that Jimmy and Ellie are being looked after the way their mother looked after us. I could feel the tears streaming down me face and brushed them away, feeling a terrible loss. And poor Emmy and Missus Redmond. There never seems to be any rest from the pain and suffering of the poor people.

'She was a great character,' I smiled. Remembering the things she used to say when people annoyed her.

'Oh, God! Don't remind me,' laughed Missus Redmond. 'I remember her husband before she got rid of him. He used to turn up mouldy drunk, oh Jaysus! Mouldy drunk he would be. Turnin up and bangin on the winda, threatenin teh annihilate her and smash the winda if she didn't let him in. Oh, be God! She was well able for him. No better woman, I can tell you. Then one night . . .' and Missus started to roar her head laughing. I waited wit me mouth open, smiling and holding me breath. 'Do yeh know wha she did?'

'No, tell us.'

'Well! She waited till he fell asleep in his usual place under the winda. Then opened it, an upended a bucket of shite she'd been savin specially for him an poured the lot all over him. Tha was the last time she ever clapped eyes on him. He cleared off and never came back. Jaysus! We were talkin about tha for years. We never got tired of askin her teh tell us the story about it, over an over again we heard it. It was the way she used teh tell it tha made me laugh. God! An I'm still laughin, Martha. Oh, God! Indeed she was a great aul character,' she laughed. Wiping her eyes listening to me screeching me head off, with the picture of Missus Dunne getting her own back on the husband.

'Do you remember the time me and Emmy sold the periwinkles out at the gates?' I said, laughing.

'Ah, Jaysus! Will I ever forget? We went off out teh the Sandymount Strand the day before. I had them all wit me. We took the train out an brought the two metal buckets, wit poor Emmy carrying all the stuff in them. The bottle a milk an the cold bottles a tea an the sambidges, an we even brought a big workman's shovel,' she laughed. 'One a the Corporation fellas stopped leanin on it, restin himself, after doin nothin all day, an threw it in the hole in the middle a the road they'd been digging for months. Anyway, one a mine spotted it an brought it back teh me, thinkin it would come in handy. Well, it did! Little Christie had teh carry tha, an it was twice the size a himself. Yeh shoulda seen the sight of us. We spent the day diggin up the sand lookin for mussels an winkles, the whole lot of us, even the babby. Mind you, half a them wasn't even born then. We were so busy we didn't even notice the bleedin tide was comin in till it started lappin aroun our feet. Then we had teh make a break for it. Holy Jesus! Everythin was soppin wit the water, an we were goin mad tryin teh gather up all our things. By the time we made it up the steps, we were like drownded rats. Soppin wit the wet we were, Martha. We had teh wade through inches a water wit me carrying the babbies, one in each arm. The babbies were only small then. Wit only nine months between them, and me shoutin teh poor Emmy, "Come on. Hurry! Make sure we don't leave anythin behind." God almighty. Tha was a grand day out all the same. The childre never stopped talkin about it. How old would Emmy a been then?' Missus said, thinking.

'Nine! She was nine, just like me. We were the same age.'

'Oh! Indeed I know. There was only . . . wha was it? A few months between the two of youse!' she said, looking at me and thinking about Emmy.

'Yeah! We stood outside the gate with the winkles and mussels in the two buckets after we cooked them in your big pot,' I said, pointing under the sink.

'Yeah, I remember,' she said, shaking her head sadly. 'We sold them for ten a penny and five for a half-penny. At first we just gave handfuls, then we had the idea of counting them to make more money.'

'I think we made about twelve shilling and nine pence, if me memory serves me,' I said, remembering the two of us counting up all the coppers and half-pennies.

'She was a very good daughter! I was blessed wit her,' missus said, looking like her heart would break. I sat quietly, looking into the fire, leaving her with her memories while I had mine.

'Do yeh know, Martha?' she said, her mouth twisting in pain. 'Even up to the last she was thinkin about me. Do yeh know how they found me?'

'No,' I whispered, waiting.

'They found a letter in her bag addressed teh me, and inside it was a pound note. She was goin teh post me the letter wit the money in it, but she never got the chance. I still have tha pound! I won't ever spend it. Do yeh know wha I want teh do some day, Martha? I want teh get enough money saved up. So tha one day I'll have enough put by, an I can bring her home teh rest wit me own mother up in Glasnevin Cemetery! An I won't rest until I have tha done. Every spare penny I have I put away for her! Yeh can do tha! Can't yeh? They will let me take her up and bring her home? Wouldn't they?'

'Oh, yeah! Of course! She belongs teh you. Nobody can stop yeh burying yer own. Have no fears about that, Missus Redmond.' She shook herself, nodding her head in satisfaction, and went back to staring at the fire.

I began to stir, thinking about the time. 'I suppose I better be thinking of making a move. If I am to catch the last bus back. Yeah.'

'Oh, God, yes! Where are yeh off teh? Are yeh goin home teh yer mammy?'

I hesitated, wondering if I should tell her. I didn't want to upset her. 'I'm not goin back near Jackser!' I said, looking at her. She stared, trying to work this out. 'I'm starting work in a house out on the Northside, near Malahide. I don't want to go back near him, he'll only expect me to start robbing for him again, and I've done me time getting locked away in that convent, Missus Redmond. I want to make something of me life. So I'm not looking back.'

'Yeah! Yeah, yer right there! Tha aul bastard was a swine in his heart. Just like the bastard I'm married teh. If it wasn't for him, I'd still have me beautiful Emmy! Yer right! Don't look back. Make a decent life fer yerself, an be happy. God knows, yeh went through enough, in yer young life. When I think about yeh dragging tha big bag around sellin tha butter. An in the end it was all for nothin. Yer the only one tha suffered. He frittered away all tha money an it was you tha had teh pay for it! Go on, love. Hurry an catch tha bus. An may the blessings a God go wit yeh always. You mind yerself now! And keep away from the fellas! They're nothin but trouble. Find yerself a good man one day, somebody tha will mind yeh an be good to yeh. An remember this! It's better teh be an aul man's darlin than a young man's slave!' she laughed. 'Tha's wha my poor aul mother used teh say teh me, God rest her. She's up in heaven now wit my Emmy, an the rest a them. Pity I didn't listen teh her,' she said, looking mournful, shaking her head with regret.

'Yeah! That's a good one,' I said, laughing.

'I must remember that,' I whispered quietly to meself and laughed again. I picked up my bag and opened the purse. Inside I had eleven pounds and ten shillings. I never spent much of me wages I got for working in the convent. 'Here! You take this,' I said quietly, rolling up the ten-pound note and pushing it into her hand. She looked at it and I could see the colour draining out of her face. I grabbed me coat and slapped me French beret down on me head. Or Bonny and Clyde hat I like to call it from the film I saw about two bank robbers in the 1920s.

'Jesus Christ almighty,' she breathed in shock. 'I can't take all yer hard-earned money from you. Sure, I'd have no luck doin tha! No, yer very good. Here! Take it back,' she said, shoving it back into me coat pocket.

'No, Missus Redmond. I'll be very upset if you don't take it. Go on! If you don't want to spend it, then take it for Emmy. You can put it towards bringing her home. Sure, I'm on me own now. I have no one to think about but meself. And aren't I well able to look after meself? I'll never go hungry! Go on! Take it,' I said, shoving it back into her hand, picking up me suitcase and shoving me hat further down on me head.

'I hope yer right,' she said slowly. 'I know there's no better one than yerself for gettin by. Sure, wasn't it you tha kept them all goin? OK! The blessins a God on yeh! I won't forget yeh, Martha. An if yeh ever want anythin, sure my door is always open to yeh.'

'I'll go now,' I said, opening the door. 'You take care of yourself, Missus Redmond. And remember, Emmy is always looking out for yeh from heaven. It must have been her idea for us teh meet today, so that will tell you! She's still looking out for yeh!'

'Bye-bye, love! Look after yerself!'

'Yeah, thanks for everything, Missus Redmond. I'll see yeh again.'

She waited until I hit the stairs and only then shut the door. I made me way down the dark stone steps, hearing voices at the bottom. 'Who're you?' asked a young fella blocking me way at the end of the stairs, while the other two stared at the wall sayin nothing. I sized them up, putting the suitcase behind me back on the stairs, wrapping me handbag around me wrist and folding me arms, hanging onto the bag. I saw the skinny one with the pimply face throwing the eye at me bag. 'Have yeh any money in tha?' he said, nodding at me bag.

'No! An if I had, you wouldn't be even gettin a smell of it,' I hissed.

'Where yeh from?'

I knew there was no point in trying to squeeze past them. They would only rob everything. 'Listen, fuck face. Don't make any mistakes about me! I know your face, Whiney Lynch!'

'Wha! Who the fuck are you?' he roared in astonishment.

'Listen! I know these flats like the back a me hand. I was eatin fellas like you when you were still gettin yer ma teh wipe yer arse. Now, get outa me fuckin way! I'm goin teh miss me bus!'

'I know her!' shouted a young fella wit a dying scurvy-looking face. 'Yer tha young one who used tch come here sellin the good butter. Aren't yeh?' he roared.

'Yeah, course I fuckin am!'

'Jaysus! We heard yeh were locked up! Did ya just gerout now?'

'Now yeh have it!' I said, reaching around and grabbing me suitcase and pushing past them still standing in me way.

'How long did yeh get?' they shouted after me, making me move to hurry out of the flats and get going to catch that bus.

'Fuckin long enough!' I shouted back, making for the gate.

That would have been one helluva fight, with me screaming me head off, and bringing everyone in the flats down on their head. Only they have the good sense to know that, and don't rob one of their own.

That's the thing. If I had any doubts before this, I know now. I don't belong here any more. I'm moving on, I'm going to lift meself out of this, no matter what it takes. I'll work day and night to do that.

3

I climbed on the bus and took the first seat away from the conductor. The bus was empty and I didn't want to have to start
making conversation with him. It had been a very long day and
I still had to face these people. They may turn me away from the
door, not wanting someone they thought they couldn't depend on.

Me heart was fluttering with the nerves, and I stared out the
window into the pitch-black night, seeing my own reflection
staring back at me. The white face with the haunted, worried look
in the eyes, under the black beret. That is not the little Martha
looking back at me who used to worry herself sick at the thought of
what Jackser would do to her. No! That is a grown young woman.
It's me! Yeah! I don't have to answer to anyone! I don't have to tell
them my business. I will just say there was something important I
had to do, and Sister Eleanor was mistaken when she said I would
come early. I will say I am sorry for disturbing them this hour of
the night, and I know I am reliable as the reverend mother said
in her reference she gave me. So if they don't like it, they can take
a running jump and find somebody else for themselves. I will just
go and look for another job. Right! That's that sorted out.

I sat back and closed my eyes, feeling the exhaustion hitting me,
but also a sense of peace. I will never set foot in my old haunts
again. The places I lived, or see the people I used to know. It does
no good. Before I would know it, I would be right back where I
started. No, never again. That is the past.

'Fares, please!' I looked up into the face of a tired aul fella resting
himself on the back of me seat, clinking the coppers in his hand

and rattling his leather bag with all the money. I could see he was annoyed with the sour look on his face at having me make him walk the six paces up to my seat, instead of sitting inside the door, making it handy for him to reach over and take the money off me. Pity about him, I sniffed. Looking up at him and asking how much is it to this place? Showing him the address on the piece of paper. 'Four pence,' he snorted, letting the address fly back and land in me lap.

'What? I'm half fare! And well yeh know that!' I shouted.

'No!' he drawled, looking up at the ceiling, delighted to get back at me. 'I know no such thing. What age are yeh?' he asked the ceiling, snorting and looking slowly down at me.

'Fourteen!' He curled the top of his lip, making quick sucking noises on his teeth, rattling his money bag, thinking about this. Feeling he had the power of God with me in his grip. While I waited, me head thrown back, and me nostrils flaring, staring up at him with me mouth open, listening to me breathing, and ready for a fight.

'Gimme the money.'

I dropped two coppers into his hand, and he rolled his machine and slapped the ticket into me hand, mashing it, and moseyed off back to his seat to spread himself and go back to his doze. 'Will yeh let me know before I get to me stop, mister? . . . please!' I asked, whipping me head around to him. I waited, while he thought about this.

'I will if I remember,' he said. Stretching himself out, closing his eyes, and jerking the cap on his head down, to block out the light.

'Ah, go and fuck yerself, yeh miserable aul bastard!' I was about to roar, losing me rag. Then stopped meself in time. Jaysus! Keep quiet. He will only kick you off the bus so fast, before even your feet have a chance to touch the floor. Anyway, ye keep forgetting! You are supposed to be practising to become a lady!

I sat back, snorting out me rage and pressed me nose to the window, seeing only dark fields, trees and bushes flying past, hoping to catch sight of something that will tell me if I'm near me stop.

* * *

I stepped off the bus holding me suitcase, barely making it to the footpath. Before he banged hell out of the bell, getting the bus to take off so fast, I nearly tripped almost breaking me neck. 'Aul bastard! I hope yeh die roaring!' I screamed after him, seeing him watching me from the platform. He had the cheek to pull his lips apart, stretching them across his face. Showing me his big black mouldy teeth, looking like someone saying 'Cheese' for a photograph.

There was no call for that carry on, I thought, picking up me suitcase and looking round to see where I'd landed. Jaysus! I'm in the arsehole of nowhere! Three shops. One a post office, a sweet shop and a chemist. Straight ahead, a long line of houses behind high walls surrounded by trees. Then to the right, a hill with more houses and an old Protesdant church behind an ancient wall. I could see the spire sitting on top of the roof. Then nothing but fields and hedges towards the city, back the way the bus just came.

So much for landing in the middle of the bright lights! This is just a one-horse town. Everyone has been dozing in their beds for hours by the look of this place. Not a light on in any of the houses. What am I going to do? I can't turn up at someone's door this hour of the night. It must be after half-eleven. I'm really going to need a brass neck now, if I want to sleep in a bed tonight. Right, no harm in trying. They can only bang the door in me face. That won't kill me.

I stood under the street lamp to get a better look at the address: King William Road. Wonder which way that is, I thought, squinting up the hill, not liking the idea of going up there in the dark. I'll have a look down here, see if the name of the road is written up somewhere. Bleeding conductor! I could have asked him, if he'd been any way human! Be thankful, Martha, yeh don't have to live with someone like him! Chestnut Road. No, not down here. I'll try up that hill.

I set off, hiking up, nearly on me tiptoes, not wanting to make a sound in case anyone was hiding in the bushes on the other side of the road. I might see them before they hear me, then I can run for all I'm worth.

I stopped outside a heavy, black old gate, not seeing the big man-eating dog until it leaped up the gate, baring its teeth and growling, slipping back down and barking its head in rage. 'Jaysus! Help! Mammy!' I screamed in fright, staring at its mouthful of sharp teeth. I started to shake like mad, terrified out of me life at the sight of the dog. I turned and ran for all I was worth, not daring to look back. The case was rattling like mad from me hands shaking. Ohh, please don't let him get loose, I prayed. Running faster than I ever ran in me life. I shot across the road, stopping at the bus stop before I had the nerve to look back up. Oh, God! A dog! And a savage one at that! I'm even afraid of little dogs, never mind a big one like that thing. That's it. I'm not moving another step, until I know what I'm doing.

I sat down on the side of the footpath, the cold going right up through me. God! What kind of an eejit am I. Getting meself into this mess. I looked around at the dark silent road, with the damp and fog swirling just a few feet off the ground, and could feel a tight band wrapping itself around me head. That's all I need, a bloody headache. I feel chilled to me bones. Think! No, I'm definitely not heading off again. I might meet another dog and won't be so lucky next time. OK, I'm taking the bus back into town. That's it.

I stood up and reached for my suitcase, heading over to the bus stop on the other side. I can catch that bus back into town. Oh, bloody hell! It will be that aul conductor. So, to hell with him. If I keep me mouth shut and pay the fare, he can't say anything.

I stood waiting, not a sign of it. Not even another car passed in all this time. Then I heard it. I looked up, seeing the bus flying towards me and put my hand out to stop it. I watched as it flew past, with the 'Garage' sign up. I couldn't believe it. It's not going back into town. That's the last bus! What am I going to do, I said to meself, feeling me heart sink down into me belly. Bloody hell! That's me snookered. How do I manage to get meself into so much trouble? I should have left earlier! Ah, hell! I was enjoying meself, and so was missus. It was lovely to sit and talk and feel for a little while I was with someone who wanted to be with me. It was almost like I belonged there. Anyway, I'm me own person, I can do what I like. This family I'm supposed to be going to don't own me. They're only buying me labour, not bleeding me. Yeah!

I looked around, hearing the silence around me. It's not so bad being stuck out in the middle of the night. I'll be glad of the heat and rest when I eventually get to lie in a bed, wherever that will be. So, there's no hurry on me. I'll ramble over to the shops and see if there's somewhere I can snuggle in for the night.

I stood up just as a big silver car came up the road. I watched it passing, with a man driving and a woman sitting in the front passenger seat. They both looked over at me then slowed down. I watched as the car slowly turned and came to a stop beside me. 'Are you OK?' a middle-aged man asked me, leaning out the window. I looked at the woman. She was leaning across, looking to see what was going on. She seems OK. I looked at him. He had dark wavy hair with silvery grey at the sides and black-framed glasses. They look respectable.

'I'm a little lost, I wonder if you would know where this road is?' I said, whipping the address out of me pocket.

'That is the road parallel with Chestnut Road,' he said quietly to his wife, looking at the address.

'Yes, to the left of Conquer Hill,' she said, leaning over to look at it. 'Sit in the back, we will take you there,' she said, leaning over to me. I hesitated for a second. They're fine. I opened the door, landing in me suitcase and sat in beside it, sliding along the cream leather seats. I could smell aftershave lotion, and looked up at the woman, she was all done up with a new hairdo. 'Goodness! What a time for a young girl like you to be out, dear!'

I slammed the door shut and sat back while the man drove off. 'Thank you very kindly,' I said, hearing Sister Eleanor always saying that.

'Not at all! My goodness! I couldn't imagine our Heather being stranded on the streets this hour of the night. Have you come far?' she said, leaning over to look at me.

'Eh, far enough,' I said, not wanting to give away any information.

'But are you expected? Will somebody be waiting up for you?' she asked, staring into me eyes. Not being able to figure out what was going on.

'Eh, I hope so,' I said, not believing a word of it. Jaysus! This is going to take some explaining. I felt a bit panicky! I'm definitely going to look very foolish. Waltzing up to strangers and banging on their door this hour of the night.

'It must be rather late,' she said, squinting at her little gold watch on her wrist. 'My heavens! Do you know it is twelve forty-five?'

'Yeah!' I croaked. Wanting to get back out of the car and wait until morning. I would rather freeze then cause ructions at this late hour. They will definitely send me packing, deciding they can do without the likes of me. Fuck! I definitely am a daft cow!

I could feel me heart fluttering, and leaned across to get a look and see where they were going. We drove up the hill past the savage dog and turned left, driving alongside smaller-looking houses, not as big in the front, but big enough. 'Number twenty-seven,' the man muttered, leaning across to read the numbers of the houses on the walls.

'Yes, dear! I think a bit further on. This is number nineteen. Oh, here we are, Richard. Another two doors up on the left.' He cruised to a stop outside a house with a wide drive in and a silver Jaguar and a little Mini sitting in the drive. I looked out. Help! The house is in pitch blackness. I didn't move, not wanting to get out and knock them up.

'It looks like no one is awake,' said the woman, quietly mumbling, staring at the house.

'Would you like me to go in and knock, dear?' the man said, looking at me. I stared at him, feeling very worried. He stared back, reading my eyes. 'Are they relatives of yours, my dear?' he asked quietly.

'Not really,' I said, trying to decide what to do. Then I grabbed my suitcase and made a move, opening the door. Deciding to take the bull by the horns.

'I am very grateful to you,' I said, smiling and making to get out of the car. I pushed open the gate, thinking a dog could come lashing out and that would put the tin hat on it. But I couldn't care less any more. Enough was enough. In for a penny, in for a pound, I giggled inside meself. Feeling a bit hysterical. I let the case down and looked for the door bell. It was hidden under all the ivy growing around the walls. I pressed it, hearing a chime of ding-dong, ding-dong. Then I stood back and held me breath waiting. The car sat outside, the two people, both pairs of eyes sat watching and waiting, too. Nothing happened!

'Do you have their phone number, dear?' the woman whispered in a loud voice. 'We don't live far! It might be a good idea if we telephone them from our home.'

'No, sorry,' I whispered, shaking me head. I felt so foolish, I could hear meself humming a tune in me head, and looking up at the moon. Things can't get any worse. I have an awful fear of going where I'm not wanted. Making an eejit of meself.

And this is it! I pressed the bell again, harder. Ding-dong, ding-dong. It sounded louder, flying around the house, then I heard movement. A door opening and shuffling. Then the light went on somewhere up on the landing. Oh, oh! Here we go. I smiled a sickly smile at the people in the car, giving a little wave. I wanted them to go, not see me getting roared at and sent marching off back down the road again. I won't mind if I'm on me own. But they will only prolong the foolishness, seeing me make an eejit of meself.

I could hear the bolts on the door being whipped back and the key turning. A curly-brown-haired man in a pair of pyjamas and wine dressing gown wearing leather slippers squinted out at me, with one eye closed, trying to make out what's happening. He squinted one eye at me and tried to open the other one to land on the two people leaning out the car window to stare up at him. 'Yes?' he barked at me. Me mouth dried up. 'Can I help you?' he said, holding onto the door and trying to fly both eyes open at the same time.

'Eh, hello! I'm Martha, the nuns sent me,' I said. 'Sorry I'm a bit late.'

'Who?'

'Eh! The person from the convent.' I was listening to meself talking like I wasn't the full shilling, but I couldn't help it. Me mind had shut down.

'What is it, Greg? Who is it?' a woman's voice came from up the stairs. I could hear her, but I couldn't see her.

'I think you have the wrong address,' he said, looking at me and making to close the door.

'Is this . . . twenty-seven . . . King William Road, Missus Andrews?'

'Yes, yes! Doctor and Mrs Andrews,' he said, shaking his head up and down like mad, hoping things would now start to make sense. 'But! Who are you?'

'I'm the girl from the convent. You wanted someone to help you with the children when you went away!'

I heard footsteps running down to the door, then it was whipped open, and a curly blonde head appeared. 'You must be Martha. Heavens above! Come in. What on earth happened to you?'

I stared at her for a minute, trying to take in she was smiling. Then grabbed me suitcase and whipped around, waving and smiling at the people, shouting in a whisper, 'Thank you very much!'

'OK.' They smiled, happy and waving. Then drove off, knowing I was safe, the people were going to let me in.

I stepped into the hall, and the woman started to close the door, first giving a look out to the car moving off, to turn around, and go back down the road. I watched the man head off down the hall, slapping his leather slippers on the old Victorian tiles. He headed into a room with his head lowered, and his neck drooping, then the woman turned to me after sliding the bolts across the door and turning the big key. 'Are you all right? Go on, go down to the kitchen.'

I walked slowly down the hall, hanging onto me suitcase, still not sure if yer man was going to roar the head off me. The lights blazed on in the big kitchen and I looked around at a big cream Aga stuck inside an arch in the wall, with a wide overmantel lined with loads of little ornaments.

'We had given you up,' laughed the woman, showing a gorgeous smile with lovely white teeth and shiny blue eyes.

'I'm really sorry. This was the last thing I meant to happen,' I said, lifting me head to look at her, then over at him, standing in the middle of the kitchen tearing lumps out of his head. Both his hands were tearing through his scalp, his nails scratching like mad through his big mop of curly brown wavy hair, and staring at the floor. Then I heard a little mewling sound and it got louder.

'The baby! Aoife is awake. Oh, save me from young girls and babies!' he moaned, lowering his head to the floor, bending his back and dropping his face in his hands.

The woman smiled, watching him. She was hesitating, waiting for him to do something. Then she said, 'Will you . . . or will I?'

'No, I'll go,' he said, springing out of the kitchen, leaving his slipper behind, then coming back and throwing the eye to me and grabbing his slipper, saying, 'I told you a young girl would be trouble. We should have gotten one of your mother's cronies in to help. Even mothers-in-law and their pals are better than this.' Then he was gone. Taking the stairs two at a time. I could hear him heaving out off the banisters, trying to get up in a hurry.

'Take no notice of him,' she said, laughing at me. 'He hates to be disturbed from his night's sleep. But don't worry, Aoife is giving him plenty of that at the moment. Would you like a hot cup of tea? You look frozen! What happened to you?'

'I, eh, got a bit delayed,' I said, watching as the man came flying back in carrying a little newborn baby bawling its head off, with its little bud mouth wide open.

'Here you are, darling. She needs her darling mamma. Go to Mamma, precious,' he clucked, dropping little kisses on her face and handing her over, letting her land into the mammy's outstretched arms.

'You go on back to bed, dear,' she said.

He whirled around, first looking at me then down at the baby then up at her. 'If you're sure,' he said, with his hands held over his head, stopping his scratching for a minute.

'Yes! I can manage. Go on,' she laughed. 'Back to bed with you.'

'Oh, you're a treasure,' he said, giving her a quick kiss and a tap on the arse and took off happily, flying out the door and up the stairs.

'We can do without the theatricals this hour of the night!' she laughed in a whisper over to me. 'Men! They make a song and dance about nothing,' she said, stretching her face and staring her eyes to heaven. I laughed, seeing the picture of his big mop of wavy hair bouncing on his head as he flew out the door. With his belly going first, and his elbows stabbed back, making himself in an awful hurry. Like someone had set fire to his arse.

'Put on the kettle there,' she said, nodding over to the worktop and sitting herself down in an armchair by the Aga, with a bottle in her hand and snuggling the baby into her, putting the bottle in her mouth. The baby made growling sounds and settled down to slurping hungrily. I could hear it going down her belly.

'Ah, she was hungry,' I whispered, smiling down at the baby, watching as she clapped eyes on me for the first time. She stopped sucking, letting the bottle slip and her mouth drop open with the milk dribbling out the corners, and stared up at me in shock. Her big blue eyes hanging out of her tiny white face gawked like mad at me. Then she shifted herself for more comfort and went back to sucking, ignoring me and looking up at her mammy, making sure she was still safe.

I half-filled the kettle and opened the presses overhead, finding two mugs and the canister of tea sitting on the worktop, and lined everything up ready for the water to boil. 'Do you like your tea weak or strong, Missus Andrews?' I whispered.

'Oh, for heaven's sake,' she laughed, 'don't call me that. My name is Clare. So call me Clare. And call him Greg!' she said, waving her head to the ceiling, making a face and laughing.

'All right,' I said, smiling happily, feeling she was a very nice person altogether, a real lady! And she's gorgeous-looking, I thought. Staring at her lovely white curly hair, and her white face with the big sky-blue eyes. But most of all, she's very gentle.

'Are you hungry?' she asked me, taking the bottle out of the baby's mouth and winding her.

'No, no! Thank you.'

'Are you sure? It wouldn't take me a minute to throw on a couple of eggs and make an omelette or something!'

'Ah, no thanks. Honestly, I'm grand.'

'Well, put on a couple of slices of bread in the toaster, I'm feeling a bit hungry. I have to keep up with little Aoife here! She has a great appetite! Haven't you?' she said, landing a kiss on the baby's head. 'It's twenty-four hours with her! She has me run ragged, the little dote,' she said, whipping Aoife down to change her nappy.

I poured the boiling water into the teapot and rinsed it out to warm it, like Sister Mercy taught me. That's all I know how to do, make tea. I can't cook! I hope she doesn't ask me to cook anything. Maybe I can watch how she cooks. Yeah, that's a good idea. I put two teaspoons of tea in the pot and covered it with the tea cosy sitting on the worktop and brought everything over to the table and sat down.

'Well . . .' she said, hurrying back in the door, her long cotton nightie flapping over her rosy-red slippers with fur around the edges. 'That gives me a few more hours before she starts bawling for another feed and the little men start marching on the move,' she breathed, laughing and sitting down, grabbing the toast and plastering it with butter and marmalade. 'You look all done in,' she said, staring over at me, munching on her toast.

'Yeah, I'm a little bit tired,' I said quietly, not wanting to wake anyone else up. Me head felt heavy, like I was getting a bad headache, and me eyes were burning. I felt like I could take me eyeballs out, and put them in a cup of water to cool them down.

'Come on, I'll show you your room, and in the morning you can sleep late. You look like you could do with some rest.'

'Ah, no! What time do you want me to get up at? Sure, look at yourself. I bet you never stop going from morning till night!'

'I won't argue with you there,' she said, yawning and stretching her arms into the air. 'Come on. Grab your case.' Then she was flying out the door, stopping for me to grab me suitcase and switching off the light as we headed up the stairs. We walked along a corridor with a night light sitting on a little table in the corner and went to an end room down a couple of stairs and into a lovely big bedroom.

'Here! Pop into bed,' she said, switching the lamp on the bedside table and pulling down the covers of a big single bed. She folded back the huge gold eiderdown then said, 'Goodnight! Or what's left of it,' she whispered, laughing, and closed the door. I opened me suitcase and rooted at the bottom for me pyjamas, and stripped off, diving into them, and flew into the bed, switching off the lamp.

4

I woke up staring over at the light coming in through the heavy yellow cotton curtains on the big window in front of my bed. It must be late, I thought. Staring around the room, taking in the big mahogany wardrobe behind the door and the dressing table with a big mirror and a stool sitting in front of it. I listened to the sounds of traffic coming from far down the hill on the main road. Thinking I could be still down there wandering around like a lost soul. I'm definitely very lucky to have landed meself here in this lovely family. The woman is a dote altogether.

I listened to the voices coming up through the ceiling. A little child's voice squealing and the baby crying, and the murmuring of the mammy. I better get up and give her a hand. I was out of the bed and rooting around in me suitcase for me clean skirt and blouse. I didn't want to be wearing me good clothes, the frock the reverend mother bought me. I picked up me coat collapsed over the chair, where I landed it in the early hours of the morning, and hung it on a hanger in the wardrobe. Then rushed out to the bathroom, seeing it open, lying empty, and dived in, brushing me teeth and washing me face in the sink and out again, feeling in an awful hurry. I quickly brushed me hair, and dressed in me old skirt, but it is washed and ironed, and put on me white blouse and me blue granny cardigan I got for Christmas, and took the stairs two at a time and walked down the hall.

Then I stopped before I got to the kitchen. I felt a bit nervous. Being in someone else's house, especially after landing meself at all hours of the night and causing ructions waking the baby.

Gawd! They must think I'm an awful person, not giving a damn about anyone!

I knocked on the door quietly, feeling more foolish, but not wanting to make things worse by steaming in as if I owned the place. I listened for a second, hearing a child squealing, making sounds like he thought it sounded great, then stopping for a listen and squealing again. I took in a deep breath and turned the handle of the door, walking into the kitchen. 'Eh, good morning,' I croaked to the back of Clare, standing at the sink washing up dishes.

'Hello! Good morning!' Clare smiled, looking around from washing the breakfast things in the sink and taking me in. 'How did you sleep?'

'Oh, I slept the sleep of the dead, Clare,' I breathed, sounding mournful, like I had never been so tired in a long time.

'Here, put on the kettle, I'll have a cup of tea with you, and then I'll start the dinner. There's cornflakes and bread, help yourself, take a look in the fridge. Do you want fruit? Throw in a banana. They're lovely in cornflakes, otherwise the only goodness is in the milk. Cornflakes are a waste of money, they do nothing for you!'

'Thanks, Clare,' I said, putting on the kettle and sticking bread in the toaster. I looked back, hearing screams behind me, jumping with the fright seeing the little boy behind me twisting himself laughing at me, lepping at the fright he gave me. 'Oh, what's your name?' I said, dropping to me knees looking into his little white face with the big blue eyes staring back at me, examining me. Deciding if he was going to like me or not. I shook me head slowly from side to side, staring into his eyes, saying, 'That was an awful fright you gave me. You make an awful big, big noise, you sound like a big, big giant! Are you a big giant?' I said, putting my arms in the air. His eyes got bigger and bigger, thinking himself a giant, and he shook his head up and down, his white hair bouncing, with his mouth open, agreeing with everything I said.

He's the spitting image of his mother, I thought, watching as he whirled around on his hunkers, holding a little car in his hand, and kept grinning at me. 'Ah, he's lovely,' I said, wanting to grab him up in a hug.

'That's Timothy!' Clare said, laughing. Watching him twirling like a monkey, his little arse nearly skidding the floor.

'Look, Mummy!' he said to me, showing me his car.

'He's calling me "Mummy"!' I laughed, staring at the size of him. Ah, he's so small, with his little legs and arms, but he looks like a miniature little boy.

'Yes, he calls all the ladies "Mummy". He's two, into the terrible twos!' she said, looking up at the ceiling. Straining her eyes and face to the heavens.

'Would you like me to make you a cup of coffee or tea, Clare?'

'Hmm! Listen, let's have a fry-up! I fancy a rasher and egg. What about you?' she said, her eyes staring at me, waiting for an answer. I hesitated, not wanting to make work for her. 'Ah, sure, why not?' she said, looking over at tiny baby Aoife sound asleep in her little basket over beside the armchair, keeping nice and warm beside the lovely heat coming out from the Aga. 'She's gone out cold. She had her last feed at six o'clock this morning, it's after nine now, she probably might not stir for about another hour or so. That gives me plenty of time to get a few things done,' she said, drying her hands and making for the fridge.

'Will I put on more toast for everyone?' I asked, wanting to make meself useful.

'Yeah! Go on! Toast! Toast, Mummy!' Timothy said, looking up at me with his big blue eyes and tapping his chest.

'Ah, listen to him,' I laughed. 'He's gorgeous! Just look at the size of him. Ah, Clare. Ye could pick him up and put him in yer pocket and run away with him, he's so lovely.' I suddenly dropped on me hunkers, grabbing him in a hug and kissing him on his cheeks before he had a chance to push me away, roaring in a rage.

'No, no, no! Toast, toast!' flapping me face away with his little hands. I laughed, delighted at getting me hug, and jumped up, buttering him a slice of toast.

'Will I put jam or marmalade on it for him? What will he drink?'

'Give him orange juice out of the fridge, Martha. And he likes jam, but give him marmalade. He has to develop his tastes,' she said, slapping down rashers and sausages on the grill over the cooker.

'Come on! Orange juice,' I said, watching his head spinning, trying to keep up with the toast going in one direction, and the smell of the fry in the other. His head snapping to the cornflakes and bananas landing on the table. He rushed over to the drawer, pulling out a huge serving spoon, and lashed back to the table, grabbing the cornflakes, upending half the packet in the bowl, spilling cornflakes everywhere. Then made to grab the heavy jug of milk. 'OK, OK, little man!' I said, grabbing hold of the jug. 'Let me help you.'

I picked up the bowl to empty half of it back and put in the milk, and he went into a rage, giving the table an unmerciful bang with the spoon, roaring, 'Mine, mine!'

'Yes, yes, of course they are yours. Oh, look what Mummy is doing!' He whipped his head around to look at her, and I dumped half the bowl back in the box and handed him the rest, putting in the milk. His head shot back, staring down at the cornflakes, trying to remember if that was all he had. 'Yes, yes! All for Timothy. Nobody is going to take them. Gawd! He has a great appetite,' I said, looking at Clare, laughing at the state he gets himself into over his grub.

'Oh, he would eat you under the table,' she laughed, watching him spoon half the bowl down the front of his pyjamas and open his mouth, trying to get the big shovel in.

'Will I get him a little spoon, Clare?'

'No, don't bother, if you don't want a fight on your hands. Let's eat,' she said, whipping two plates of rashers and sausages and fried eggs down on the table.

I sat down and started to butter the toast, and Timothy banged down his shovel and grabbed a rasher off my plate. 'Me, Mummy!' he said, holding the rasher in front of his face, knowing full well they were supposed to be mine.

I roared laughing at the little eyes pleading with me, his head cocked to one side. 'Yeah, you and me,' I said, shaking me head at him. He nodded agreement, and started to make short work of the rasher.

'These are the perks of being a mother,' she said, diving into her breakfast. 'Greg leaves early in the morning, to arrive at the hospital in the city centre. I get up to get his breakfast, but he wouldn't have time for this,' she laughed. 'I have to drag him out of the bed, then watch him running to the car still eating his breakfast, and grab the empty bowl out of the car before he takes off like a scalded cat. He's hopeless at getting up. His mother warned me about that, just before we got married,' she laughed. 'He's hoping to start his own practice when we get the money,' she sighed, her jaws working slowly, chewing on the breakfast, thinking about this. 'Goodness knows when that might be!' she said, letting air out through her nose, staring down at her plate, looking to see what she was going to eat next.

'Is it expensive to become a family doctor?' I asked.

'Oh, yes,' she said, shaking her head. 'You need the premises. We couldn't have it here. There's no access from the front. Unless we want patients traipsing through the house, staring at me eating a fry for breakfast,' she laughed, making a tinkly sound, like someone tapping gently on crystal. 'His brother Francis is also a doctor, so the two of them are planning to go into practice together.'

I stared at her, thinking she was really very, very pretty. Wondering how some people could be born so lovely. She has milky white skin that glowed like a pink hue. And her eyes are sky-blue, with the whites nearly shining. And she has natural blonde wavy curly hair that bounces around her head. 'Eh, you're very pretty,' I said. 'You must have had all the men going mad after you!' I said, grinning.

'Will you stop! They see blonde, and they think dumb! It's very hard to get men to take you seriously, with this,' she said, whipping her hand around her hair.

'Why, what's wrong with that?' I asked. 'I'd love the men chasing me all the time!'

'Ah, come on, Martha. They just want to drape you around their arm like a trophy. Then it's trying to get you drunk and have their wicked way with you!' she squealed. Picking up a bit of the fat off the rasher and throwing it down again.

'Still, you must have been on lots of dates,' I said, thinking about the idea of having men queuing up to take me out.

'No, it's not like that. The decent ones wouldn't come near you, because they think you are out of their league, and anyway! They think you're fast. Their mother wouldn't approve. A loose woman,' she screamed. Roaring her head laughing.

'Yeah! But you got a lovely one in the end. Greg is very handsome. The pair of you together look like film stars!' I gasped, not being able to get over the idea of being so pretty and getting a lovely husband to match you.

'Oh, tell that to Greg and he'll dine out on it for the next six months,' she said, roaring her head off with the laughing.

I started to munch on me toast as Timothy gently leaned over to take me other rasher, giving me a big smile, showing all his little teeth, and leaning his neck into his shoulders while he put the rasher in his mouth, watching me. I looked at the egg and sausage left sitting on me plate and dived into it before he got that, too.

'Yeah, eat that quickly,' Clare said, eyeing me plate. 'He really has taken a fancy to you. He thinks he's helping you!'

'Go on over and help Mummy,' I whispered to him. 'Look! She has sausages!'

'Ah, no chance. I'm well up to him,' she said, shoving the two sausages on her toast and biting into half of the sandwich, watching him staring over at her, thinking about it. 'I don't know where he gets his appetite,' she said, shaking her head and wondering about it. 'He would eat anything that doesn't move.'

'What about your other little boy?'

'Oh, Oliver! We have to collect him at one o'clock,' she said, looking over at the clock sitting on the back wall over the door into the garden. 'Yes, Martha. That's what I really need you for. To take him to school in the morning. He leaves at eight-thirty. And it's a twenty-five, thirty-minute walk there. I timed it walking back with him last week. Then you leave the house at twelve-thirty to collect him at one o'clock. My mother will be coming to stay here while we are away. We're going for three weeks. So you can take care of the children, you'll be in charge of them. My mother will do all the cooking.'

'Oh, that's a relief, Clare. I can't cook.'

'Oh, don't worry about that. My mother loves cooking. My little princess here,' she said, lifting her head to check over on the baby still clapped out cold, 'she's going to Greg's mother. I will pay you ten shillings a week. It's not much, but you don't have to do much. Just help with the children and collect Oliver from school. Maybe the odd bit of babysitting. We don't go out much, but you wouldn't mind that, would you?'

'Of course not,' I said, looking at her worried face.

'Now, it will only be for a total of five weeks. Then you will have to get another job. The nun said you will find work yourself, so it will give you time to look around. Is that OK?'

'Yeah, that's grand, Clare. I'll have another job fixed up by then, so don't worry. How old is Oliver?'

'He's five! Going on fifty!' she laughed. 'He's in senior infants. This is his second year at school. We started him at four. These two are like chalk and cheese. Timmy could charm the birds off the trees with his cheeky little grin, but poor Ollie has to work hard to make friends at school. He takes life far too seriously, and the other little boys give him a hard time. He questions everything and goes around giving them lectures on why he thinks they are being silly. Naturally, that doesn't win him many friends. He even contradicts the teacher,' she said, shaking her head laughing, but her eyes were sad. 'He's very intelligent. That can cause its own problems.'

'Do you mean he doesn't suffer fools gladly?' I said, trying to understand.

'Yes, I suppose that's one way of putting it, Martha,' she suddenly laughed. 'He probably needs to move up a class. We'll have to see. Anyway, I better get a move on,' she said, looking up at the clock. 'The time is moving quickly.'

She stood up, taking her dishes over to the sink, and I started to clear the table. 'I better make a start on the dinner. Baby is going to wake up any time now, wanting her next feed.'

I put the dustpan and sweeping brush in the press and looked around at the lovely clean kitchen. The sink was gleaming and everything was in its place. Lovely, I thought, giving a big sigh and dropping my shoulders, feeling contented after doing a good job.

The door whipped open and Clare flew in carrying Timmy under her arm, squealing and kicking his legs. 'Don't you dare send that poo flying out of that nappy,' she roared, trying to keep him at a distance and still hang onta him.

'Gawd! I can smell him from here,' I laughed, watching the nappy full of shit slip down his legs.

'Don't complain,' she said, laughing. 'You're safe over there, I'm the one in the firing line. Given half a chance, he'll tear it off and sling it everywhere, and not for the first time. Where's that Sudocrem?' she muttered, swinging her head around the kitchen. 'Martha, grab the baby's changing bag and give me out the cream. Quickly, before this fellow has a fit.'

She took off with the cream, swinging Timmy under her arm, and glanced up at the clock, shouting back to me, 'Goodness! Look at the time, Martha. You better get going now! And collect poor Ollie. He'll be left standing at the gate thinking we've forgotten about him.'

'OK, right. I'm on my way,' I said, flying up the stairs behind her to head to my room and get me coat.

'Now, you know where it is! Turn left at the top of the hill, and keep walking. Then right, up the hill, after the chuch. You can't miss it.'

'Right! I'll be there in a flash. Don't worry, I never have a problem finding my way around anywhere,' I said, rushing in to take me old green coat out of me suitcase, and dump the case back in the wardrobe, and tear off down the stairs.

I slammed the hall door shut behind me and took off up the hill, forgetting about the big dog that nearly scared the life out of me last night. Suddenly, out of nowhere, I heard a deep growling, and before I knew where I was a huge big brown hairy dog threw itself at the big black gates, rattling the hell outa them. Ah, help! Mammy! Me heart froze in me mouth as I whipped me head around, looking straight into the open snarling jaws of the biggest dog I ever saw in me life. I stared at it for a split second, and its mad red eyes stared back at me. Me jaw dropped, watching as the

muscles rippled along his back, then stiffen, getting himself ready
to spring. I flew me eyes the length of the gate, judging if he can
jump it, then another split second spent judging if I should run, or
stand me ground. 'Stand! That's always better!' I gasped to meself
outa breath. Then it slowly, deliberately, stepped backwards on its
paws, the eyes never leaving mine. It was as if he could read my
mind and was going to attempt to spring over the gate.

I blinked, swung me head, threw back me shoulders, and tore
off up the hill, me feet not touching the ground, running for me
life. I dare not look back. I blocked out everything, letting the
quiet around me settle, listening for the sound of racing paws
tearing up behind me, me skin on alert for the feel of hot wet
breath on the back of me neck. I rounded the corner at ninety
miles an hour, and kept running. 'Ah, help! Mammy!' I moaned,
me elbows flying like propellers. Me arse pulled tight, tingling
with the heat, waiting for the jaws to lock onta me, any minute
now! I could hear a car coming up behind me and shot out in
front of it, me whole body tingling, waiting for the knock, hoping
I'd left enough distance not to get meself killed and maybe slow
down the dog. Giving me time to throw out one eye to see if he
was behind me. No sign!

As I whizzed past the windscreen, seeing the driver look
shocked, flying the steering wheel for all he was worth, hearing
the screeching brakes, heading the car away from me, sliding over
towards the high wall. Jaysus! Am I kilt stone dead, I wondered as
I whirled around, me eyes peeling from him yanking the steering
again, trying to wrestle the car away from the high stone wall,
and fly along the footpath, then me eyes slid down the road. No!
The dog didn't make it.

Oh, Jaysus! What a fright I got for meself! Me heart was
pounding, and I could feel me face icy cold. Oh, Mammy! I
never want to go through the like of that again. I'm afraid of
me life of dogs, especially the size of that one. It looked like one
of them big hairy cows ye get in Scotland. I saw a picture of
them in a book, and that one was definitely bigger! I collapsed
back against the old stone wall, dropping me head, sliding down,

hanging onta me chest, trying to get a breath. Me legs seized up, feeling like lead.

'YOU THERE!' I snapped me head up just in time to see an aul fella, white as a sheet, leap out of the car making straight for me. Leaving the door wide open and the car wheels still up on the footpath. His head was bent forward with his fists clenched down by his side, wanting to get at me in a hurry, looking like he really meant business, because he was going to kill me when he got his hands on me. I watched him, not able to take me eyes off him, with his long gaberdine coat trailing out behind him. Fuck! I'm really for it now.

'YOU BLOODY MENACE!' he shouted, waving his fist at me.

'I . . . oh . . . eh, it was an accident,' I said, waving me arms, leaving me hand hanging in the air. Watching him get closer. Bloody hell, run! He looks like he might hold onto me for the police! They're very fond of them in places like this.

I took off, heading in the direction of the school, hoping he wouldn't follow me. Jaysus! I could lose me job. If the people find out I'm liable to be throwing meself under the path of cars . . . Well, that's the end of me. There's no way they would let me loose with Ollie! Fuck that bleeding dog! I'm never daring to go past that gate again!

I kept running, hearing the car come up behind me, and slowed down to get a look, ready to run back in the other direction. The car slowed down, and the baldy-headed aul fella started turning the handle on the window like mad, desperate to give me an earful. Then swung his head out, shouting, 'You bloody mad young horror! I shall find out where you live, and complain vigorously to your parents. How dare they let you loose on the unsuspecting drivers! Stand still when I am speaking to you!' he screamed, going purple in the face, really losing the rag altogether.

'Sorry, I'm in an awful hurry,' I mumbled, taking off again, knowing I was right. He would hang onta me, causing ructions. He's not the sort to let things go. That kind of aul fella would hang you for looking crooked at him. I can see he has nothing else to do with his time! Jaysus! I don't like the sort of people living around here! Many's the time in the city centre I raced out under a car and all they do is curse you out of it. Threatening to knock the head offa ye if they get their hands on ye.

'Right, Baldy! Catch me if you can!' I muttered. Turning right and flying up the hill, along the narrow road with the high walls, wrapping around huge houses hidden away in their own grounds. I looked back ready to stop and dare him. Then I could duck back, going in the opposite direction again, giving him no chance to turn the car around because the road was too narrow.

'No sign of him,' I muttered, staring down the hill into the distance. Hearing only the quiet of the trees rustling in the breeze behind the high walls. I felt the wind going out of me. Pity! I was beginning to enjoy meself. The thought of driving him mad when he couldn't get his hands on me. Ah, well! I took in a big sigh, dropping me shoulders, and let out a big breath, feeling better now me heart had stopped threatening to burst, and felt plenty of fresh air in me lungs after that run.

Right! Next time keep your eyes peeled for trouble. There's plenty of guard dogs round these parts. They must have plenty to rob and want to make sure no one gets their hands on their ill-gotten gains! I heard once, no one gets rich unless they first had to crawl on the backs of some poor unfortunates to get it. The poor are too honest, and they share the last penny in their pockets with you. Well! You certainly never become filthy rich unless ye came by it robbing someone. Hmm! Takes one robber to know another! I sniffed, looking up at the big mansions sitting on top of the hill. I was only in the half-penny place when I was doing me robbing. Yeah, well! One day I'm going to live in a big house like these, and I'll get there through hard work. No more robbing for me! I thought, straightening me shoulders and moving up the hill, feeling light as air, with not a care in the world.

I neared the school gates, seeing the mothers coming out holding little boys' hands and carrying their school bags. I started to hurry, wanting to get to Ollie. I rushed in the big gates and slowed down to get me bearings. The school was massive! It looked like a lovely old castle. With big arched brown doors and narrow long windows that went down to the ground. I could see a long winding avenue. With green lawns and trees around the high walls. Mothers were standing around talking to each other, while the boys went mad, chasing and pulling hell out of each other.

I passed two aul ones nattering away, one interrupting the other. Neither one was listening. The pair of them screaming at each other until one said, 'Stop, Simone! You just have to hear this.'

'Do tell!' gasped the other one. Thinking what she was going to say next, all the time shaking her head up and down while the other one yacked away for all she was worth in your woman's face. I could tell she wasn't listening. Her eyes kept blinking, with her neck leaning forward, ready to spring in, getting her turn when the other one paused for a breath.

One very glamorous woman was wearing a fur coat with black high heels, and a big black fur hat to match. I stopped to stare. Them high heels don't go with that fur hat, I thought. She should be wearing boots. Like she was really dressed for the snow that's not coming. I moved on slowly, earwigging and gaping with me mouth open. She was screaming in a high-pitched voice to another one with blonde hair curling around her fawn cashmere coat. 'My dear, he came crawling back on all fours with a huge bouquet of flowers clutched in one arm, and an enormous bottle of Miss Dior perfume in the other! And a box of After Eight mints gripped under his arm, grovelling! He was then positively drooling when he saw me standing there, in my long chic transparent night ensemble, giving him one of my "you may look but you are certainly not having me for dessert" looks! I rasped demurely, then swanned off in a sultry pout after polishing off half a bottle of Dom Bénédictine all on my poor ownsome.' Then she threw back her head, giving a piercing laugh.

The other one screamed her head off, neighing like a horse. Saying, 'Oh, Miranda! You really are terrible! Poor man. It must have cost him a small fortune!' The Fur Hat spluttered, dropping her head, bending herself in half, trying to get a breath with all the laughing.

I could smell the perfume as I slid past, not looking where I was going, and knocked against the handbag hanging off her arm. Suddenly, she noticed me and whipped her arm into the air, looking to see if it was still there, giving me a withering look. Then she slid her eyes sideways, taking me in from head to toe. Looking from me green coat that had seen better days, down to me bokety shoes that someone left behind when they were in a hurry to get loose from the convent. Now I was getting the wear outa them. She turned away, closing her eyes, and started whispering to the other aul one, the pair of them looking in my direction and saying something about me. Then your woman sniffed, and turned away from me like she had a bad smell under her nose and muttered something to the other one, and the two of them roared laughing.

I could feel me belly getting hot, with the rise coming up in me. I stared, boring holes in them. The cheek a her! Giving me dirty looks. I wonder who she thinks she is? Then I heard meself saying, 'Is that animal dead, missus? Or does it just smell like that? And while I'm asking, do you put all that face paint on with a trowel? You would need more then that, missus, to hide your hatchet face,' I said. Looking very sorrowful that someone could smell that bad and look so ugly. All the time pointing at her fur coat, then nodding me head slowly at her face.

'What? Did you say something?' she snapped, knowing full well what I just said

'Ah! Don't worry about it. We all have our afflictions. Look at your woman standing beside you. That poor aul one is mutton dressed as lamb. Tut, tut! What aul ones will do to try and look young.' Then I lifted me head into the air, twitching me nose like I just got a bad smell and marched off, trying to wobble me arse like Marilyn Monroe does in her films. Hearing them take in sharp breaths and mutter like mad, the pair of them going into shock. I could hear them agreeing like mad I was an insolent little bitch.

Jaysus! That one has so much paint and powder on her face, I wonder does her husband get an awful fright when he sees her without it? Fur coat an no knickers! They probably live on bread and margarine to afford this place. Real ladies don't carry on like that lot. They're all done up like a dog's dinner. I bet she looks like a dying aul hag first thing in the morning, after all her eating and drinking and getting up to no good. Huh! They really fancy themselves no end, the people living around here.

I sniffed, feeling better at having me say on what I thought about them. Yeah! That put them aul ones in their place, the annoyance at their insults vanishing outa me. Right, to hell with them! Now, where's little Ollie?

I spotted a teacher with books in her arms, standing with her ankles crossed and a pained look on her face. She was listening to a mother who was gabbing away like she was desperate. With her mouth working up and down, rattling her head like she was chewing on something. And all the time trying to hold onta the hand of a little fella hopping his hand up and down in the mammy's and doing a tug of war trying to escape. No, I won't bother asking her. That mother looks like she would eat the head offa me if I interrupted her in the middle of moiderin the poor aul teacher.

I wonder where Ollie is? I know what he looks like. I saw him in the photograph, and the mammy told the teacher Miss Prune to expect me.

I heard shouting coming from me right and saw three little fellas tearing lumps outa each other. 'Give it back!' screamed a little fella with shiny brown floppy hair as a young fella grabbed his school cap off his head with one hand, and with the other grabbed a hold of his school tie, trying to strangle him. The second young fella managed to tear the school bag away from the brown-haired little fella after tugging at it like mad. The little blackguard ended up flat on his arse when the little fella suddenly let go. He was now being dragged along the wet grass, desperately trying to grab hold of his tie to stop the life getting choked out of him. The fella with the hat then grabbed up the poor kid's blazer thrown on the grass and ran, waving it around his head, laughing and squealing like a hyena.

'I'm going straight to Miss Prune and tell her what you've done, Georgie Hillsop, and you too, Sebastian Fryer,' the little floppy-haired boy shouted, getting to his feet. Then it hit me. That's Ollie. Poor Ollie! Them little beggars!

'Hey! Cut that out!' I flew over, grabbing the hat and blazer off the little bully, and reached over to the other fella for the school bag, seeing the leather strap broken and the little demon wouldn't let it go.

'That's my bag! Give it back,' screamed Ollie, nearly losing his mind, red in the face, his eyes burning with rage, and tears.

'Let it go,' I said quietly, prising the fingers of the fair-haired, curly-headed little fella with the face of an angel, and the big blue spiteful eyes daring me to get the bag off him. 'Let it go,' I said again quietly, staring hard into his overfed white face with the knowing look in his baby-blue eyes that said, 'Nothing in this life will ever be refused to me.'

'How dare you touch me!' he screamed. 'I shall tell on you at once! My father will have you up before the bench. He is a High Court judge! You will go to prison!'

'Yes!' screamed the other fella. 'Tell Miss Prune, Sebastian! Let's go and tell her at once.'

'No, you don't,' I said, grabbing hold of the two of them. 'Now! You pair. Listen to me,' I said quietly, bending down and looking hard into each of their faces. They stood stock still, staring at me in shock, as I held them clamped together, side by side, staring daggers into their eyes. 'I am going to come to this school in the morning and tell all the boys you are both cowards! Do you know what that means?' They shook their heads in shock. 'No! You don't,' I said. 'Well, it means you are not real boys! You are not brave. You are two sissies. Do you know what that means?' They shook their heads up and down. Their eyes locked on mine. 'Now, if the big boys hear you are both sissies! Cowards! Not brave! What do you think they will say? They will laugh at you, and shout every time they see you, "There go the two little cowards. They are bullies. They have to pick on other little boys who have no friends to protect them!" Do you think that might happen?' I said, looking very shocked. 'And, what's worse . . .' I took in a deep breath, 'All the other boys in the class will laugh and call you names because you bully other little boys! So, do you want me to come here in the morning and tell all the mammies and the other boys in the school what you were doing to Oliver? I will, you know!' I said quietly. They shook their heads up and down, and side to side, not knowing what was happening, and trying to take everything in at once. 'Do you want that to happen?' I whispered, looking very sad.

'No!' the blue-eyed little angel with the demon gone out of his eyes whispered. Now gone into complete shock. Nothing had ever happened to him like this before. No one had ever chastised him. Poor cocky little fella. If something went wrong, he wouldn't be able to manage. I can see no one has ever threatened him in all his born days. Now he had the fear of God in him.

'So, if you don't want me to tell, what do you think you can do to make up to poor Oliver for tormenting him?' I asked.

'We are sorry,' the pair of them whispered.

'Hmm! I don't know if that's enough,' I said, shaking me head. 'What about if you all become friends? You make Oliver your best friend as well, then you'll be three best friends and you can become heroes! Do you know why?'

'No!' the other fella said, moving closer, wanting to hear more.

'Well, if someone else tries to hurt Oliver, you will be able to rescue him. You can become his protector. Like Ivanhoe! Did you ever see him on the television?'

'Yeah! Yes, we did!' they shouted, getting all excited.

'Right, so which one of you is going to be Ivanhoe?'

'Me!'

'No, me!' they shouted, thumping their chests.

'Right! So, you can talk to Oliver tomorrow when he comes into school, and decide what names you are going to call yourselves. Yeah? Or I have a better idea,' I said. 'You can be the Three Muskeeters!'

'I know that book,' shouted Sebastian.

'So do I! Daddy read me that story when I was little!' shouted Georgie, hopping up and down with excitement.

'Yes, I have that book as well, and I can read it myself!' shouted Oliver.

They stopped to look at him, the air going out of them at the thought of Oliver being able to read for himself.

'He will be in charge of reading and writing down all the orders you want to give to your men,' I said, looking at them. 'You need someone who can read, right?'

'Right!' they shouted. Grabbing Oliver around the shoulders, one each side of him.

'You are our new best friend,' whispered Sebastian.

'Yeah, three best friends,' laughed Georgie, shaking himself with the excitement, then looking very seriously into Oliver's eyes. 'Do you want to be our best friend?' whispered Georgie, sounding like this was the most sacred thing in the whole wide world.

Oliver was confused, looking hopeful, but suspicious at the same time. 'Do you mean you will play with me?' asked Oliver. 'And not fight with me?'

'Nooo, never!' they squeaked. Looking shocked at the idea.

'OK,' Oliver said, letting out a big breath, agreeing, like he was doing them a favour. 'I will speak to you in the morning when I have a think about what names we should call ourselves.'

'No, I'm going to decide my own name!' shouted Sebastian.

'Me too!' shouted Georgie.

I saw Oliver heaving in a big breath, about to say something else, and I laughed, saying, 'You have plenty of time tomorrow to work out everything. Just remember the Three Muskeeters' motto, what they always say to each other, "One for all, and all for one!"' I laughed, wrapping me hands around them, pulling them together. Then whipped Oliver ahead of me, saying, 'Bye-bye, now! Remember, you are all very brave muskeeters! You look after each other.'

'Bye, Sebastian! Bye, Georgie!' shouted Oliver, waving his hand like he had been friends with them for years.

'Bye, Oliver!' they shouted.

I waved at the teacher, making her way down to me, saying, 'I'm collecting Oliver!'

She smiled down nodding her head, then shouted at the two little fellas, 'Come along, boys. Down here to me, where I can keep an eye on both of you!'

I stopped at the gate, calling Oliver. 'Come on, Ollie! Put on your blazer and your hat.'

'No! I don't have to. You carry it! We must only wear those for school.'

'OK! You're the boss. Let's go,' I said, hanging onta the stuff and wondering how I was going to get past that dog.

We moseyed our way home slowly, with Ollie stopping to bend down and get a look at every leaf and bits of bark lying on the road, and wild bushes growing along the ditches, and looking up to see if there were any owls nesting in the high old trees.

'Look, Ollie! Conkers,' I shouted. Pointing to the brown chestnuts lying further down the path from the branches of the big old chestnut trees hanging over the wall. We flew down the path, and stopped, bending down to pick them up and load up Ollie's school bag. 'We can put holes and string through them tonight, and bring them to school in the morning, and you can have great gas having conker fights! What do you think?'

'Yeah!' Ollie said, the idea of it just dawning on him.

'We can test them out when you get home, see which one is the best. Then you will have the champion one!'

'Yeah? Yeah!' Ollie screamed.

'We'll make some for your new friends, Georgie and Sebastian.'

'No!' Ollie said, stopping to think about this, his face dropping. 'They won't really be my friends,' he said, looking very mournful, a faraway look in his eyes.

'Why not? Course they will!'

'Nooo. I don't have any friends. They don't like me. Everyone is very mean to me.' I felt me heart sinking, looking at his poor face. He's not as good-looking compared to Timmy. His red apple-shaped face, with the big freckles and the grey eyes don't exactly jump out at you! And if you put the two of them together . . . well, poor Ollie has no chance at all. Fuck. He's gorgeous in his own right! The kids just need to get to know him.

'Ollie! Do all the boys have best friends? Or are there any like you, wanting to take their time about who they want to be friends with?'

'Nooo, everyone got a best friend last year, when we started in the baby class. Except Wally Wilson . . .'

'Yeah! Maybe he could be your friend.'

'Nooo! He doesn't count!' Ollie said, seeing me eyes light up. 'He still wets his pants, and cries for his mummy all the time!'

'Oh! What about the other boys? Can they read like you?'

'Nooo, they are only starting on the baby books. I'm the only one who can read properly!' he said, sounding even more mournful, stabbing at the weeds coming out of the holes in the wall with a stick.

'Right, come on, Ollie! We are going to get you new friends. Let's get these conkers home, and we'll do loads of them up for the morning. Then at breaktime you can hand them out to Georgie and Sebastian, and only people who want to play with you! Right, Ollie?' I said to him flying up behind me. 'And you can help them with their reading. They need you to help them. But you have to be patient, they are not as clever as you! Do ye see what I mean?' I said, looking at him, seeing him thinking about this. 'You see, you have a big, big brain. They only have little brains. So they don't understand what you are talking about. So, pretend you don't know lots of things, and ask them to help you sometimes!'

'Do you think that would work?'

'It would make them think they are like you. They've got a big brain, too. So if they feel important, they might think you are great! Whadaye think, Ollie?'

'Hmm!' he said, rattling his head, trying to work this one out! 'Do you mean I have to stop interrupting people and telling them they are wrong? And they won't fight with me because I keep quiet?'

'Yeah! Yeah! Let them figure it out for themselves! You just play with them. Bring in the conkers. Then another day you can bring in a football.'

'I don't like football,' he said.

'Oh, right! Well, what about a yo-yo? Bring in a couple of yo-yos.'

'Yes! I'll ask Mummy to buy yo-yos for me and my new friends!'

'Great! And I'm going to be taking you to school and collecting you at lunchtime. So, if you're not happy about the way things

went, you can tell me then, and I will sort it out for ye! What do
you think? Is that a good idea?'

He shook his head up and down, agreeing. But still thinking
hard about this, saying nothing, and just put out his hand for
me to take, and we set off for home. Both of us lost in our own
thoughts. Me thinking how I'm going to get past that dog, with
the fear of God in me at the thought, and him thinking how he
was going to get around this business of making a friend.

5

I finished washing up the pots and pans and dishes after the dinner, and wiped around the sink, giving it a good rub to bring up the shine of the stainless steel. 'Right! That's done,' I sighed, putting me hand on me head and feeling how hot and dry it is. Gawd. I really don't feel too good.

I folded the cleaning cloth and dropped it into the little dish for holding the washing-up stuff. Happy now I was finished at last. I didn't move, feeling it was too much of an effort, and stood looking out the window into the garden. Oh, me bloody head is dizzy and I feel a bit chilly. It must be the damp, I thought, looking out at the grey mist hanging in the air, with the evenings getting darker very fast now. It must be the foggy nights, I thought to meself, thinking I started to feel this way for the last few nights and first thing in the morning. It always comes on when the night starts drawing in, making the air chilly. It looks cold and damp out there, I thought, staring tiredly, looking at the nearly bare trees, and the wet damp from the mist settling on the grass.

I think I'll go up to bed. Clare doesn't need me any more, she has got Ollie down for the night after reading him his bedtime story. Right! That's what I'll do, I decided, staring at the floor, wanting to get meself moving. I moved slowly past the sitting-room door, hearing the television on, and Greg roaring his head laughing at it. I climbed the stairs thinking, God help anyone old or ailing. Now I know what it feels like to be ninety and trying to climb Mount Everest. It can't be any worse than these stairs when you're feeling banjacked. I opened the door to me room and sighed happily, seeing me lovely bed waiting for me. Oh, just let me in there, I shivered with cold and exhaustion. I threw off me clothes and dived into me pyjamas and slid under the bedclothes, giving a huge sigh of contentment, enjoying the feeling of me eyes going very heavy, and sinking very fast down into a deep sleep.

I heard a voice from the distance and tried to lift me head off the pillow. 'Martha! Are you awake?'

'Yes, yes! I'm coming.' I struggled to bring the room into focus, everything was foggy. I could hear Clare calling me to get up and take Ollie to school. But everything was spinning and I couldn't make out anything. Jesus!

'No, stay there!' I heard Clare say. I could see her shape standing in the doorway.

'No, no! Just wait. I'm coming now,' I said, trying to get meself out of the bed. Wanting to get up and go about me business.

'No! You have to stay there. You look terrible,' Clare said.

I gave up and dropped me head back on the pillow, thinking I should get up, and sank back into sleep. I woke up with an elderly long skinny man looking down at me, with his bushy eyebrows raised over a pair of glasses sitting on his nose. Then he lifted his head, talking to Clare, while the two of them stood next to me bed.

'Good girl. Sit up,' he said, holding one end of a stethoscope wrapped around his neck and the other ready to plank on me. Clare lifted the back of me pyjamas, and the doctor said, 'Breathe in for me.' Then he listened to me sounding like I was on me last gasp, heaving me chest for breath, and wheezing like a kettle letting ye know the water is boiled. 'Hmm! Bad case of bronchitis,' he said to Clare. 'Antibiotic, warm drinks, keep her warm in bed, Clare, and get her to cough it up.' Then he was gone, and I was out like a light again. Me last thought, thinking poor Clare! Now she has gobshite me to put up with, as well as the children, and I'm supposed to be helping her! I felt really ashamed of meself, because I never, ever got sick, not even for one day, when I was in the convent, more's the pity!

I woke up hearing the muffled sounds of laughing and shouting and the television roaring coming up through the ceiling. I opened my eyes, staring straight ahead at the rain lashing against the window pane, and leaves blowing off the trees in the front garden. I could hear the wind howling around over me head in the attic, and I snuggled down deeper, sinking into me lovely soft mattress, and pulled the heavy green satin eiderdown over me, right up to me chin. 'Ah, lovely!' I sighed, feeling snug and warm and sleepy, letting me eyes slide around me lovely warm cosy room and the wind and rain howling outside, and the sound of cars hissing through the wet roads, all rushing to get home after a hard day's work, wanting to be resting just like me. Snug as a bug in a rug.

The door opened and Ollie marched in, with Clare coming in behind him carrying a tray. 'Hullo, Martha. What happened to you? Why are you sick? Can you get up and take me to school? I have loads and loads of things to tell you,' he puffed, trying to get everything out at once. 'But Mummy said I can't disturb you!'

'Hi, Ollie!' I croaked, pulling meself up in the bed and starting to cough.

The door flew in, hitting the wall, and Timmy came flying in, landing on the floor. 'Me, Mummy, me!' he shouted, picking himself up in an awful hurry, not wanting to miss out on anything.

'Everybody out!' shouted Clare. Landing the tray down on me bedside table.

'Nooo!' Ollie said, twisting himself in half to stop Clare grabbing him. 'I have big important things to tell Martha,' he said, looking up from the floor, half of him bent in two, with his eyebrows raised, pleading in a quiet voice. She stared at him for a minute, then he stood up, waving his finger, bending into her. 'It won't take long, Mummy!' he whispered, sounding like he was the mammy and she was the child.

'How are you, Ollie?' I croaked, pulling meself up to a sitting position, and spluttering, taking a fit of coughing, me mouth filling with thick gobs of phlegm.

'Spit that out,' shouted Clare, looking around at the side table, grabbing a white Styrofoam cup. Just as Timmy came flying over screaming, 'Me, me!' reaching up to grab a hold of the tray.

'No! Don't touch that. It will fall,' screeched Clare, grabbing his hands pulling at the tray.

I could hear the baby screaming coming up the stairs, and Greg flew in the door laughing, with the baby roaring in his arms. 'Princess is having a major wobbly, darling,' he said, stretching his long legs across the room with the baby red in the face, her eyes flying around the room and landing on the mammy. Then she stretched herself the full length, opening her little bud mouth wider and stuck out her tiny fists, letting her tongue hang out, and went even redder in the face, with her eyes shut tight and went mad with the rage, nearly having a fit. Greg carried her across his outstretched arms, letting her sit in the palm of his big hands, and landed her into the mammy's arms.

Clare's face creased into a half-cry and half-smile, looking around at all the confusion, not knowing what to do next. 'Get the boys to bed!' she shouted, reaching out with one hand to grab Timmy.

'How's the patient?' Greg said, laughing down at me with his hands on his hips, taking no notice of the roars around him.

'GREG!' screamed Clare. 'Get them out of here! Martha, grab that tray before it ends up on the floor. Everybody out!' she roared, flying for the door. 'I'm going to see to this little minx, you get them started on their baths, Greg!'

She stopped to look back, seeing Greg lean down to me, saying, 'You have to cough that up, young lady! No swallowing it back.'

'Right!' I croaked, as I held onto the tray, trying to stop Timmy from upending me tea. Feeling foolish at all the confusion I was causing.

'Gawd almighty! Give me patience,' huffed Clare, staring at the ceiling with the baby hopping herself up and down in her arms screaming. 'Bed!' she shouted. Then flew out the door and down the stairs.

'I have a champion conker!' roared Ollie. 'I have him in my bag. He's called King! He knocked out seven other conkers! Do you want to see him? Do you, Martha?' roared Ollie in one breath as he was being heaved out of the room.

'Tomorrow! You can tell Martha everything tomorrow! Now it's bedtime, young man!' shouted Greg. 'Come here, you! Timmy! No!' he raced over to take me omelette out of Timmy's mouth.

He had managed to climb up on the chair and grab it while I was looking at Ollie. 'Naughty Timmy!' the daddy said, giving a little slap to Timmy's fist to make him drop the whole omelette he was dangling in his mouth. 'Take your tea, Martha, or what's left of it,' he muttered, half laughing. Then he grabbed up Timmy, dangling him under his arm, and whipped Ollie out the door, dangling him under the other arm, saying, 'Come on, you holy terrors! Bath, book and bedtime. What are we reading tonight, boys?'

I could hear the shouting fading away as Greg put out his long leg, kicking the door shut after him and I stared at it for a few minutes, wondering if the room really was silent again. Then me eyes lit on the tray with the half-eaten omelette and the fried tomatoes sitting on the plate and I reached over, grabbing hold of the tray, and landing it on me lap. I looked at the other plate with the three slices of melted butter on the toast, and poured out a cup of tea from the little teapot and put in milk from the little stainless-steel milk jug and dived into the egg and tomatoes. Lovely. Yum, delicious! With bits of rashers inside and thick melted cheese on the outside. I wasn't in the mood for eating up until now. I still wasn't bothered until I tasted this. Gawd! Clare is the best person in the whole world. She's a real lady, not like them gobshites in their fur coats at that very grand school! No, they're only tuppence half-penny looking down at tuppence. Clare is the real thing. Greg was very lucky to get her! She's the best mammy as well.

I suppose Clare is lucky, too, to get Greg! He worships the ground she walks on. They match each other great. Even though he's a bit dopey when it comes to helping Clare with the children. She has to tell him every single thing. He pretends he can't do anything. Then she gives up and does it herself, saying it's quicker that way. He laughs, and beetles off, rubbing his hands together, and planks himself down to watch the television and read the newspaper. Huh! I'm well up to his game! So is Clare!

'Oh, it's all go!' gasped Clare, puffing and struggling her way down the stairs with two heavy bags and another one thrown over her shoulder. With me banging down behind her dragging the carrycot,

and Ollie and Timmy pushing behind me, carrying a big bag of
terry-cloth nappies between them. 'Greg, get them blasted bags out
of the hallway, we can't move with them there!' she roared, trying to
squeeze past the big suitcases stacked against the wall, blocking the
stairs. Then we heard a car pull in and a door slamming, then the
doorbell rang. 'Oh, for the love of God! Someone open the door.
That's Granny. GREG! What are you doing up there? I only asked
you to bring the pram down. Not make it!'

'Coming, my sweet!' Greg roared in a sing-song voice. Then he
was towering above us, swinging the pram at the top of the stairs.

'Will you move, darling? You are blocking the whole stairwell!
I can't get out!' she screamed. 'These bloody cases are blocking
everyone in!' Then she muttered curses under her breath, looking
back with her face twisting, and trying to lift the heavy bags up
in the air.

'Everybody back up!' Greg shouted, landing the folded-up pram
back on the landing and grabbing the bag off Ollie and Timmy, who
were fighting over wanting to carry it by themself. I turned around
with me bags and went up the stairs again, and Greg snatched it off
me and landed it on the landing, then belted off down the stairs and
squeezed past the mammy, grabbing up the cases and landing them in
the sitting room. Then he whipped the door open, shouting, 'Mother-
in-law! It's marvellous to see you. Come in, come in. Goodness!
You get better-looking and younger every time I see you,' he said,
grabbing the woman with a smile about to light up her face. I was
watching from the crack in the door. But before she could draw the
next breath, he was steering and swinging her into the hall.

A little woman appeared in the door wearing very high heels
and staggered to her feet, trying to steady herself, as Greg grabbed
her again with one hand around her waist, and the other one on
her shoulder, making her head disappear under his arm, because
she was so small. 'Darling, it's your mother!' he roared, looking
up the stairs, then peeling his eyes back down again, landing
them on Clare standing right in front of him, forgetting she was
there. Clare stared daggers at him, looking like she wanted to
shout curses at him this time. 'Here we are,' he said, talking to

the granny as if she was a child. Then letting her go, shutting the hall door, and stretched his face, making his eyes turn, crossing them, then rolled up inta the back of his head. Tormenting Clare behind the mammy's back. And he vanished into the sitting room, humming a tune, taking the bags with him that Clare dumped out of the way.

'Mother! Thank God you're here! It's like a mad house! It's absolute bedlam. We're trying to get the baby's things organised!' Clare screamed, sounding like she was crying.

'Oh, darling! I'm here at last,' gushed the mammy, looking up at Clare, then sweeping past me and staring down at all the stuff coming down the stairs, and vanishing, with Greg flying up and down into the sitting room. 'Greg, dear! Would you ever run out to the car and bring in my suitcases?'

'Did you drive yourself, Mother dear?' Greg beamed, rushing back and staring down at her with his hands on his hips, a big grin spread all over his face.

'Oh, you have no idea what I went through. I got stuck in Nenagh, right on the bridge, with a herd of sheep running in all directions. I thought the lot of us was going to end up in the river!'

'Mother! Greg! Sorry to interrupt, Mother. Greg! Please do something. Bring in Mother's cases from the car. Don't just stand there!'

'Right, darling. On my way!'

'No, stop! Bring down the baby's cot first.'

He stopped dead, with his head and foot out the front door and his arse still stuck inside, and whipped himself back in, saying in one breath, 'Whatdoyouwantmetodofirst!' He puffed. Standing still, like a statue, waiting for his next orders.

'Oh, really, Greg! You would try the patience of a saint,' Clare said, hearing the baby wake up and start to roar her head off. 'That's all I need,' she muttered, swinging herself off, sounding like she was going to cry her eyes out, and ran into the kitchen to grab up the baby just as she was working herself up for a piercing roar.

'Sorry, darling. Do nothing. You go and put your feet up. Leave everything to me!' he roared down the hall.

Then he tore up the stairs, and Ollie roared. 'Granny! Did you bring us something nice? Have you got a present for us?' he said, tearing over to grab at her big brown leather handbag.

'Oh, Oliver darling! Let me look at you,' she squealed, grabbing him and pushing him out to stare at him, then whipping him back, crushing him in a big hug, roaring, 'You got so big since I last saw you. Give Granny a great big kiss,' and she plastered his face with red lipstick. He rubbed his cheek like mad, keeping his eyes glued on her handbag and trying to whip it off her arm.

'Me, me, Mummy!' screamed Timmy, flying over and tripping himself up in his hurry.

'Sorry, Mumsy. Gangway!' roared Greg, humping the pram down the stairs, squeezing past her with the pram in the air.

'Oh, did you bring in my luggage, Greg, dear?' she breathed, her head whipping up to him and flying around in all directions, trying to take everything and everybody in all at the same time. 'Come on! Come on, darlings! Let's go into the kitchen and see our new baby sister,' she roared, whipping away her handbag and flying off down the hall in her big pointy high heels.

'Presents!' screamed Ollie, still holding onto the bag, getting himself pulled down the hall.

'Me, me! Sweeties!' roared Timmy, flying after her.

Greg staggered in with two huge suitcases, landing them down behind the door and muttering, 'My worst nightmare! She's come to stay for good.' Then he gave the door an almighty kick with the back of his foot. Just as the bell rang again.

Then the letter box rattled and a voice shouted in, 'Cooee! Greg, let me in. It's me. Mummy.'

Greg dropped his head, and started to tear his hands through his hair, scratching like mad, mumbling, 'I give up! All hell is about to break loose.' Then he stared at me for a second, standing on the end of stairs, and whispered, 'These two hate each other,' he said, stabbing his thumb down the hall. 'Never the twain shall meet. It's the war of the grannies!' Then he whipped himself to the door, opening it and letting out a roar. 'Mammy! Come in, come in,' wrapping his arms around a huge woman wearing a black three-quarter-length wool coat, with a brown fur animal wrapped around her neck and a big felt hat with a feather sticking up.

'Oh, Greg, sweetie! Don't be so common!'

He wasn't listening. He was too busy sucking on her cheeks, and whipping back to roar into her face, waving his arms around, singing, 'I'd walk a thousand miles for one a dem smiles. MA A AH . . . MEE . . . MAMMEEEE!'

'Oh, really,' she said, laughing and twisting her face in disgust. 'Go away out of that with yourself, you silly boy,' she whined, flapping him with her soft kid-leather beige gloves. 'Where is everybody? Are they in the kitchen? Cooee! It's meee! Granny's here! Where's my boys?' she sang, rushing herself down to the kitchen and stopping dead just inside the door. 'Oh! How nice to see you, Mrs Enright,' she said in a low moan, not sounding like she meant a word of it.

'How are you, Mrs Flynn?' squeaked the other granny. Making it sound like a threat. There was a silence for a minute and I tore down the hall not wanting to miss anything.

'Come and see what Granny has for you!' Greg's mammy shouted, waving at the boys and landing her big bag down on the kitchen table.

'I think they are about to have their tea. Isn't that right, Clare?' said the little granny. Looking woebegone. Hanging onto a big bag of lemon sweets nobody wanted any more. She stood, holding them out in the air, letting them dangle, but still nobody was interested in them.

'What did you bring us?' screamed Ollie, flying over to grab at the big shopping bag as the granny landed out big bars of chocolates, bags of Tayto crisps, packets of biscuits.

'And a lovely teatime express cake for your tea, dear,' she said, handing Clare a big box with a yellow ribbon tied around it. Then the little granny flew over and whipped the baby out of Clare's arms, saying, as she settled her in her arms, throwing her eye to the other granny, much as to say, 'Well, you're not getting your hands on this one!'

'Oh, Clare, love,' she said, sitting herself down in the armchair next to the Aga, making the baby comfortable in her arms. 'She's the spitting image of your great-aunt Mindy, who went out on the African missions and never came back. Every bit of her the spitting image of my side of the family.'

'Nonsense!' roared the big granny, whipping her head around, making the feather shiver on her hat, busying herself in the middle of peeling the silver paper off the big bars of chocolate, leaving Timmy trying to get the whole bar bigger than himself shovelled down his neck. 'Where do you think she got that beautiful strawberry blonde head of hair from?'

'Not from him,' the little granny snorted, pointing her finger at Greg bending down, grinning with his hands in his pockets, looking from one granny to the other. 'Sure he has brown hair,' the little granny sniffed, lifting her baldy eyebrows. She had to paint in eyebrows with an eyebrow pencil. But she didn't get it right. One side of her face had an eyebrow going halfway across her face, nearly to her ear. While the other side was up in the air, nearly working its way to her forehead. Making it look like the two halves of her face didn't belong to each other. Ahh! I felt a bit sorry for her, staring at the almighty show she made of herself with the baby-blue eyeshadow sitting over one eye, where it had smudged.

'Of course he was blond when he was a baby! Weren't you, Greg, dear?'

'Oh! The car keys, Mother! I want to start loading up the baby's stuff.'

'Yes!' Clare sniffed, disgusted at the way her mother was being treated. 'Time is running out. We still have a lot to do!'

'Yes, yes, of course, Clare, dear! Will your mother be staying to look after the boys? Naturally, I am taking baby. It would be too much to expect of your mother at her age of advancing years!'

There was a terrible silence while they all swallowed this. Then the little granny exploded. 'On the contrary! You would have to be in your full health and be on your toes looking after two fine healthy strong boys! Someone in your condition wouldn't be able for all that running around.'

'I am sorry!' the big granny snapped, whirling herself around, stopping the peeling of the chocolate, and narrowing her nose, squeezing her mouth into a pucker. 'Might I ask what condition would you be referring to?'

'Oh, I don't mean to cause offence!' mewled the little granny, delighted she'd caused an awful lot of offence. 'I just meant with you having to carry all that weight. It must be an awful burden on your heart. I know of course you can't help it. It's in your nature. Being such a big woman and all that!'

'MOTHER, IS THE CAR OPEN? WHERE'S DAD?' screeched Greg, whipping himself into action, looking around at the hall, then giving a quick look over at Clare, who was staring stony-faced down at the baby's feet kicking like mad to get out of the granny's arms.

'YES, IT IS!' screamed the big granny, raging at being interrupted while she was trying to think of something vicious to throw back at the little granny. 'He's gone on walkabout!' Then she lifted her huge breasts, taking in big breaths, and marched over, snatching the baby out of the little granny's grasp, cooing, 'Come to Granny. You must surely be making strange, with all these foreign faces huffing and puffing around you, you poor little precious diddledums. But you know your Granny Flynn! Of course you do!' she said, tickling the baby under the chin, who just gaped back up at her, her huge big blue eyes starting to water, and her tiny little mouth starting to wobble, wondering when she should start crying, with all this snatching going on.

'Yes, I was the first to see you after you were born!' she rasped, nodding her head up and down, sounding hoarse from all the insults she was flying around. 'Except for my son, of course,' she cooeed over at the little granny, who shut her gaping mouth, clamping her lips together, her eyes narrowing, looking like she was thinking it would be worthwhile doing time in Mountjoy Prison just to wipe the smirk offa that aul one's face.

'Come on, Martha. Give me a hand to load up,' said Greg, then he was out of the room and tearing out with the pram. 'Bring the carrycot!' he shouted back to me.

I raced into the sitting room, grabbing up the cot, and was out the door, standing in next to no time beside a big black car. 'Gawd! This is very grand,' I breathed to Greg, watching him opening the big car boot and throwing in the pram. 'Your parents must be very rich.'

'No, Mother just lives beyond Father's means. He spends so long hidden away in that dusty old office, you would have to send in a search party to find him. Then dig him out buried underneath all those boxes and files. The poor man sits day and night poring over figures, I expect he's covered in cobwebs by now.'

'What does he do, Greg?'

'He's an accountant,' Greg sniffed, 'not a millionaire, as Mother would have people believe. Mothers!' he moaned, curling his lip and rolling his eyes. 'Here! Give me that cot. We'll put this in the back seat for baby to sleep in. Now! Back into the fray.' Then he threw himself back into the house.

I laughed, racing in behind him again, to bring out the tons of bags the baby was going to need. 'That's the lot,' Greg said, standing with his hands on his hips, eyeing the car with the back wheels nearly sitting on the ground from so much stuff we packed into it. 'Would you ever believe one tiny girl would need so much stuff?' he asked, shaking his big mop of curly hair. 'Any more than this and we will need to hire a removal truck to send her off. Oh, Dad's coming,' he said. Waving at a tall, thin, grey-faced old man with a grey moustache. Looking like his head was too heavy for his shoulders, he was so stooped. He was wearing a grey pinstriped suit, with a trilby hat sitting on his head, sucking on a pipe. The old man took the pipe out of his mouth, giving a big smile, and waved back.

'Good girl, Martha! Thanks for all your help,' Greg said, smiling down at me then taking off, slowly running to meet his dad.

'How are you?' I heard the old man say, clapping Greg on the back.

I turned and rushed back into the house. Clare was filling the baby's bottles with milk she'd made up and looked around at me with a very tired look on her face. 'Everything's packed up for the baby, Martha,' she said quietly, as I moved over to stand beside her.

'Yeah, we couldn't squeeze another thing in, Clare. The car is filled to the brim.'

'Oh, don't say that,' she whispered, looking at me very seriously. 'I hope you left room for the old battle axe over there!' And she lifted her eyebrows, throwing her eyes back over her shoulder.

'Yeah,' I laughed in a whisper. 'But she's going to have a tight squeeze.'

'Good enough for her. So long as I get her out of here, the sooner the better,' she whispered, jumping her eyebrows up and down, her eyes laughing. I snorted, wanting to give a big laugh. 'Don't you dare,' she said, giving me a dig with her elbow. 'Come on. Get me the Milton steriliser over from the worktop. I want to empty it. Then we can get her moving.'

'Right,' I whispered, flying over and handing her the big box holding all the soothers sitting inside, getting sterilised.

We loaded the stuff into a big leather bag, then Clare said, 'Is there room on the back seat for this? Where's Greg got to?'

'Oh, he's talking to his dad.'

'Here we are,' Clare said. 'Are we all ready, then? Say goodbye to Granny, boys. She's going to take care of baby while Mummy and Daddy are away.'

'I'll take the baby. You go on out to the car and seat yourself in. Give Granny a kiss, boys!' the big granny shouted, wondering if she was getting the bum's rush out the door or not.

'Bye-bye, Granny,' Ollie said, wrapping his arms around the granny's neck. Timmy came tearing himself up from the floor, covered from head to toe in chocolate. His hands were soaked in it, and he held them out in front of him, just as the granny turned around, with her eyes suddenly turning to shock, and not getting a word out before he had his hands grabbing hold of her furry animal with the head and eyes staring out, and the two paws dangling at the other end. He grabbed a hold of it and swung out of it, planting a lovely big kiss on her eye, covering it in chocolate. I stared, then burst out laughing as she grabbed for her handbag, squealing, 'Oh, no! Naughty Timmy!

Don't touch Granny. Wait until I get my handkerchief. Where is it?' She searched her handbag, squinting, with one eye closed. Then rubbed her eye, making it worse.

'Me, Mummy, me!' Timmy shouted, looking up at her, not finished with his kisses.

Oliver stared, then said, 'Granny, you look terrible! Your eye is covered in brown chocolate.'

The little granny screeched, laughing, saying, 'Oh, dear. Poor Timmy! Look at the state of your poor Granny Flynn. Tut tut! What a shame he ate all that chocolate. Now you will be sick!'

'Somebody get me a tissue. Oh, goodness! My make-up will be ruined. What am I to do? Is there a mirror down here? Do I have to go up to the bathroom? Oh, this is too much. Clare! Clare! Wait a minute, I have to repair my make-up!'

Clare whipped her head around, standing at the car talking to the granddad. Then she whipped it back for a second look and let out an almighty laugh. 'Oh, Greg! You are dreadful for saying such a thing,' Clare roared, trying to cover up the laugh, by slapping Greg on the arm, and holding the baby in the other, while the granny stared, wondering if she was laughing at her.

'Wha . . . what!' Greg barked, spinning his head, wondering what was going on. Clare buried her face in the baby's blanket, while the granddad looked up at the granny under his bushy grey eyebrows. Then looked at Clare with a glint in his eye.

I rushed back in, closing the door, and whipped Timmy over to the sink, lifting him under the arms, keeping him well away from me, and turned on the tap, grabbing his hands and holding them under to wash them. 'Now! Lovely and clean,' I said, grabbing the washcloth and rinsing it under the tap to wipe his face and hair. 'Oh, oh! Somebody is going to need a bath tonight,' I said, looking at his little white face beginning to turn a different colour. It looks a bit green, I thought, staring at him as he licked the water from his chin, tasting the soapy facecloth. 'Hmm! You look a bit sick to me. For once, Timmy, I don't think you will be wanting any grub for your tea! Will you now?' I said, leaning into him and landing a kiss on his face. It felt wet and cold, and still smelled of chocolate. He shook his mop of blond hair up and down then all around. Not sure what the right thing to say was.

'Come on,' said the granny. 'Let's get up to the bathroom.'

'Eh, I think Missus Flynn is still up there,' I said, looking at her. Watching her thinking, then seeing her face crease into a big grin.

'Oh, you are so right, dear,' she said, giving me a mouthful of yellow false teeth with the lipstick plastered over them, and half of her face. Then she grabbed Timmy and sat him down on her lap, saying, 'Now, tell Granny what you have all been up to since I last saw you.'

'Granny! Where's Granny Flynn?' asked Clare, steaming into the kitchen.

'She's up in the bathroom repairing her make-up, so she calls it. Gawd help us! More like looking for a chisel and hammer to take it off, I say,' sniffed the little granny.

'Oh, I hope she gets a move on. The baby will be due another feed before she gets her home at this rate of going,' Clare moaned, rushing out to the hall. Then she came flying back in. 'Mother, why don't you go upstairs and get yourself settled? You haven't even taken your coat off yet,' she said, eyeing the canary-yellow coat with the big silver buttons, and the wide wraparound collar.

'I was going to give Timmy his bath,' the granny said, looking down at Timmy sitting on her knee, sucking his thumb, looking dead tired now.

'No, you go on upstairs. You are in our bedroom. I've made the bed up for you. Come on, Mother! I'll get Greg to bring up the cases as soon as I get rid of the one upstairs.'

'Yes, now that you mention it, darling, I am feeling very tired after that long drive from Tipperary! Do you know,' she said, putting Timmy on his feet and holding his hand, taking him with her, and Ollie grabbing her other hand, the three of them following Clare up the stairs, 'I was actually sitting in the drive of the house, after pulling the car to a stop. Before I realised I had actually arrived! Can you beat that now?'

'Oh, Mother! I worry about you driving that car,' Clare said, sounding definitely very drained.

I stood in the kitchen, wondering what I should do to help. Clare usually gets the tea. Hmm! Maybe I should wait to see what's happening. I looked around the empty kitchen, thinking the life has gone out of it now. It's funny the way a room can be teeming with life one minute, then cold like a morgue the next. Wonder if I could nip in and watch the television?

I wandered out to the hall, seeing the grey emptiness in the sitting room, and looked out through the open front door, seeing Greg standing at the driver's side of the windscreen, leaning on the car chatting to his father. It felt freezing cold with the door open, and the dark night creeping in already made me shiver. It couldn't be any more then around four o'clock but the day is gone already. Gawd! I'm suddenly feeling flat as a pancake. It must be because Clare is going tonight. I'm going to miss her! The house already feels empty without her.

Me eyes peeled back at the kitchen, and I wandered back in again, sitting meself down in the armchair and leaned into the heat from the Aga, feeling glad of the bit of heat. I must still be under the weather from that aul dose of bronchitis. Jaysus! It really knocks the stuffing out of you. I listened, hearing the big granny and Clare coming down the stairs. With Clare sounding very worried the granny might not know everything there is to know about taking care of little baby Aoife.

'Yes, she's sleeping in the carrycot. Greg is out there keeping an eye on her, and talking to his father. Now, you know her routine. Generally, she takes a feed every four hours, but if she wakes before that, give her a bottle. You know the formula, and how to mix the feed. I've written everything down on the lists for you.'

'Don't worry, Clare, dear!' the big granny laughed, making it sound like a cat being strangled. 'I have reared three of my own, you know! They are all still hale and hearty. You should know. You are married to one of the great big lumps.'

I wandered out to get a look, seeing the big granny take her compact out of her bag and put more powder on her face, squinting into the compact mirror, and rubbing it hard into her purple nose. Then she slapped it back into her big handbag, and slammed the clasp shut, and fixed her hat, pulling it down and over to one side. Then she put on her leather kid gloves and took off out the door, stopping to look back at me and wave. 'Well, I'll be off, then! Goodbye . . . eh, dear!' Then she was gone, with Clare trailing out the door after her, and standing on the footpath with her arms folded. While Greg came around to stand beside her and put his arm around her, pulling her in beside him. She kept bending down and looking in the back seat at the baby, making sure she was OK. I stared at the two of them standing side by side, even though Clare looked a bit cold and lost, without her baby, and even Greg's arm around her didn't make up for her loss.

The car started up and the granddaddy waved and the granny turned around, waving and smiling underneath the big hat! I rushed back into the kitchen, not wanting them to see me watching. I felt out of place. Like it wasn't my business to be hanging around taking in everything that somehow seemed a bit private. Like I knew I'm not one of the family. It's times like this when I'm caught off guard that make me realise just how much I miss not having that. Underneath all that guff, I do be telling meself that it's just grand being on me own with no one to tell me what I can and can't do. When really underneath I would give anything, just to belong to a family like this. Maybe one day I'll meet a lovely man like Greg, and be just like Clare. Have me own family, and make them all happy. Just like Clare does. The room lights up when she comes into it. A good mother is everything. Yeah! And a good man to back her up, just like Greg. You can't have one without the other! You definitely need a good man to make a happy family. I think that's maybe more important then having loads a money. What good would that be when you're cold and lonely?

6

I stood at the back door, puffing on me cigarette, staring out into the darkness, enjoying the feel of the dry cold air making me skin tingle, after being stuck in the house all day. I lifted me head, staring up at the few stars glittering far above in the inky-black sky. Ah, this is the life.

I shivered. Keeping an ear out for the little granny. Yesterday morning when she called me out of bed to get the day going, it was just me and the granny. Clare and Greg had gone off to the airport late the night before. Gawd! She never stops fussing. Flying around in her big fluffy slippers, making much ado about nothing. Giving me orders left right an centre. Getting nothing done! Now nobody listens to her. Not even Timmy!

The door opened suddenly without any warning and a voice roared, 'Shut that back door! You are letting all the heat escape. What's that smell?'

I got such a fright, I sent the half-smoked cigarette flying through the air, sending it landing on the damp grass. I watched it for a split second, glowing in the dark, hardly any of it smoked. Ah! What a pity to waste all that! I whipped me head around, staring into the granny's white tired face. Her new perm with the red dye was flattened on her head, and her eyes were hanging out of her skull and she had on a frilly apron covering her aul black skirt and a yellow blouse with the top buttons missing, showing off her grey wrinkly neck with the skin hanging down. I could see she had somehow shrunk very quickly, and looked like the next gust of wind would blow her away.

'What's that smell?' she barked.

'What smell? I don't smell anything.'

'Were you smoking in the kitchen?'

'No, definitely not. Why? What's wrong with you, Missus Enright?'

'Wrong? Nothing's wrong! Why should there be anything wrong?' she snapped, lifting her neck, trying to make herself look bigger. 'I have everything under control,' she snorted. 'Now, don't you dare ever smoke in my kitchen!'

'Right!' I snorted, marching out.

'Wait! Where are you going?'

'To switch the television on in the sitting room.'

'No, there will be no television unless I say so.'

'Wha?' I screeched, leaving me mouth hanging open, ready to give her an earful.

'Go upstairs this minute and read those bold boys a bedtime story. Then I expect them to go quietly to sleep,' she said. Looking up at the wall clock, seeing it was half-past eight at night and they were still not asleep.

'But didn't you just read them a story?'

'Yes, of course I did. I spent the last hour and a half reading them stories. But they are still unsettled. They are missing their parents.'

I scratched me head, thinking. 'They won't go to sleep for me either, Missus Enright. Last night there was murder. They belted each other around the room, flying the pillows and toys and anything else they could get their hands on, having great gas for themselves.'

'Yes, but who do you think was in and out to them until half-past twelve last night?'

'Me!' we both said together.

'Indeed you were not. I was sitting in their room on my own, and when I called you that last time you refused to get up!' she screamed, losing the rag at the thought of it all.

'What about me? I had a hard time getting meself out of that bed this morning, yeh know! I was banjacked,' I said, beginning teh lose me own rag.

'Stop talking rubbish!' she screamed, going purple in the face. 'Who do you think had to get up and call you? Me!' She slapped her chest, snorting and roaming her eyes around the kitchen. Wanting the walls to hear what she went through. 'You are supposed to be helping *me*! But I am having to run around after you. Now! This will all stop. I am . . .'

'Don't you dare!' I screamed. 'I'm the one doing all the running, while you fly around the place like a headless chicken!'

'How dare you speak to me in that tone! I will be reporting you to Clare when she gets home. You may be assured of that, madam!'

'You reporting me?' I screamed, starting to choke, because I nearly strangled meself with the rage flying through me. Then I started a fit of coughing, and tried to hurry it up to get me breath back. Desperately wanting her to know just how in the wrong she was. She stared for a minute, watching me face turn blue. Then she beat me to it. Opening her mouth wide and throwing her head back and shouting again, 'Yes, I am in charge here!'

'No, you are not! I am in charge. Clare left me in charge. She said that specifically. You are only here to do the cooking. I am in charge of the children.'

'Well, really!' she puffed, wringing her hands and turning away, making for the kettle to make herself a cup of tea. I could hear the ructions upstairs and headed out the door, flying up the stairs.

'Martha! We are having a fight!' Ollie laughed, clouting the little shape hidden under the blankets laughing its head off. Me eyes took in the state of the room. The shelves were empty, all the toys ending up all over the floor, and the wardrobe hanging open with the clothes on the floor, and Ollie's eyes flying with devilment, looking like he had enough energy to last the night.

'Bedtime!' I clapped me hands, going over to make up Timmy's bed, with all the blankets lying on the floor.

'Nooo! We are having loads of fun,' Ollie moaned in a low keen.

'Bed!' I said, quickly finishing making the bed and whipping little Timmy into his own bed. 'Now, I am going to tell you a story. Not from a book. But only if you promise to be very quiet! Is that OK?'

'No! We want to play,' Ollie said, making his mind up.

'OK, Ollie. Stand off the bed until I make it first, then let's see what is going to happen next,' I said, leading him onta the floor.

'What? What are we going to do?' Ollie roared.

'Wait and see! Now, you grab that side and tuck it under the mattress. The sooner we have this room tidied up, the quicker you will find out. OK? Quickly!' He panted, pulling the blankets up on the other side of the bed.

'Timmy, pick up the toys and put them on the shelf.' Timmy let go of his bit of slip from Clare's underwear. He drags that everywhere when he's tired. Then he started to throw all the teddies and soft toys at the shelf and landing them on the floor again. 'Right, Ollie. You hop into bed and wait until we see what happens next.'

I whipped Timmy up and put him into his bed, giving him his bit of silk, and covering him up. He started to suck his thumb, rubbing the silk on his cheek, with his eyelashes flapping, and I knew he would conk out if I could get ten minutes of keeping him quiet.

'OK, Ollie,' I whispered. 'The next bit is you lie down under the bedclothes and wait to see what will happen.' I saw him wriggling, dragging the bedclothes over him and waiting patiently, watching my every move.

I flew around the room, grabbing up all the stuff and putting them back in their places, and fixed the wardrobe, shutting the door, and closed the curtains again, to keep out the cold. Then I whipped over to put out the overhead light, and switched on the night light, that sits just outside the door on a little table. 'Now,' I whispered, sitting down beside Ollie on his bed, 'I am going to tell you a true story.'

'What's it about?' mumbled Ollie, his eyes closing, now he had settled down.

'It's about magic, and fairies, and very, very special teddies, and all about the adventures of two very special little boys called Ollie and Timmy. Once upon a time . . .' I whispered.

'. . . and Ollie and Timmy flew back through the open window on the magic carpet and landed back in their own room. Then the snow bear gently lifted the two sleeping little boys and put them warm and snug back into their beds and wrapped them up. Then gazed out at the soft white snowflakes gently falling onto the earth. All was quiet, everything still, and in the distance he thought he could hear the tinkling of bells. "Time to go," he whispered. "Santa is on his way."' I ended the story, barely above a whisper.

Out cold, I thought, staring from Ollie with his mouth open, giving a little snore. To Timmy, totally clapped out with his arm thrown back over his head, and the little silky slip lying in his outstretched hand beside him on the pillow. Gawd! They're exhausted, poor little things. I stood up gently, not wanting to make a sound, crept out of the room, closing the door over, letting the light shine in through the gap in the open door, and made me way quietly down the stairs.

I opened the kitchen door quietly, seeing the little granny sitting at the kitchen table drinking a cup of tea and munching on a crumpet. She looked far away, and a bit lost. Listening to the radio sending out lovely old music from long ago. 'That was the Glenn Miller Orchestra,' a man's voice announced, speaking in lovely soft tones with an English accent.

'They're asleep,' I whispered, smiling and creeping over to the table. 'Are you all right?' I said. 'I'm very sorry for losing my temper. I shouldn't have spoken to you like that. I had no business. It won't happen again,' I said, looking at her poor tired old face that had seen a lot of life. Now she looked really drained.

'No, forget all about it, Martha. You are really a good girl. I had just run to the end of my tether. I'm certainly feeling my age. Here, help yourself. Have a crumpet. I have just heated them up under the grill, and they are lovely and warm. Do you want raspberry jam? I love them that way.'

'Yeah, thanks, that's lovely,' I said happily, staring at her lathering on the good butter and topping it with jam.

'Now, you can finish the rest of them. I bought them today in the local shop. They had just arrived in with the breadman. By tomorrow they will be stale. Oh, it's lovely to enjoy the peace and quiet, and know the day is over,' she sighed, taking a big bite of the crumpet.

'Yeah, they're a handful when they get going,' I said.

'Oh, I had forgotten what it was like to be taking care of young children. My days of doing this are well and truly over,' she sighed, staring at the table. Forgetting to eat the rest of her crumpet.

'Ah, don't worry. It will be grand. We'll manage fine between the two of us. Here's what we'll do. You look after the cooking, and I'll do all the washing up and cleaning. Now, if you give them their bath in the night-time, I'll get them down to sleep, and I'll take care of the boys, do all the running around. Then you only have to worry about the shopping and the cooking! What do you think about that idea?'

'Oh, that will be marvellous,' she said, happily, thinking about it and rubbing my hand. 'Clare said you were a great girl. I think you are a treasure,' she said, smiling at me. I felt meself blushing at all the praise, and delighted she was now easier in herself and feeling very happy. 'Mind you,' she said, 'I'm delighted to be here. I jumped at the chance to stay and take care of my grandchildren. I don't see them very often. In fact, only a couple of times during the year. I travel up by train usually, and stay with them for a few days over Christmas. Then maybe for a week in the summer. Other then that . . . well, I'm on my own. Rattling around in that big old house with nothing much to do. Clare says I should get rid of it and move into something smaller and more modern. But I couldn't be bothered. It's too much effort at my time of life. Besides, I spent most of my life in that house. It was my husband's family home. We started our married life together in that house. Reared our two children, and he died there. Prematurely. He should never have died so young. He was only sixty-one. Nearing retirement, he was,' she said, shaking her head, a look of pain crossing her face. 'We had so many plans. So much life to catch up on. We were going to go on a world cruise, you see,' she said, looking at me like she still couldn't understand what went wrong. 'We had been saving for that for years. Then one morning, it was just after eleven o'clock – I remember hearing the grandfather clock ring out the chimes in the hall as I rushed to answer the phone. It was Mr O'Driscoll, my husband's partner. "Mary," he said, sounding very serious, speaking very slowly and precisely. "I have grave news," he said. I knew straight away something terrible had happened. It was the way he spoke, using the word "grave". I just knew.'

She shook her head, letting the whole thing happen to her all over again.

'Then he coughed, I remember holding my breath, feeling a terrible sense of dread. "What is it?" I said, wanting him to get on and tell me. Dreading to hear what he was going to say. "Mary, I'm afraid it's Kevin. He collapsed here in the surgery. Doctor Geoghan came straight away, but it was too late. There was nothing anyone could do for him. I'm . . . afraid he has passed away." He said that so quietly, I could barely hear him. "I'm sorry I'm not there with you, to give you the news personally, but I'm still at the hospital. I was waiting for news. Hoping he would pull through. But I'm afraid he was gone by the time we got here, the doctor told me. Father Finnigan is on his way over to you right now. He will drive you out here to the hospital. I'll wait here for you, if you like? Would you like me to ring anyone?" "No, no," I said, putting down the phone. I remember staring at the clock, hearing the time ticking away. Hearing no other sounds. I was completely alone. I knew then that was it. My Kevin had gone. We had lived for each other, and the children. Now they were all gone. John, my son, the eldest child, was a missionary priest out in Africa. I knew I might never see him again. It had been fifteen years since he went on the missions, and we had never seen him again. Not once. Clare was up here in Dublin doing her hospital training. That was it,' she said, staring down at her hands, talking quietly, lost in that terrible time back then.

'The savings we had so carefully put away? Well, that was spent for the funeral, and putting up a headstone. I even paid a large lump sum for the perpetual care. Wanting to make it up to him for losing the long life he should have had left to him.'

Then she lifted her head slowly, looking around the room, bringing herself back to the here and now. Sitting in the kitchen eating and drinking and listening to the radio with the two of us enjoying the quiet talking. Then she landed her face on mine, and we stared into each other's eyes. Her shaking her head gently up and down, filled with terrible regret at all the loss she missed out on. Being with her husband and enjoying their old age. Just the two of them together again, after rearing the children. But it never happened.

'My goodness!' she said slowly. 'That is the first time in nine years I have spoken about it. Not since that fateful morning have I really allowed myself to think about it, never mind speaking about it! I just went on without him, feeling numb for years, trying to blot out the horror that kept threatening to engulf me. I suppose I have thawed out a bit. I try to keep busy. But really, it's just filling in time. I do enjoy my Wednesday nights, though, when my friends come to the house to play bridge. Kevin was a great bridge player,' she laughed. 'Oh, I can just hear him now. Getting very vexed with me because I didn't follow through with a good hand he was holding. He used to get very cross with me and would keep threatening to change partners. "I am going to swap you for Molly Clarke," he would shout. "She's a smashing bridge player." Then he would look over at poor old Molly, giving her a long slow wink, while the poor woman used to blush from ear to ear, then start tittering like a school girl, telling him he was a very naughty man. But all the time loving it. I think she still misses him, too. She was the old spinster from the local library. Oh, he loved the old game of bridge. He took it so seriously. I would laugh, watching him bluster, getting all excited over losing on a particularly good hand. "Ah, Kevin, sure it's only an old game of cards," I would say. "Sure you know I am hopeless at bridge!" "Yes, it's just as well I didn't marry you for your bridge playing," he used to mutter.'

'What was his work?' I said.

'Oh, he was a dentist. I always thought that was a very depressing old job, staring into people's mouths day after day. It was probably that job that killed him,' she snorted.

'Yeah,' I said. Getting the picture of looking down all day long into people's gobs. With the smell of bad breath and rotten teeth.

Then having to yank like mad, trying to get hold of a piece of rotten tooth stuck down in the gum. You'd probably have to stand your leg up on the chair and yank like mad to get it out, pulling the guts out of yerself. Then have to put up with people whingeing and wriggling around in the chair, dying to get away from you, afraid of their life at even the look of you. With you telling them to sit still, or you'll never get it out. Then manhandling a big drill, the noise going through your head, making your teeth rattle. I suppose that's what it's like. Judging by the way people used to talk about it when I was a child. They only went to get their teeth pulled out when they couldn't stand the pain any longer. Then I thought of Jackser. He used to wait until he got the labour money, then he would go down to a fella on the North Strand, and hand over a red ten-bob note. A whole ten shillings. Jaysus! You could feed a houseful of children for a week on that.

'I never went near a dentist. All me teeth are fine, and they're snow white. So I'm very lucky that way. Oh, I remember going to the dentist once. I must have been no more then two or three years old. Jaysus! It was early in the morning, and I got nothing to eat. I remember they lifted me into a huge big black-leather chair. I was frightened out of me life. Yeah! I remember staring down at a pair of old granny slippers someone had left behind in the foot rest. Then a man grabbed me from behind, and put a mask over me face, and started counting, while I was being gassed. I kicked like mad, because I was suffocating. Then I woke up and me ma took the scarf off her head and wrapped it around me mouth, to stop me catching cold, she said. Letting me lean into her as we walked home, because I was still groggy and sleepy from the gas. That was at the old dental hospital in the Corn Market. Yeah! I can still see it as if it was only yesterday. No, I don't like dentists,' I said, coming out of that memory. 'I wouldn't go near one if you paid me.'

'You have a lovely set of teeth,' she said, staring at me mouth. 'They are all so white and straight. You must look after them.'

'Eh, yeah!' I said. Not bothering to mention I never got a toothbrush near me mouth until I went into the convent.

'I suppose it's time we started to move,' she said. Stirring herself and standing up, looking at the clock on the wall.

'Yeah, I'll just wash up these dishes and head off straight to bed.'

'Yes, we'll get them out of the way, then set the table for the breakfast. It's always a rush in the morning,' she said, helping me clear the table, and start to wash up the few dishes. 'I'll dry,' she said, 'then see you off to bed before I check the house for the night, making sure all the electric plugs are pulled out of the sockets, and the lights switched off.'

'Ah, no! I'll keep you company,' I said, seeing her look white as a sheet.

I followed her around the house, after we finished in the kitchen, and trailed into the sitting room after her. She threw her eye over to the fireplace, seeing the fire guard was tightly wrapped around the fire, and it had died down, with only a few bits of coal still glowing, but they would soon die out.

I searched the job vacancies in the *Evening Herald*. Me eyes flying up and down the columns. 'Office staff wanted. Junior copy typist. Must have at least fifty words per minute, accuracy, good spelling essential. Must be able to work on old Underwood manual typewriter.' No, no good. 'Office clerk.' Definitely not. 'Wanted. Secretary to Managing Director. Must have at least one hundred and twenty words per minute in shorthand, and eighty words per minute typing. Must be smart, well dressed and prepared to travel. Must have at least five years' experience of running an office.' Yeah, definitely. That job would suit me down to the ground. Pity I can't do that stuff. Still an all! I might learn to type and do shorthand one of these days, when I get settled in a job and save up a few bob.

Hmm! What's next? 'Medical. Junior Doctors.' No, no hope of ever wrangling me way into that. 'Factory work. Experienced girls wanted for jam factory. Must have at least two years' experience.' No good. 'Machinists wanted, for skirt factory, experienced girls only need apply.' No, hate knitting and sewing! 'Medical representatives. Ambitious male wanted for large medical supply company. Must have own car, will pay travel costs. Minimum of five years' experience necessary. Good conditions and pay.'

'Domestics wanted. Housekeeper wanted for large private house, to take care of four adults. One invalid needs special care. No cooking necessary, as cook on staff. Full bed and board given. Free day off Sundays. Excellent pay and conditions for suitable woman.'

'Groundsman wanted for private boys' boarding school in the west of Ireland. Duties include odd jobs, so must be handy. Small cottage available for married couple. Must have references, and come highly recommended.'

'Protestant school. Church of Ireland couple preferred. Housework. Woman wanted for heavy-duty cleaning. Other staff employed in large private house. Must be strong and able-bodied. Older women in mid-twenties to thirties need only apply. Full bed and board given. One day off per week. Good pay. Must have excellent references. Apply to Nelly Dobbins Agency, suppliers of domestic staff since 1851.'

'Mother's help wanted. Strong country girl wanted to help mother with seven children. Cleaning, cooking and gardening, as well as help with children. Only experienced girl need apply, must be a good plain cook. Live-in only. Own room. References necessary. Sundays free.'

Me eyes slid down the page, seeing nothing for meself. I stared at the picture of a miserable-looking aul fella with a bald head. 'Hair restorer,' the advertisement said. 'Works like magic. Thousands of men in America swear by it! Now it has come to Ireland. Freddie tried it out, and after only six weeks, his hair is now fully restored. Hurry! Hurry! While stocks last. One bottle costs only seventeen shillings and sixpence. Guaranteed to work right away.'

I stared at the picture of Freddie, now grinning from ear to ear with a big mop of curly hair standing up on his baldy head. Gobshites! That's a wig! Hmm.

Ah, bloody hell! There's nothing in the paper. Not even one job for me. I kept searching, me eyes sliding up and down the pages. Nothing! What am I going to do? Clare and Greg will be back on Sunday. That's only three days away. I have to find something by then. Because I have to leave one way or the other. They only wanted me for five weeks. Now that's just about up! Gawd! I'm up the creek without a paddle.

Oh! What's this? 'Shop assistant wanted for shop near Drumcondra, close to city centre. Country girl wanted to work in grocery and tobacconist's shop. Must live in. Accommodation given. Must have experience of shop work.'

That's me! Work in a shop. Oh, yes, definitely. I always wanted to work in a shop! It's definitely one step up from being a domestic. They are offering accommodation! That's unusual. Gawd! That would suit me down to the ground. The best thing about it as well, would be the work is most definitely easier. No doubt about that. Experience? Right, what will I say? Yeah! Me granny used to own a shop in the country! But I haven't got a culchie voice. Never mind. I'll think of something. What's the number?

I flew out into the hall and picked up the phone. 'Hello, I'm ringing about deh job for the counthry girrel! Is it gone yet?'

'No, we are still looking for someone. Why? Is it yureself dat is looking?'

'Yesh . . . I mean, yeah 'tis.'

'Have yeh any experience of dat class a work?'

'Oh, begad, indeed I have. Ha, ha. I was born behind the counter yeh might say, because I have dat much experience behind me!'

'Where are yeh from?'

'Eh, deh yeh mean originally like?'

'Wha deh yeh mean originally? Where are yeh living now?'

'Dublin! The big smoke!'

'Oh, right! Will yeh come to see us for an interview? Would tomorra suit yeh?'

'Oh! Eh!' I was trying to think fast. 'No, I have me day off on Saturday! Would dat be all right?'

'Yeah, dat would be OK. Are yeh working at the moment?'

'Yeah, I am! I'm mindin children, but I'm looking teh change.'

'Oh, right so! Have yeh a pen handy dere? Take down dis address! Now, yeh don't come here, yeh go teh anuder place. Dey own a few places. Dat place yer asking teh be working in is anuder place dey have. Do yeh follow me?'

'Yeah, yeah, I'm following yeh, right enough.'

'Good! Now, yeh ask for the owner, Missus Murphy, she's called. Come around two o'clock! That's the best time teh catch her. She's cummin in dis afternoon, an I'll tell her teh expect yeh! Where did yeh say yeh hail from?'

'Eh!' Think, think! 'Bally ma gash!'

'Wha? Where's dat?'

'Oh, yeh wouldn't know it! It's down in the very heart a deh counthry!'

'Wha part?'

'Eh, Mayoh!'

'Oh, yeh are a Mayo woman, like meself! But yeh don't sound Mayo! Yeh lost yer accent. Wha age are yeh?'

'Oh, I'm a lot older than I sound.'

'Right so! Have yeh got all dem details I gev yeh?'

'Oh, I have! Thank you very much. Goodbye now. It was nice talkin to yeh!'

'Goodbye so. Hope yeh get the job!'

'Thanks very much.'

I put the phone down with me heart racing. Jaysus! I would never keep that up. It's no good. When I see that aul one, Missus Murphy, I'll tell her straight out I'm from Dublin. Fuck them. I'll do the job as well as the rest of them. I'm not changing meself for no one. I'm a born and bred Dubliner, and that's the way I'll stay. Right! Good, now that's decided. I'll tell your woman as well, that I have no experience. But I'm willing to learn, and I'm a fast learner.

I put me head in the kitchen, seeing the little granny busy heaping flour into a bowl then breaking in eggs. 'Martha, Granny and Timmy and me are baking a cake specially for Mummy and Daddy when they get back home tomorrow. Do you want to help?' Ollie asked. He stood there wearing a long apron belonging to Granny, and his hair was standing up stiff with white flour. I laughed, seeing his face and nose covered in chocolate.

'Is it a chocolate cake you're baking, Ollie?'

'Yeah! How did you know?'

'Did you dip your nose in to test it?'

'Yeah! No! I was stirring it for Granny. Look, it's all melted in the saucepan.'

'Cakes!' Timmy shouted, laughing and waving the wooden spoon, examining it and then giving it a good lick. He was covered from head to toe in flour, with the apron Granny put on him trailing the ground.

'Sorry, Ollie, I have to go out on a message. Missus Enright, I'm off now! I should be back around teatime.'

'OK! Have a nice day out. Enjoy yourself, and don't spend all your money!'

'No fear of that,' I laughed. 'Bye, Ollie. Bye, Timmy. Have a great time with your baking, and cook me something nice.'

'Wait, wait! Give me a kiss.'

'OK,' I said, putting out me hands to grab him in case he got his mucky little paws all over me lovely new clothes. 'Now, there's a smacking big kiss for you. Bye-bye, have to run.'

'Me, me!'

'Oh, right!' I tore back and grabbed little Timmy, swinging him into the air. Ah, fuck! I thought, seeing a shower of dusty flour landing down on me head. Hmm! 'Two big kisses for Timmy.' Then I landed him back on the floor again, and tore out the front door, banging it shut behind me. I rushed off down to catch the bus into town. Smacking the dust like mad off meself. Wishing I could see what I looked like in a mirror. Hope I'm not covered in chocolate.

I hopped on the bus, with only a five-minute wait. Great! This is lucky. No long wait. I wonder what questions she will ask me. I better think up something good. It's best to be prepared.

I looked up, seeing we were just heading into O'Connell Street. Jaysus! That was quick. The bus was flying. I hopped up quickly, checking to see I had me handbag. Then waited with me back twisted, until the old man sitting next to me huffed and puffed himself to a standing position. I watched him, waiting patiently for him to let me out of the seat. But he's barely moving himself. He's spent the last five minutes with his arse in the air, thinking about making the next move. 'Ah, for the love a Jesus. Will yeh hurry up, mister! I'll miss me stop,' I muttered to meself. I could feel meself beginning to lose me rag.

'Sorry, mister, could you please let me out?'

'I'm gettin there, I'm gettin there. Hold yer horses! You young ones have no patience these days. In my young days—'

'LET ME OUT! I'm missin me stop.' I panicked, looking down at the conductor, seeing we were stopped. 'HANG ON! I'M GETTIN OFF!' I roared, pushing past the old man still giving out, and rushing down the aisle. The conductor banged the bell, making the bus pull off, just as I got to the platform, and I had to jump off backwards. 'Swine!' I shouted after him, watching him stick out his tongue and cross his eyes at me.

I stood on the footpath getting me breath back and snorted in air, then let it out slowly. Right! I pulled me hat down on me head, fixing me coat, and tightened the belt. Then started walking, looking at all the bus stops to see which one takes me to Drumcondra. 'I could walk. It's not really that far,' I muttered to meself, thinking about it. 'But I don't want to be late.'

I threw me head across the road, looking up at Clerys' clock. A quarter to one. No, it's better to take the bus, then I'll have a bit of time to get me bearings and take a look around. I milled me way through the crowd, all rushing in different directions, wanting to get their Saturday shopping done before the shops ran out of the good stuff and there wouldn't be any bargains left, especially for the Sunday dinner. I gave a shiver, remembering me robbing days in the shops. Jaysus! Don't start thinking back on that now. It's all behind me, thank God.

The bus! Which stop? Ah, come on, Martha. You're just wasting time. I saw a bus man lounging outside the Carlton Cinema, hanging onto his money bag and ticket machine. 'Hey, mister, which bus do you get to Drumcondra?'

'There! It's right there, under your nose. It's not far. Why don't yeh walk? Yeh could take me wit yeh, if yeh like. I'd be grand company for yeh and I might even buy yeh a bag of chips, if yer not careful.'

I stared at him with me mouth open. Taking in the state of him. Watching him wink and narrow his eyes, turning his head sideways, trying to make himself look gorgeous. Jaysus! He must be hitting forty, if he's a day. 'No, I'm not that desperate. Ask me when I have one leg in the grave. But by then you'll be long gone. Pushing up daisies by the look of yeh.'

'Go on outa tha, yeh cheeky little cow. Women would give their eye teeth teh get their hands on me. Ask the wife, she couldn't wait teh get me down the aisle,' he said, shaking his shoulders, and wriggling his neck. Looking like he believed every word of what he'd just said.

'There yeh go! The poor woman was desperate,' I roared over. 'By the time she got around to making up her mind, you were the only thing left sitting on the shelf!'

'Ah, now, I was saving meself for you! But the poor woman threatened teh throw herself in the Liffey if I didn't make an honest woman a her.'

I roared laughing, watching the size of him, standing there wriggling himself, bouncing up and down on his toes, trying to make himself look bigger, and stretching his eyeballs, doing everything he could to make himself good-looking. Jaysus! He's a gas character, I thought, standing at the bus stop, waiting on the bus. Enjoying meself no end.

OK, here we go. Drumcondra. I walked past shops looking for Aladdin's Den. Luxury clothes shop for ladies' wear. Ah, here we are. I stood looking in the window at a dummy standing naked, waiting for something to be put on it. I stared down at big corsets, and long pink knickers, and long petticoats to go underneath the frocks. Gawd! They're very hickey. I put me head in the door, seeing a long wooden counter with a brass surround. Shelves of wooden boxes had jumpers and nylons sticking out. Jaysus! Luxury? Sure, they're only for aul grannies! I took me head out again, not wanting to be seen. And moved off, wanting to find out the time.

Next door was a toy shop with the name Aladdin's Cave. Jaysus! She must own that, too. I wonder where she got the name from? Maybe she made her money in them far-off foreign parts. Where they go around in turbans hanging off their heads, and fancy slippers with the toes looking up at you. Like Sinbad! No, he was a sailor man. That's what the song said anyway, when I was a child.

I looked down at me patent black shoes, seeing the lovely shine. Yeah! The Pond's Cold Cream did wonders for polishing them, it brought up a lovely shine. I put on me black wool gloves I bought, to go with me Bonnie and Clyde hat the reverend mother bought me when I was leaving the convent. Now I look very respectable altogether. If she doesn't give me the job looking like this, then she can stick it up her arse. She won't get any better then me. Right, it must be time to go in. I straightened me shoulders and headed back to the shop.

'Hello, I have an appointment to see Missus Aladdin.'

'Who? Missus—'

'Oh, sorry!' I whipped me piece of paper out of me pocket and looked at it again. 'Missus Murphy, the owner,' I smiled.

'Oh, yes!' A grey-faced aul one with glasses sitting on her nose, and the bit of thin grey hair wrapped behind her head tied in a bun. You could see her scalp, where she should have had hair. 'It's just to the side of the shop. Push in the door, and knock on the first door on your left. When you get to the landing.'

'Right! Thanks very much,' I said, making for the door after the shop. I pushed in the hall door, sending it flying against the wall, and held me breath. I hope she didn't hear that. She'll say I'm wrecking the place before I even get in the door. I walked up the narrow stairs, breathing in years of dust. The carpet had seen better days and looked like nobody had swept it for years. This one still has her communion money, I said to meself. I bet she's very mean with the money.

I knocked on a brown wooden door with a spyhole in the middle, and moved away, not wanting her to see me before I got a chance to see her. 'Come in!' I turned the handle, walking into a room covered in cardboard boxes, looking around for Missus Murphy.

'Are you the girl come for the interview for the shop assistant?' I looked to see where the voice was coming from. 'Come in. Sit down.' Then I spotted her buried behind a big desk. 'Shut the door,' she said, standing up and pointing to the door I left open.

I gaped at her. Jaysus! The size of her. She must weigh a ton. A little woman with a big red fat face, and a flat nose with little beady eyes was studying me, as I took her in. She was breathing hard. Making snuffling sounds. Jaysus! Her chest and arse and belly are massive. And her legs look like two tree trunks grown together. I dropped me eyes down to her ankles and they fell in rolls of fat, folding themselves down into a pair of old men's slippers.

'Sit down. Take the weight off your feet.'

'Thanks very much,' I said, sitting meself down on a dusty old chair, after moving a load of magazines off it.

'Now, the shop is the next street up from here,' she said, getting down to business straight away. 'You have to work shift hours. That means you get up and be in the shop for seven a.m. For the newspaper deliveries. You work from seven to three one day. Then you start at three in the afternoon the next day, and finish at eleven at night. Then you are on again at seven a.m. for the early morning shift. We get the airport traffic, so that's why we stay open late. It's right on the route to the airport, so we get a lot of business from that end.' She smiled, showing a mouthful of gums, with tiny black teeth.

I stared. Some of them are rotten. Gawd! She's ugly. Just as well she has the money. I looked to see if she really had a wedding ring on her finger. No! I knew it. She's calling herself missus in case anyone tries to rob her business. 'I'll get me husband onta yeh!' she can roar. Because men take no notice of women. You have to have a man. But she's right there! I'd do the same.

I blinked, leaning forward to catch up with what she was saying. 'There's a flat goes with the job. The wages is three pounds ten shillings a week. Naturally, you are paid on the Friday. The first week you work a back week. That means you don't get paid that week. But you get it back when you are leaving the job. Is that understood?'

'Yes, mam.' I shook me head, taking everything in.

'Now, you pay one pound ten shillings rent, and ten shillings a week for the electricity bill. That means you get one pound ten shillings into your hand after the deductions.'

'So I really only get thirty bob a week wages! Is that it?'

She stared at me, her beady little eyes disappearing, the way she narrowed them. I could see her thinking, reading me from head to toe. I dropped me face, relaxing it, and keeping me mouth closed, and me eyes steady with me hands sitting limply across each other in me lap, closing meself down and giving nothing away. I just waited quietly for her to make her judgement. I didn't want to let her think I might be trouble, by questioning everything. No, I want this job.

She took in a big breath, saying, 'No, you are forgetting you have to pay rent, and the electricity doesn't pay itself. So, in fact, you are getting it cheap. Now, do you want the job?'

'Yes! Yes, please. I'll take it!'

'When can you start? I want someone straight away.'

I thought about this. Clare and Greg will be home on Sunday. Monday! 'Will Monday be all right?'

'Yes. But can you get here on Sunday night? I want you to start on the Monday early morning shift. Molly will show you the ropes. You can work the shift with her. Then take over in the afternoon. Then Paddy, that's my manager, he runs the bookies for me. He has the keys to the shops and will lock up and check the takings. You are going to have to learn how to do that. Because he just double-checks. But I'll get him to help you, or maybe Molly. By the way, are you any good with figures? I hope you can count.'

'No problem, mam!' I breezed out. Shaking me head like I was born counting.

'Good. Because you will be responsible for any deficits in the till at the end of your shift.'

'Oh! Do you mean if I'm short of money when we count it up, I have to pay out of me own pocket?'

'Of course! I'm not running a charity for fools!'

'No,' I said slowly, thinking no wonder she has her money made.

This fucking aul one would sell the clothes off her granny's back if there was any money in it. Hmm!

'So, just to be sure I understand everything, I work a shift, then start late the next day. Is that right?'

'Yes.'

'Well, if I work two shifts on Monday, I will be getting the time off for that. Isn't that right?'

She stared at me, thinking, looking shocked. This idea hadn't even hit her. 'Eh, I don't think so. Because we will have to give you training.'

'At that rate of going, mam, you can have someone stay with me on my shift to give me all the training I need. But by the sounds of it, I should pick it up fast.'

'But then I would have to pay Molly to work an extra shift!' she said, the shock at losing money really hitting her now.

'Well, her or me. I am a very hard worker and I pick things up quickly. But, like you said, mam, my life is not given over to working for charity either.'

'Right, well, anyway, let me think,' she said, sounding like she was caught out at her own game. 'Hmm!' she said, thinking, trying to work out how she could milk me. 'Right so,' she said, scratching her head. 'I'll ask Molly to keep an eye on you working your shift on the Monday morning, she'll probably be hanging around anyway. The flat is just above the shop. Yes, I'll do that. She's very obliging that way.'

Good, I thought. She can milk the obliging Molly, and more fool her. I've learned me lesson well, after working for them bleeding nuns, milking every last ounce of obliging I had in me bones.

'Here is the address. The house is next door to the shop. That's where the flats are.' Then she handed me a piece of paper, saying, 'Right! That's it then.'

I stood up, saying, 'Thank you very much, Missus Murphy. I'm delighted with the job.'

'Good. I'm glad to hear you say that. I hope you settle in well. It's a good job, you know?'

'Yes. Indeed it is, Missus Murphy. Well, thanks again.' Then

I was out the door and down the stairs, flying down the road, jumping through the air with the excitement. Working in a shop! Off at three o'clock. Sleep in late in the mornings. I won't have to get up early, only every other morning, and it's close to the city centre. Oh, thank you, God, for looking after me. I'm so happy, and the best of all was, she did all the talking. I didn't have to give her any information about meself, so I didn't have to say I'd just come out of the convent, and watch her counting up all the dollar signs spinning through her head at the thought she was going to get a right eejit she could milk for all its worth. Someone who was just let loose after being locked up for years, and knew nothing about the world and its ways. No, now I'll be able to keep quiet about that, and just say I worked in a shop. That's when I move the next step up the ladder, to do whatever job that's going to be. Probably office work next. I'll save me money, and pay for the night school to get the training. I tore off, heading into town, not waiting for a bus. I can't wait to get back and tell the little granny. I have a job.

I woke up seeing the light coming in through the curtains. It's Sunday! I don't have to get up early. Great! I stretched and yawned, giving a little shiver, feeling the heat of the blankets, and snuggled down again, to go for a bit of a snooze, laughing under me breath at the luxury of it all. Then me eyes opened slowly again. Sunday! I'm leaving today. Clare and Greg will be back. Jaysus! I better get up quick and get meself going. I have to pack.

I dived out of the bed and into me clothes, opening the door and heading down for me breakfast. I could smell a lovely fry coming from the kitchen, and hear laughing and voices. I leapt into the kitchen, landing me eyes on Clare sitting at the table with Timmy on her knee, helping to eat the sausages off her plate. 'Look who's here!' Greg roared, standing there large as life with his hands on his hips, wearing his dressing gown and brown leather slippers. Laughing at the sight of me face at clapping eyes on them.

'Clare! You're back!' I shouted, rushing in and standing beside her at the table, staring at her, still trying to take in the sight of her. 'How was your holiday?' I laughed, getting all excited. Looking from her with the lovely golden face and her hair snow white. Then whipping me eyes over to Greg, looking brown as a berry, with his brown curls gone a goldie colour.

'Great,' he laughed. 'It was a second honeymoon! Isn't that right, darling?' he laughed over to Clare, who was smiling, looking at him, closing her eyes like she was very tired but regretting it was all over.

'Oh, it was marvellous. We had a wonderful time, Martha. How did you and Mother get on with the children? Was everything all right?' she said, putting a bit of rasher in her mouth, and buttering a slice of toast. Timmy sat on her lap, watching the rasher going into her mouth, and wringing his hands, having them at the ready. I could see he was biding his time, getting ready to grab it.

'Watch that last sausage, Clare!' I laughed. 'You're about to see it vanish.'

'Oh, I was looking forward to this. But most of it has already found its way down his little tum-tum,' she laughed, squeezing his belly, making him fart, and squeal laughing.

I peeled me eyes back to Clare, saying, 'Oh, everything was fine. We had no problems whatsoever. Do you know, Clare, I think your mother is great. She's a real dote!'

Greg threw back his head and screamed laughing. 'Greg! Behave yourself!' Clare snorted, getting annoyed with him making a joke of her mother.

'Ah, no! Seriously, though. I told you they would get on like a house on fire. The elderly and the young always do,' he said. Shaking his head up and down, trying to look serious, and looking very contrite at Clare, then at me, and back to see how Clare was taking it. Hoping he had made peace with her.

She gave him a look from the corner of her eye to see if he meant it. Then she smiled at me, saying, 'I'm delighted to hear that, Martha. It eased my mind knowing my mother had you to help. She was delighted with being left with the children, but she's not getting any younger. Well, everything seems to have been fine without me!' she said. Looking around the kitchen then laughing down at Timmy, wrestling with a whole sausage. He was trying to chew the lot at once, but he couldn't get his teeth around the size of it. Clare pulled it out of his mouth, and gave him a piece, leaving the rest sitting on the plate. He swallowed the lot without chewing, and grabbed the rest, jamming it in his mouth. Then started to choke, and pulled the lot out of his throat again, making a sick-looking face, and stared at it in disgust. Then he flung it on the plate, jamming his two little hands under his arms, shivering his face, his whole little body rattling. Like he had just eaten something horrible. I roared laughing, looking at the carry on of him.

'That's put him off sausages for a while,' I said.

'You must be joking,' Clare said. 'Some people eat to live. Others live to eat. Especially this little glutton here,' she said, shaking him and giving him a smacking kiss on his head.

'So! Here we are. Back to the grindstone,' Greg said, scratching his head like mad, then stopping, with his head bent to the floor, looking like he was thinking. 'Oh, by the way, Clare, I better check the diary for this week! I think that conference is coming up on Thursday.' Then he was out of the kitchen, flying up the stairs, heading into their bedroom.

'Clare, I'm leaving this afternoon, after lunch. I got meself a new job,' I said, watching her eyes open wide with her mouth dropping, staring at me in shock. 'Yeah! I got a new job working in a shop! I have to start early in the morning. So they want me to arrive there this evening. I get a flat with the job.'

'You are leaving today!' she said, dropping her head on the word 'today'. Trying to take it in. 'Gracious! I didn't expect you to leave so soon. I know we said five weeks but . . . I suppose you are right. Where is the shop?'

'Drumcondra, Clare. It's not too far from the city centre.'

'Well, I certainly am going to miss you. The boys really did take a shine to you. Especially Ollie! He really will miss you,' she said, thinking about this. 'Right, I better get moving and get the dinner started. You don't want to arrive late!' she laughed, looking at me with meaning, her mouth shut, then letting it drop, and her eyebrows hitting the ceiling. I roared laughing, remembering how I arrived in the middle of the night, waking the whole house up.

'No,' I said, shaking me head. 'Definitely not that. I won't be making that mistake again.'

'Come on then. Let's get moving. You start the washing up, while I take this little scruffpot up and change him.'

7

The bus stopped and started, letting people on and off, slowly making its way out of O'Connell Street.

'Jesus Christ almighty, that's a terrible dirty aul night! Yeh'd be blown clean offa yer feet, if yeh hadn't a pick on yeh!' I heard an aul one roar, huffing and puffing, talking to everyone and no one as she hauled herself along the bus, holding onto the back of the seats with one hand, and shaking her wet umbrella with the other. Sending sparks of rainwater flying in all directions. I moved away from the window, shuffling meself fast down the seat, not wanting to make any room for her. Then I lifted me head again, looking up to see a big fat aul one with a dripping-wet face, stripping a soaking-wet scarf off her head. I could see by the way she was looking at me, she was intent on planting herself down beside me.

Jaysus! She's standing there waiting for me to move in. I could hear her heavy breathing in me ear, and feel the hot breath on me neck. She hesitated at my seat, not sure what she was going to do. I whipped me head over to the window, pretending to stare out. Not seeing anything through the dark glass with the condensation running down. I gave it a wipe with me hand, pretending to be busy. I could see her reflection standing there with her mouth open, waiting for me to move.

'Eh, you! Would yeh not move up and make room for me?' she roared. 'Hey! I'm speaking to yeh!' she moaned, poking me on the shoulder.

'Oh, eh, yeah, sorry!' I said, making a half-hearted attempt with a few shifts up the seat. 'Can you get in with me case?' I said, looking up at her face with the water streaming out of her hair.

'Jaysus! I'll sit somewhere else,' she muttered, making for the long seat at the back. Gawd! That was lucky. She would have ruined me good coat, with the size of her! Sitting on top of me. And all that wet. Not to mention the smell! It must be years since that aul one had a wash. Jaysus! Yer very mean, Martha. Yeah, that was cruel. Still and all! I have to think of me good clothes. They don't come cheap! Then again, I might get stuck some day ending up looking like that meself! She didn't always look like that, I'll bet. Hmm!

I smiled up at her, hoping she might smile back and I'd make meself feel better. She saw me looking and stared for a minute. Looking like I had an awful cheek to be smiling at her after what I'd just done. Then she curled her lip up under her nose and turned away from me, like I was an awful bad smell.

Jaysus! That didn't go very well! I felt like laughing at the carry on of meself, but just stared out the window seeing nothing. Afraid to look back up at her again in case she roared down and asked me what I was looking at.

I moved back over to the window and wiped the glass, watching the pool of water roll down and catch in the window frame. Then I stuck me face to the glass and stared out. All the shops along Dorset Street were pitch black with the shutters pulled down. The bus slowed down, stopping to let on people trying to make it off the footpath, with the wind and rain driving them back. The lights from the street lamps glowed orange in the dark, and I watched the rain blowing through the light, making it look bluey black. People struggled across the road, with their coats blowing out behind them, getting soaked to the skin. An umbrella blew inside out. I watched, as the woman got yanked backwards with the force of the storm pulling the umbrella clean out of her hand. It took off, flying through the air, and sailed over the high wall of the Bishop's Palace. Without warning, the wind went mad. Gusting across the road, lifting her off her feet. She staggered, dancing backwards with her arms flying, like she was trying to swim.

'Oh, my God! She's going to fall under that car coming up right behind her!' a woman roared out, sitting behind me on the bus.

'Where?' people shouted. Everyone pushing their heads against the glass and wiping it like mad. We all watched, holding our breaths as the car skidded, sending water gushing into the air, and swerved away from the woman flying backwards heading straight for the wheels under the car. The car stopped dead in the middle of the road. I could hear the gasps of shock from the other people as we all stared out, seeing her struggle to get her balance. She rocked backwards and forwards with her arms held out, then planted her feet on the wet road, letting herself balance against the bonnet of the car, and took off again. Ignoring the car and everything else in her path. Fighting into the wind and the rain with her head down and her back bent. She slowed down, throwing her head sideways to take in the bus slowly moving off, making its way towards her. But she just kept going, bus or no bus.

The driver decided to take no chances and stopped. Waiting to let her get back across from the other side of the road. Knowing she was making it her business to get across the very wide road and wasn't stopping for nobody.

'Jesus!'

'That was lucky!'

'Holy mother of God.'

'She's one lucky woman!' people all said, shaking their heads, nobody feeling the better of it. God! She nearly got herself killed stone dead, I thought. She could have ended up on a mortuary slab, in the dead house. God! You can be alive one minute, and dead the next. It's hard to understand that! Instead now, she's probably thinking about getting herself home and out of her wet clothes and into a big cushy armchair beside a roaring red fire, and eating a lovely hot fry, with a steaming-hot pot of tea. Then toasting herself with the feet up, resting on a stool. Then later on, go to bed with a delicious hot cup of Horlicks, and climbing into the bed with a hot-water bottle. Getting all snug and cosy. Well, that's what the little granny used to do. Go to bed with a mug of Horlicks. I didn't like the taste of it, even though she said it was good for me. I prefer cocoa, made on milk. But I'm really thinking that's what I would like for meself.

Me clothes are going to be ruined! And I'm hungry again. What bloody put the idea into me head of leaving on a night like tonight? I should have stayed another night with Clare. All wrapped up and cosy in me room.

Gawd! I hope me flat is cosy. I wonder if it has a fireplace? I could get coal and light the fire. Tomorrow I could do that. It's too late to go looking for coal now. Everything's shut up for the night. Anyway, you wouldn't put a dog out on a night like tonight. Never mind walk the streets yourself in that weather. Maybe the shop sells coal. No, it would have to be a hardware shop.

Where am I now? I pressed me nose to the window again, seeing we were coming to me stop. 'Quick, move yourself! The next stop is mine,' I muttered to meself, sounding like an aul one. I jumped up, grabbing me suitcase, seeing all the steam on the bus and people dozing in their seats with the heat rising up from their damp coats. Oh, bloody hell! Me lovely coat and hat and even me shoes will be destroyed. Why didn't I wear me old green coat? Jaysus! I'm a right gobshite.

The bus stopped to let me off, and I hesitated, seeing the black dirty water running along the gutters. I didn't want to splash me coat. The bus started to move off and I leapt onto the footpath, missing the rushing water and taking me suitcase down with me. The rain immediately lashed into my face, with the wind lifting the hat off me head, sending it flying through the air. I grabbed out, catching hold of it before it hit the ground, and jammed it into my coat pocket. Jaysus! What a night to come out!

I lowered my head, keeping me face down, and started to push against the wind and rain, with the suitcase banging against my leg. All I could see was the rain hammering against the footpath as it drove into the ground. The lights from the cars rushing past made the water sparkle and dance above the ground, lighting up the path. Then the quiet and darkness again, as the cars faded into the distance. Leaving me with only the wind howling, and the lashing rain beating against me legs.

Jaysus! Am I there yet? I lifted me head slightly, to see how far I'd got, seeing the lights of the shop in the distance. It was the only one lit up. The rain got heavier, and the wind blew it full force, smacking against my head and face, making me lose my breath and soaking me to the skin. 'Nearly there,' I muttered. 'Thank God it's not far from the bus stop. That's handy for getting into town.'

The rain belting me in the face made it hard for me to see ahead. I could feel the water running down me neck, soaking the collar of my frock. I stopped, putting the case down on the wet ground and closed the top buttons of me coat, getting blown backwards and knocking the case on the ground. 'Ahh! What am I doing, bringing meself out on a night like this?' I screamed, opening me mouth and nearly crying, tasting the water spilling into me mouth. Then I saw how foolish I was, crying in the wind. 'Right!' I sniffed. 'Get yourself moving.' Then I picked up the case, setting off again, trying to think of something happy.

I'm going me own way! Yeah! It's just dawning on me now. I started feeling nervous and excited at the same time. Imagine! I'm all grown up now! Out in the world on my own. I have me own place to live, and a job. I need never again put up with anyone's madness, or get the life beaten out of me, or work for nothing, or have people even thinking of telling me what to do. No! Now I'm me own person. The rest is up to me. I can sink or swim. Yeah! That's right, I told meself. Trying to buck meself up at the thought of losing me lovely home comforts with Clare and Greg and the boys, and little Aoife.

I could see the bright lights from the shop as I passed a laneway with a door at the side. Wonder if that's where the flat is? I walked on, pushing in the door of the shop, and stopped, putting me head in first, seeing shelves stacked with tea and bread at one end, and cigarettes and sweets and newspapers at the top end. The long wooden counter ran the length of the big room, then across at the end, and up the other side. Gawd! It's big. Look at the size of it! Me eyes stretched along the shelves, seeing on the right side a long showcase under the counter, stretching the length of the room. With fancy-looking chocolates, and biscuits where they sell them loose, by the ounce. They were all sitting in their boxes with the glass lids, so you could see what you're getting.

I walked over to the counter, letting me case drop down on the floor, and waited for the shop assistant to finish serving a man. I stood, letting the rainwater drip down the length of me. In no time at all, I was standing in a pool of water. Bloody hell! I thought, moving away from the water and looking down at meself, flicking me wringing hair out of me eyes to see what was going on. I'm saturated from head to toe. I still can't get over the stupidity of me not wearing me old clothes.

The woman serving behind the counter had short brown hair, curled in a tight perm on top of her head. The back was cut short like a man's and dead straight. It stood up like a flower pot. I stared at her, seeing the red culchie face, with half-dead-looking grey eyes. The only movement was from her mouth, twitching into a straight line, showing how annoyed she was with the man for not being able to make up his mind about what he wanted. His eyes flew up and down the shelves, moving himself from one foot to the other to get a better look past her, blocking his view of the sweets.

'Gimme a packet a them wine gums,' he said, rooting in his trouser pocket for the change.

'Sixpence,' she muttered, making it sound like a snarl. 'Yeah, can I help you?' she said, turning her head to me and raising her eyebrows, waiting to hear what I wanted. I hesitated, waiting for the man to come up with the money he was counting in his hand. 'What do yeh want?' she barked.

'I, eh—'

'Sixpence! Is tha right?' said the man, interrupting me and throwing down coppers with a thrupenny bit. Raising his eyebrows and giving her a dirty look, not liking the way she served him. She said nothing, just picked the money up and pressed the keys sticking out of the cash register. It tinkled and flew open, then she dropped the money in and slammed it shut. The man stopped to open his sweets and stuck one in his mouth, then pulled up the collar of his coat, making his way out into the terrible stormy dark night.

'Shocking weather! You wouldn't believe how bad that storm is until you have to go out in it!' I said, smiling at her, hoping she might smile back. She said nothing, just stared at me. I could hear me voice fading into the distance and me smile going with it!

'Do yeh want something?' she said, raising her eyebrows at me.

'Yeah!' I said, hearing meself saying, 'I don't want you to smile. Yer face might crack. Still, you have enough to worry yeh when you look at yourself in a mirror. That face is an awful affliction to be carrying!' I snorted, lifting me shoulders, giving her the same treatment.

'That's it! I'm not serving you. You can get out,' she said, throwing her arm at the door.

'I'm not asking to be served. By any chance, would you happen to be Molly?'

'Who wants to know?' she snapped.

'Listen, you can tell me where the flat is for this shop. I'm going to be working here first thing in the morning.'

'Oh!' she said, whipping her head up, as if I was challenging her for a row. Staring me up and down the length of the floor. I stared back at her, taking in the flowery aul blouse thrown over her big bulk, with a huge chest sticking out. The blouse had definitely seen better days. It was covered in all colours, and the long aul moth-eaten Arran cardigan with the torn pocket hung on her like a rag. The big grey wool skirt wrapped around her massive arse went well down past her knees, hiding her big legs. That skirt looks like something she made out of an old horse blanket. Jaysus! What a culchie!

'What's your name?' she snapped.

'What's yours?'

'Go on then. Around to the side of the shop, down the lane and bang on the door. Someone will let you in.' Then she turned her back on me, pretending to fix the packets of sweets hanging at the side of the shelf.

'Thanks,' I said, whipping up me case and handbag, and marching out of the shop, leaving a trail of water behind me, dripping me way back out into the storm. 'Fucking culchie aul fucker,' I muttered under me breath. 'If yer not happy, then youse should all go back to the bog where youse came from!' I heard meself say, listening to the way I used to speak not too long ago.

I banged the letter box, seeing there was no bell. Then waited, the wind whipping up me coat, and the rain lashing the legs and face off me. Fucking weather! You would know it's December. I hate the winter. I stood waiting, starting to shiver, and nothing happened. No one came to open the door. So I banged again, rattling the hell out of the letter box, then waited.

Fuck this! I was just about to go back to the shop when I heard feet coming down the stairs. A big woman with black-framed glasses and a man's haircut stood looking down at me, trying to take me in. 'You're the new girl?'

'Yeah! Martha is my name,' I said, pushing past her to get in out of the weather and making for the stairs. There was no room for the two of us in the entrance.

'Right! Up the stairs. You're in with me,' she said, rushing up and trying to squeeze past me. I followed up behind her, the two of us making our way down a passage past doors, with the whole corridor blocked by big cardboard boxes. 'That's the kitchen,' she said, waving her hand at a little room with a table and a cooker with shelves and an aul kitchen dresser with glass doors. 'Come on. This is my room,' she said, holding the door open for me. 'You are sharing with me,' she sniffed, not looking too happy about it.

I walked in, looking around a big musty old room with two windows, one at each end. 'This is my bed,' she said, pointing to a single bed sitting under the far window on the left. 'Your bed is up that end.' I looked up, seeing a single bed pushed into the corner, with a big old wardrobe beside it, and the door hanging off its hinges. I looked at the dressing table sitting between the two windows and it was covered in face powder and all her make-up and stuff. Nylons hung off the mirror, and the place was covered with her clothes and shoes dumped everywhere. Even on my bed. 'You keep to your end,' she said, rushing up to yank her stuff out of the wardrobe, and dump it into the bottom of another wardrobe sitting in the corner at her end.

'Are you a Dubliner?' she said, waiting, with her hands on her hips, for me answer.

'Yes, I am. You're a country woman, right?'

'Yes! I'm from Kerry.' There was a silence between the two of us. You could hear the room holding its breath. I felt heat rising in me belly, waiting for her to say something bad about the Dubliners. But she thought better about it, seeing me staring at her, with my eyebrows lifted and me eyes spitting venom.

'What's your name?' I said, seeing her turn her back.

'Molly!' she snapped.

'Well, Molly, I have nothing against culchies, I've met some lovely ones,' I said, wanting to get back at her for being a miserable cow.

'I've nothin against jackeens!' she snapped.

'But sure why would you? Aren't we very good to you? Here you are invading our city and we give you all plenty of work, feed you and clothe you! What more would you want?' I said, hanging up me wet dripping coat in the wardrobe. All I heard was the slamming of the door and she was gone. I was left talking to the empty room.

Oh, oh! There's definitely going to be trouble by the looks of the people working in this place. Jaysus! All a shower of fucking red-neck culchies! They hate us Dubliners.

I sat down on the side of the bed and looked around the room. The bulb was weak and didn't give out much light. Mother a God! What a kip! I thought, looking around the place, feeling miserable inside meself. The place had no life in it. Jaysus! It looks like the store room, with the bare grey plaster walls. There's a terrible musty smell. That Molly one probably never throws open the windows to give the place an airing. I could feel the damp. I looked around, seeing no heaters. Jaysus! There's no heat, no pictures on the wall, nothing that would make it look like a home. Only the sight of her smelly clothes thrown in a heap everywhere. Ah, fuck! She really doesn't want to have to share the room with me. I don't blame her. I thought I was coming to something lovely, cosy and warm. Or at least to have me own room. I knew it! You get nothing for nothing. There had to be a catch somewhere. Flat, me arse!

I lifted me head from the half-dark room with the bare-naked bulb hanging from the ceiling. Seeing the rain lashing at the window, and the panes of glass rattling like mad in the window frames, and wondered if I did the right thing being in such a hurry to leave Clare's house. I could feel me heart slipping down into me belly, and I felt cold and miserable. I shivered, with the cold in the room hitting me after sitting in this soaking wet frock, and the collar sticking to me neck with the sopping wet. Jesus, this is worse than nothing. On top of that, I will have to work and live with these culchie cows! Ah, to hell with it! I can always move on if it doesn't work out, I sighed, standing to me feet, and humped the suitcase onta the bed. I'll make the best of it, just for a short while anyway, see how it goes. I can always look for something else.

I took out me working skirt and blouse with the navy-blue jumper Clare gave me, and left out me old bokety brown shoes. Then left me dressing gown, slippers, nightdress and washbag sitting on the bed and shut the case. Leaving it standing on the floor in the wardrobe. The door wouldn't shut, it was hanging by one hinge. Ah, leave it.

I turned around and peeled the wet frock off me, and looked for a hanger in the wardrobe. None! Not even one to hang me coat. I looked down to where your woman had stuffed her clothes, seeing a load of hangers sticking out of the end of her wardrobe. Mean cow. She robbed them all. I bent down and picked up a handful, listening to make sure she wasn't coming back. I didn't want her to start thinking I was trying to rob her stuff. I hung me wet coat up inside the wardrobe, and got another hanger for me frock. Then I peeled the rest of me clothes off, throwing them on the bed, and dived into me nightdress and dressing gown, wrapping the belt tight around my waist, and slipped me damp feet into the new red fluffy slippers I'd bought meself. I shivered again, feeling the lovely heat from the dressing gown going through me.

Right, I'll feel better when I get into the bed. I threw back the couple of brown thin blankets to fix the bed. Jaysus! The sheets are damp. The cheek of that aul one taking ten bob for the electricity, when she has no heating in the room. The fucking robbing aul fucker! No wonder she has her money. I stripped the bed, looking at the sagging mattress with a hole in the spring underneath. Ah, Jaysus! This is criminal! Me arse is going to be tipping the floor.

I could feel me belly getting hot with the rage. 'That fat, poxy aul overfed, fucking good-for-nothing aul one has another think coming if she thinks she's getting ten bob a week outa me for the electricity,' I muttered, hearing meself crying. Then I remembered. She stops it out of me wages! We'll see about that. I can help meself to eight bob's worth of stuff from the shop! That's only fair. She can have two bob for the electricity. Yeah, I'm satisfied with that. Right! Enough moaning. Just keep moving before yeh drive yourself mad.

I finished making up the bed and looked around to see what else needed doing. That's it. Everything is sorted out. OK, that's me all ready for the morning. A cup of hot tea would be nice! I'll go down and take a look in the kitchen, and see what there is to eat. Maybe I'll see that Molly one and ask her what time I have to get up in the morning. But first I'll give me hair a rub. Jaysus! It's still dripping with the wet. OK, that will do.

I put the towel hanging on the back of the chair sitting next to my bed and combed my hair, then put the washbag under the chair. Bloody hell! Not even a little bedside table to put me stuff on, I thought. Looking around to see if Molly had more then her share. No, nothing. She has only the one little locker. Right, I'm off.

I flapped me way down the concrete passage, slapping me new slippers against the hard ground, hearing voices and seeing the light was on in the kitchen. Great! Someone's in here. 'Eh, hello!' I said, putting me head in the kitchen, seeing Molly sitting at the little formica table talking to a man with snow-white grey hair. The two of them stopped talking. Molly looked busy, examining her mug. 'God! It's gone very quiet in here,' I said, laughing and smiling down at the man. Molly wouldn't look at me. The man half-smiled, throwing his eyes in my direction, then stood up, grabbing his dishes and making for the sink, saying, 'Right, I better be off then. I'm hoping to get an early night. Another week starts tomorrow.'

I stood looking, wondering if he was including me in what he was saying. But he kept his back to me and rinsed the dishes under the hot tap and left them stacked to drain on the kitchen sink. 'Goodnight, Molly. See you tomorrow,' he said, rushing out the door, giving me a little nod and a jerk of his mouth, to show it was supposed to be a smile. Hmm! I sure know how to empty a room, I thought, watching his back flying out the door. I poked around the worktop, looking for the tea canister.

'Eh, Molly! Where's the tea?'

'What tea?' she muttered, not bothering to look up at me.

'You know. That stuff there. What you're drinking out of that cup,' I said, getting fed up with her sulking. She said nothing. Just sat there with her hands wrapped around the mug to keep herself warm, twirling it around in her hands and staring at it. 'Ah, Molly. Come on! You know. Where's the tea canister to make meself a cup of tea?'

'You have to buy your own,' she said, 'or put money in the kitty.'

'Wha? What do you mean, no tea? And buy me own? And who the fuck is Kitty?' I roared, losing me rag.

'There's no need for that kind of language here,' she sniffed, standing herself up and taking in a deep breath, pushing out her overgrown milkers. 'This is a respectable establishment,' she said, whipping up her mug and plate and knife, rushing them over to the sink and rinsing them out. I stood with me mouth open, staring at her hands moving from the hot tap, and flying her fingers in and out of the mug, then rubbing the plate. Waiting for her to explain to me what she was talking about.

'Kitty is the jam jar we pool our money into every week to buy the tea and sugar and milk and cornflakes.'

'Oh, you have to buy your own,' I said, not believing it.

'Of course! You don't expect Missus Murphy to pay, do you?'

'Eh, no, I suppose not. How much do you put in?'

'Five shillings,' she said.

'Five shillings!' I roared. 'What for?'

'I just said!' she shouted back. 'But if you don't want to do that, then you can always buy your own.'

'Right, I'll buy my own!' I snorted, looking for a cup to get meself a drink of cold water. She was out the door, slamming it shut behind her. Me head whirled around looking. Right, where's the bleedin tea? Miserable aul bastards! I hope they come to a bad end. God forgive me!

Jesus! I'm starved. I got no tea. I haven't eaten anything since me dinner at one o'clock today. I'm now used to being well fed. Three meals a day. I still haven't got over me hungry days. I never waste an ounce of grub. I always make sure to clean me plate, never even leaving so much as a crumb. I think it's terrible to waste good food when people are out there starving for the want of a bit of grub.

Cornflakes, lovely. I emptied half the packet into a bowl, keeping an eye on the door in case someone came in. Oh, bread and a bit of cheese in a box. Damn! May as well get hung for a sheep as a lamb. I took the lot. Lathered on good butter from the fridge, and helped meself to a banana left sitting in a bowl on top of the press. The kettle boiled, I put two spoonfuls of tea into the teapot and let it draw for a minute, sitting it over a low heat on the cooker. Lovely! I carried the teapot over to the table and poured out the tea into Molly's mug. I could smell the tea pouring out of the teapot as it went up me nostrils. The smell of the tea somehow bringing me back in time to days of being cold and hungry. Ah, lovely. I dived into the cornflakes, slurping on the milk, and milled the cheese sandwich, making short work of the banana. Then poured out another mug of tea for meself, and lit up a Major cigarette.

Ah, this is lovely! I leaned back, watching the smoke curl into the air, feeling nice and warm now, and happy I had got me own back on Molly. Bloody hell! She'll go bananas when she sees her stuff gone. Bananas! Ha! Yeah, thanks, Molly. It tasted lovely. Jaysus! She'll go off her head. Serves her right. There's no need for the way she carries on. I was barely in the door, in fact she left me standing out in the pouring rain. Only I pushed me way in. I'd probably still be standing out there right this minute. Culchies! I'm definitely going off them now.

* * *

I woke up with a shock, staring into the dark. Me heart was flying. Jaysus! What's happening? Then it hit me. A bell ringing. I stared around the room, trying to make out where I was. Oh! It's an alarm clock. I could barely make out a huge mound buried under the blankets at the other end of the room. The shop! Me new job! I better get up.

I raised me arms outside the threadbare blankets and the cold hit me straight away. I whipped them back, not feeling too much warmer. Jaysus! I couldn't get to sleep last night with the cold. Me head was still wet, and I spent the night shivering around in the bed trying to drop off to sleep. I suppose I better get up. I don't want to be late. But your woman, the Molly one, is not stirring herself!

Right! I leapt up, throwing off the blankets, and dived out, feeling me way around the chair, groping for me clothes in the pitch black. I didn't want to put on the light and have her start giving out to me. Not until I was dressed anyway. I tore into me clothes, and slipped on me shoes, and took off out the door and fell over a box sitting in me way. I went down sideways, spinning around and landing on me arse with me foot under me. 'The curse a Jaysus on that aul Murphy one! Her and her fucking boxes,' I muttered in a loud whisper, rubbing me arse and sitting down on the box to rub me ankle. I got up and limped down the hall, making me way into the kitchen, seeing the aul fella from last night.

'Hello! Good morning,' I said, rattling over to see what he was cooking. 'Are you frying an egg?' I said, looking at the two eggs sizzling around in the frying pan.

'I am!' he said, not taking his eyes off the eggs and flipping them over with the lifter.

'Eh, is there any chance I might borrow one of your eggs and give it back to you when the shop opens?' I said, looking up at him hopefully.

'Have a look in the box,' he said, throwing his head at the egg box sitting on the worktop.

No! Empty. 'There's nothing in it.'

'Sorry,' he said, knowing full well he had got the last of them.

'Thanks anyway,' I said, feeling a bit foolish at getting caught out like that.

Right! I whirled around, seeing if there was any grub lying about. I can't start the day on a empty stomach. I opened the kitchen cabinet press, seeing if there was anything worth eating. Bread! I'll grab some of that, and plaster it with a bit of butter. Before Molly starts mooching in looking for her grub, and finds it all missing, I said to meself, whipping out the bread left sitting behind the glass panel of the kitchen cabinet. I buttered it, leaving it sitting on a plate, and grabbed the kettle to fill it. Then looked around for the teapot.

'Tea's made,' he said. 'You can have a cup of mine, if you like.'

'Gawd! Yer very good! I don't know what I would have done without you,' I said. Not meaning a word of it. Watching him slide the eggs onto the plate, the smell making its way up me nostrils, tormenting me. I saw the bottle of milk sitting on top of the fridge and grabbed it, taking down a bowl and filling it with the last of the cornflakes. I rattled the box, hearing it empty. Oh, dear! Nothing inside. I had a look just to make sure. No! Definitely all gone! Somebody is going to go mad!

I grabbed a mug and poured meself a cup of tea, putting in plenty of milk and sugar, then making short work of the bread and slurping down the cornflakes. I didn't bother me head saying a word to the aul fella and he didn't bother me. The two of us just sat, busy concentrating ourselves eating the grub. I heard footsteps and jumped up, banging me dishes into the sink and rinsing them out rapidly and tried to make me way out the door just as Molly came in. She stood in the doorway, squinting around the kitchen with one eye open and her hair stood up like it had a mind of its own. She had her mouth hanging open, trying to make out what was happening.

'I hope you did not touch my groceries!' she roared, rushing over to the kitchen cabinet.

'Oh, no, Molly! I never saw your stuff,' I said, racing down to get me washbag and get to the bathroom before the ructions started.

I came flying out just as she headed out of the kitchen. 'I told you not to touch my stuff!' she screamed after me, flying meself into the bedroom. I dumped me washbag in the wardrobe and rushed to the dressing table to comb my hair in the mirror, pretending I didn't think she was talking to me. 'Did you hear what I said?' she roared, rushing over at me.

'Wha? What's the matter with you, Molly? It's too early in the morning to be listening to that kind of carry on,' I said, making me face look confused and upset.

'I'll give you carry on!' she screamed. 'Just you wait until I speak to Missus Murphy. Now get away from that dressing table. I want to get ready.'

'Hold yer horses, Molly. I was here first. Anyway, you don't own it. Half of it is mine!'

'That's all my stuff on that dresser!' she screamed, pushing me out of the way.

'Fuck you, Molly. Big and fat as you are. Touch me again and I'll have you plastered on that floor. Now why don't you stop acting the fucking eejit. What age are yeh? Thirty?'

She was white as a sheet with the rage on her and at the insult of making her older then she was. I watched as her nostrils flared, and her eyes whipped around the dresser, taking in all her stuff, then back to me, her eyes turning in the back of her head with the torment in her. 'I am twenty-seven!' she roared. 'You are only a slip of a thing. You better start showing me some respect, miss! I am in charge here. Now get out of my way, or I'll have you fired on the spot!'

'Yeah, you're right, Molly,' I said, taking in a big breath and letting it out through me nose. 'I should have more respect for me elders. It's not right for me to be talking to people of your age like you were a young one. I'm sorry about that,' I said, sounding mournful, and rambling back down to me own side.

'Are you being insulting again?' she snapped, grabbing up her wash stuff and stopping halfway to the door, waiting to hear what I had to say.

'No, definitely not, Molly. You're the boss, and I think we got off to a bad start. I don't think you like the idea of having to share the room. I'm sorry about that. I'll stick to my end of the room, and try to keep out of your way. Can we start again?'

She stared at me, saying nothing. Then went out the door muttering to herself, but looking a bit more appeased. Jaysus! Enough is enough, Martha. She's right! You'll be out on your arse before you know what's happened if you don't stop tormenting her. Right! She's got the message by now. Don't mess with me.

'Here! Come over here and lift them newspapers over to that shelf there.' I looked around, seeing the empty shelf she'd pointed to, and whipped up a heavy pile, sending the half at the bottom of the pile landing on the floor in a heap, seeing all the pages spilling out. 'Jesus! You're less then useless!' she roared, staring at the upended newspapers splattered all over the floor, and me standing there with another pile upended in me hands, after grabbing them up the wrong way. 'Put them on the counter!' she roared, gritting her teeth.

I slammed them down, happy to get rid of the weight, then stood looking at me hands covered in dirty black ink. I looked at me lovely jumper Clare gave me and it was smudged with the black. 'Jaysus! I'm destroyed! Them papers are filthy!' I roared.

'Yes, you fool! You should have been more careful,' she hissed, grabbing up the stuff off the floor.

'Is anyone serving here?' We both looked up over the counter, seeing an old man leaning across looking down at us. 'Ten Carroll cigarettes, please,' the man wheezed, sounding out of breath.

'Will I—'

'Yes, serve that customer!' roared Molly.

'Yeah, would youse please hurry up! I'm in a hurry and haven't got all day to stand around listening to the likes of youse,' he snorted, landing his sights on Molly and drawing in his breath with impatience.

'Certainly, sir!' I breathed. Whipping meself around to look at all the cigarettes. I couldn't see them.

'They're right in front of you,' he said, pointing his hand at the second shelf.

I whipped up the packet, putting them on the counter, saying, 'Will that be all, mister?', delighted with meself to be serving me first customer, even if he was grumpy. Well, not with me. It's with that gobshite Molly, I thought to meself.

'Yeah! Just gimme the change,' he said, 'and make it a few coppers. I need that for the phone.'

'Certainly, half a crown you gave me,' I said, smacking the big keys hanging out of the cash register, hearing it tinkle and fly open. Then I smacked it shut, landing the change on the counter, saying, 'Thank you, call again.'

'Not on yer nelly,' he said, giving me a dirty look. 'Youse left me standing here for at least ten minutes. It's the likes a me that's keeping youses in a job, yeh know!'

'Oh, yer right there,' I said. Shaking me head agreeing with him.

'Will you ever get a move on and sort out them newspapers?' Molly roared. Staring up from the floor at me. Getting herself all red in the face.

'That man was complain—'

'Never mind him!' she roared. 'The bread man will be in on top of us any minute, and so far you are more of a hindrance then a help.'

'Ah, you get up off your knees, Molly, and let me do that,' I said, hoping to put her in better form.

'Stack them in their separate piles,' she said. 'Make sure you sort them out properly. I don't want someone bringing them back complaining we gave them the wrong newspaper.'

'God forbid I would do that,' I said, sounding very pious.

'And watch your language. Stop making a show of this establishment, with your filthy tongue.'

'Excuse me!' I roared, whirling around with me hands on me hips.

'Don't start again! I'm warning you!' she snarled, sucking in her lips, looking like she wanted to make mincemeat out of me.

'Right! But I don't use bad language,' I said quietly, looking hurt.

'Then you should stop and listen to yourself,' she moaned, making out she was a holy Mary.

Fuck! Any minute now I'm going to lose the rag if she keeps

this up. I snorted, letting me breath out, making a big noise so she should know she was going too far.

'How're yeh, girls?' I shot around from stacking the sliced bread on the shelves to see what was going on. 'Do yeh have a nice box of chocolates?' a fella with long hair past his ears, curling in a quiff, and hanging down over one eye, laughed. Swaggering his way into the shop and making for me.

'What kind do you want?' I said, smiling at him, delighted he wanted me to serve him.

'I'll get these,' Molly said, raising her head from the milk crate and stacking the bottles in the fridge.

'No! Yer all right. The young one will do me,' he said, waving her away.

'Do you want chocolates or not?' she said, barking at him, holding her hands on her hips.

'What's a lovely young thing like you doing working in a kip like this?' he said, waving his head around the shop, giving a dirty look to Molly.

'Waiting on a lovely young fella like you to come and buy me a box of chocolates,' I said, leaning on the counter and giving him a big smile, showing off me white gnashers.

'Right! What time do yeh knock off?' he said. 'I'll pick yeh up after work. Where do yeh want to go? The pictures?'

'Get back to work!' Molly roared. 'You are not being paid to have idle chatter with the customers.'

'Jaysus! Where did yeh get yer woman from?' he said, stretching his neck back and letting his eyeballs hang out, looking down his nose at Molly. I was delighted he was getting a rise out of her, but I kept me face straight.

'No, sorry, I have a boyfriend,' I said, getting all serious. Enough was enough. I didn't want to lose me job. Anyway, he's not my type. He's too full of himself. I want better when I start looking.

'Molly will serve you,' I said, wanting to placate her, and not give your man the wrong idea.

'Your loss!' he said to me back as I planted the bread on the shelves.

'What price do you want to pay?'

'Give me a box of them Dairy Milk,' he said, pointing to the big box of chocolates. 'Are you sure you won't change your mind?' he roared at me as he was making for the door. 'I bet your boyfriend won't buy you a box of these. Look, these are for me ma. She's in the hospital, but I can buy you a box as well, if you like?'

I looked around at him. Seeing he wasn't acting so full of himself. He looked a little lost, more like a little boy. 'What age are yeh?' I said, laughing.

'I'm sixteen!'

'Oh! So am I.'

'Well, then! Will yeh come out with me?'

'Ask me another time,' I said, seeing he was really shy, and was just covering up, trying to make himself look like a man of the world.

'Yeah, right. I will. I'll do that then,' he said, backing out of the shop with the chocolates under his arm, wrapped in a brown paper bag.

'Bye! See yeh! Bye! Be seeing you!' I laughed. Thinking that could be my very first boyfriend if I wanted. I even felt a bit sorry for him, God love him, and he's very good. Buying his ma a box of chocolates because she's in the hospital. Yeah, I might think about it. Because I know he wouldn't do me any harm. I don't trust fellas, so that's saying a lot for him.

'That's a very cheeky young fella,' Molly said, bending down to put the milk in the fridge.

'Ah, he's only showing off, Molly. There's no real harm in him.'

'How would you know? Sure what experience do you have? You better watch yourself. Mind who you keep company with!' Molly snorted, raging no one had asked her out. Jaysus! I would hate to be stuck in a dump like this when I get to her age! I'd rather hang meself. No, I'm going to be moving up in the world.

'Keep an eye on the shop. I'm taking my break,' Molly suddenly said, making over for the cakes the bread man delivered early this morning. I watched her taking two big sugary jam doughnuts and take off up the stairs to the kitchen, to make herself a cup of tea.

'Right, I'll be in charge,' I said, stretching me arms and leaning me hands on the counter. Then she was flying back down the stairs just as quick.

'Don't do . . .' she snorted, whipping herself back into the shop, coming to a standstill, trying to think. 'Make sure you know what you are doing,' she said, looking worried. Her eyes watching me carefully, then flying around the shop to make sure everything was OK.

'Don't worry, I know exactly what I'm doing, Molly. Everything will be as right as rain.'

'That's what I am afraid of,' she said. 'You better not make any problems for me, I'm warning you!'

'Like what, Molly? Sure I have been at this job all morning. There's nothing to it!'

'I'll be upstairs, if you want me. Just open this door and shout up.'

'OK, Molly.' Then she was gone.

I'm on me own! Running the shop by meself. Who would have thought it? Me eyes flew around the length and breadth of the shop, taking in all the sweets. Then I landed me head on the glass case over the other side. The one with the fancy sweets. I listened for a second. Right, she's gone. I dashed over, and flew around the counter and shot down to where the lovely soft nutty brown sweets were sitting, waiting for me. I picked up one, sniffing it. Hmm, gorgeous. It smells like toffee and coconut. I'll just have one. They're very expensive. Well, maybe two. Oh, have another one. Jaysus! Have two more. It's only a few. Gawd! This is definitely a marvellous job. Working in a shop. I can help meself to whatever I want.

I had me fill of the sweets and was just starting on the Kimberley Biscuits when the door flew open. I nearly choked with the fright. 'Where are yeh?' Molly roared, flying her head around the shop, looking the length of the place for me.

'I'm over here,' I croaked, lifting me head out of the biscuits, raising me eyes above the counter, trying to swallow the biscuit whole.

'What are you doing over there?' she roared, eyeing the sweets, seeing me cheeks bulging.

'Eh, fixing the sweets, Molly! A man wanted some then changed his mind. I, eh, had to empty them back.'

She stared, looking at me very suspiciously. 'Them sweets are very expensive, you know.'

'Yeah! They're very dear at that all right,' I agreed, shaking me head at her.

'So keep your hands off them!'

'Of course! God forgive yeh, Molly, for thinking such a thing,' I said. Flying around the counter to stand beside her. 'Can I go for me break now, Molly? You've had yours.'

'Go on, and only take ten minutes!'

'Right, I'm off,' I said, belting up the stairs, dying for a cup of tea and a cigarette. Then I remembered and came flying back down again. I helped meself to two doughnuts and was just whipping out the door again when Molly let out a roar. 'Come back here, you!'

'Wha? What's wrong?'

'You have to pay for them, you know. You pay for everything you take out of this shop.'

I didn't know that, I thought, seeing her not paying for the doughnuts. Then decided to chance me arm. 'Ah, I won't bother after all so,' I said, hesitating, and putting it to me mouth, looking like I was thinking about it. 'I suppose I better put them back.'

'You can't put them back. You've been manhandling them.'

'Yeah, I know. What will you do? Will I dump them in the bin?'

'You will do no such thing. You can pay for them now.'

'No, I most definitely will not. I thought you were getting them for nothing. I didn't see you paying for them,' I snorted, feeling the heat rising in me, because, now that I remember, she didn't pay for them.

'Go on! Get out. Eat your bloody cakes. But don't let me catch you doing that again. Or I'll report you to Missus Murphy.'

'Right, thanks very much, Molly. You're very good.'

* * *

The shop was crowded. I was on night duty, with Molly doing overtime. Because she had to do stocktaking, she called it.

'Give me an ounce of ready-rubbed tobacco,' an elderly man said, pointing at the big jar behind me. I dipped me hand in, and pulled out a square piece of tobacco, looking at the price, and handed it to him. 'Thanks, love,' and he was out the door, then back in a few minutes later. 'You might as well give me another two,' he said, pointing at the jar. Before I knew where I was, there was a great run on ready-rubbed tobacco.

'Gawd! This stuff is flying,' I muttered, handing it to a young fellow. 'What do you use that stuff for?'

'It's me granddad that smokes it in his pipe,' he said, handing me back the tobacco I gave him. 'I only asked for an ounce,' he said. 'That's two ounces.'

'What?' I looked at it, seeing the near-empty jar.

'The other one,' he said, pointing to the jar at the far back of the shelf. 'That's the smaller one, yeh can easily see the difference,' he said, being very obliging to point that out to me.

'Thanks!' I whipped the money off him, thinking, Jaysus! I'm for it now. I've been giving out two ounces for one ounce all day. The fucking robbers! They knew what they were up to. Waiting on me to serve them. I was wondering about that – why me and the ready-rubbed tobacco was so popular. Now I know. Jaysus! That stuff is very dear. If Molly finds out, it will cost me a month's wages, judging by the amount I gave away. Better hide the jar. I swapped them around, putting the full jar of one-ounce in front and the empty one in the back, hoping she wouldn't notice.

I was sweeping the floor after the shop shut up for the night. 'We're down seventeen shillings and nine pence,' Molly was saying, looking very worried, to the grey-haired man checking the money with her. The pair of them gave looks in my direction. They better not blame me. When it came to giving out the change, I was very careful. I always make sure to count it out to the customers as I hand it over. That's what I always did as a child. I always made sure I got the right change.

'Let's start again,' he said, emptying out the bags of money.

'Molly, I'm going up to bed now,' I said, making for the door.

'You better wait! The day's takings are short. You may be liable.'

'No chance,' I said wearily, dropping me shoulders and leaning me elbows on the counter further down the shop. Nobody is taking one penny out of my wages. If there's one thing I can do, it's count. I wasn't running me own business at the age of nine for nothing, I thought to myself.

'I'm going up for a cup of tea. I'll be back,' I said, moving out the door.

I heard the side door being locked, then someone drawing the bolt across and I held me breath. Molly came into the kitchen, making for the teapot. The grey-haired man followed her in behind. 'Is it all OK?' I asked her, holding me breath.

'Yes, it balanced,' she said, not bothering to look at me.

'Right, goodnight, then. See you in the morning,' I said.

She nodded at me, and the man muttered goodnight under his breath. I walked off down the hall making for me bed, feeling this job would not be so bad if the people were nice.

I leaned on the counter, opening the pages of the *Evening Herald*, seeing the shop was quiet. Molly threw her eye at me, giving me a dirty look but saying nothing. She just tutted, shaking her head, and went back to the business of stacking the shelves with cans of beans. She'd got fed up giving out to me. I had worn her down.

Ah, here we are. Night classes. Me eyes lit up. 'Classes in shorthand and typing. Why get stuck in that dead-end job! Come and join us. Earn big wages as a secretary' the advertisement said. 'Apply to Taylors College. Phone number . . .' Right! That's what I'm looking for.

'Molly!'

'What?' she said, giving me a withering look.

'I need coppers for the phone. Can I run upstairs to me handbag or can I borrow it out of the till?'

'You will do no such thing. Keep your paws out of that till.

You are not going anywhere. You can do your business on your own time.'

'Well, I have to go to the toilet, Molly. You can't stop me doing that!' I roared, opening the door and flying up the stairs before she could say another word. I grabbed two pennies out of me purse and flew back down again.

'Right! I'm back. You didn't even know I was gone, I was that quick,' I puffed, trying to appease her.

'You won't last in this job,' she sniffed, letting out her breath.

I went to the phone box at the side of the door and put the money in. When I heard someone say 'Hello,' I listened to the money drop as I pressed the button A. 'Is this Taylors College?'

'Yes, can I help you?'

'Yeah, I want to enquire about the night classes in shorthand and typing.'

The woman at the other end listened then said, 'Are you a beginner? What standard are you at?'

'Standard?'

'Yes. Have you done any before?'

'No, I want to start.'

'Right. It's a bit late now, the classes are nearly finishing up. But if you come in January, the classes will be starting over again. They start on the twelfth of January. You just come along on the night and enrol straight away and pay. What way do you want to do it? You can pay nightly. Five shillings for two hours one night a week. That way if you don't turn up, you don't lose any money.'

'Oh, that's grand. That will suit me down to the ground.'

'OK, the classes start sharp at seven p.m. And end at nine p.m. It's to allow for people working during the day. Is that all you need to know?'

'Yeah! Oh, wait a minute! Do I need to bring anything with me?'

'Yeah, you need to buy a shorthand notebook, and a pencil and rubber. You can get that in Eason's. Is that OK?'

'Yeah, yeah, that's lovely. Thank you very much for all your help. Oh, by the way!'

'Yeah?' the woman said, getting a bit impatient to get off the phone.

'How many classes are there in the college? Will I be able to find the one I want? I don't want to be late and miss the beginning.'

'No, this is only a secretarial college. We have students coming in full-time during the day, and we only do one class at night. It's always on a Tuesday night.'

'OK!'

'Goodbye now,' she said, making it sound final.

'Goodbye. Thanks again.' I put down the phone, feeling me heart flying.

Right, I'll be there on the Tuesday night in January. But I forgot to ask her how many classes I would need before I can do the shorthand and typing and get a good job. Well, we'll see. I'll work hard, that will hurry it along.

I could see Molly was earwigging. She put on her long face with the woebegone look, much as to say, 'It's a pity about yeh, thinking we're not good enough for yeh!'

8

'There you go, mam. Thirteen shillings and sevenpence half-penny change.' I watched the woman count her change and put it carefully into her purse, looking to see what she had left.

'That's grand,' she said, shutting the purse and putting it at the bottom of her shopping bag.

'Here's your bread and milk,' I said, holding the two bottles of milk while she fixed the bread and tea in the bag.

'Bye now,' she said, waving to me.

'Thanks, and a very happy Christmas,' I said, smiling at her.

'And a very happy Christmas to you too, love,' she said, making for the door. Molly whipped it wide open, shaking the door, impatient to close it, then slammed it shut after letting the woman out.

'That's the last of them,' Molly sighed.

'Right,' the grey-haired man said, flying around the shop switching off all the lights, letting the Christmas lights in the window go off. Then rushing out the door to slam down the shutters on the two big plate-glass windows and slam the shutter down in front of the door on the outside. Then he locked the front door as Molly whipped past me shouting, 'Don't go near that bathroom. I'm having a bath now. I need to run for that train leaving Heuston station at ten past four.'

'Right so, Molly. I won't bother. See you after Christmas.'

'Yes! Wednesday we open again. So just you make sure you are back here on Tuesday night. You are on the early morning shift.'

'OK. See you. Have a lovely Christmas!'

'Yes, you too,' she said, flying up the stairs.

'Happy Christmas, Mister O'Brien!' I shouted to the grey-haired man checking to see if everything was turned off.

'Oh, yes. Happy Christmas to you too,' he said, looking miles away, not really taking much notice.

I was up the stairs and into the room, making for me green coat and handbag. Molly was already gone down to the bathroom. That was quick. She really is in a hurry. I could see her big brown battered old suitcase standing next to the bed, with her purple wool coat folded on top of her black old handbag sitting on the bed waiting for her. Then I spotted the string nylon shopping bag thrown in the corner. Great! Just what the doctor ordered. I need that for me shopping today. I'll just borrow it.

I grabbed it up, rushing to get me coat and handbag, taking out the little brown envelope with the big green one-pound note, and the red ten-shilling note, all new and shiny. Right, I'll take it all into town with me. I might as well spend the lot. After all, tomorrow is Christmas Day. It's the one day of the year I should be good to meself. I can start saving again after Christmas. You always need money in your pocket, you never know the hour or the day when I could really need it. I don't want to find meself suddenly out of a job and without a penny in me pocket. Jaysus! That would never do. I could end up walking the streets just like me and the ma. I shivered even at the thought of it. No, I'm never going to let meself get into that position. At the mercy of the world. I will always make sure I have another job to go to before I leave what I'm doing.

I combed me hair, putting on me coat, and picked up me bag, checking to make sure I had the hall door key to let meself in. Grand. It's there. Right! Better hurry and catch the bus into town. The shops are going to be crowded.

I opened the door as Molly came flying down the hall. 'Are you off, then, for the Christmas?'

'Yeah!' I said, trying to rush past her. Not wanting her to know I would be staying here, and have to start answering awkward questions. I'm telling no one my business. Who I am, and where

I come from is no one's business, I huffed to meself, taking off down the stairs.

I got off the bus in O'Connell Street and turned right, crossing the road, flying under buses and cars, with people and traffic nearly running into each other. Everyone was in a hurry. Rushing to get the last-minute bit of shopping. I turned right, heading up Henry Street. Seeing all the Christmas lights streaming through the air. With Santa on his sledge and his reindeers flying out behind him, hanging from the tops of the buildings strung out across the street. The noise was deafening. People were crushing each other to get up and down and sideways, in and out of the shops. I pushed me way into the centre of the road, discovering it made no difference. Everyone had the same idea.

'Get yer Cheeky Charlies,' I could hear the Moore Street aul ones shouting. Now they were along this street for the Christmas. With their stalls lining the edge of the footpaths, catching all the people crushing past. They wouldn't take no for an answer.

I made me way onto the footpath, hoping to make it up to Woolworths. 'Here, love. Take one a dem for the Christmas. Yeh'll get hours a enjoyment outa it. Lookit! Take it!' an aul one with grey curly thin hair sticking out of the scarf on her head roared at me, her tired, faded old blue eyes boring into me, as she danced the grinning monkey up and down on the string, then shoved it in me face.

'Ah, no, missus! Thanks, I don't want it,' I laughed, trying to push past her.

'No, wait! Come back,' she said, grabbing the sleeve of me coat. 'Lookit! Yeh can give it as a present to yer sisters and brothers. Mebbe yeh might even play with it yerself. It's not too long since yeh used teh play yerself. Go on! It's only a half a crown, love. Lookit! I have only a few left,' she said, waving at her stall. 'Or lookit! What about a few decorations? Yer mammy would love dem! The best quality ones they are. Here, come back!'

'No, sorry.' I shook me head, pulling away from her. Feeling sorry as I pushed me way up the street. Poor woman is desperate to make a few pounds. But that's no good to me. I never played with toys in me life, and I can't give it to anyone. I don't know many people these days. I haven't made any friends yet. Just the customers who come in and out of the shop. But I don't really know them.

I couldn't get in near the door of Woolworths. I stopped to look in, seeing the mad crush of people all milling around, pushing and shoving each other. Ah, I won't bother meself going in there. It's only a waste of time. Sure I won't be able to get near the counters.

I turned away, moving slowly through the crowd, making me way back out onto the road, and looked up at the Woolworths café overhead. I could see people sitting at the tables, looking out through the big glass windows enjoying themselves, eating and watching the crowds going past. I used to do that, I thought. Looking up at them. That was me greatest enjoyment after the terrible fear of going around robbing in the shops all day. Then when it was over, sit there at the window enjoying me chips and eggs and beans and bread and butter, with the pot of tea. Feeling an infinite sense of peace that it was all over and I had the money in me pocket, and the food in me bag, and I was safe for another week. It might be nice to go up now and have something to eat, and watch the crowds. But somehow, I don't think it would feel right. It would remind me too much of them days. No, I'll keep moving. That part of me life is now dead and gone. Thanks be to God.

I made me way down Moore Street. 'Sixpence the Christmas pineapples. Do yeh want some, love? Lookit! They're only massive. Here! Feel one,' she said, humping it up and down in her hand, making to land it in my hand. I kept me hands in me pockets, and smiled at her, moving on.

'Here, missus,' she said to an aul one trying to make her way past me. 'Take one a these home for the Christmas. Go on! Try one out for after the dinner. They are ony gorgeous! I'm tellin yeh, missus. Yeh won't be able teh get enough a dem. Here! Have ony the one then. Tha won't break yeh!' she roared. Her face curling up in disgust at the aul one, who pushed past her, saying, 'Excuse me, please. I am in a hurry,' speaking in a very grand voice.

'Jaysus!' the dealer roared after her, standing with the pineapple in one hand and the other hand on her hip, with her feet planted, going in different directions. 'If anyone needs a pineapple, it's you, missus! It might take tha sour, hungry, dyin-lookin look offa yer face. Yeh should start spendin tha confirmation money yeh made all a dem years ago. Yeh can't take it wit yeh!' she snorted, taking her vengeance out on the aul one rushing past me, looking mortified. I roared laughing, looking back at the dealer. 'Them aul ones wouldn't give yeh the steam offa their piss,' she snorted. 'Bleedin fur coat an no drawers,' she moaned. Looking down mournfully at all the pineapples still left sitting on her stall. Then throwing her head at me and anyone else listening. 'Go on, you!' She waved her arm at me in disgust, not liking me laughing. 'Don't spend yer money all in the one shop,' she said, starting to get even more annoyed with me.

Jaysus! Them aul ones would kill yeh if you crossed them, I thought, laughing and pushing me way through the crowds. They really know how to make a show of you.

'LAST OF THE TURKEYS! GET YER FRESH TURKEYS! Come in an lookit dem. Only beauriful, they are. They're so fresh they'll eat yeh alive!' a small skinny little aul fella wearing a blood-spattered white apron down to his ankles was shouting through a megaphone into the faces of all the people going past the butcher shop.

'Are they very fresh?' a little aul one stopped to ask him, carrying a shopping bag so full with the Christmas shopping her head was nearly tipping the ground with the weight of it.

'ARE THEY FRESH?' he roared through the megaphone, letting the whole street know, and pointing it at her, blasting the ear offa her, making her jump back with the shock. 'Missus,' he roared, 'they're so fresh they haven't had the time to know they're dead yet! Sure weren't they ony eatin their breakfast this morning. Not knowin they were goin teh be sittin on your plate tomorra!'

'Gawd! I'll go in an take a look,' she said happily after looking at them all crowded on top of each other, sitting in the window with their eyes sticking outa their heads. Looking like they still couldn't get over their misfortune at having gotten themself killed. I looked in to see what else they had. I stared at sheeps' heads. Ugh! Jaysus! That would turn your stomach.

I moseyed on, wandering with the crowd, getting meself carried to the other side of the street. I stopped to look in the window at the pork and bacon shop next to the laneway. I stared at the big hams and black-looking spiced beef, and corn beef, with nice-looking sausages and all sorts of different kinds of rashers. I could see the shop was crowded. I wonder what I'll get for meself to eat over the Christmas? Right, I better get something in here. It's as good as any, all the shops are full anyway.

I shuffled me way in, following behind an aul granny with a shopping bag wrapped around her arm. The scarf was getting pulled off her head and we were getting battered by the people trying to get out. 'Take it easy, will youse! For the luv a Jaysus. They're not givin the stuff away for free!' she huffed, looking back at me. As if I was the one pulling the scarf off her head.

'Yer right there, missus,' I said, muttering behind her.

She lost the rag and thumped an aul fella falling backwards and standing on her feet. 'Me corns! Mind where yer fuckin goin! The lot a yehs!' she roared, pulling the scarf tight around her head, working her chin up and down. Then pushing her hands out in front of her to keep people moving, and stop them knocking her down.

We got in as far as the door, and she pushed her way through, making for the counter. 'Outa the way, the lot a yehs!' she roared, pushing and shoving everyone. 'I lost me place in the queue wit yehs pushin me back. Have youse no respect for the likes a me? Old an crippled, I am!' People moved slightly to look back to see who was doing all the shouting and roaring and hitting. 'Here! Let me in!' she shouted as soon as someone made a little gap, looking at her.

Then she was up to the counter with me behind her, pretending I was with her by shaking me head and puffing out me cheeks and raising me eyes to heaven, muttering, 'The granny is a terrible woman. She has no patience.'

One aul fella looked back at me and blocked me, saying, 'Well, youse can wait yer turn. Yer not gettin yerselves in front a me!'

'Here, you! I was standin here before you turned up! Ger outa me way or I'll swing for yeh!' Then she gave him a dig. Pushing out her bony elbows and squeezing past him.

'Are yeh all right, Granny?' I said, squeezing after her.

'No thanks teh him, I am!' she said, fixing the scarf on her little head and tying it under her chin. Giving the aul fella such a dirty look it was enough to stop a clock. 'What have they got?' she said, trying to stretch her neck to see over the counter to the shelves behind the far wall. Seeing long strings of sausages, black and white pudding, cooked ham, and trays of eggs, then looking up at the ducks and chickens and turkeys and hams hanging outa the big hooks coming outa the big beams. 'I ony want something small,' she said. 'Just to do me teh get by for the Christmas.'

'Yeah, me too,' I muttered, wondering what I was going to get. I can't cook yet. I'm only starting to learn.

'Listen, son! I'm next. Have yeh any nice chickens? I don't want antin toooo big! Just enough for meself,' she said, smiling at him, showing the one rotten tooth she still had left in her head.

'Here's a nice little one,' he said, holding it by the legs and showing her, with the head and feathers still stuck to it.

'Here, get rid a tha head first! Are yeh chargin me be the weight?'

'Well, this one is three and six, but you can have it for two and six. Me Christmas box to you! How's tha?' he smiled, showing dimples in his cheeks and a lovely set of white teeth.

'Yeah, tha will do me lovely,' she said happily. 'But take tha bleedin head off first. I don't want teh be wakin up with the nightmares after lookin at tha thing!'

'Now. Anythin else?' he said, wrapping the chicken and landing it down on the counter.

'Yeah, give us a half-pound a dem Hafner's sausages, and a bit a black an white puddin. Make sure yeh put plenty a seasonin on dem! I'll be watchin teh see wha yer doin,' she warned him. He laughed, grabbing the sausages and cutting a bit of black and white pudding and lashing on the seasoning from the metal canister. 'Yeah! I'll take a dozen a dem big eggs there, an make sure yeh seal dem tight. I don't want no one breakin dem on me, before I can get dem home!' He slapped on an empty egg carton on top of the eggs then covered them all the way around, sealing them with the Sellotape. Putting the eggs now nicely packed on top of the counter.

'Leave it at five shilling,' he said, watching her rooting in her purse and coming up with two half crowns, landing them on the counter. Then she happily put everything in her bag, sticking out her elbows to make sure no one nudged her and ended up breaking the eggs before she could get them in her big cloth shopping bag.

'Goodbye now! An a happy Christmas to yeh. Hope yeh have a bit a luck for givin me dem few things,' she said, using her elbows to make her way out of the shop again.

'Give us a half-pound a Hafner's sausages!' I roared up, before he could finish saying 'Right, who's next?', looking down the line at the crowd of people all pushing and shoving, squeezing and suffocating us at the counter.

'Here, I'm next!' the aul fella with the red face shouted as the young fella asked me what else I wanted.

'I'm goin teh get to you next,' he said to the aul fella roaring in me ear behind me.

'Tha one! An tha aul hag just gone out the door skipped the queue!' he roared. Pointing his finger in the air, then jabbing it in me, stabbing me in the back. 'Yeah! Scandalous, it is. An we all takin our place in the queue, an that's the thanks we get for it! He's servin them tha has no respect for anyone. Just walk in, if yeh please. An get yerself served straight away!'

All the mutterings came from behind me, and everyone started roaring, giving out like mad. I couldn't think fast enough what I wanted. So I copied the old woman. 'Give us a bit of white pudding and a quarter of streaky rashers, and two nice big pork chops,' I gasped, in an awful hurry before I ended up getting eaten alive and thrown out of the shop on me arse. 'And don't forget the seasoning. I want plenty of seasoning,' I said, copying the aul one just gone out the door.

The young fella wrapped them in white paper and slapped them down on the counter. 'Anythin else?' he grinned at me. Knowing I was in trouble for skipping the queue.

'Yeah, I'll take a dozen of them eggs there. The big ones,' I said, pointing at the trays of eggs.

'Four shillings and ninepence to you,' he said, grinning at me.

'Make it four shillings,' I laughed, 'and I'll light a penny candle for yeh!'

'If yeh promise to come in again,' he said, 'I'll see what I can do.'

'Get a fuckin move on there!' roared the aul fella, giving me a smack on the back of me head. 'We haven't all day!' he roared into me ear.

'Yeh aul—' I started to roar, whipping meself around.

'Give us the half crown. And what else have you there?' the young fella said quickly, seeing me with the half crown and the shilling in me hand after I stopped rooting in me purse for the rest, because I was going to give the aul fella behind me an earful. 'Here!' he said, grabbing me hand and taking the half crown and the shilling. 'That will do.'

'Right! That's lovely,' I said happily, delighted with me bargains. Then putting the eggs in me string bag along with the rest of me stuff and holding it in front, making me way out through the crowd, saying, 'Go easy! Let me out. Don't break me eggs.'

'The curse a Jaysus on yeh!' the aul fella snorted, giving me another dig on the shoulder, with his face turning blue at the sight of me after getting me shopping, and half of it for nothing, while he still had to wait. I just grinned, knowing he was annoyed enough with me, and pushed and fought me way over to the grocery part of the shop, hanging onto me eggs.

Jaysus! This is no good. Me eggs will be smashed. I spotted empty carton boxes lying against the wall next to the counter where the girl was going mad trying to keep up with the paying customers. I reached in and grabbed a big one, mooching meself closer to the chair she was sitting on. Smiling up at her as she wondered what I was up to. 'I'm just putting these things in the empty box,' I said, scraping her nylon stockings with me hand getting pushed against her.

I put the bag sitting in the box and used it as a battering ram to work me way around the shop. I put two bottles of milk into the box then headed down for a pound of good butter and a box of cheese. What else? I spotted the biscuits and put in a packet of me favourites, Kimberley. Then I went mad and put in a box of Dairy Milk chocolates. Lovely! That's the lot. I made me way down to the queue, thinking I could easily make me way out the door now without paying. But I have no intention of doing that. Me self-respect is worth more then the few pennies I would save. You can't put a price on self-respect.

I felt really happy with meself standing in the queue waiting patiently to pay. Feeling I was really free at last. 'Two shillings and elevenpence,' the young one said.

'Oh, you might as well give me twenty Major cigarettes while you're at it,' I said, pointing up to the shelf behind her. 'Make it two packets of ten,' I said, wanting to make them stretch. I handed over the money and made me way back out into the crowds. It was even worse now. It was beginning to get dark and the people were getting desperate to get their last-minute shopping. I battered me way down Moore Street, keeping the box out in front of me, pushing me way through the crowds. I stopped to look at tomatoes sitting on a stall. 'Sixpence a pound' the sign said.

'Do yeh want dem tomatoes, love?' an aul one said, diving on me and whipping open a brown paper bag ready to grab a pound of tomatoes for me.

'Only if yeh give me the ones at the front,' I said, staring at her.

'Here, they're all lovely,' she said, grabbing the rotten ones she had hidden at the back. They always do that. Get rid of the rotten stuff first.

'No, the ones from the front. I'm payin yeh good money,' I said, wanting her to know I was no dopey posh young one.

'Here, keep yer money,' she roared at me, grabbing me arm and pushing me down the road. 'Bleedin young ones! No respect for man nor beast. Some of dem have no rearin in dem. Their aul ones just dragged them up!' she shouted after me.

'Go on!' I shouted. 'Yeh should have respect for yer betters!' I roared back at her. Knowing she would go mad at the thought of someone looking down on her.

'Yeh won't be sayin tha if I catch hold a yeh!' she roared, waving her fist at me. 'I'll soon put manners on yeh!'

'Ah, yer all hot air,' I laughed, sticking me tongue out at her, and crossing me eyes. Then I laughed, feeling a bit mean for tormenting the poor aul woman. Still and all, I'm not paying good money for just rotten tomatoes!

I stopped outside the bread shop, seeing the loads of black-crusted loaves of bread and fresh turnover all piled in the window. Right, I'll get some of that lovely fresh bread to go with me good butter. I made me way into the shop, standing in a big queue, miles a bodies well away from the counter. Every time someone pushed out, the crowd milled in. I held the box in front of me, shouting, 'Let me in!' and forcing people to part away from each other, slowly getting me way to the counter.

'Give us a black crusty loaf, and a fresh turnover. Make sure it's very fresh,' I said to the aul one serving me.

'It's all fresh,' she snorted, breaking two loaves stuck together, and doing the same with the turnover, and putting them in a paper bag, then slamming them down on the counter, thinking I had a cheek. 'One shilling and sixpence,' she said, holding out her hand for the money. I landed the box up on the counter, whipping me purse out of me pocket, and handing over the money. Then I was out the door again.

I stopped further down to look at a stall with only a few tomatoes left. They look nice and hard, I thought. 'Give us a pound of yer good tomatoes,' I said, watching her grab the paper bag and feel and manhandle them, throwing back the hard ones and looking for the soft ones. 'Have a heart! It's Christmas. Give us the nice ones, missus!' I said, thinking I'm going to end up with a load of squashed tomatoes if she keeps this up.

'Go on then,' she said, landing the tomatoes back on the stall and picking up the nice hard ones.

'Thanks very much, missus,' I said, delighted with her being generous as much as getting the good tomatoes.

'Do yeh want antin else, love?' she said, holding out her hand for the sixpence.

'Yeah, give us a nice bunch of bananas.'

'Righ! That's ten pence,' she said, landing the bananas in me box.

I walked on to the end of Moore Street, then turned right, heading past the Rotunda Hospital. I could see men flying in and out, some had teddies and bunches of flowers. Ah, the maternity hospital. Imagine having a baby today! Or even better still, tonight. A baby born on Christmas Day. Still and all. Them mothers will be delighted to have it over them for the Christmas, and can go home carrying their new baby. I hope that's a nice present for all of them, I thought. Thinking of the poor women who had too many children, and the last thing they needed was another one.

Ah, well. Some poor people never get it easy in this life, I thought. Then the picture of the ma came flashing into me mind. I stopped dead in me tracks, thinking of the ma and the poor children. I could feel meself sinking down straight away. Just seeing the picture of them all. No, don't! It's not your business any more. She will only drag you down. Nothing was ever enough for her. That's the way she is. Forget it. But it's Christmas! They'll have nothing, I thought, feeling the pain come over me at the thought I was only thinking of meself. Don't be bleedin stupid! I've spent me whole life trying to help the ma, and look where it got me! Locked up for three years, and all she could worry about was when she could get her hands on me, to start milking me again. Then I'd start getting meself into trouble all over again. Anyway, as long as she stays with that aul fella . . . well, I'm never having anything to do with her. You promised yourself in the convent, Martha, you were never going to look back. It's all over. Now I have to make a life for meself. You are going to have a grand life. You have given her enough. Yeah, I have. Enough is enough. I am going to make something of me life, I said to meself. Desperate not to look back. God knows where that might take me, I thought, getting pushed sideways by the crowd, and starting to move again, making me way down, heading over to Parnell Street.

I stopped and went into a hardware shop, asking the aul fella behind the counter, 'How much are yeh charging for a hot-water bottle?'

'Here's one for a shilling,' he said, landing a hot-water bottle on the counter.

'Have yeh anything cheaper?' I asked him, watching him dozily twirling his whiskers.

'No! Do yeh want it or not?' he said, getting ready to whip it away.

'Yeah! It's too late to go looking in Woolworths,' I said. 'Pity! I would have gotten it cheaper there.'

'Yeah, an if I had Mister Woolworths' money, yeh could buy it cheap from me, too,' he said, sticking out his hand for the shilling. 'Furthermore, I wouldn't have teh be listenin teh the likes a you complainin about me prices.'

'Jaysus, mister!' I said slowly, getting annoyed meself. 'Don't take yer vengeance out on me. It's too bad yer not knocked down with the rush of people wanting to buy yer stuff,' I said, looking around the empty shop. 'It's not my fault yer place is as dead as the morgue! Maybe if yeh lowered your prices a bit, people might think of coming in. Christmas, how are yeh! This is supposed to be the season of goodwill!' I snorted, slamming down the shilling and grabbing up me hot-water bottle and putting it in me box. Now brimming over with me shopping.

'Yes! And a happy Christmas to you, too!' he said, shouting at me back.

'Yeah! Don't choke on yer turkey,' I said, making me way out the door.

I walked on, standing at the traffic lights to try and get across O'Connell Street. I looked up and down, seeing no gap in the traffic. 'No! Wait, yeh gobshite. You'll get yourself killed,' I muttered to meself, not used to waiting at traffic lights to get across the road. The box was too heavy and I could hardly see over it. But it was grand and handy for getting me through the crowded streets.

Finally here. I made me way into the second-hand bookshop, smelling paraffin oil smouldering out from the wreck of an aul heater, standing upright on four legs. 'Hello!' I said, smiling at the old man sitting on a stool behind the counter, warming his hands wrapped in grey wool gloves with the fingers cut out. He had a soft battered old hat sitting on his head and a scarf wrapped around his neck, to keep out the damp. 'Mister, can I leave this box behind yer counter while I have a look around at the books?'

'Yeah, go ahead, love. Feel free to see if there's antin yeh want. Go on! Put it under the counter. It will be safe there. I'll mind it fer yeh!'

'Thanks.' I bent down, pushing the box under the counter, and rambled around the little book shop, throwing me eye at all the shelves stacked with piles of books. I wandered up and down, seeing some that might interest me, but hoping for something that would make me mad to read it. John Steinbeck. *Of Mice And Men*. I read the back, and flicked through the pages, not wanting to read it and spoil the story. Just to get an idea of what the book was like. Yeah! That looks good. I'll take that.

I wandered on, taking me time, looking at anything that caught me eye. Then I picked up one that said Harold Robbins, *The Carpet Baggers*. Yeah! That sounds good. I'll read that.

Right! I let out a big sigh of contentment, and headed off down to the old man at the counter. 'How much do you want for these two books, mister?' I said, putting them on the counter. He looked at the price on the back. It said three shillings and sixpence to buy new.

'Give us half a crown for the two,' he said.

'Make it a shilling each! And I'll sell them back to you at half that. Then buy some more from yeh, if yeh go easy on the price,' I said, reaching for me purse.

'OK, fair enough. Give us the two shilling,' he said, taking the money out of me hand and putting it in his pocket, looking very happy.

'What time will yeh be closing at? It's a bit cold for you to be sitting in the draught coming in from that door,' I said, looking at his watery red eyes and his nose streaming. He took out a dirty aul white hankerchief and wiped his nose.

'Ah, maybe I'll get a few more customers in like yerself,' he said, looking hopefully at the door.

'Yeah, well, have a nice Christmas for yourself. Will you be having your family come to see you?'

'No, the poor wife is long dead this ten year. God rest her. But I'll be all right. I'm going to take the bus out to Cabra and stay with the sister. She has a big crowd of them all piling in on top of her. Her daughters are very good to her. So I'll be grand there.'

'Have you no children of your own?'

'Oh, indeed I do, daughter! I have seven of them. Four boys and three girls. Now they are all away. Living in Birmingham and Manchester and London. All over the place, they are. But they have families of their own now. They couldn't be making it home just to see me! I wouldn't want them to anyway. I have me own way of doin things. And I don't want to be bothering anyone. As long as I can keep moving, I don't care. Mind you, havin said tha, I do have trouble wit me aul hands. The arthritis does be crippling me. That's why I wear the aul gloves,' he said, lifting up his hands, showing them to me.

'Ah, God help yeh. Old age is an awful curse! It's without mercy,' I said, seeing the swelling of his knuckles through the gloves. 'Well, it was lovely talking to you. I better make a move, it's beginning to get late,' I said. Looking out at the darkness coming down fast. I reached in under the counter to take up me box and put me books in, lifting the box into me arms, and made me way out the door, hearing the bell ring overhead, letting the man know when customers were coming into the shop. 'Goodbye now. Look after yourself, and a very happy Christmas to you,' I said, making me way happily out the door.

'And a very happy Christmas to you, too,' he said, holding the door and gently shutting it behind me, making it ring again.

I wandered out into the dark streets, seeing the Christmas lights glittering in the dark night, with the rain drizzling down. The air was alive with the excitement of people rushing for buses to take them home, and others making a mad dash to reach the shops before they closed for the Christmas. I waited at the traffic lights again, wanting to get back on the other side of O'Connell Street to get the bus back to Drumcondra. I made it across and wandered down, looking at the big cars stopping outside the Gresham Hotel. I stared over at the very glamorous-looking women, all made up with their hair shiny and piled up in curls. They had themselves wrapped in fur coats, with long frocks trailing underneath. I watched with me eyes hanging out of me head as they tottered on big high heels, holding onto the arms of men in long expensive overcoats rushing into the hotel for their dinner. One gorgeous woman swung her legs out of a big Rolls-Royce, then put out her hand, waiting for the man to take her arm and help her up while the doorman wearing a uniform held the car door open for her. She stood up, taking the man's arm held out for her, and swept towards the hotel with a long brown fur coat rushing out behind her. Wearing her honey-coloured-looking hair pinned at the back of her head, with the top coming back in waves. I watched her, with me eyes hanging out of me head on stalks. She swept herself up the steps like she owned the place and marched into the hotel with her head held in the air.

Mother a Christ! That takes more than money! I bet her face isn't even that good-looking close up! But she acts with the greatest of ease, like she is the most important person in the whole world, and nobody is more beautiful then her. Hmm! How do you get to be like that? I wonder what it must be like to be one of them. Imagine going in there all dressed up to the nines. With loads of money in your pocket, and not have to worry about the prices! No! That's a long long way from where I am now. But one day I will be able to do that. There's only one way to go in this world when you are at the bottom. Start climbing right to the top. Yeah! There's nothing to stop me. I will get there some day!

I put me box down on the ground at the queue waiting for the bus and looked behind me at the film showing in the Carlton picture house. Alfred Hitchcock. *The Birds*. People were standing in a queue waiting to go in. I wonder if I should go in now and see it? I'm not going anywhere in a hurry, and I can please meself!

I couldn't make up me mind. I stood at the bus stop, looking around at all the people rushing in all directions. Mothers hurried past, carrying big shopping bags with food bursting out. The husbands carrying big boxes wrapped up in brown paper. One man carried a child's two-wheeler bike, with ribbons hanging off the handlebars and a silver bell. He carried a big box under his other arm in a Clerys bag. The box stuck out at the top, showing the face of a big doll with long fair hair with a red ribbon tied in a bow. I stared at it. The doll was standing upright behind the see-through plastic cover.

'Come on, hurry. We might yet catch that bus,' the woman puffed, looking at the man and trying to run with the heavy bags.

'Here! You take this,' he said, stopping to take one of the heavy bags off her and handing her the long narrow box with the doll. They swapped over and took off again, rushing to get the bus coming to a stop further down. Everyone seemed to have someone with them. Even the ones rushing somewhere seemed to have a purpose. Except the very old. I watched an old woman walk past slowly, taking her time, carrying her few messages with a far-away, distant look in her tired old face.

I suddenly felt a bit lost. I could feel me heart sinking. Everyone seems to have someone. Maybe it's not such a good idea to go back to the room just yet. I could stay in town a bit longer, keep with the crowds. I looked around, seeing the cars and buses and vans flying past, puffing out blue smoke, stopping and starting in a mad rush, blowing their horns at each other, and the twinkling of the Christmas lights, making it feel like I was a part of something magic. I might meet someone nice, have a chat, pass away a bit of time. Then I wouldn't feel so left out. I could go down to Caffola's Café and have a cup of coffee made on milk. I could sit there and watch the crowds coming and going. Once I'm back there in the room, it will be very quiet. Pity I don't have a little transistor radio. That would be great company. But they are too expensive. I'm sure one of them would set me back about ten shillings. No, forget that.

Ah, bloody hell! Make up your mind, Martha. Will I go in and see the film or not? I love chillers. Alfred Hitchcock is great. But on the other hand it might frighten the life out of me, now that I'll be in the place on me own. I might start getting all sort of mad ideas, like someone trying to break in! Jaysus! I think I'm just tired. Maybe I should keep moving. Anyway, this box is too heavy and awkward to be dragging around the town. On top of that, it's getting very dark and late. Maybe I should get the bus and go back. I was in great form earlier. Yeah! I have me books to read. No bleedin Molly watching me every move, screaming at me night and day. Yeah! It's grand. I'll have the time of me life. Eating, sleeping, reading me books, and no one to bother me. What more could I want? Right! I can always go to the pictures another day. I'll go back, and take it easy. Get meself sorted. I can even have a nice warm bath and get into bed with me new hot-water bottle and have something lovely to eat. Yeah! That's what I'll do. I'll get the bus back. I'll be grand. Happy Christmas to me! Happy Christmas to me! 'I'm go . . . ing to ha . . . ve a lovely! lovely time!' I sang to meself, happily waiting for the bus to come.

The bus heaved in, coming slowly to a stop. I could see it was chopper blocked. People were standing, holding onto the bars. The queue moved up, with everyone tightening in behind each other's backs. I picked up me box and checked to see I had me handbag on me arm. The queue waited to let people off, and the conductor leaned out off the platform with his arm outstretched, letting some of the people on. Then he barred the way of the rest, shouting, 'That's it! We're full up! There's another bus on the way.'

'When will it get here, Conductor?' a woman asked, standing at the top of the queue.

'It's about five minutes behind me.' Then he banged hell out of the bell, hanging off the platform to make sure no one jumped on. The bus moved off slowly, rocking from side to side, threatening to overbalance with the weight it was carrying.

'More like five hours!' the woman at the top muttered to the crowd of us all staring after the bus. I would walk it easily, only for this heavy box, I thought to meself.

I looked over to see the crowd had started moving into the picture house. Girls and fellas laughed, the girls holding bags of sweets and some even had little boxes of chocolates. I have a box for meself for over the Christmas, to go with me books, I thought happily. Yeah! It will be nice to get in out of the cold.

I started to stamp me feet up and down, feeling the chill going up through me. A man standing in front of me rubbed his hands together, and started banging his feet on the ground. 'Cold aul night,' he said, looking past me to the woman behind.

'Indeed it is. We'll get our death a cold standing out here in this damp miserable aul night before we're done!' she said, wrinkling her mouth and turning her nose up in disgust, then leaning off the footpath to throw her head down the road, looking for any sign of the bus coming.

'Ah, I intend milling in to the aul drop a whiskey when I get home,' he said. Rubbing his hands faster together, smiling, and grinning from ear to ear at the lovely thought hitting him.

'Jaysus!' she said, shaking her head from side to side at him. Looking like she was going to start crying any minute. 'I can't wait to get in the door and boil the teapot for a hot sup a tea, and get me feet up for a few minutes. Dem shops was black with people today. I should have had more sense then to go into town, today of all days. Jaysus Christ almighty! The crush was something terrible!'

'Ah, don't talk,' he said, like he had something even better to say. 'I'm just knocking off work now. The missus will be going ninety to the dozen giving out when I get in the door. Complaining about gettin knocked senseless. Sure she had to do the same thing. Rush into town this morning to get a few last-minute things,' he said, thinking about it.

'Yeah, the whole world and his wife was in dem shops today,' the woman sighed, the energy going out of her face, feeling tired now it was over. We all stood in silence, waiting and stretching our necks down the long street, hoping every bus coming was ours.

'No, not stopping!' people would say. Staring like mad after a bus flashing past us, with passengers hanging out of it. 'Too full to take us.'

The bus was finally coming. Everyone moved up, staring to see if there was room. I looked behind me, seeing a long queue of people stretching far behind, nearly going to the next bus stop. I held me box in front. 'The first six people!' the conductor roared, hanging off the bus with his arms wrapped around the pole showing six fingers. People made a dive, and I held me ground.

The woman up front was pushed sideways. 'Here! Stop pushing. I'm first!' she screamed.

'Everyone back!' the conductor shouted, putting out his hand to stop people skipping. 'Let that woman on. Who's next?' He stood on the side of one entrance, watching people carefully, doing a head count. I was the fourth and jumped up, pushing me box forward to get me going. 'That's it! No more room!' the conductor roared, racing to bang the bell and keeping his eye on the people trying to jump on. 'Off! No more!' he shouted, pushing the people off trying to lift their leg onto the moving bus. 'Move up along the bus!' he shouted. 'Come on! Move up there.' He was pushing people behind me and they were pushing me. I held me box out in front of me, and it was getting crushed into me chest. Jaysus! Pity I can't put this thing down.

I held on, with the bus waving from side to side with the weight it was carrying. Then I was landed into the lap of a big fat woman wearing a long see-through plastic raincoat. I was still holding onto me box, and for a second it was lovely to get the weight of the box off me, and feel like I had a cushion under me, sitting on her soft lap. 'Do you mind!' she roared in a very grand voice. Pushing me up with her two hands outstretched. I heaved meself to a standing position, pushing the box out in front of me, then trying to plant me feet, with the bus waving from side to side. A man standing in front of me was leaning over a seat, hanging onto the bar, and I rested the box on his back. He kept looking back at me with a glare on his face, and trying to move away from me. But there was nowhere for him to go, and he had to put up with it.

The bus was finally picking up speed as we left Dorset Street, and I tensed meself, watching out for my stop. I could now see it coming up ahead, and tried to move with the crush of people behind me. 'Excuse me! I'm getting off!' I shouted, wanting to make me way down to the platform before it was too late, and I would end up having to walk miles back again. People were hesitating, looking at me, then at each other. Everyone waiting for the next person to make the first move. They were afraid of losing their place on the bar. 'Excuse me!' I roared. 'Conductor! Stop the bus! This is my stop coming up, I want to get off!' I shouted. Straight into the ear of people standing next to me, trying to make meself heard by the conductor. Because I couldn't see him. The people standing beside me moved away fast, not wanting to get another blast in their eardrums.

I pushed me way down the bus, using the box as a battering ram to get people to squeeze out of me way. Then I was off, standing on the footpath, breathing in the fresh air. 'Oh! Am I delighted to get off that bus!' I puffed, making me way up the road, seeing the shop in the distance was in pitch black. Great! I'm going to have the place to meself.

At last! Back again! I put the box on the ground and rooted in me bag for the key. Here we are. I put the key in the door, pushing it in, and landed the box on the stairs, reaching back to the wall and switching on the light. 'OK!' I muttered, wanting to break the silence of the place by hearing a voice. Even if it is me own. I slammed the door shut, then looked at the bolt. I better put that on, seeing as I'm in the place on me own.

I humped the box up the stairs, and stopped in the hall to work out where the light switch was. I flicked it on and the hall lit up. Showing the boxes stacked against the wall, nearly the length of the passage. I made straight for the kitchen, flicking the switch, and the room filled up with light. The silence hit me straight away, and I stopped breathing for a minute, taking in the dead-quiet stillness. Jaysus! This place is like the dead house! And it's bleedin freezing. There's no heating, they have it switched off for the Christmas. Right! I can fix that.

I rushed over to the cooker and switched all the knobs on the electric hobs, watching to see if it would blow up with all the amount of power it was suddenly using. Feeling afraid of me life, because I'd be down the swanny with no way of cooking. Nothing happened. Grand. That should heat the place up in no time.

I emptied out the box, putting the rashers and sausages and chops in the fridge, along with the cheese and milk. Then I left the eggs and bread and pound of butter sitting on the worktop. Lovely. I filled the kettle, leaving it on the cooker to boil, and went down to the room, taking me books and chocolates with me. I switched on the light and pulled the curtains across. Then hung up me coat and put away me handbag and left Molly back her string bag, where I'd found it. Now for something to eat. What will I have?

I made me way back to the kitchen and the hobs were turning red. The heat hit me as soon as I walked into the room. Gawd! This is great. The kettle was boiled already, and I decided to fill me hot-water bottle to get me bed warming as quickly as I could. It's freezing in that bedroom. Lovely! That's better. I fixed the blankets over the hot-water bottle, seeing the little hump in the bed, and me heart lifted. Great! All me little comforts. I can eat meself stupid, then have a bath and dive into the lovely warm bed and read to me heart's content. Yeah! That's what I'm going to do! Eat sleep read, and do what I like for the next four days. Right! Now for the grub.

I flew down to the kitchen, enjoying the blast of heat as soon as I hit the room. What will I have? Chop? No, save that for tomorrow, and the next day. Rashers! Two! Better not burn them. I rooted around in the press, coming up with the frying pan, and looked for a bit of dripping. Borrow theirs. Where do they keep everything hidden? I looked in all the presses. Nothing! A mouldy packet of flour. They must have cleaned out everything for the Christmas. Butter will do. I lashed on a big knob and slapped on the rashers, then whipped them off again. Cook the sausages first. They take longest. Jaysus! I'm really coming on. I learned a few things watching the little granny and Clare doing the cooking. Yeh stab them first to stop them exploding, Clare said.

They were beginning to turn black very fast. The butter was making them black. Jaysus! They're not turning out right! Wonder what's wrong? I stared at them, seeing the smoke pouring out of the frying pan and the kitchen was beginning to fill with the smoke! I started to cough and me eyes were watering. Maybe I should turn down the heat. It's on too full. I whipped the knob down to one and flew out of the kitchen, wanting a bit of air, and watching from the doorway the sausages turning black. Pity! Wonder how that happened? Then I flew in again, whipping the pan off the cooker. I stared at the two sausages, burned to a cinder! They'll do. I'm not wasting good food.

I put on the two rashers and cut the tomatoes in half, putting the four halfs on the pan and kept turning them. I'm taking no chances this time. I watched them like a hawk. The rashers gave out a lovely smell and I whipped them off as soon as the fat was going crisp. Lovely! I put them beside the burned sausages and took off the pan. I put on another knob of butter and dropped in the two eggs, hoping for lovely white, and gorgeous soft yolks in the middle. They went black and greasy straight away. Never mind. Maybe it's not a good idea to cook stuff in good butter!

I left them cooking away and put on the kettle to boil for the tea. Then started to cut me black-crusted loaf. Fuck! This knife is not sharp enough. It's only for eating your dinner with. Then I spotted the sharp little knife sitting at the bottom of the cutlery drawer. I had a go with that, stabbing at the loaf and sawing away. Smashing! I cut two big thick slices. Then lathered on the good butter, making it inches thick. I looked at the golden-coloured butter spread across the soft white bread with the black crust, and me mouth watered and me belly rumbled. When I think of me days starving as a child, dreaming about this . . . Now I can eat as much as I want to me heart's content! I still can't believe I'm free as a bird. I can go me own way through life. Oh, this is lovely!

I slid the greasy, black, curled-at-the-edges eggs and overdone in the middle after the yolks burst onto the plate, and made the tea, putting two teaspoons into the pot, and poured on the boiled water. Then I left it on the hob for a minute to stew. That's what Sister Mercy used to do in the convent. So, at least I can make tea. I sat down at the table and started to mill the grub. The sausages are not too bad. You can taste the charcoal a bit, but I've eaten worse.

Ah, that was lovely. Maybe just another slice of that bread! I took one more of the Kimberley biscuits, feeling stuffed. I've eaten six. I looked at the packet in me hand. Nearly half of them gone. That's enough. I better spare them. I'm feeling tired now. Me face is red hot. Think I better go to bed.

Right! I looked around the kitchen, getting the smell of burned cooking, seeing the smoke was beginning to clear out the door. I'll get these washed up and clean up the kitchen then have me bath and head off to bed. I gathered up all the dishes and put them in the sink, turning on the hot water. It's stone cold! The water's cold! What will I do? There must be something to turn on. Jaysus! I don't know how you work these things. I never had anything like this with me ma. We never had hot water or anything electrical. Not even an iron to press the clothes. Because we didn't even wash them! They spent years sitting in the bath, floating under the disgusting, smelly water, and every now and then Jackser would look at them and roar, 'Missus! Yeh should get up off yer arse and wash this stuff!'

'Ah, don't be annoyin me wit yer washin!' the ma used to mutter, looking at the wall, curling her fingers like mad through her hair, looking for lice.

I rushed into the bathroom, turning on the tap. Cold! No hot water here either! Ah, Jaysus! What do I do? Maybe there's a switch. I looked around the old bathroom, seeing the copper pipes snaking along the edges of the wall, and stared into the dirty white enamel bath with all the brown stains and the white enamel chipped out, leaving the metal showing. There's nothing here! Only the bath and the one chair for putting your stuff on. Oh, there should be a box. I flew out to the hall, seeing it sitting up high on the wall, and rushed into the kitchen to get a chair, then flew back and planked the chair underneath. No! Wait! That's dangerous! You shouldn't be interfering with the electricity. Jackser always said that. Every time a fuse blew in the house he would stand up on the chair, looking at the meter, afraid of his life to touch it. 'Sally! Eh, you! The Martha one,' he would roar at me. 'Listen teh me carefully. This is a very dangerous thing here,' he would say, stabbing the air with his finger, pointing at the box, looking afraid of his life. 'I can get blown up! I'm warnin yehs! If anythin happens teh me, don't come near me. Or youse will go the same way! Run and get the sweepin brush and make sure not teh touch me. Push me away from the danger wit the brush, then call the ambulance! Do youse get tha?' he would say. Looking at us with the fear of God on him, and a warning look to make sure we understood he was preparing to lose his life, and we better make sure we didn't get ourselves kilt so that we could save him. We would stand looking up at him. Me prayin like mad he would get kilt stone dead.

The ma stood holding a candle up, eating like hell the inside of her lip. Blinking and getting impatient, saying, 'Yes, yes! We heard yeh! Now will yeh ever get on wit it an get the fuckin light back on!'

'I'm warnin yeh, missus!' he would say, whipping his hand back an throwing a look at the ma. 'If I get kilt, it will be on your head!'

'I hear yeh! I hear yeh! Holy Jaysus Christ al-mighty! The fuckin carry on a him,' she would mutter to the wall, afraid of her life to go near it herself. I would stand, watching up at him, holding me breath and keeping well back. Prayin like mad he would go up with an unmerciful explosion! Nothing ever happened! It's hard to kill a bad thing. Now here I am about to do the same thing.

I stood up on the chair, staring at the black meter with the wheel flying around, and numbers underneath. Right, that's the box showing how much electricity it's using. Yeah! I got that. Now! All these big white fuses are for . . . to keep it going! But how do you get the water to heat? I looked at a big black switch. Wonder what that's for? It has to do something. Could be to heat the water. Right! I put out me hand, afraid of me life to touch it. Aaaaah, here goes! I grabbed the switch, pulling it down, and the place plunged into darkness! HELP! MAMMY!

I leaped off the chair, crashing me hands against the wall, and groped me way down the hall screaming. Ohh, somebody save me!

The place might blow up any minute. Wha did I do? I started shaking like mad, the sweat pouring out of me. Where's the hall door key? Where's the fucking key?

I felt me way along the wall, making me way into the bedroom and felt me way over to the window, opening the curtains to let in a bit of light. What will I do? I can't stop shaking with the fright. I'm afraid of me life of electricity. I could see if the light is on here. Maybe it's only the hall and the kitchen. I put me hand out for the switch. No, I could get electrocuted. No, fuck yeh! Get on wit it! I could hear Jackser's voice in me head. I felt like a child again.

Switch the fuckin thing on, missus! I reached out me hand and flicked down the little switch. Nothing happened! Oh, sweet Jesus. What have I done? Calm yourself down. Where's me cigarettes? I groped over to the wardrobe, rooting for me bag, taking out me packet of cigarettes and struck the match, seeing me hands shaking. I don't even think I'm supposed to be in this place for the Christmas. I think that aul one Missus Murphy would go mad if she found out! I can't let them know I have nowhere to go. No home to go to. They might get rid of me. Say I'm too much trouble. No, I have to work this out meself. Sit down and have a cigarette. The place is not going to go up in fire!

Right! That must have been the switch to turn off the electricity. That's all. Nothing more and nothing less. So all you have to do is switch it back on again. Right! I'll do that when I've finished me cigarette.

I made me way into the kitchen and put the cigarettes sitting on the table. I'm going to have another smoke and a cup of tea, if this works out OK. But I can't see me way around the fucking box. I could put me hand on something and get blown up. Oh, Mammy! I wish someone was here to do this for me, but I don't know anyone. And anyway I couldn't let strangers up here in the first place. The boxes in the hall could get robbed. Or the shop get broken into from the door downstairs leading into it. Jaysus! Me nerves are gone. Right! Just do it.

I groped me way back into the hall and held onto the back of the chair, putting me hand out ready to steady meself against the wall if I fell in the dark, or wanted to jump down quickly. I could barely make out the box in the pitch black. There's not a chink of light coming in anywhere. I felt the little door hanging open and pushed it against the wall. Now for the switch. Keep your hands away from any wiring. I felt the top of the white fuses, and when I felt air I let me hand go in further. Right! Got it! Here's the switch. I put one hand out, ready to jump, and the other one on the switch, and flicked it up, holding me breath for one split second, with me body locked, ready to sprint, and the lights blazed on. I blinked, looking around. I'm not blown up! The lights are back on! Me heart leaped with the excitement. I did it! Everything is OK again. That's it! Never again. Leave everything well alone.

I grabbed the chair and flew down to the kitchen and looked at the cooker. The hobs were starting to heat up. Oh, thank God for looking after me. I'll boil the kettle and use that for washing up. To hell with the bath. I can boil water in the kettle for that, too, and wash meself in the sink. Who needs the bath? I can wait until they get back. Right! Where's the washing-up liquid, and the stuff for cleaning the cooker?

I washed the dishes, putting them away, and cleaned down the table then stood back, looking at the cooker gleaming white again. The smell is well gone out of the kitchen. Right! Just sweep that floor, then I can brush me teeth and wash me face in the sink then hit the bed. Where do they keep the sweeping brush?

I whipped open the long press in the corner next to the sink and stared at a copper boiler. Me eyes travelled to the top of the press. A white box with a fuse and a switch beside it said 'Immersion'. This is for the hot water! It was in the 'off' position. I flicked it on. Hot water! Oh, my God! All that trouble . . . it was here all this time. Now I have hot water, and everything is grand again. Oh, this is great.

I rushed over to the long narrow press in the other corner and there was the sweeping brush with a mop and bucket for washing the floor. Fuck that! I'm never washing that floor. I'm the shop assistant here. My days of being a skivvy, as the young ones in the convent used to call me . . . well, not any more!

I grabbed the brush and swept up the floor, then slammed it back in the press and rushed off down to me room to get me stuff ready for a nice hot bath. I put out me clean pyjamas. That nightdress is no good here. It's too cold in bed. I must get meself another pair of pyjamas, but I have to watch the money. If aul Murphy has her way, she'd take the lot off me. As it is, I have to pay for me food out of the one pound ten shillings a week she gives me for me wages. So I have to pay for everything. Tea, sugar, milk, bread: it doesn't seem to last long. I think the others must be using my stuff. I keep it separate from theirs. My tea is in a big coffee jar. They can keep their aul tea canister! And me sugar is in an empty jam jar that I washed out. The money flies out of me pocket. I can't cook properly, only boil an egg, with bits of cheese on my bread, and sliced ham. That's very dear altogether. So I'm not eating too much! But the money still goes. I only get me bus fare into town and buy ten cigarettes a day. Other than that, I don't spend money on anything else. Hmm! This job is even less then I was getting in the convent. At least there I could save the five shillings they gave me every week for working up in the convent. Now I seem to have nothing left at the end of the week.

I put out me washbag with me toothpaste and toothbrush, and the new bar of Palmolive green soap I bought meself when I was living with Clare. It's still new. I didn't have to use it, because I could use their stuff. Even here I use Molly's soap. She always forgets it and leaves it sitting in the bath. Then stares down at me, giving me suspicious looks when she sees her soap getting smaller, after remembering to take it back in with her. Right! I'm using me own, especially as it's Christmas. I pressed it to me nose. Hmm! It smells lovely. Wonder if she has any bath salts? I whipped me head down to her side. No, leave her stuff alone. She'll know you were touching her things. Anyway, you wouldn't like it if she touched your stuff. OK, get yourself ready.

I put on me nice warm dressing gown and slippers and made me way down to the bathroom, putting me stuff on the chair. Then switched on the hot tap. No, it's not hot enough yet! I want it scalding. Right, put on the kettle and have a drop of tea and a cigarette. By the time I finish that, the water should be hot enough. Oh, God! There's nothing like having the few comforts. This is the life. I could feel meself getting back to me old self as I sat and smoked and drank the lovely sweet hot cup of tea. I haven't a care in the world. No one to please but meself. For a while back there I could feel exactly as if I was a child all over again. Shivering in fear. With Jackser screaming and barking out his orders in me head. Even in me mind's eye I could see him. It was like as if I had never moved away, grown up, and was well out of his clutches. That he was long gone behind me. No, for that short while, nothing had changed. I am locked with him again. Waiting for the terror to pass, then waiting for the time to pass, so I can escape him.

Even now, deep inside meself I don't really feel safe. It's too soon since I got away from him. Anything can happen. That's why I don't want anyone knowing who I am. Or meeting anyone who knew me then. I even went into the Custom House and searched for a birth certificate to take back me own name. The one me ma gave me. Her own maiden name. Long! Jackser always put his name down for me. Pretending he was my father. So it was a shock when I went in and discovered he had put his name on me birth certificate when he met me ma. I now had two names down on me birth certificate. 'What's this?' I roared at the fella behind the desk. 'How did this happen? That aul fella is not my father! How could he put his name down as my father when he only met me ma when I was six years old?'

'Hold on!' he said, after looking at it. 'I'll get someone to come out and talk to you.'

'Yes? I am the supervisor here. Can I help you?'

'Take a look at this and explain it to me,' I said, pushing the big book around to a grey-haired aul fella squinting at me through a pair of dispensary glasses hanging down on his nose. I stood, me breath coming in gasps, white with the rage, waiting for him to read it and explain how someone can just walk in and claim to be a child's father.

'Come into the office,' he said. 'We can talk in private.'

'Fuck this,' I snorted, banging me hands on the big thick wooden counter. I then followed him in through a door, waiting while he sat down at a desk covered in a mound of papers.

'Take a seat,' he said, opening the big book at the page where I was registered.

Then I started. 'The world and his wife knows that aul fella is not related to me. I was with him when he went to the dispensary to talk to the aul fella there. Fucking Jackser wanted to get the labour money for me and Charlie!'

'Please! Don't use that kind of language,' the aul fella said, shutting his eyes and putting out his hand in front of his face.

'LISTEN!' I roared. 'I heard him talking to me ma about it. The same fucking week we moved in to live with him. THAT AUL FELLA IS NOT MY FATHER!' I screamed. The supervisor went white. 'Me ma's sisters and brothers know that! And let me check my brother's. Charlie's! I want to check Charlie's!' I roared. 'Because I can certainly tell you this. Jackser is most certainly not his father. I know the name of Charlie's father. I remember every detail of him. Let's see what's on his birth certificate. What's his date of birth and his full name? Charles Edward Long. I don't know his exact date of birth. But I do know he was born five years after me. I remember everything. I even remember when me ma went into labour with him. There's nothing I don't remember.'

'OK, hang on a minute. I'll just go and get the book . . . Right, here we are,' he said, finding it and putting his finger on the entry. 'There you are. His is changed as well.'

'Look, he has me ma's name. Long. And now that Jackser bastard's name is added. So explain how he was able to do that.'

'It's very simple,' the supervisor said. 'He went with your mother to a commissioner for oaths. Then in front of the commissioner he swore out an affidavit saying he was your father, and the father of your brother Charlie.'

'Just like that?' I said. Not able to take it in. 'But people go through the mill, going to court to adopt children who are not their own, and this bandy aul bastard could just walk in and do it as easily as that?'

'Yes. He was able to get the right information. As you say, the man in the dispensary that he talked to must have been the registrar for births, marriages and deaths. He would have known exactly how the process works.'

'So what do I do now? This man is neither mine nor my brother Charlie's father. They are not even married. Jackser was married to someone else, long before he met me ma. She never got married.'

'Well, unless you can get your mother to admit he is not the father . . .'

'But we both know that, me and the ma. The ma knows I know he's not. Sure he always made sure to let me know I was not his bastard!'

'Yes,' the supervisor said, trying to get a word in and waiting for me to finish. 'Unless she admits in an affidavit, in front of a commissioner for oaths. Then there's nothing we can do about it. She swore under oath he was your father.'

'Well, I am definitely not taking his name on my birth certificate.'

'No, you don't have to. See, here is the name you were registered with at birth. "Sally Long, Mother. Father unknown." You are Martha Long. That is what your mother first put down when you were registered at birth. So you can have your original birth certificate with your mother's name. That is the name you will be recognised with for the rest of your life. Whenever you apply for a birth certificate again, this is what you will be given. But you can't have the long form of birth certificate. That will show Jackser as the father.'

'OK,' I said, feeling weak from the shock. 'One day I am going to do something about this,' I said. 'That can't be allowed to happen. A child's name is robbed just like that! I thought birth certificates can never be changed. Well, in this instance . . .'

'But in fact it's not changed,' he said. 'The original entry is still there. Jackser's name has just been added alongside it.'

'Even years after I was first registered?' I roared.

'Yes! It's all down to your mother,' he said.

I took the short form of my birth certificate, seeing my name and date of birth. That's all it said. I kept staring at it, thinking at least I have me name back. That was the first thing I did when I got out of the convent. I even left the children's home where I was supposed to be training as a children's nurse. The first time they let me out when I had the day off, I made me way to the Custom House to claim me name back, never realising he had added himself to mine and Charlie's birth certificates. I thought all along he was just pretending his name was ours, never realising for one minute he had actually made it legal, getting himself on our birth certificates. They'd always said you can't change that. But he did. You can do anything you like in this world to a child. It only took the ma to say I was his and the authorities jumped to do his bidding.

I walked away feeling a burning anger with Jackser and the ma. But most of all with the authorities. What had kept me going through all them years was the thought I was in no real way connected to him. He wasn't married to me ma, because he was already married to someone else. So he couldn't have married her anyway, even if he had wanted to. Me ma was never married. So I knew there was nothing he could do about making us his stepchildren. But all along he had worked it out. Straight from the very beginning. Fuck! That would have killed me if I had known. But I knew I would go back to my own name once I was grown up. So now I have.

But the authorities taking the word of a bastard like Jackser and the no-good ma! One day I will do something about that. I will fucking force the ma to admit she was a lying whore. That is all I had. The one thing me ma gave me. Her name. Jackser is not going to rob me of my identity.

I don't know who my father is, and I'm not bothered to find out. He's probably a tramp like Charlie's father was. Walking the streets picking up cigarette butts. Begging for the shilling to stay at the Back Lane homeless hostel for men in the Liberties of Dublin. Then fucking off and leaving her to face her family, and the three of us ending up on the streets, looking for somewhere to stay. No! I'm not bothered about a father. He was the first one that got me ma into trouble in the first place. After that it was all downhill for her, until she fell into the clutches of that mad bandy aul bastard Jackser! So, whoever you are, Father, you can go and fuck yourself! I'm never going to go looking for yeh!

Anyway, I saw what that kind of carry on did to some of the girls in the convent, when they finally caught up with their mothers. Some of them had the door shut in their face. You never find the fucking fathers. Men! I started to roar me head off crying. I hate fucking men. Especially Jackser.

No, I hate that stupid selfish whore of a ma even more! The good-for-nothing cowardly bitch. I wouldn't have even minded if she was a whore! At least she would have gotten paid for it. Then we would have gotten something to eat. And maybe a roof over our heads! No, she was even too stupid to work that one out. Jaysus! If I ever find that I am going to have sex with a man, then I would start charging for it. To hell with that! If you're going to sleep around, you might as well not be giving it out free! No, I'm never sleeping with a man unless I am going to marry him, and that's not going to happen for a very long time. So no fella is going to get his hands on me. Never! I'll never be like the ma.

Jaysus! When I think of all the men she slept with. Stupid cow! The most she got was one shilling and sixpence from the fella who used to sell the newspapers on the corner. Even then I had to drag it out of him when me ma sent me after him. Jaysus! I can still see her now. Sitting up in the bed, leaning herself on one elbow. 'Jaysus, Martha. He didn't leave me any money! I have no money to even buy a bottle of milk. Run after him quick an ask him teh lend us a few shillins.'

LEND US! Fuck! If I'd been her after giving him what he wants, it wouldn't a been a lend! I would have turned the little bastard upside down and shaken every penny out of him. No, me ma had no sense. I would never let a man use me like that. Never mind let him make dirt of me. I think sex and money is at the root of all trouble. No, I'm going to live like a fucking Carmelite nun. Hunted and haunted, not having anything to do with sex. So that's that!

I lifted me head, wiping me snots with the back of me hand after bawling me head off, feeling me anger going away. Gawd! Wait until poor Charlie finds out when he turns up some day looking for his birth certificate. Still, he can do what I did. Get a copy of the original one. At least I can use me own name again.

It's funny how the rage only really started hitting me now when I started to think about it. I suppose I went into too much shock. I couldn't really take it in. Yeah! It's taken me until now to sit and think about it. Well, there's nothing much I can do about it now. But the time will come. There's a time and a place for everything. Right! The water must be scalding by now.

Me eyes shot wide open. It's morning. Christmas Day! I stared around the room, seeing the light still on. Gawd! I went out cold, leaving the light on all night. Good! I'm getting me money's worth for the ten shillings, that aul Murphy one is robbing off me.

I could see the light coming in the window through the thin curtains. I moved in the bed, feeling the cold hot-water bottle beside me. Gawd, that was lovely last night. Having all that heat with the lovely hot-water bottle. I must have been shattered. As soon as I hit the bed and snuggled up with me book and the lovely heat I went out for the count. I don't even think I got past the first page. Where is it? I lifted me head, seeing *The Carpet Baggers* sitting on the floor.

Right, up you get. I leaped out of the bed, feeling rested and full of energy. I could hear church bells ringing to announce the start of the next mass. Right, I'll have me breakfast and get ready for the mass after this one. What time is it? I walked over to take a look at Molly's old clock sitting on one leg held up by a holy ornamental mug from Lourdes. Twenty past eight. Gawd, that's great! It's still very early, I'll have the whole day to enjoy meself.

I pulled back the curtains, letting the early morning bluey-grey light make its way into the room. Then made up me bed and left me book and hot-water bottle sitting on the bed, waiting for me to come back and enjoy meself no end with a good read and the lovely comfort of a warm bed. I folded me pyjamas and left them on top of me pillow. Then stood back to see everything looking nice and neat and tidy. Yeah, I love that. The nuns trained me well. I love the order of having everything in its place. It's a long way from what I was used to.

Now for breakfast. What will I have? Two boiled eggs and black crusted loaf with thick good butter plastered all over it. Right! I headed into the kitchen and switched on the cooker and filled the kettle. That's going to take a while to boil. I think I'll go and get meself ready. I rushed down and got me wash things and gave me face and neck a good wash and brushed me teeth. OK, what will I wear, I thought, as I headed up to the room. I'll wear me best clothes – the frock and shoes and hat and coat the reverend mother bought me when I left the convent.

Ready! Gawd, I look lovely.

I slammed the hall door shut behind me and set off, walking down the road to the church, looking down at meself, seeing I looked lovely. I could smell the Palmolive soap off meself and I felt as good as anyone.

'How many of you here would open your door to welcome Joseph and Mary carrying the Christ child in her womb? The child who was to become the king of all kings? How many of you would invite them in? Give them refuge? Sanctuary? She will not be carrying a sign saying "I am to be the mother of the Christ King!" NO!' the priest boomed, frightening the life out of everyone. Bringing us all back to our senses. Making us all sit up and gape at him in astonishment. Instead of sitting here, taking in all the style. With the lot of us all dressed up to the nines, and me wondering what I'm having for me Christmas dinner. Will I put me pork chop under the grill along with the sausages and rashers? I'm not taking any chances this time and burning them! No, I want to enjoy meself, have the best time of me life. I can eat me chocolates, keeping some for tomorrow, St Stephen's Day. That's a very important day.

'YOU WOULD PROBABLY SLAM THE DOOR IN THEIR FACES!' he screamed, making everyone jump, me included.

Interrupting me thoughts for a lovely day. I stared up at him along with everyone else. People's faces had dropped. They even stopped coughing. You could hear a pin drop. All the mammies had muzzled the kids to shut up. Afraid of their life he would roar at them from the altar, even though we knew that wouldn't happen. No, not on Christmas Day! But with the mood that aul priest was in . . . well, everyone was craning their necks looking up at him hanging out of the pulpit. His big bald shiny head and his matching shiny red face gaped down at us with disgust that we would not let Mary, carrying the baby Jesus, come into our homes and share in the Christmas dinner. Everyone looked very annoyed with him at the idea of him spoiling their lovely day with the stupid question of whether they would let Mary, the mother of Christ, born on this day – on this day, for God's sake – into their homes! Of course they would!

'The mass is ended. Go forth in peace,' the priest said, making the sign of the cross, with his hand held stiff and sideways. 'I wish each and every one of you a happy, holy and joyous Christmas,' he said, looking to every side of the church. Then he bowed to the tabernacle, and swept himself off the altar, with the four little shiny-faced altar boys in their snow-white soutanes following his footsteps. One each side of him and two behind holding onto his alb. The people stood, with their bodies braced, waiting for him to clear the altar and disappear into the sacristy. Then everyone made a move out of the benches and we slowly made our way down the aisle and out into the Christmas morning. With the sun trying hard to make itself seen.

The air felt cold and dry, and I stood for a minute, still part of the crowd stopping to wish friends and neighbours a happy Christmas. Everyone was very excited. All gaping at each other's style and leaning into each other, listening for the bit of gossip with gaping mouths, then laughing, and looking around for each other. With people wanting to make a move and get home to start the feast. Children ran in and out of the crowds of mammies and daddies and uncles and aunts, and grannies and granddads, and relatives and friends who had come specially to stay, and enjoy the

Christmas together. I felt the excitement, and I was all dressed up, too. I was just like them, a part of everything that was going on. I could talk to any of them and they would not turn away from me because I was a pauper, dressed in rags and bare feet and covered in sores. No, I look lovely.

I didn't see anyone I could strike up a conversation with, because they were all busy talking to each other. So, it's really a day when people only have time to talk with you for a few minutes if they know you, because they have to rush home and get everything going.

People started rushing off, the crowds disappearing very fast. It was getting quieter now. I suddenly felt a bit lost. Which way to go? Up to the room or head left, slowly walking in the direction of town? There wouldn't be many buses today. Anyway, I could walk. I'm not in a hurry anywhere. No, I won't bother going back to the room. It's far too early. I'll take a walk in the direction of town then mosey back and cook me dinner.

I turned left out of the church grounds and started walking, keeping me hands in me coat pocket. Ah, here we are, the Bishop's Palace. I stopped to look in through the big black gates. They're locked. I looked in at the dark avenue with the huge trees covering the path, and wondered what the bishop was going to eat for his Christmas dinner! Probably a huge big roasted turkey served on a big silver platter, with mounds of roast potatoes, and gorgeous black Christmas pudding dripping in whiskey and shovelfuls of brandy butter. Hungry fucker! I bet if I went up there now and banged on his door demanding to share his dinner . . . 'Why?' he'd ask.

'Because I like turkey and pudding and the rest of the lot that goes with it!'

'So, why should I let you in? Give me one good reason why I shouldn't call the police and have you arrested for trespassing,' I can hear him saying.

'Because that red-necked priest was roaring at everyone in the church that we should share. That's why! And because you're the bishop. You have to show good example!'

Yeah, if you want to get yourself arrested, Martha, go on! Climb over the gate and have a go. Jaysus! The things I think of. I wouldn't want to sit with him anyway, and probably end up praying with him for the rest of the day in the chapel, giving thanks for the lovely grub I got. Not on yer nelly! I got enough of that with the nuns. Hmm!

I looked around, seeing the empty streets, and spotted the bench. I sat down, feeling I hadn't a care in the world. Ah, this is the life. Gawd! I remember the last time I sat here. It was years ago. I was in an awful sweat after robbing all the packets of cigarettes out of that priest's saddle bag sitting on the back of his bike. There he was, minding his own business, up on the altar saying mass for the nuns in the convent, and I come along and rob him blind. I wonder what he thought when he saw the bag empty. Probably cursed me to hell! Then I robbed that bag with the chicken, out of the shop up the road. Gawd! Here I am now. All dressed up and nobody to answer to, nothing and nobody worrying me! I still can't get over that. Yeah, life is definitely a bowl of cherries. Right, move on. It's getting freezing cold sitting here.

I moseyed on, stopping at Binn's Bridge and looking over the wall into the dirty canal water. My Gawd! This brings me back. How often have I turned here, walking up that Whitworth Road there on the way to the convents with me ma and the kids. All of us walking from town, or going over this bridge and heading up the road on me way back out to Finglas. But we walked it more times then we took the bus.

I haven't been around these parts in years. Not since I went to the convent. Now here I am, back again, but on me own terms. Yeah! I wanted to shout and laugh. I looked around, seeing no one, keeping me happiness to meself. You don't laugh on your own. You get arrested for madness and disturbing the peace. Ha! That thought made me laugh. I feel I can do anything, whatever I like. Who is going to stop me?

I headed on down through Dorset Street, seeing a few cars on the move. People sat in the cars with their new hats and coats on. Most of them had grannies and granddads in the back of the car, with loads of Christmas presents all stacked in the back window. They're probably getting collected to go for their dinner with their grown-up children, I surmised, looking after the cars. Some cars had children in them, hopping around, tearing open presents. They're probably going to a relation for their dinner or visiting the granny or an auntie to give her a present. They're all the respectable people I used to look up to. Now I could pass meself off as one of them. Funny, they don't seem that big and important any more! Just ordinary. It must be because I'm ordinary, and if I'm like them, then they must be ordinary, too.

I stopped when I got to the corner of Gardiner Street. Will I turn left down there, and end up on the Liffey? Or will I go straight, head on down Dominick Street, and continue on down to the Broadstone? I'd even end up beside the Richmond Hospital. Then if I went up the hill, I would be up outside the Morning Star Hostel, where that Jackser fella said he first met me ma. He used to talk about that. He'd even say if it wasn't for me running off with that aul one's high heels from the women's part, the Regina Ceoli Hostel, they would never have met!

Yeah, I remember that day very well. I took off, running down the hill in a pair of women's high heels. The ma had started talking to an aul one in the hostel. Then me ma made herself comfortable, sitting down on the aul one's bed with the babby, Charlie, sitting on her lap. I spotted the high heels sitting under the bed and tried them on.

'Don't touch my things, young one!' snapped the aul one at me. I couldn't help meself. I took off running, straight out the door, onto the street and down the hill. With the ma carrying the babby in her arms and roarin at me teh bring back them good shoes. The aul one was flying behind her, screaming; 'Mind them heels! Don't break me bleedin heels!'

This was the best thing that ever happened teh me. The ma giving me a chase with the aul one roarin up behind her, and me gettin teh wear a pair of women's high heels. I flew past a pack of aul fellas all sittin on the steps. I was clattering along like mad, hammerin the heels up and down on the concrete, tryin teh keep me balance. The aul fellas' heads shot after me, roarin their heads laughin when they saw me in the shoes bigger then meself. Then the women whippin past trying teh catch me. Charlie was gettin a bounce up an down in the ma's arms as she flew after me. He was screamin laughin, too.

Yeah! Then I remember me ma and her friend going over to talk to the men. They were there for hours, until the aul ones who ran the women's hostel came out and chased me ma and her friend back to the hostel. But I don't remember seeing Jackser. I was too busy hoppin up and down on the steps. Not takin any notice until the aul ones came running out of the hostel to eat the head off me ma for talkin to the men. I still remember what the aul sister said. 'Come away at once! You are not allowed to stand here engaging these men in conversation. Get back to the hostel this instant!'

I remember staring up at the ma, as she shook Charlie in her arms, saying, 'Ah, no, sister! I only wanted teh know the time because I have teh take the babby over teh the hospital teh get him looked at. Lookah! He's not well at all.'

I started pullin the babby's leg and he roared his head laughing. 'Ma, there's nothin wrong wit our babby!' I shouted, lookin up at her wit me mouth hangin open, wonderin why she was sayin tha. 'Lookah, Ma! He's laughin at me!'

'Keep quiet, you! Fuckin big ears!' the ma roared, losin the rag. Disappointed at her enjoyment getting cut short. Yeah, that was one of the few rare times she ever went for me. The ma used to be very gentle until she met that toerag!

'This is your last warning!' the sister roared. 'You will all be barred from the hostel, if you do not come back at once.'

I remember the ma takin us and runnin back in. Afraid of her life we might get locked out. But I knew she was disappointed, because she had been laughin and havin a great time with the men. God help her! Come to think about it now, she very seldom had much to laugh about. But them aul ones made short work of her little bit of enjoyment. They called themselves sisters. They were the Legion of Mary. Very holy aul ones altogether. They spent most of their time on the lookout for loose women. They even managed to get the prostitutes off the streets in the 1920s. Up around the Monto, it was called. Around Gloucester Street, and all round Corporation Street. Where I used to live. The Monto was famous in its day. I heard so many people talking about it. They even had a song about it. 'Take her up to Monto! Monto!' Yeah!

So that's why when me ma met him that night when we were walking through Church Street on our way back to the hostel, they stopped to talk, saying, 'There yeh are again!' It never really dawned on me. I was the one responsible for them clapping eyes on each other in the first place. So that was the beginning of their great bleedin romance! And the worse thing of all is that it's all down to me! If I hadn't robbed them high heels, they might have passed each other by in the church grounds, without saying a word to each other. He would never have told her he'd got himself a place and we could move in with him. Jaysus! I curse the day they met.

No, if I walk down that way, I'd even end up in the Liberties. By crossing over the Halfpenny Bridge, then mosey along the quays, past Usher's Island, then turn left, and head up into the Liberties. All me and the ma's old haunts. Me heart really started to sink. God! What's wrong with me at all? Why am I wanting to wander all around them places on Christmas Day? This is not the time for that. It would cause me no end of heartache. I would end up remembering, and wanting them times back when it was just me and the ma. We had nothing, but we did have each other. The really hard times started when poor Charlie came along. Then Nelly, me ma's sister, had enough and took off to England, leaving me ma to get on with it. Yeah, you were right all along, Nelly. The ma was nothing but trouble, getting in with the likes of Jackser!

Ah, bloody hell! I can feel the pain hitting me all over again. Wanting! Always wanting to get back to a time when . . . I was happy with the ma! When was that really? No, we didn't feel happy. We were only happy when we had a few bob, or somewhere to stay. Most of the time we were tired. But I think we were happy. I must have been. Because I keep wanting them times back. Oh, God, please help me!

I suddenly started feeling the tears spilling down me cheeks. I pulled the hat off me in frustration and started to scratch me head like mad. Wanting the terrible feeling of loss, and the pictures in me head of me and the ma, even walking the streets of the Liberties homeless, back a long time ago, in the old days . . . I want that longing to stop. It's just me! There's no ma. I want to enjoy meself. Now suddenly I feel like I'm completely alone in the world.

'Fuck yeh, Martha! Why could yeh not keep yer fuckin mind on what's goin on aroun yeh?' I heard meself screaming inside me head. It was like I was a little child again. I could hear the voice of meself as a child. I'm never far away from that. Being the small child again, with the street kid way of going on and speaking. 'That's who I really am!' the child screamed in me head.

I will be respectable, though. It will all work out! I'm only starting off in life. I need to be patient. I'll make friends and have people around me, and have somewhere to go as well. Just like all the other people. I just need to be patient.

OK, I'll ring someone and wish them a happy Christmas. Who will I ring? I can ring Sister Eleanor. Me heart lifted straight away. Yeah! I started to root, searching me pockets for change. Sixpence! I came up with sixpence and took it out of me pocket. I wonder where I'll get coppers for the phone? Then it hit me. Sister Eleanor would eat the head off you for ringing her on Christmas Day. It's a time only for the nuns. They probably even have the phone switched off. Me heart sank at the picture of her getting very annoyed with me, because I disturbed her peace. She had enough of the children in the convent. She probably only managed to get rid of the last of them at the last minute. Like last year.

No, forget that idea. Well, who else do you know? Clare! Yeah! No, she was nice to me . . . but I don't belong. They have their own family. They don't want strangers disturbing their peace. Yeah, leave her alone. OK, forget that. Just keep walking down towards the Liffey. See what might be happening.

I walked across Mount Joy Square, and down the hill. Looking over at the Father Scully flats. Everywhere is locked up. There's not a soul around. Jaysus! Where is everyone? The streets are empty. I was hoping for the crowds, and looking to see the style of people all dressed up. See what the fashions are.

I stopped at the traffic lights, blinking red to green, with no one wanting them. I looked up Summerhill, then right, looking down Parnell Street. I could see onto O'Connell Street, with nothing happening except the odd car in the distance. Which way now? Will I go straight ahead, then turn right, up Sean MacDermot Street and onto O'Connell Street? Ah, Jaysus! I can't make up me mind. I could always turn around and head back to the flat. No, that would be a bit of a let-down. I was looking forward to something happening. What? What's eating at yeh? What are you looking for? People, someone to have a laugh with! All these dead streets are making me feel I'm on me own. But yeh are! Yeah, but I didn't really think that. I'm always on the move, chatting and laughing no matter what I do or where I go. In the shop when I'm serving the people, or rushing to get ready to go out on me afternoon off. All excited after getting me bath and doing meself up in me good clothes. These ones! I looked down at them. Then I'm off to the pictures or in and out of the shops, looking at the latest fashions. Or going for a cup of frothy white coffee in Caffola's. Watching the people going by. Fuck! Suddenly I'm all dressed up with nowhere to go. Jaysus! I definitely don't like Christmas after this. I never did, up until I went to the convent and got people to go out with for the Christmas holidays.

Hmm! I know what I'll do. I'll mosey on and turn up Talbot Street and see what's happening on O'Connell Street, and head back to the flat that way. Then by the time I get back I'll be in great form after me long walk. I can have me lovely dinner, me pork chop, and sausages and tomatoes and two . . . yeah two fried eggs. Then a couple of biscuits and hop into bed with me hot-water bottle and read me book and start on the box of chocolates. Smashing! I could feel me heart gladdening at the thought of all I had ahead of me.

Right, here we are. I stared the length and breadth of O'Connell Street, really seeing the size of the road, for the first time, without any buses, cars or people. Only the odd straggler, like the man across the road, stopping to take a swig of the bottle of red biddy in his hand. Then making his way, staggering, with his head pointed straight ahead, looking like he wanted to get somewhere in a hurry. His head suddenly whipped over in my direction, seeing me looking at him. 'Happy Christmas to yeh!' he roared happily, waving the bottle over at me and stopping to take another swig, lorrying the drink down his neck. I laughed.

'Happy Christmas to you, too,' I shouted, thinking he's rushing to get himself a bit of dinner somewhere. Probably down the quays to the Adam and Eve's church. No, I don't think they give out anything on Christmas Day. Suddenly, I shouted over without thinking, 'Where are yeh going for your dinner?'

'To the Mansion House. The Lord Mayor's place.' Then he roared laughing. 'I don't care if he's there or not, so long as they give us out our Christmas dinner! By the look a you, yeh don't need it. But if yer lookin, make yer way over there. They do give out a lovely dinner.'

'Thanks. That's good of yeh. But I'm grand. I'm on me way home.'

'Right, I'll keep movin. Enjoy yerself! Because if you don't, no one else will do it for yeh!' he said, rushing himself happily off in the direction of Dawson Street, going for the free Lord Mayor's dinner.

I wonder why he thought I might need a free dinner? I'm all dressed up! Does he think I might be homeless like himself? Gawd, I'd hate to think that. Maybe it's because I asked him. Funny how people can read yeh! Mind, I'm like that meself. I can read people a mile away.

Right, time to get moving back. I'm dying to get there now and have me dinner, then start on me book. This wandering around, going nowhere, would put years on you. I'm just getting lost in meself with nothing to do, or see. No wonder I've gotten meself into a state.

I pulled the plug, letting the water out of the bath, and took off down to my room. Ah, that was a lovely hot bath, I thought, looking in the kitchen, seeing it all nice and clean after me Christmas dinner.

I could still get the smell of the rashers and pork chop I had for my dinner. That was lovely and tasty. I managed to cook it lovely. I think I have the idea on how to cook now. You watch the frying pan like a hawk, and keep turning everything. But it still cooks too fast. Then comes out a bit dry. Wonder why that is? Still and all, it was lovely.

I threw me washbag under the chair and climbed into bed, bringing me book and chocolates with me. Oh, where's me cigarettes? On the kitchen table. Ah, leave them. I can smoke in bed to me heart's content. Who's going to stop me? But it's better to keep the air fresh in here where I'm sleeping. Now for the bit of comfort.

I sat in, propping me head against the pillow, and sank back, hitting me head against the wall. Fuck! Me eyes peeled down to Molly's bed. I leaped out, grabbing hers. She has two! I only have the one. All the better. I can put it back before she finds out. Now, here goes. At last.

I opened the box of chocolates, dipping me hand in, and opened the first page of the book. Lovely! I couldn't ask for more. No one's having a better Christmas than me.

I looked over towards the window, hearing shouting. People coming up the road roaring at each other. I listened. 'Will yeh come on outa tha, for Christ's sake?' a fella was shouting at a woman. Ah, yeh can leave them to it, Martha. It takes Christmas to bring out the worst in some people. I took another chocolate, going back to me book, getting lost in the story.

9

I was just heading out the door on me afternoon off. I'm not due back at work until three o'clock tomorrow afternoon. 'Wait!' Molly shouted, coming down the stairs after me. 'You are to give me your hall-door key.'

'What? You must be joking! I need that to get in.'

'No, Mrs Murphy said I'm to take it off you.'

'Why? What business is it of yours or Mrs Murphy's?'

'You are too young, at sixteen years of age, to have a hall-door key.'

'No, you're not getting it. I'm working here like the rest of youse. What I do after that is nobody's business.'

'Give me the key,' she said, holding out her hand, glaring at me.

'How will I get in then?'

'It's OK. I'll let you in, or someone else will. There's plenty of people around at night to open the door.'

'So you will let me in when I come back?'

'Yes,' she said, looking like she meant it.

'Do you promise?'

'Providing you are not back later then eleven!'

'Oh, that's all right then. The last bus is at eleven anyway, so I'm always back before that.' I handed her the key, looking at the loss of it. She put it in the pocket of her blue work smock. I wore me ordinary clothes. I didn't want to be reminded of wearing the working smock when I was in the convent.

'Right, I'm off. Don't forget to open the door for me tonight.'

'Don't be late!' she shouted after me.

'No, I'll not be later then eleven o'clock.'

I took off, heading down the road to catch the bus into town.

I stepped off the bus and walked back to stand at the traffic lights on O'Connell Street, waiting to cross the road. Right, where will I go today? I'll go up to Clerys and wander around the shop, maybe I'll start buying meself a bit of make-up. I could buy some of that liquid eyeliner I see them all wearing. But it's hard to put on, trying to get a straight line without getting it all over your eyes, and ending up looking like someone gave yeh a black eye. That's no trouble, I can practise in me spare time before I wear it out. Great! I can even get some mascara to go with it. It will make me eyelashes look like brushes.

The lights changed, letting us get across. On second thoughts, I'll head down Aston Quay, and go around by the seaman's mission and get meself a plate of chips in the café down the road. I might even get a big ray! Yeah, fish and chips first. Lovely!

I took off, passing the big newsagent's on the quays, when me eyes lit on two little young fellas and I whipped me head back staring at them. I couldn't believe me eyes. There they were, mooching around the shop. 'TEDDY! HARRY! What are youse doing here?'

'Martha! It's you! Where are yeh goin? Where did yeh come from?' they roared, their eyes lighting up at the sight of me.

'Jaysus! Where did youse come out of?' I said, trying to get me breath back with the shock. Then grabbing a hold of them and squeezing the life out of them.

'We're doin nothin. Just goin fer a ramble,' they said, lookin me up and down, with the lot of us all getting excited and delighted at seeing each other.

'Where's the ma? Are youse on yer own?'

'Yeah, we are,' Teddy said.

'But how did youse do that? How did yeh get into town?'

'We walked!' Harry said, laughing and looking at Teddy.

'Jaysus!' I couldn't take it in. 'Come on. Come with me. I'm going to buy youse fish and chips. I want to know what you have been up to!'

'Here, get that into you,' I said, pushing the two plates down in front of them when the waitress landed the three plates of fish and chips on the table.

'Anything else?' the waitress said, holding up her notebook and pencil.

'Yeah, give me a large pot of tea and two plates of bread and butter.'

'Right, will that be all?' she said, looking at me.

'Yeah, thanks,' I said, watching her write down what we had ordered, and putting the bill on the table. I looked at it. Twelve shillings and sixpence! Fuck. That's a lot! Never mind. It's worth every penny.

'How did youse two get out of the house?' I said, looking at them shovelling down the chips and picking up the fish with their two hands, and making short work of it.

'We were supposed teh be gone tch school, Martha,' Teddy said, nearly choking on his grub.

'Take it easy. Don't try teh eat it all at the same time,' I said, looking at them, their faces bursting with the grub. I ate me fish and chips slowly, waiting for them to have their fill before I said another word. 'Here, take half of that between the two of you,' I said, dividing up most of me fish and chips, not feeling very hungry. I wanted them to have it. God knows when they will get another feed.

'Are yeh sure yeh don't want it, Martha?' Teddy said, his eyes bulging at me plate, wanting it, but not wanting to deprive me.

'Yeah, course I don't. Go on, eat it up! Do yehs want more bread?'

'Yeah! We do, don't we, Teddy?' Harry said, shaking his head with the woolly hat wrapped around it, covering his forehead.

'Why are yeh wearing that hat, Harry?'

'Cos he has sores, Martha! His head is covered in sores!'

'Oh, my God! When did that happen?'

'It's been like tha fer weeks, Martha. Me ma's puttin ointment on it. An he has teh keep it covered. Don't yeh, Harry?'

'Yeah!' Harry said, shaking his head up and down. Smiling at me.

Fucking hell! Jaysus Christ almighty, I moaned to meself. That's fucking sheer neglect. 'So, come on, tell me. Why are yehs hanging around the town? What are youse doing out on your own?'

'We were supposed teh be at school. But we're not. We're mitchin!' Teddy said, looking at Harry wit a devilment look on his face. Then the two of them grinned at me.

'Yeah, me da doesn't know or he'd kill us. But we know he won't find out this time cos he's gone off drinkin wit the labour money.'

'Yeah, he was drinkin yesterday. An this mornin he grabbed the money left in me ma's purse, and ran off out the door sayin he was goin for a drink. Me ma went mad an started roarin an screamin. She sent us out after him teh get the money back but we watched him get on the bus an then we took off ourselves! Didn't we, Harry?'

'Yeah, we did!' giggled Harry. 'We walked inta town teh have a look aroun.'

'But what happens when yeh go back home now? Won't he find out then?'

'No, he'll be too drunk teh know!'

'Yeah, cos he'll be flat out on the sofa. So we can sneak back in!' laughed Harry. 'Yeah!'

'But member the last time he caught us, Harry?' Teddy said, with the fear of God coming across his face. Teddy shook his head at me, remembering. 'He founded out we were mitchin, Martha. So we hid in the field down the road from the house. But he found us when we fell asleep in the night time. An he picked us up be our necks, an dragged us home like tha. Then he thrun us in the bath, an he got a rope an tied it aroun our necks and tied us together. Then he wrapped it aroun the tap in the bath and turned on the tap, makin the water pour out, an tried teh drown us! Our tongues were hangin out cos we were chokin and we went all black!'

'Yeah, me ma said our faces turned all black. She was screamin, an we weren't breathin no more! She stopped him. Yeah! Ony fer tha we woulda been dead. Yeah! We were nearly goners,' Harry said, shaking his head, his eyes staring out of his skull, with his mind wandering back to that time of hell.

'Oh, Jesus! What am I going to do with youse? He'll kill you for good this time, if he finds out!' Me heart was going like the clappers, looking at the two of them sitting there watching me, waiting to see what I could do next for them. 'Listen, Teddy, Harry. Where's Charlie?'

'We don't know! He just keeps runnin off from the house.'

'What? Where is he now?'

'We don't know! Me da's givin up lookin fer him. The first few times he ran away me da used teh go out an find him. He was hangin aroun the fields wit the big young ones. An me da bate the hell outa him. But Charlie doesn't care. He just runs off again when me ma sends him for the messages!' They laughed. 'Yeah! Ever since you left, he was gettin inta trouble wit me da. He wanted him teh do all the things tha you did. But me da said he was too stupid. An he wouldn't do anythin for them. He wouldn't even go fer the bread up to the convents. So, the first time me da threw him outa the house he thought Charlie would come back. But he didn't. So Charlie wouldn't come back ever since. He likes teh stay away, so he does. An me da went mad. Cos he wanted him teh go fer the messages, an look after things the way you did, Martha. Yeah! But Charlie won't do it. He doesn't care how much me da kills him cos he knows he can run away. Yeah! So are we, aren't we, Harry?'

'Yeah, we don't care neighter,' Harry said, shaking his head and looking at Teddy. The two of them trying to make themselves brave.

'No, come on. You're going home. I'm putting the two of youse on the bus. You are too young to be on the streets! Are you listening to me?'

'Yeah,' they said, the light going out of their eyes. Not wanting to go back home.

'Listen, my little darlings,' I said, putting me hands across the table and stroking their little cheeks. 'You have to go home to the ma. She'll be worried sick looking for youse. The streets are very very dangerous! There's people walking these streets who would grab hold of you and you'd never be seen again. They would murder you! Did you know that?'

'Yeah!' they said, the terrible thought just occurring to them now.

'You have to wait another few years before you can live on your own. I'm big. I'm sixteen so I can go where I like now! It seems a long time for you to wait, I had to wait when I was your age. I thought the time would never come, but it did. You need to go to school every day and learn to read and write. Life is hard if you can't write your name! Have youse learned to write yet?'

'No, but we don't like school.'

'We can't read nor write. An the master kills us. Doesn't he, Harry?'

'Yeah, I get kilt, too,' Harry said, shaking his head, looking fearful.

'Oh, Jaysus! Learn the letters and you can teach yourselves like I did! Do you know your letters?'

'Yeah, we know the letters, don't we, Harry?'

'Yeah, we can say all the letters, Martha,' Harry said, looking more happy.

'Right then, reading is easy! Just spell them together, getting the sound then keep saying it, go around spelling everything you see. Break down the word, get the sound and soon you will be able to read. That's how I learned. Now I want you to do that. Are you listening to me? Then school will be easier. Anyway, it gets you away from that aul fella. Right, will you promise me you will go to school?'

'Yeah, we will,' they said, shaking their heads, meaning it for the moment.

I paid the bill, looking at me change. Four shillings and sixpence.

'Come on, let's go and get the bus!'

'Are you comin wit us, Martha?' they said together, their eyes staring out of their heads with excitement.

'No, what would I be doing going back there? Can you see me living with Jackser?'

'No,' they laughed, then their faces dropped.

'We miss you, Martha,' Harry said, with his little face looking very mournful. 'Me ma is always talkin about all the stuff you used teh get!'

'Yeah, me da really misses the money yeh used teh bring home,' Teddy said, shaking his head at the memory, thinking about all the loss they had. 'He's always talkin about it. Yeah, yeh used teh bring us toys an everythin,' he said, the pair of them agreeing with each other. Their heads hanging along the ground.

'Ah, come on, you two. Your time will come! Then you will be able to leave and get yourselves a job. Now, isn't this lovely, the way we met? Did you like your fish and chips, eating in that café? Wasn't it great?'

'Yeah, we never had anythin like tha before, did we, Harry?'

'No! Tha was great, it was!'

'OK, let's rush up to Woolworths and buy cornets. Would yehs like that?'

'Yeah! Yeah! Can we do it now, Martha?'

'Course we can. Come on!'

We headed up Henry Street and went into Woolworths. 'Give us two ninety-nines,' I said, handing the girl two shillings and waiting for her to give us two creamy ice creams with two chocolate flakes stuck in the middle. 'Right, boys. Here you are,' I said, putting one each in their hands. 'Come on! Take a bag and put a few sweets in and get yourselves a big bag of pick 'n' mix each. Look, you can take your pick of all the sweets and put them in the bag. Here's a shovel. Wait, I'll do it meself. I'll get yeh some of all of them, and I want to get a bag each for Dinah and Sally and Agnes. How are they?' I asked smiling. 'Are they OK?'

'Yeah, they go teh your old school, Martha!'

'Yeah,' Harry said, getting all excited.

'Shurrup, Harry! I'm tellin her,' Teddy said, looking very annoyed at Harry.

'Yeah,' Harry said, smiling and looking at the ground, disappointed he couldn't tell me.

'Ah, Teddy! Let Harry tell me one bit then you can tell me the rest.'

'But I want teh tell yeh! I was the first teh start talkin, Martha!'

'Yeah, I'm dying to hear you, but I want to hear Harry first. Go on, Harry. Tell me what you were going to say.'

'Dinah is goin teh yer old schule. An she's makin her communion next year, so she is. An . . .'

'It's muy turn teh talk!' roared Teddy, putting his hand over Harry's face and mouth.

'Fuck off!' roared Harry, losing the rag.

'Stop! No fightin or yehs are not gettin any a them sweets!' I said. 'Now be nice. Tell me, Teddy, what you were going to say.' I heard meself getting back to me new voice. Forgetting meself for a minute, going back to me old way of speaking.

'Yeah, she's gone inta the first class, so she'll be makin the communion next May. An Sally is in the high babbies an she's goin teh be goin inta the first class next year. But Agnes won't be goin teh schule yet cos she's not big enough yet. An the new babby is a boy! Me da called him Gerry.'

'Ah, is he lovely?'

'Yeah, he has black hair, an me ma's eyes.'

'Yeah, me ma says they're her eyes!' shouted Harry.

'But she's not able fer him, Martha,' Teddy said, looking pained in the face at this idea. 'She's complainin she's tired all the time. She keeps him in the bed wit her. An me da goes mad! They're always fightin an shoutin. We can't get no sleep wit them at night time. Sure we don't, Harry?'

'No, they keep roarin an shoutin,' Harry agreed.

'Then he always goes out on the drinkin! We don't care, do we, Harry?'

'No, cos then he doesn't be at home all day!' Harry said, shaking his head, thinking that was a good thing.

'No! But when he gets back then tha's when all the killins does start,' puffed Teddy, lookin shocked at the thought of it.

'Yeah, there does be killins,' said Harry quietly, shaking his head, thinking about it.

'Bastards!' I muttered.

'Where are yeh livin, Martha? Mebbe we can come an stay wit you?'

'Can we do tha? Yeah! Yeah! We want teh come teh live wit you, Martha!'

'Jaysus!' I said, scratching the hat off me head. 'Believe me, if I could, I would do it this minute! But I have nowhere to take youse. I share a room wit another one, an aul one from the country. She thinks she's doing me a favour by letting me sleep in the room. No, Teddy, Harry. It breaks me heart to say this. But I can't take you to live with me. I hardly have anywhere to go. I have to be careful not to lose me job, or then I'm sunk! I'd have nowhere to live.'

'Oh, yeah,' they said, the two of them shaking their heads, understanding what I'm saying, and looking at the ground feeling very miserable.

We headed out of Woolworths, the pair of them sticking their noses into the white bags and taking out a boiled sweet to suck on. 'Come on! Let's go up to Parnell Street for the bus out to Finglas.'

'Oh! Yeh didn't know, did yeh? We moved outa our old house!' roared Teddy, getting all excited.

'Yeah, yeah!' shouted the two of them together.

'We swapped wit a man an he gev us money!' Teddy explained.

'What? Are you not living in Finglas any more?'

'Yeah, yeah, we are,' they said, shaking their heads up and down, getting outa breath and all excited.

'We only moved down the road,' puffed Teddy. 'It's just a bit far down. But we don't like it, and me ma an da doesn't like it. Everyone is very rough! An one day me da got inta a fight wit another man, an me ma tried teh help him an a gang a people jumped on her, an beat her up somethin terrible.'

Oh sweet Jesus! I could feel me heart drop down into me belly, the shock making me head go light and the colour leaving me face. 'Was the ma all right?' I whispered.

'Yeah! It happened before she had the new babby. An she had a go inta the ambulance teh hospidal. Tha's why we came down teh you! In the convent. Me da said we was teh keep our traps shut and not teh tell you or the nuns. So we kept quiet,' Teddy said, his voice trailing off into a whisper. The memory of that time hurting him.

I looked at Harry, his eyes standing out of his head, and his mouth open, listening and remembering. 'Come on! You're OK here and now with me,' I said, pulling the two of them under me arms, one each side of me. 'Do we still get the bus on Parnell Street?' I said.

'Yeah! We know the bus teh get. It's still the same one. We just have teh get off sooner!'

'OK, here we are,' I said, making for the bus stop. 'Now, here's the bag with the three bags of sweets, one each for Dinah and Sally and Agnes. I got a packet of silvermints for the ma because she likes them. They're in the bag, too. OK? Now, Harry. You carry them. Listen, Teddy, I want you to do something for me. I am going to trust you to do this for me, OK?' I said, opening me bag and taking out what money I had left. 'First of all, this is for your bus fare. It's twopence each. Right?'

'Yeah, right,' Teddy said, looking at me handing him the fourpence for the bus.

'Here's two shillings each to spend on yourselves. Now, I want you to give this two pound to me mammy. She needs this to buy food because I bet she hasn't got a penny left after that bandy aul bastard spent the lot on the fucking drink. So give her this and don't lose it! Are yeh listening teh me carefully? Here, have yeh got pockets in them short trousers?'

'No, there's a hole in me trousers, Martha.'

'Fuck, I don't want you going and losing all this money.'

'Give it teh me, Martha! I promise I'll take care not teh lose it!'

'OK, here's what I'll do. Harry. Give me that bag with the sweets. I'm going to put the money in here. You carry it, Teddy.

Make sure you give it to the ma, and don't let that bastard Jackser get his hands on it, will you!'

'No,' he said, shaking his head up and down, listening to me very intently.

'Now, will you give me ma that money? You wouldn't keep it for yourself, would you?' I asked him, kneeling down and looking into his eyes.

'No, I promise we won't spend it on ourselves! I cross me heart and hope teh die,' he said, looking at me, his little face so serious.

'I want the ma to buy you a bit of dinner,' I said, in a whisper. 'Especially Dinah and Sally and Agnes. You wouldn't want them to go hungry after you had a lovely time, would you?'

'No, we will give me ma the money. I promise on me word a honour, Martha.'

'Right, love,' I sighed, knowing they would.

I stood up, drawing the two of them close to me, holding them under me arm. Trying to wrap them in me coat, treasuring the minutes we had together, waiting on the bus. With nobody saying a word. We just stood in out of the cold, in the doorway of a house. The three of us, holding onto the warmth of each other, me wishing I could protect them and take care of them meself and they standing hanging onto me, snuggling closer in behind me, trying to shelter from the cold wind blowing up from the Liffey, feeling safe now just for the moment, knowing I would protect them with my life, but soon we will be going our own separate ways. Them back to the hell on earth, and me going back to a job where I was not going to last. Molly's trying her best to get rid of me. I didn't suit her ways.

'Here we are,' I whispered in a sigh, seeing the bus pull into the terminus. 'Come on, sit on the seat next to the driver.' I got on the bus with them and put them sitting down where the conductor could see them. 'Sit there for a minute. Give me the name of the stop where you get off,' I said.

'It's four stops before our old one,' they said. Looking very small and tired now. The pair of them looking lost. They look so run-down and neglected, and they're only little. Jesus! Teddy and Harry are too small for this, far too little to be running around wild.

'Ma, fuck yeh!' I muttered to meself, going over to talk to the bus conductor. Then waiting, seeing him lift his left leg, dropping himself against the wall, letting the wall take the weight of him. I watched him light up a cigarette, then went over to him. 'Are you going to be the conductor on this bus out to Finglas?'

'Yeah, she'll be going out in five minutes,' he said, taking a deep drag on his cigarette, and holding his breath, letting the smoke go down into his lungs. Then letting it out slowly, lifting his head back to watch the smoke going up into the air.

'Listen! Do you see the two little fellas there sitting on the long seat just inside the door?' I said, pointing at Teddy and Harry watching me out the window. 'Will you make sure they get off at the right stop?' Then I gave him the name of the stop. 'Don't let them off before that. Keep your eye on them. They're a pair of ramblers! Do yeh know what I mean?'

'Yeh mean they were mitching from school today?' he said, holding the cigarette halfway to his mouth.

'Yeah! Yeah, that's exactly what I mean. I want them to get home in one piece.'

'Right, you needn't worry yourself any further. I'll take care of them. Don't you worry! I'll keep me eye on them like a hawk,' he said, leaning around me to get a better look at Teddy and Harry watching us out the window. 'Ah, they'll be all right. I'll make sure they get off at their own stop!'

'Oh, thanks very much, mister! That's very good of you,' I said happily, me heart lifting, knowing they would get home.

'Now, eat your sweets and be good for me. The bus man is going to keep his eye on the pair of you to make sure you don't get off at the wrong stop.'

'But we don't need tha! We know our own ways home! Don't we, Harry?' Teddy said, screwing his face up at the thought I was treating them like babies.

'Yeah, course you do. But I don't trust anyone else! You're not the problem. Someone else might be watching yeh. You are too young to know the world and its ways. That's why you have to promise me you won't run off again. It's very dangerous! Do you want me worrying about youse and having me hair turning grey before me time?'

'No,' they laughed, not used to the idea of having people fussing over them so much!

'Well, give us a kiss and a hug! The bus is going to be going any minute now!' I wrapped me arms around Teddy, feeling his skinny little frame with the ribs not having a bit of flesh on them. 'You two mean the whole world to me. Just because you don't see me doesn't mean I have forgotten about you or I don't care! I'll always be your big sister, and I'll always look out for the lot of yehs. Tell Charlie I hope I run into him one of these days. I'm going to be looking out for him. Will yehs tell him that when yeh see him?' I said, looking at them and grabbing Harry in a bear's hug and kissing the face off him. I could smell the dirty, manky clothes off them. Jesus! The ma hasn't washed them rags since the day she put them on the poor kids. Me heart bled, looking at the state of them, with the little white faces half-starved, and the eyes looking huge. Hanging outa their heads from years of neglect and the fear and worry of living with them two fucking good-for-nothing bastards. There's times when I hate that ma. She does fuck-all to help the kids.

'Right, we're moving off,' the conductor said, jumping on the platform and steadying the money bag around his neck. Holding his hand on the bell ready to give it a whack.

'Right! Be good! Go straight home,' I said in a panic. Looking at the two of them staring at him, the pain and fear in their faces at the thought of me going away without them. I couldn't think of anything else to warn them about, or how much they meant to me. I had to get off the bus. 'Goodbye now! Straight home!' I shouted as the bus moved off. I saw them jumping up on the seat to wave at me, the pair of them pressing their heads to the window, trying to keep me in their sights as the bus moved up Parnell Street.

I stopped looking and waving when the bus turned left at the top of the road, heading up through Gardiner Street making its way out to Finglas. I turned slowly, looking down across O'Connell Street towards Capel Street, feeling a terrible sense of loss. I feel completely empty inside meself and cold. Me vision was blurred and I could barely make out the people and the traffic all around me. The noise seemed very far away. I suddenly felt I had been part of a different world for a few hours. I was a part of me own family. Me brothers! Then it was gone, just like that. I was on me own again, but not on me own. Jackser and the ma was back in me life. Just a bus away! It made me feel like I had never escaped.

I walked on, wanting to get somewhere. Away from them bastards. The ma and Jackser. Feeling a slow burning rage with the thought the boys were going to end up getting killed or something terrible was going to happen to them.

And Charlie! Where the hell is he? I have to find him! But then what? What can I do with him? How would I be able to keep him with me working in the shop? He would have to go to school. On top of that, if I start taking meself out to Finglas, what good would that do? There's nothing can be done to help the ma. She doesn't want to change anything. She would only be happy with me giving her money. Fucking Jaysus Christ! There's nothing I can do. I would change nothing, and instead end up in the clutches of that aul fella again. No, Martha! Keep well away from them bastards. I would only end up destroying meself. Right, leave it be. Maybe I could talk to Sister Eleanor about it. If she could take them into the convent. Yeah, I'll give her a ring. Right, I'm going to do that straight this minute.

I made me way down O'Connell Street and into the General Post Office. I need tuppence for the telephone. How much have I got left? Jaysus! Ten shillings! I looked at the ten-bob note, and one shilling and sixpence left. That's all I have left outa the four pounds I had. Jaysus! It didn't take me long to get rid of that money. Still, it was money well spent. Teddy and Harry were delighted to be eating in that café, and the ma needs the money for the children.

OK, I better watch me money carefully from now on. Thank God I still have all me savings left. I have a whole ten pounds saved up, hidden in me suitcase. That's including the double money Greg gave me as a going-away present. Instead of the two-pound ten shillings they owed me, he handed me a whole five-pound note. I was gobsmacked. Some people are very good. They certainly were. I still miss them!

So, anyway. I'm doing grand. That should keep me going if anything ever happened. Now I know why it's always good to save me money. It means I'll never be stuck if I end up out of a job and need to find somewhere to live. As the ma used to always say, you can eat and drink on the streets, but you can't sleep on them! Fuck that! No, I had enough of that as a little child. Look what happened to her! She ended up with that fucking Jackser because of that. Not me. Not on yer nelly!

OK, I only need two pennies for the phone. I looked around, wondering who I could ask for change of a sixpence, and went over to the counter. 'Will you give us change for the phone out of that sixpence, mister?'

'Do yeh want all pennies?'

'Eh, yeah, I might want it for the bus fare.'

I went into the phone box and shut the door. I knew the number off by heart and dialled it after putting the money in the box and waiting for it to ring. I held me finger on the A button, ready to answer, then looked at the B button. 'I hope this box gives me back me money if I don't get through. Some of them bleedin boxes rob yer money!' I snorted to meself.

'Hello, Holy Redeemer Convent!' I heard a squeaky voice say, then hold her breath.

'Yes, I would like to speak to Sister Eleanor, please.'

'Who is it? She's not available at the present moment,' a young one's voice squeaked down the phone, trying to be posh.

'Where is she then, please?' I said in me best voice.

'Who's this?'

'One of the girls,' I said. 'Where's Sister Eleanor?'

'Who's that?' she roared.

'Jaysus! Will you hurry and get her? I might be cut off. It's me. Martha Long!'

'Oh, how're yeh, Martha? What are you doing? Are you working?'

'Yeah, I am. Now, listen. Who's that?'

'It's me! Remember me? Sofie, from the middle group.'

'Oh, yeah! Listen, Sofie, where's Eleanor?'

'Oh, her! She's gone off on her retreat.'

'Ah, Jaysus! When will she be back?'

'Not until next week. My nun is in charge of your old group. Do you want to talk to her?'

'No,' I said, me heart sinking down into me belly button at the terrible loss of her not being around when I wanted her. 'OK, thanks,' I said, feeling weak with the disappointment.

'OK, bye!' Sofie roared down the phone.

'Bye,' I said, putting down the phone and making me way out into the crowds now rushing home from work.

The noise of the traffic hit me straight away. I barely knew where I was for a minute. Not being able to take anything in. Jaysus! She's gone away. I really feel empty. I don't know anyone, and I have nowhere else I could go to talk to someone about what to do. I feel sick at the thought of the poor children. If only I knew what to do! I thought Sister Eleanor might be able to take them into the convent. So that's the end of her! She's gone away. What will I do? Ah, to hell with it. I'll go over to Caffola's and buy meself a white cup of coffee and sit there in the comfort of the bit of heat, and maybe somebody might put sixpence in the juke box and I can listen to a bit of music. Some hope! That very seldom happens. Sixpence is too much money for people to be wasting on bleedin juke boxes.

I made me way across Nelson's Pillar and walked into Caffola's. Most of the seats were full. Then a country woman stood up, and the husband came back from paying the bill, and I dived on the seat. Getting meself a table right by the window. Now I can sit and stare out at the passing traffic and people for hours. I am not in any hurry, there's no one waiting for me. Me time is me own. So, thank God for that. I can please meself. If only I could have the kids with me!

Yer bleedin mad, Martha. Stop the nonsense. There's fuck-all you can do. Jackser and even the ma would kill you first. They need them children to get the social welfare and everything else they can get! The convent in its own way is not the answer. They might do more harm than good. The children might fret. Them little bastards in the convent would bully them, the clannish little fuckers! I could take it, but the poor little children couldn't. They might even end up getting split up. Sent off to different homes! So, it looks like their suffering will go on for another while, until they are old enough to leave. Judging by the look of things, they are already doing that!

Jesus! Please take care of my little brothers and sister. Especially Charlie! He's now on his own, by the way things are going. What age would he be now? Eleven. Jaysus! He won't find the time flying until he can start getting himself a job just like me. I wish I could see him. No, I can't go out to bleedin Finglas looking for him. That would bring me into dangerous territory! I don't want to get caught by that bastard Jackser on his own home ground. That would really be looking for trouble. No, he would only come after me. It would only draw his attention onto me. He'd probably think I am interfering in his business. He knows now where he stands with me. Ever since I wouldn't leave the convent for him. So, as far as he is concerned, I'm his number-one enemy!

Right! So, I'm keeping well away from his territory. No, I have to watch meself. I'm not home and dry yet as far as that bastard is concerned. He could still come looking for me. Start hounding me the way he hounded the ma when she tried to escape him. Searching the streets night and day, looking for her. Dublin is a very small place.

Oh, Jesus! I gave an almighty shiver, with the sudden cold fear running through me, making me see stars and everything turn black, at the thought of having him come after me. I would have to run to England. Or, God forbid, kill the bastard! No matter what it took and I know I would! He is never getting the better of me again. I am a match for him.

I felt meself gritting me teeth. A rush of rage flying through me. The picture of me ma letting him get away with murder. It

made me want to crucify the bastard, nice and slowly. Watching
the fear in his eyes and the thought that it was a woman doing
it to him. Yeah, he better not ever cross me. I'm no Sally!

I blinked, shaking me head to clear the terrible picture of getting
involved with them all over again, wanting to put them clean out
of me mind. I stared out at the passing traffic. It's easing off now. I
could see people starting to congregate outside the GPO across the
road. Fellas and girls lined themselves up outside the big building
of the post office, waiting for their dates to turn up. Gawd! I'd love
to be standing over there now waiting for a lovely fella to come and
take me out. Probably to the pictures, then back here for a plate of
fish and chips. He would have to be really nice. Definitely have a
good job and be very respectable. Yeah, someone who dressed nice
and spoke lovely. Imagine that. Or me turn up and he's waiting for
me. Yeah! It will come, everything takes time.

The door pushed open and an icy-cold wind blew in with two
girls laughing their heads off. 'Blind date, me eye! Did you see the
cut of him?' roared a young one. Wearing a midi-long black coat
with a belt tied around, and tight white-leather boots that clung to
her legs. I looked up at her hairstyle. It was back-combed, going
nearly two inches inta the air, looking like a bird's nest. She had
gathered the hair up, pinning it in place with loads a clips. I stared
with me mouth open at her false eyelashes, flapping against her
eyebrows they were so long. She had half a box of blue eyeshadow
on her eyebrows and one was smudged with black eyeliner! The
pink lipstick was smudged on her front teeth. Jaysus! She looks a
holy show, I thought, staring at her with me mouth open.

'That was your fella!' the other one said, wearing a Mary Quant
look, with the wide tent frock, looking like she was expecting. And
red boots the same as her friend with a trench coat like mine. It
didn't suit her, with the big fat legs and the massive chest! Her hair
was cut in a page boy, and she wore false eyelashes and thick eyeliner,
curling up at the edges, heading for her ears. One side is longer
then the other, I thought, turning me head to look after them.

'Jaysus! I wouldn't be seen in a dead fit goin out with the likes
a them. Your fella was covered in boils!' roared the bird's nest.

'Yeah, but it was only a date, for Jaysus sake! We weren't expected teh marry them!' the page-boy one roared.

'Well, we left them standin there,' the bird's-nest one said. Sounding a bit down at the loss of the fellas. 'Jaysus! I wonder if they're still waitin for us teh turn up?' she said, with her eyes widening and a laugh spreading across her face.

'Gawd! Oh, Mammy! Do yeh know wha just came inta me head?' the page-boy one suddenly said. Letting the eyes hang outa her head in sudden shock, and putting her hand over her mouth. 'I hadn't thought a this. It just struck me this minute.'

'Wha? No, wha? Tell us!' the bird's nest said. Staring at your woman with her mouth hanging open, waiting for page-boy to get over her shock.

'Yer man will get me tomorra when I turn up for work. An your fella is his best pal! Jaysus! There's goin teh be ructions for us after makin the fool outa them.' There was silence for a minute, while the two of them stood there staring at each other, thinking about this. Then they suddenly threw back their heads and screamed with the laughing, slapping and falling against each other, getting hysterical. Then they staggered their way over to a seat at the back of the café, and collapsed into it, still laughing their heads off.

I took in a big sigh, looking back out onto the street to see what was happening. The street lights were on, and all the buildings had lights blazing against the darkness outside. People were hurrying past, with their shoulders hunched, and their heads stuck inside their coats, against the icy-cold wind blowing up from the Liffey. I looked at their faces, seeing them throw their eyes into the warmth of the café, hesitate for a second, then face their head, set for home. Hurrying on, wanting to get home in a hurry. In safe, out of the treachery of the cold, dark January night.

'I should think about moving,' I muttered to meself, having no intention of moving just yet out into the cold. The bright lights in here, and the lovely heat, with the murmuring of the voices of the two waitresses, standing at the counter staring out into the night, like they were miles away, tired after running on their feet all day, was sending me off inta a doze. I'm content to just sit here and be with all the other people doing the same. A lot of people were sitting on their own. Just staring out, lost in their own thoughts. No one in a hurry anywhere. Not wanting to leave the comfort of the place, enjoying being a part of people, even if you were not with anyone.

Suddenly, music rose up, and I turned me head, seeing the bird's nest singing along quietly with the song, while page-boy tapped her fingers and shook her head up and down in time to the music. 'Gene Pitney! Oh, I love him, I do! I can't get enough of him,' moaned the bird's nest, closing her eyes and dropping her head back on her shoulders. Looking like she was crying and singing mournfully.

'AND THEN SOMEHOW BACKSTAGE I'MMM . . . LO-HONEH-LEEEE!' The singer's voice rose. I listened, holding me breath. Gawd, he has a powerful voice! The music made me heart rattle inside me chest. He was singing like he was crying with the pain of loneliness. It made me feel like I wasn't the only one feeling like that! Him and me. We feel the same. Somehow it made me feel better. I knew what was wrong with me, and I wasn't alone.

The song ended, and there was a silence, like everyone had been holding their breath. A woman sitting in the other corner shifted herself slightly, catching my eye. She had a tight perm in her hair that was beginning to grow out, making the top look straight, and it was thin and straggly-looking. She looked about in her thirties, I would say. Her brown overcoat was folded up nice and neat and left sitting beside her on the seat. Making it clear she didn't want anyone sliding in beside her and disturbing her peace. Her headscarf was loosened, and she let it slide down and sit around her neck, on top of a baby-blue matching twin set, a thin nylon jumper and cardigan. The top buttons of the cardigan were open, showing off a gold chain and cross. She was wearing that over a dark-blue wide skirt.

She's a country woman, I thought, seeing her barely move her mouth in a little smile over at me, then shift her head back to stare out the window again. She looks very lonely to me, too. Just like meself. I suppose she has no one in Dublin to go out with. Probably all belonging to her are back down in the country, or maybe gone away to England. She was sitting here when I came in. That was hours ago. It must be her day off work. I bet she does housework. Or shift work, like me. Most people don't get their day off work until Saturday afternoon, then go back on Monday. Ah, God help her! She's not married, there's no ring on her finger. I don't suppose she has any chance now. What has she got to look forward to? She's already given up, by the look of her.

Her eyes stared into the distance, seeing what was happening, yet not seeing anything. She was looking beyond the here and now, probably far back into some distant loss at what might have been. Maybe in her younger days she had some fella. But he went off to England or America, and she didn't go with him. Maybe she regrets it to this day. He was probably the only one she ever had any time for. So now she thinks no man will ever match up to the first fella.

God, all the lonely people! You only notice them when you have time to sit and stare, seeing in them what you are going through yourself! Only I have me whole life just starting ahead of me. I'm very lucky! I stirred meself, getting up and slowly made me way out the door, seeing the woman shift her head, letting her eyes rest on me, like the two of us had been part of something for a while. I nodded over, giving her a smile, and she smiled back, nodding her head at me. Much as to say, 'It's a pity when the lovely comfort of sitting here comes to an end.'

I pulled up the collar of my trench coat, gripping it tightly around me neck, and took off out the door. Straight into a blast of freezing-cold wind that knocked me backwards, taking the breath out of me. Oh, I can't wait to get out of this cold and into me bed. Right, I better get moving fast down to the bus stop. I don't want to be late back. I'm raging I don't have me hall-door key. I should have stuck to me guns and not given it up. I'm going to go to that aul Murphy and demand it back. They have no right to tell me what to do. I'm only working for them! The bleeding cheek a them. Acting like they're me lord and masters. Thinking they can take it on themselves to tell me what to do.

Anyway, back before eleven, she said. It can't be any more then after ten. I looked back, seeing the Clerys clock. Twenty past ten. That's grand. I should be back in time. I hope I'm not waiting too long for the bus.

I stood waiting at the bus stop, getting more and more frostbitten by the minute, hopping up and down, stamping me feet to keep out the cold. Bloody hell! When is that bus ever going to come? I stared into the distance, seeing no sign of it. Oh, for Jaysus' sake! The one night I'm wanting to get back in a hurry, and I'm going to be late. Usually I'm back well before this.

At last! Me eyes lit up at the sight of the bloody bus coming. I could see it flying up the road, looking like it might not stop. I leaped off the footpath, putting me arm out wide, leaving him in no mistake I wanted to get his bus. It stopped a good bit ahead of me and I had to run to catch it. I swung onto the platform and the conductor smacked the bell hard a few times, and the bus took off flying.

I looked, seeing another bus flying past. Two bleedin buses at the same time! My bus took out after it. The two of them looking like they were racing each other. Fucking eejits. Taking their time getting here, then coming together!

I snorted at the conductor, taking out me tuppence and handed it to him as he rattled his machine in me face.

Right, I'm here. I stood up in good time to make sure the driver didn't fly past me stop with the speed he was going. I jumped off, with the bus barely slowing down, and headed up the road, seeing the lights going off in the shop. 'Just on time! I made it, no thanks to that bus!' I snorted, looking at it vanishing up the road in a puff of black smoke.

I rang the new hall doorbell and waited. Nothing happened! I rang again. Still no sound of anyone coming to let me in. I kept me finger on the bell. Nothing! Jaysus! She won't open the door. I rattled the letter box. Nothing! Then I shook hell out of it. Still no answer. I rang and rang but nobody would let me in. Then I ran around to the front of the shop. I was left looking in at the dark shop. It's all closed up. Nobody there. I felt like crying with the rage. The fucking bastards! That fucking Molly one won't let me in. She promised she would open the door. Why is she doing this?

I went back and rang the bell and rattled hell out of the letter box at the same time. Still no answer. Then I kicked the door, screaming me lungs out. 'MOLLY! OPEN THE DOOR! LET ME IN!' I could hear someone coming. The bolt was pulled across and the door whipped open. The grey-haired man stood looking at me, then opened the door wider and let me through, into the hall and up the stairs. 'Thanks very much! I was locked out. Molly was supposed to let me in,' I said, nearly crying.

'Come on. That's all right,' he muttered, then locked the door.

I tore up the stairs and belted into the room, switching on the light. 'WHY DIDN'T YOU LET ME IN, MOLLY?' I screamed at the lump hiding under the blankets. She didn't move. 'I'M SPEAKIN TO YEH! ANSWER ME, YOU CULCHIE LYING FUCKING COW! YOU PROMISED ME YOU WOULD OPEN THE DOOR WHEN I GOT BACK! MORE FUCKING FOOL ME, I BELIEVED YEH!' I was sweating with the rage, and the fright. At thinking I was going to be left out there, stranded in the street all night. She just completely ignored me. I stamped over to me bed, taking me clothes off after switching out the light. Then stamped out, banging the door after me, heading down for the bathroom. When I stamped back in, making as much noise as I could to annoy her and get me own back, she was gone. Her and the mattress! I gaped at the springs on her bed. She's gone! Taking her mattress with her. That was quick. I was only a few minutes cleaning me teeth.

Jaysus! Imagine stripping your bed this hour of the night. Wonder where she's gone? To hell with her. I climbed into me bed and was out for the count in no time.

The grey-haired man appeared in the shop as I was serving a customer and made straight for me. 'Hmm, eh, Martha,' he said, trying not to look at me, his eyes slipping over mine, then landing somewhere on the far wall. 'Mrs Murphy wants to see you straight away, over in her office at the bookies.'

'Me? Now?'

'Yes, you better run over.'

I looked at Molly listening, then turning away quickly from me. Making herself busy with the bread delivery, putting it on the shelves. 'OK,' I said weakly, getting a fright. It must be something to do with last night. Molly not letting me in. Wait until I tell her what that Molly one did. I rushed around the counter and out the door, making for the bookies across the road.

'Missus Murphy is looking for me,' I said to the girl behind the cage taking in the bets.

'Hang on and I'll let you through,' she said, coming out of her little office. I could see men with the arse out of their trousers looking like they could do with a good feed. Studying the newspapers hanging on the walls. Everyone looked very intent. 'Go right through and up the stairs,' the girl said, lifting the counter and letting me walk through, in a door and up the stairs. Onto a little landing with two doors. I knocked on the one straight ahead.

'Come in,' a voice said from the other door. 'Oh, it's you! Come in and sit down for a minute,' Missus Murphy said, counting wads of green pound notes, and red ten-bob notes, and even big fivers and ten-pound notes. Jaysus! I wonder who would have gambled with ten-pound notes. Imagine that! Someone having whole ten-pound notes to throw away!

She went back to examining her notes along with the bags of silver coins, leaving me sitting there with me eyeballs springing outa me head. They were left hanging, sitting on me cheekbones, at the sight of all that money. I blinked away the fog in me eyes, getting a better look. Gawd! Yer woman is rolling in the money! That's all on the back of the poor, judging by the poor unfortunate wasters downstairs, spending the only few bob the family have! I looked up at her fat red ugly face with the greedy look in her beady little eyes that had sunk into the back of the mound of flesh that passed for a face. She pulled all the notes and coins away from me, wrapping her big fat arms around the money and dragging the lot towards her, looking to make sure there was nothing left at arm's distance for me to rob. As if I would even bleeding think about it. I didn't like her not trusting me, miserable aul cow.

'I got a bad report about you,' she said, looking at me.

'About what, Missus Murphy?' I said, keeping me face steady and looking her straight in the eye. She stared back at me, her little beady eyes narrowing, taking me in. I waited.

'You came back at all hours last night and drove poor Molly out of her bed.'

'What? I did no such thing, Missus Murphy! I was back by eleven o'clock and she wouldn't open the door to let me in. I was left standing out in the freezing cold nearly half of the night,' I snorted, feeling very annoyed she was taking that one's part.

'Nooo, that's not what I heard. You were certainly not back by even half-eleven at the latest. I asked her. She said it was well after twelve.'

'Yes, it was well after twelve by the time I was let in, frostbitten, by the grey-haired man, Mister O'Brien. Only for him I would still be left standing out there waiting to get in.'

'Well, you were not in by eleven o'clock, that's for sure! I believe what Molly tells me. I know she is very honest.'

'How could I not be back by eleven? Or even half-eleven, if it comes to that? The buses stop running after eleven o'clock,' I snorted, trying to get her to believe me.

'Well, anyhow,' she puffed, 'that poor girl had to sleep in the storeroom all night. It was freezing cold in there. You came in making an almighty racket. Roaring and screaming at the poor girl in her bed, which is where you should have been!'

'But she took me key and said she would let me in,' I said, trying to make her understand. 'She had no right to do that!'

'Yes, she did. I told her to take the key off you. I didn't realise you were only sixteen! Where are you from? You are a Dublin girl, aren't you?'

'Yes,' I said, on me guard. 'So?'

'Why don't you live at home with your mammy?'

I said nothing, thinking it's none of her business. She studied me, her beady little eyes trying to work this out. 'Are you by any chance out of a convent?' she said slowly, making it sound like I had killed someone. Her eyes lighting up, then narrowing like I had definitely done something wrong.

'No,' I said quietly, shaking me head slowly and holding her eyes.

'Well, I don't want to know your business. But whatever it is, I don't want to be involved. You are too young. I'm going to have to let you go.'

The shock hit me like a blow in the stomach. I felt the blood drain outa me. 'But . . . surely you had no complaints about me work? I'm a hard worker! What complaints could you have had with me? Why are you letting me go? I've never interfered with anyone. I'm always behind the counter on time . . . I'm—' I was desperate to plead me case. But she just stared at me.

'Look,' she said, interrupting me, 'I can't have my staff getting upset by you. They have worked for me for years. Molly has been with me these last ten years. Now, I can dispense with you, but I can't afford to lose someone of her calibre! She's very experienced. Now, you needn't bother working out the rest of the week. You can pack up your stuff and collect your wages, I'll pay you the back week you're owed and for the rest of the week. So, go on! Get ready,' she said, throwing her head to the door. 'I'll get your wages made up for you now, you can collect it from downstairs. I'll leave it with Collette.'

'Right, OK,' was all I could say with the shock.

I stood up, walking to the door, staring at the floor, trying to take in what had just happened. I went down the stairs and through the door into the bookies, hearing the tinkle of money jangling in an aul fella's pocket as he stared, looking nervously up at the racing paper on the wall, moving himself from one side to the other, searching for a winner.

I ducked under the counter, not waiting for the girl to lift it, and went out the door, heading back to the shop. I walked through, seeing Molly serving a customer, her eyes flicking up, seeing me then suddenly looking very shifty, pretending to be all business while serving the customer and not taking any notice of me. I went up the stairs into the room and stood looking around for a few minutes. So, that's it! I'm gone from here. Just like that. I liked working in this place. Having me time off and going into town every second day, with no one to bother me.

Jesus! I'm going to have to find another job today, or I'm out on the streets! Me heart leaped with the fright. No, I'm all right. I can pay for somewhere to stay for a few nights. I have me savings and whatever Murphy gives me. OK, I had better get a move on. I've no time to waste.

I headed over and opened the wardrobe, taking out me suitcase, putting me night stuff and hot-water bottle and wash things in. I put in me two books. I haven't finished *The Carpet Baggers* yet. It's good, and I still have the second one to look forward to. Oh, me coat. I took all the stuff out again and left me green school coat sitting on the bed. Gawd, I'm still wearing that for everyday wear. But it's better then me new trench coat for keeping me warm. This one is wool. Right, I'll wear me old clothes, the ones I'm wearing now, and put the good clothes in the suitcase. I folded them, keeping them nice and neat, and put them in the suitcase, with the rest of the stuff sitting at the side. Then closed it shut and took down me handbag from the shelf in the top of the wardrobe. Nothing left! I looked up and down the wardrobe, seeing it empty, and shut it, watching it swing open.

'Right, Molly! Yer welcome to the aul wardrobe back,' I muttered, looking at me bed and stripping it. I was doing this out of habit from the convent, when we had to change the sheets. I folded the blankets and left the pillow sitting on top, and took one last look around the room. It really did grow on me, I thought, looking sadly around at the room, feeling empty at me loss. Reminded of all the happy times I spent here on me days when I had to start work in the afternoon. I never went out on that day, knowing I would have to start work at three o'clock.

Now I better go across and collect me money. I'll leave the suitcase here. I'm not going out the front carrying this, letting Molly think she's got the better of me, with her thinking I'm going with me tail between me legs. Anyway, I want to make sure Murphy gives me the money she owes me. I don't trust them bastards, not one little bit after the fast one they just pulled on me. They know only too well I was back on time. Taking the key off me was just a ruse to walk me inta a trap! Fucking Molly didn't like me, that's the long and the short of it. No matter what I did, she always found fault with me. I was quick with the till, being able to calculate a bill like greased lightning, even faster then her. I learned very fast the prices of everything, not making the same mistake twice with the ready-rubbed tobacco once I found out what was what. I even stopped eating the expensive sweets, knowing you can't do that. The first time I had the stupid idea that if you worked in a shop you could help yourself to the sweets and loose cakes. But Molly soon put a stop to me gallop there. No, she just didn't want to be working with me and having to share the room. I think she treats this shop as if it's her own, and she could run it by herself. Stand morning, noon and night behind that counter, not bothering to take her day off. She never went out anyway. So aul Murphy was right. If I had a gobshite running me shop for me like Molly, then my feet wouldn't touch the ground I'd be out the door so fast! But, then again, I don't think I would throw someone out onto the street. No, I know I wouldn't, not even for money. I'm not that bleeding heartless! I'd give them time to find another job. Me ma was right. The more money people get, the more they want!

Right, better get me money or that aul one won't be moving me until I do. So, I'm leaving me suitcase here. I went down the stairs, out the side door and across the road to the girl behind the cage. 'Hello, did she leave me wages with you?' I asked the girl, holding me breath in case of trouble.

'Yeah! Here, she left that.' I took the little brown envelope with the wages and opened it, checking to see what was in it before I left the bookies. I took out three green pound notes and four half crowns. Three-pound ten shillings? How did she work that out? A back week is three pounds and three pounds for this week. That should be six pounds. Hold on. She stopped the money for the electricity and the rent for the room in the back week. So that's one pound ten shillings she owes me. So she's giving me two quid for this week and only stopping thirty bob. OK, that will do me. 'Thanks,' I said to the girl watching me count me wages from behind her cage.

I flew back into the shop, catching Molly's eye, and she turned away from me with a shifty sleevin look on her face, expecting me to start fighting with her. I ignored her and dashed up to the room, grabbing me suitcase and lifted me handbag. I opened it and put in the three pound notes, putting them together with the ten pounds I had saved. Grand. I have thirteen pounds saved to keep me going until I get a new job. I will use the five shillings for bus fares and eating. Oh, and to buy a newspaper to look for a job. Dear God, I hope I get one today. I need somewhere to stay.

Right, have I got everything? I looked down at me handbag and suitcase sitting on the bed and checked me pockets. Me cigarettes and matches! I left them downstairs under the counter for when Molly's back was turned. Then I usually had a quick puff. Huh! I'm not leaving them behind.

I raced down the stairs and into the shop, coming up behind Molly staring at herself trying to squeeze out a blackhead in the mirror over the wall advertising Coca-Cola. 'Don't waste yer money on face powder, Molly! It's Polyfilla you need for the bleeding cracks!' I shouted up behind her. She screamed and jumped with the fright.

'Aaah! You nearly frighted the life out of me!' she roared.

I grabbed me cigarettes from under the counter and waved them at her, saying, 'Mine! Tell aul Murphy yeh don't want a cheap aul pine coffin when they carry yeh outa here, Molly. And don't forget teh tell someone where yer burying the money yeh never spend. She might spend a bit of it on a headstone for yeh. Otherwise she'll fling yeh inta a pauper's grave, yeh aul haunted and hunted-lookin spinster! Stick yer shop up yer fat arse!'

Then I was gone, hearing her spluttering insults after me, tearing meself back up the stairs and making for me suitcase. No, wait!

Them fuckers are not having the last word. I rushed over and whipped up the mattress, looking at the spring. Yeah, as I thought. The springs all tie in together! I uncurled them, taking out as many springs as I could, and put them in me bag. Then I went over to Molly's bed and pulled up the mattress. I took out seven springs, leaving a great big gaping hole in the middle, then I let the mattress fall down. It sank right in the middle, falling through to the floor. Then I flew down to the kitchen and brought back a pot of cold water and soaked the two mattresses. Now, see how you like being without a bed tonight, Molly, seeing as you're doing the same to me. And yeh can't even sleep in mine, because that's gone the same way. You too, aul Murphy. You're going to have to go out and buy a whole new bed, just to shut Molly up. That should put your nose out of joint, having to part with a few bob. Hah!

I tightened the belt around me coat and took off down the stairs again and out the side door, not letting Molly get the satisfaction of seeing me go. I stopped down the road on the way to the bus stop and took all the springs out of me pocket and handbag. Then I emptied them into an ashbin waiting outside a house for the dustbin men to collect.

Right, I'm off. I picked up me suitcase and handbag, heading down to the bus stop to wait for the bus. I better go straight into town and get the evening newspaper! Hope there's a job waiting for me. I still can't understand why they threw me out. Too much trouble? Too young? What trouble? Young? What's that got to do with anything? I did me job.

Ah, teh hell with it! Molly just didn't want me there. So forget it. Let's see what turns up next.

10

Right! Which way first? I need the evening papers. I think the *Evening Herald* is the best one for all the jobs. That won't be out for hours yet! I can go round to the delivery depot, at the back of Woolworths, when they come in. Get one before they start their deliveries. Then I'll be well ahead of the posse for any jobs going. So, what will I do for now?

I looked up and down O'Connell Street, thinking. Feeling like a lost culchie just arrived up from the bog with me suitcase in me hand. Me eyes landed on the brass-plate sign beside a hall door. 'Nelly Dobbins Domestic Agency.' Oh! She had advertisements for jobs in the newspaper last time I was looking. I'll give her a go. I went in the door, seeing it was open, and up the old rickety stairs and onto a landing. Then turned and up another flight, seeing a foggy glass door with a sign outside saying 'Nelly Dobbins, suppliers of domestic servants since 1850.' Yeah, this is it!

I knocked on the door and a woman's voice said, 'Come in!' I pushed the door in, bringing me suitcase in behind me.

'Hello,' I said, making for an elderly woman with silver-white hair tied up in a bun behind her head and a white face with the cheeks hanging down. She was wearing a navy-blue frock with a matching jacket, and a snow-white blouse underneath, with a lovely ruby and diamond brooch pinned at her throat. She smiled at me, looking over her half-moon glasses sitting on her nose.

'Can I help you?' she said, in a lovely old lady's voice.

'Yes, eh, Missus Dobbins, Nelly!' I said, sitting meself down on a chair in front of her big mahogany old desk. 'I'm looking for a domestic job, Nelly.'

'Eh, excuse me!' she said, getting a good look at me by holding down her glasses hanging on her nose. 'I'm not Nelly Dobbins,' she said, smiling at me.

'Yer not?'

'No, she was my grandmother.'

'Oh!' For a minute I was confused, wondering where I went wrong. 'Oh, yeah! Sorry! Of course you're not. Ha, ha! That would be over a hundred years ago. Sorry about that.'

'Well. You are not the first. You would be surprised the amount of women come through that door mistaking me for my grandmother! Mind you, I am called Nelly. So was my mother. The name has carried on through. So, what can I do for you?' she said, lifting her pen ready to write down me answers. 'Now, what sort of job are you looking for?'

'Eh, mother's help.'

'Do you have experience?'

'Eh, definitely. I have years of experience.'

'Oh, what age are you?'

'Eh!' I was trying to think. Should I make meself older? She might ask for me birth certificate. Then see I told her lies. 'Sixteen.'

'Hmm! You are very young. What was your last job?'

'Eh, children's nursing.'

'Oh, how long was that for? You are, after all, only sixteen!'

'Yeah, eh, I lasted a few weeks.'

'I see. What was your job before that?' she asked, looking a bit disappointed.

'Eh, I worked in a shop!'

'Oh, we don't do that sort of work here.'

'Oh, that's all right. I'm looking for something indoors. I need a live-in job.'

'Do you have references?'

'Eh, yeah . . . no!' I didn't want to show her the one from the convent.

'I don't see how I can fix you up with a job without a reference,' she said, putting down her pen, looking disappointed. Me heart sank. 'How many jobs have you had?'

'Well, I was a mother's help out in Malahide until not too long ago,' I said, hoping that would help.

'How long was that for?' she said, picking up her pen again.

'Eh, five weeks.'

'No, that's not very long. Our clients are professional people. They need a mature woman, a highly experienced housekeeper to take charge of the running of the household. Including any other staff they may employ. Like the cook, and gardener. But not all, of course. Some have small households, and may only need a general dogsbody. Someone who will cook and clean.'

'I studied cooking,' I said, thinking I had to cook for meself in the shop. 'For a little while,' I said, in case she thought I was qualified.

'How long?' she asked me, holding her breath. Not bothering to pick up the pen again.

'Eh, a few weeks.'

'Hmm, I'm sorry, but I have nothing to offer you,' she said, lifting her chest, pushing it up with her fists held together. Then letting them sit on her lap, making big sighing noises out through her nose, and looking around at her papers. Then looking up at me, widening her mouth, keeping her lips clamped together, like she was disappointed, too.

'All right! No harm in trying,' I sighed, peeling me eyes away from her, seeing no hope in her face and standing meself up. 'Thanks anyway.'

I picked up me suitcase and went out into the cold, foggy late morning. It must be hitting the twelve o'clock mark. There weren't too many people or cars around. Just buses and delivery vans flying up and down. Everyone was at work.

I stood, feeling a bit lost in meself, looking up and down the Liffey, staring into the rushing water passing under the bridge. Hearing the mournful sound of the fog horn crying, from way out at sea. The sound was getting carried up the Liffey, making itself heard loud and clear. It cut through me then lingered on the air. I listened, holding me breath, hearing it sigh away. Leaving me with the terrible feeling of loneliness and the empty streets. With little sign of life around me, to help block it out. What can I do in a hurry to find a job? Nothing! I'll just have to wait for the newspapers.

At last, I've got the newspaper! I hurried out of the lane and around by the GPO and stopped at the footpath, with me head flying up and down the street, getting ready to dash across the road. I took off, ducking in and out of the traffic and across the road into Caffola's.

I grabbed a seat at the back, putting down me suitcase and left me handbag sitting beside me, and whipped open the newspaper. Vacancies! What page? Here we are. Me eyes slid up and down the pages, looking for 'Domestics Wanted'. 'Housekeeper.' No! 'Woman wanted for cleaning and some light cooking. Live out.' No! 'Mother's help! Girl wanted to help mother with children, live in. Tipperary.' Fuck! No good. I'm not living in the country. 'Cleaning woman, afternoons or mornings. Must be flexible. May be asked to do occassional plain cooking.' No! 'Training given to factory girl. Good starting wage. One pound ten shillings per week.' No good.

Fuck, there's nothing! Sweet divine Jesus! There's no job for me. What am I going to do now? Even factory work doesn't pay. Young ones like me are usually classed as training, they don't pay much and, anyway, the girls live at home. Damn! I haven't even got a reference. Except the one from the bloody convent. That will only get me housework anyway. Then they make an eejit out of yeh! I heard that too often from the other big girls when they came back. Even the aul fellas, the husbands, tried to get their hands on them. Some of the girls sit, nursing themselves for weeks trying to get over the shock of it. Fuck! I'd like to see one of the aul husbands try that one on me! They would be fucking limpin for the rest of their life. Hmm, I wonder! Maybe the nun in charge of the children, Sister Mary Ann Augusta, will take me back for a little while, just until I get a job. It will only be for a few nights! I should have something by then. Yeah! Please, God, she'll let me. I have nowhere else to go!

Right! I whipped up me suitcase and made for the other side of

O'Connell Street again. Flying into the GPO. This place is great for making a phone call. They have lines and lines of boxes where you can shut the door and talk in private.

I dropped the two pennies into the coin box and dialled the number. I waited, hearing it ring, and held me breath, me heart going like the clappers. Jaysus! Wonder what she will say to me? It's an awful pity Sister Eleanor is away. 'Hello, yes? Holy Redeemer Convent.'

I pressed the A button, trying to get me breath. 'Eh, hello! Can I speak to Sister Mary Ann Augusta, please?'

'Who is this?' I listened to the voice. Fuck! It's Sister Benedict, the nun in charge of the chapel. She will only want to know me business.

'Eh, it's personal!' I said, not breathing.

'Is this one of the children?' she roared.

'No,' I squeaked, knowing the nuns wouldn't come to the phone for one of us.

'Speak up! I can't hear you!' she roared down the phone at me.

'Is Sister Augusta available?' I asked in a high-pitched voice, trying to change me voice and sound like someone important.

She listened, I could hear her breathing. 'MARTHA LONG! Is that you?'

'Eh, yeah, Sister Benedict. I'm looking for Sister Eleanor or Sister Augusta.'

'They're not here! Sister Eleanor is away getting her retreat, and Sister Augusta is out getting her office. She's praying along the cloister walk. What do you want? Is it important? Will it wait?'

'No, Sister Benedict. Could you please get her for me?' I asked, wanting to get hopeful.

'No, hang on. Here's the reverend mother. You can speak to her.'

I listened as she dropped the phone and shouted to the reverend mother, 'There's a phone call from Martha Long, mother. She wants to speak to the sisters in charge of the children. I told her Sister Eleanor is away, and sister-in-charge is getting her prayers. She won't take no for an answer.'

'Really!' I heard the reverend mother breathe, making to take up the phone. Me heart stopped, and I dropped the phone back into its cradle like it had scalded me. I picked up me suitcase and took off out of the phone box, dashing to get out among people again. No! I want no part of them nuns. They start treating you like they own you, if they think you can't manage. It's better to stay out of their clutches. There's no point in turning back. So what goes for Jackser, goes for them. I can add them to me list.

What was I bleedin thinking? Just hearing them speak brought back all the years of Jackser and being locked up with them. I'd rather sleep on the bloody streets than ask them to take me back. But they have jobs coming in occasionally. That would be my best bet. Ask them if any jobs came in from people looking for girls. Right! But I'll ask Sister Eleanor when she gets back. Damn! When will that be? I didn't even get to find that much out. Bloody eejit, Martha, wake up. So, now I need to find somewhere to live.

'How much is it for bed and breakfast for one night?' I asked the country woman with the sleevin eyes. Narrowing, taking me in, and wondering how much she can rob me for.

'Thirty shillings bed and breakfast,' she said, with a greasy smell coming off her, and the sudden whiff of bad breath, from a mouthful of rotten teeth. She's not very clean, I thought, pulling back as she moved herself closer to me. Bringing the sour smell of cats' piss and rotten cabbage with her. I stared at her as I was thinking about it. While she held the door half-shut, pulling it out behind her. Then she folded her arms and leaned out, whipping her eyes up and down Talbot Street. Then pinning them back on me, waiting.

'No, thanks! That's too dear,' I said, walking away from her.

'Suit yourself,' she said, slamming the front door shut after me.

'Fuck you too, missus! Yeh money-hungry-fucking-looking aul cow!' I fumed. Feeling dead tired after walking the length and breadth of the streets, knocking on one bed and breakfast house after another, looking for something cheap.

Ah, bloody hell! There's no way out of it. I think I'll take the boat to England, I have a better chance of getting a job over there. I walked on, heading back up to O'Connell Street. Going nowhere in a hurry, and slowed down to think about it. I could take the boat to Liverpool and the train to London. When I get to Euston Station, the first thing I should do is look for a room to stay. Then go out searching for a job. Right! That's what I'm doing.

I took off, hurrying to get over to the ticket office on Westmoreland Street before they close. Jaysus! It must be after five o'clock. I wonder if it's half-five or six o'clock they shut. What time is it? I don't want to spend another night in this fucking kip of a country. It's run by greedy, grasping fucking culchies! The Dubliners never get a look-in. I felt raging in meself, not knowing who or what I was raging with. With meself for losing the job, and everyone else for looking out for themselves. Especially that fucking Molly one! Ah, let them. I'll get there! I know something will turn up. Yeah, England is me best bet. I felt meself lifting, knowing now I knew what I was doing and where I was going.

I crossed over O'Connell Bridge and made me way onto Westmoreland Street. Stopping to wait for the traffic lights to change, so I could get over to the booking office on the other side of the street. Suddenly, I heard me name shouted. I whirled around with the shock, wondering where the voice was coming from. 'Martha Long! What are you doing? Where are you going?' I looked up in shock at the face staring at me, looking from me suitcase then back to me, a smile plastered all over her face.

'Laura! It's great to see you,' I shouted happily, delighted to meet someone I knew from the convent.

'Where are you off to, Martha?' she said, looking at me puzzled, seeing me suitcase.

'Ah, Laura, I lost me job, and I'm stuck. I'm heading off to get me ticket to take the boat to England. I'm going to London.'

'No, you're not!' she snapped, grabbing the suitcase out of me hand. 'Come on! You're coming with us.'

I looked at Anna Brennan, standing beside her, 'Yeah, why not! The more the merrier,' she laughed, shaking her head.

Then Laura wrapped her arm around me shoulder, pulling me into her. 'Listen, Martha,' she said, shaking her head slowly, looking very serious as she leaned her head closer into me. 'London would only swallow you up! It's a very big place, and you don't know anyone there. An awful lot of people from the convent get lost there. Some of the girls who went from our group have got themself into a terrible lot of trouble, and that's only the ones we hear about. I heard of one girl turning up with a baby in her arms. The fella she was living with dumped her. The nuns turned her away from the door. Now she's on the game. Some of them have even ended up shut away in the laundry. But they're a bit before our time. No, forget that idea. Give it a few years, you are still only finding your feet.' Then she pulled me tighter into her and dragged me off down the road, away from Westmoreland Street and the ticket office for the boat to London.

I hesitated, pulling away from her, looking back at the ticket office. 'Ah, yeah, Laura, I know what you're saying. But it would make no difference to me. I don't know anyone even here. Never mind London. I have a better chance of getting a job over there,' I said, looking at her watching me carefully. I wanted to believe she was right I should stay here. But I still thought I should take the chance.

'Don't talk rubbish. You have us now. Let's get going,' she said, laughing and grabbing me arm. Taking off down the road again.

'Listen, Martha. Wait until you hear this! We have just gotten a flat for three. But there's five of us and the landlady is very old.'

'Yeah, and deaf,' laughed Anna.

'Yeah, and half-blind,' Laura sniffed, rolling her eyes over to us and stretching her face. Looking like it was the end of the world. 'So she won't notice two more of us,' Laura breathed, talking in one breath. Then throwing her neck back, screaming her head off with the laughing. Swinging herself and me, bouncing us against each other. Making her lovely blonde hair flop like mad around her shoulders, and her eyes danced in her head, shining with the devilment. Then stopping to look at me, staring into me eyes. 'The landlady lives downstairs, we have two huge rooms upstairs. One bedroom with three beds, and a big sitting room. You should see the size of it, Martha! It's only massive!' she said, holding out her arms to show me.

'Really? If it's that big,' I said, thinking, 'you could nip down to the convent while Sister Eleanor is away and borrow the new record player I heard they got for Christmas. You could hold a dance in the sitting room and charge people to get in.'

'Are you serious?' they laughed. Staring at me with their eyes hanging out of their head.

'Yeah! Why not?' I laughed. Getting the picture of us flying down the avenue with the record player under our arms, and the young ones screaming their heads off, tearing down after us. 'We all need the money!' I said, looking serious, beginning to think it was a good idea.

'Yeah!' Laura said, looking like she, too, was thinking that it could be a good idea.

Anna stared at us with her mouth open and suddenly let out a roar. 'Would you two stop talking rubbish! The pair of you are out of your minds. Sure the landlady lives under the place and we would be kicked out so fast we'd all end up on the streets before we know where we are. Come on! You better behave yourself, Martha Long. Don't go putting mad ideas into Laura's head here. That one is worse than you. She's always getting us into trouble. We lost the last job because of her!' snorted Anna. Walking off ahead of us. 'Hurry,' she said, looking back at us. 'It's over in Harold's Cross. Come on! We'll get the bus.'

'You can take Harriet Miller's place, she's not coming until Saturday morning. So you should be OK until then,' Laura said, sitting beside me on the bus.

'Right! By then I should have found another job with living-in,' I said. Feeling very happy with me good fortune at meeting Laura and Anna.

'Right, girls. This is our stop,' Anna said, standing up and walking down to the platform, waiting for the bus to stop. We jumped off and I followed behind.

'We're here! This is the house. Now shush! Don't make any noise,' Laura said, going up the stone steps to a big house and putting the key into a heavy green door. The paint was peeling off the door and the windows looked like they were ready to fall out, the wood was that rotten. Laura watched me face, seeing I wasn't thinking much of the place as I looked around, taking everything in. Then I clapped eyes on a huge rat as big as a cat, diving out from under a pile of rubbish sitting under the basement window.

'Ah, Jaysus! This place reminds me of the old tenements we used to live in. Me and the ma and Charlie.'

'It's very handy for the bus. We just have to cross over to the other side of the road, and it gets us into town in no time,' Laura whispered.

'Shush, say nothing. The landlady is probably looking up from the basement,' Anna said, pointing down the steps.

We walked into a long hall, with the floorboards giving out from under us. Three cats came crawling up the basement stairs, crying, and looking like they might spring at us any minute. 'I'm afraid of cats . . . and dogs, girls,' I whispered, not taking me eyes off the cats.

'I don't believe it. Martha Long is actually afraid of something,' giggled Laura, creeping up the stairs. I followed up behind them and stopped on a landing. Waiting for them to open the door into the flat. '"Come into my parlour," said the spider to the fly,' moaned Laura, making a face, then laughing at us.

'Gawd! It's like a ballroom,' I said, looking around at the size of the big room. It had no furniture, and was a bit dark. The window looked out to the back garden, and it was overgrown with bushes going in all directions, growing into each other. I looked over at the big grey marble fireplace, and the two armchairs each side with the long aul couch in the middle. The place looked very bare, and when we walked on the floorboards they sprang up and down, giving me the feeling I was going to start flying through the air. Landing meself splattered in the room underneath. The noise we made echoed around the room. I looked at the wallpaper, seeing it was very old and faded. It's nearly brown, but I could see it had been red once, with little flowers in it that had faded away to nothing.

'This is grand. At least you all have a roof over your heads,'

I said. Following them into the big bedroom. I looked around at three battered old wooden beds. With a press built into two alcoves, one each end of the room, with two beds in the middle and one just inside the door. 'Where will I sleep, Laura?' I asked, wondering how five people were going to fit into three big single beds.

'You can have that one behind the door. We'll double up with Linda and Tricia.'

'Great!' I said happily. Shoving me case under the bed without opening it. Feeling delighted at getting a bed to meself. I didn't fancy sharing with anyone! 'How much rent a week are you paying for this, girls?' I asked.

'Seven pounds ten shillings a week!'

'Jaysus! That's very dear altogether.'

'Yeah, that's why we need five of us. Three of us on our own couldn't manage the rent!'

'Yeah, you're right,' I said. Thinking I would never have a chance on me own. I'm really surprised they let me stay with them. The convent girls are not too fond of me normally. I suppose everyone has changed, now we're all out on our own.

I sat down on the steps of the Liffey, looking down at the water. 'Ah, no! Don't jump! Whatever it is, it's not worth it!' an aul fella carrying a load of paper bags and weighed down with a mound of coats roared down the steps at me.

I jumped. Nearly falling with the fright. 'Ah, help, Mammy!' I moaned, looking down at the water, not realising I was only two steps away from falling in. 'Bleedin hell, mister! You nearly put the heart crossways in me,' I said, jumping up with the fright and making me way up the steps away from the Liffey. 'Jaysus! You shouldn't shout like that. I nearly ended up in the drink. That's if I didn't first lay plastered to the ground, stone dead,' I said, holding me hand on me chest. 'I'm afraid of me life of water! I can't swim!' I moaned, staring at him. With me heart rattling in me chest.

'Well, then, that's no place teh be sittin there! Wha ails yeh?'

'Who says there's anything ailing me?' I said. Looking into the face of the down-and-out I robbed all the food for when I was in the convent.

'God almighty! It's yerself! The very lovely little angel that gave me the pile a grub when the stomach was hanging outa me for the want a something teh eat! I never forgot yeh, yeh know! I lit a candle for you down in the Adam and Eve's Church the very next day.'

I felt a lovely heat flying around me, and me chest lift with the happiness of having someone think that much of me. But all I could say was, 'Thanks, mister,' I whispered, looking inta his lovely faded blue eyes that looked really tired and worn out. They must have been sky blue at one time. He stared back at me, straight into me eyes, leaning his head forward. Wondering what was the matter with me, like he could sense all wasn't well with me.

'Go on, chicken! Yeh can tell me whatever is going on in yer mind,' he whispered, looking like he really was worried about me. I could feel meself near to tears. That he remembered me, and he wanted to help me. I couldn't bring meself to say what was on me mind. 'Well, would yeh credit tha now? Imagine meeting you after all this time,' he said, trying to get us talking.

'Ah, I'm delighted to see you, too,' I said. Getting me voice back. Then looking down, seeing his feet was all black and blue and swollen badly from the walking and the frost. 'How's the feet?' I said, staring down at them. The top of the boots was burst in all directions, and he had the bit of leather that was left, tied on with string.

'Ah, Jaysus, child! Don't be askin. I'm wonderin how long more it is before I won't be able teh get one foot in front a the other!'

'Listen! Why don't you take yourself up to Jervis Street Hospital? You need to get them feet seen to!'

'Ah, I have no time for hospitals. Sure all they'll do is put a bit of ointment on them, maybe throw on a bandage, then I won't be able teh walk at all!'

'Well, will we go and find out? I'll come with you. I'm doing nothing. I've given up for the day, everything is closing up now. I'm trying to find work and I'm having no luck! So I might as well get something good out of the day. Come on! Sure it's not far. I'll take you over.'

'Ah, I won't, angel. Let me sit down over here on this bench and get the weight offa me feet.' I followed him over to the bench on the other side of the street. Watching him swing from side to side, trying to balance the pain in his feet. With his paper bags swinging out behind him. 'So, wha has yeh down these parts?' he said, settling himself on the bench and putting his bags on the other side, making room for me to sit down.

'I've left the convent,' I said. Seeing him give me all his attention, really looking like he wanted to know. 'I lost the job working in a shop. They threw me out. Because I wasn't what they were looking for. I've been searching the papers and walking the streets, hoping to find something. But nothing's turned up. I need a job living-in. Cleaning, and minding children, something like that. I can't live-out because the wages are too low, and I haven't any experience to get a better-paid job. Well, enough anyway to afford a bedsitter.'

He scratched his neck and stared at the ground, shaking his head, looking very sad. 'God, chicken! Have yeh no one teh go to?'

'No, I don't know anyone.'

'Wha about friends? Have yeh anyone there?'

'No, I talk to people. I enjoy a bit of company,' I said, looking at him. 'But I haven't really got a friend.' I said, thinking about that. Wondering why that was.

'You know, I was in the same boat as yerself many, many years ago now. God, that's going back,' he said. With his eyes beginning to look far-away. 'Yes, indeed I was,' he muttered quietly, his eyes searching the ground, like he was trying to find an answer to something. 'It was back in the 1920s. I came down this very road,' he said, lifting his head and pointing back up the quays. 'Heading for the mailboat to England, I was. I had just arrived up from Connemara, the arsehole of nowhere! Oh, a godforsaken place,' he said, shaking his head, looking down at the ground. 'It was so barren, even Jesus Christ himself wouldn't touch the place. God forgive me,' he said, blessing himself. 'It was the day I turned sixteen.

I arrived in a grey-hair suit. With me head shaved and a pound note in me pocket. I had a ticket for the boat teh Liverpool an the train to take me teh London, an a letter in me pocket with the last known address of me mother. After leaving Letterfrack, I was. The worst hell-hole that man could invent. Like animals we were treated. Not innocent childre. A dumping ground for all the sins an the dirt this bloody hypocritical people wanted teh hide away. Dirt! An the sins of our mothers! That's wha we were classed as. That's wha them bastards the brothers called us. It was run by vicious bog ignorant lunatics. Fellas tha came in off the land. The only notion on how teh act was wha they learned from watchin the animals in the farmyard. Devils spawned from hell, them Christian brothers were. Kids died like flies in that place. It was from the cold an all the beatings. Some childre were too weak. Run down from all the hardship, an the lack a proper nourishment. They just upped an died. That's one way teh escape, I suppose,' he said, looking like this idea had just occurred to him this minute.

I stared at him. Seeing him completely lost in himself. He was gone from me. Forgetting I was sitting here listening to him. He stared at the ground, with his face creased up in terrible pain. Remembering that time all them years ago. I said nothing. Just waited. Letting him have his thoughts. Then he shifted himself, moving his hands folded across his knees, and lifted his head slightly to me.

'Well, there I was, after stepping off the train an arriving here in Dublin. Jaysus! There wasn't much of it teh be seen. The whole place was bombed teh nothing. Fallin down around the ears of people, it was. Yeh see, there had been a civil war. That's what a man told me. When I went lookin for somethin teh eat. "Where's the nearest eatin house?" I asked him. We got talkin, an that was all the first I'd ever heard about any war goin on in Ireland. A nice aul Dublin man, he was. But deh yeh know what he said teh me?'

'No,' I said, looking at him lifting his head, watching me. Waiting to see what I thought about what he was going to tell me next.

'Well, tha Dublin man stood there lookin me up an down. From me shaved head down to me big black cob-nailed boots. Then, after a minute, sez he teh me, "Do yeh mind me askin, but are you just after bein let out a one a them reformatory places in the country?" Jaysus! I was quarely gobsmacked, I can tell you that!'

'Yeah, it was the way you were dressed,' I said. We could tell by them straight away. A young fella who was just let out of a reformatory. It was the shaved head and the suit and the boots. 'I know of that place, mister! I knew loads of young fellas who were locked up there.'

'Indeed you do. Most of the young fellas were from Dublin, mainly bunged in for robbin, God help them. But I was put there as a bastard. Me mother had put me there. She had teh. Then she took off for England. Deh yeh know, I went and tracked her down. I moved the length an breadth a England on her trail. I kept meself goin by workin on buildin an farm labourin an anythin I could get teh keep body and soul together. Sometimes sleepin rough. A lot of times sleepin in barns on the hay. The aul farmer would let me after givin him a day's work. Plus me bit a grub. Then eventually I found her. It took me seven year. She was be then livin in Norfolk. On the sea. It was the sorriest day I ever did. She wanted nothin teh do wit me, I was the past for her. From tha day on, I felt there was nothin left for me. The thought a findin her an makin everythin right. I thought everythin would fall inta place. Then I would be happy. All I had teh do was find me mother. Now tha was left me. I had nothin left teh search for. I turned me back on the world. I was never the same. I only wanted me own company. An tha's the way it's been ever since. I just kept movin. Never stoppin in the one place too long.'

'So you never settled down, got married and had children?' I whispered. Me heart breaking for him.

'No, angel, I did not.'

'Was it brutal for yeh?' I whispered.

'Brutal!' he muttered, lowering his head gently, and closing his eyes.

'I think I know what them Christian brothers were like,' I muttered, thinking of Jackser. 'But it didn't make you vicious?' I said, looking inta his sad and gentle eyes.

'No!' was all he said.

We sat in silence watching it get darker, and colder. I didn't want to move. I felt warm, sitting with the old man. We understood each other. I knew he cared, and I felt his pain. It was nice to feel I wasn't alone. Yeah, he knows I understand him, too.

'I only sat on the steps down there to get away for a while,' I said quietly, looking at him.

'From people?' he said.

'Yeah!' I smiled. 'I just wanted to be by meself and think. Everyone seems to be rushing somewhere, having somewhere to go, or someone waiting on them. I wanted to stop seeing that for a little while,' I whispered. Seeing him shake his head, knowing what I was on about.

'Where will you sleep tonight?' I asked him.

'Oh, I'll head over to the Back Lane Hostel over in the Liberties, or maybe down to the Ivy Hostel. One or the other will do me! That area is me usual haunt.'

'Yeah, that's where I come from,' I said. 'I was born in the Liberties.'

'A very noble, honourable people, the Liberty people,' he said, shaking his head. 'That's where you get yer lovely manner from. All the Liberty people have that special way. There's a certain noble way in their character you won't find anywhere else!'

I listened, feeling delighted, and warm inside meself. 'Yeah, they are very kind people,' I said. Remembering how good they were to me when I was a little child.

'Angel, I want you to mind yourself. Trust no one! At least not until they prove to you they can be trusted. I'll be lookin out for yeh. I'm goin teh be keepin yeh in me prayers when I do be goin inta the church teh say the odd prayer. Now, more importantly, get in outa the rain,' he laughed, showing his black teeth. I didn't mind. He has a lovely smile anyway. It lit up his lovely blue eyes. 'Go on,' he said, shifting himself, trying to get to his feet. 'You better get movin before the night settles in. Where are yeh headin now?' he said, looking at me.

'I'm staying in a flat for now. With some girls from the convent.

Listen, mister,' I said, putting me hand on his arm, 'I'm feeling a lot better now, after sitting with you. Thanks very much, for being so good to me,' I said, smiling at him. Feeling warmer in meself. 'And did you want to know something else?' I said, feeling shy at saying this. But I wanted to. 'I love the way you call me "angel" It . . . makes me feel special somehow,' I said. Feeling really embarrassed.

He stared at me for a minute, taking in what I said. Then he took me arm, laying his thick black hand caked with the dirt ever so gently on me hand, letting it sit there. I stared at it. Seeing how thick and swollen it was. But I could feel the strength and the gentleness of him coming through in that hand. 'Listen, chicken. You are an angel. I saw that the first time I looked inta yer face. Even without the grub, I knew you were one in a million. I've come across a lot of people in me time. Some were good, and some were very bad. Then again, I've met some real saints. But you have the soul of an angel. You're very special,' he whispered, leaning into me. 'Another thing I'm goin teh tell yeh. I don't waste me time talkin teh people in any depth. In fact, I have very little teh do with people if I can help it. So now yeh know! Tha makes you even more special. Now! Let's get goin outa this cold before we all catch our death. I think now is a good time to be makin tracks. So I'll make me way back over to the Liberties. Which way are you goin?'

'I'm heading up to get the bus for Harold's Cross,' I said, waiting for him.

'You go on then. I want teh make me way in me own time. I'll say goodbye to yeh,' he said. Waving his bags at me, and took off slowly. Twisting himself from right to left, trying to make his way in terrible pain. I walked on ahead, looking back and waving, giving him a big smile. Then took off up the quays, hurrying to get back to the flat and the girls. Poor man, he's at the end of his days. He's one of the loveliest people I have met in a long time. If people only knew. You have to get beyond the smell and the dirt. Then you meet someone that makes life worth living.

So that's how you end up becoming a down-and-out! You just

stop bothering! I always wondered about that. Why people don't try to make a home for themself. Me and the ma were different. We were looking for a home. Ah, Gawd love him. The life just went out of him, after the shock of his mammy not wanting him. Fuck! I would never bother wanting to know who me aul fella was. If he was any good in the first place, he wouldn't have run off leaving me ma carrying me in her belly. So fuck him! Whoever he is. He caused me ma all the trouble in the first place. So I don't want to know the bastard.

I woke up hearing noises. I lifted me head off the pillow, looking around, seeing girls shifting their heads and squinting at the door. I whirled me head around, seeing a little old woman with stone-grey thin hair pulled up in a bun making her way in the door.

'No! I'm not having this. I've counted five people in these beds. There's only supposed to be three of you. You can all get out! I want you all out of this flat today! Now get up, the lot of you, and get moving off my property.'

'Who is it?'

'What's happening?' people muttered. Trying to open their eyes from the sleep and make out what's going on.

'It's the landlady. Girls! We're caught,' someone muttered. I stuck me head back under the bedclothes, feeling me heart sinking. Ah, bloody hell! That's the end of me. I'm out on me arse! Still, today is Saturday. I knew I was going to have to go anyway. I don't want to be here when that mad cow Harriet Miller turns up this morning. I'm sleeping in her bed. Jaysus! She will go mental when she hears that. That one never liked me. I had to do all her work *and* me own when we were in the convent. Everyone was afraid of her bad temper. Especially Sister Eleanor. But, then again, she really liked the Miller one. She was her favourite. Harriet darling this. And Harriet darling that! It used to make me sick listening to the pair of them throwing bouquets at each other. They had a mutual-admiration society going for themselves. That Sister Eleanor thought the sun shined out of Miller's fat arse. That's why I ended up getting stuck with all her work. But I wasn't afraid of her. Oh no, not me! I made mincemeat outa her when she crossed me. Ah, I have had enough of that carry on.

There's going to be skin, teeth and hair flying when they all wake up and come to their senses and it dawns on them they were just flung out on their arses. Fuck! Especially when Miller gets here. Expecting to have a welcome party waiting for her. Only to be told, I can hear it now, 'No, sorry, Etta' – that's what her friends call her – 'we can't stay! The landlady has just thrown us out!'

'Why?'

'Because we had too many in the flat. Martha Long was sleeping in your bed!'

'WHAT?'

'Yeah! Well, yeh see, we found her rambling around town . . .'

'SO WHAT?'

'So we let her stay . . . in your bed!'

Right, I better make meself scarce. What will I do? Get meself off into town and ring Sister Eleanor. Oh, please, God, grant she's back in the convent, and she will be able to get me a job.

I threw off the bedclothes, hearing them all arguing. 'Whose idea was it to invite that Long one?' I threw me eye over in the direction of the roar. Seeing the Linda Bradshaw one suddenly wake herself up, flying her finger at me. 'Without her being here, the landlady wouldn't have thrown us out!' she roared, squinting at me with her lip curled up.

'Don't worry,' Laura said, yawning and throwing the bedclothes back. 'I'll say we just invited a few friends to stay. You all missed your bus home and we're sorry. It won't happen again. We will just have to hide when she's coming.'

'What do you mean hide? I'm not hiding when I'm paying the rent!'

'Well, some of us will have to!' shouted Laura.

'How can we, when she has the key and sneaks in when we're all sleeping?'

'Thanks, Laura, for letting me stay,' I said, putting on me clothes and grabbing me suitcase to make me way out of here.

'I'm sorry we can't let you stay, Martha, but there's too many of us as it is,' she said, wrinkling her face at me, and screwing her eyes up.

'Yeah, one too many,' muttered Bradshaw, examining a dirty jumper, deciding to turn it back to front, and snorting over at me. Making her hatchet face look even uglier than it is.

'Ah, no,' I said, ignoring the cow and talking to Laura. 'I understand, Laura. It was very good of you to let me stay in the first place. Thanks a million for everything. I'm off. I'll probably see you around,' I said, making me way out the door, feeling glad to be going.

I don't want to hang around with them miserable cows. They would put years on you, with the moaning and fighting and dirty looks they give you. Except Laura and Anna. They're very nice. But the rest can go and fuck themself! Anywhere and nowhere is better then having to put up with the likes of them.

II

Right, here we go! I pushed me way up O'Connell Street, hanging onto last night's *Evening Herald*, held tight under me arm. Diving in and out of the Saturday shoppers, with everyone in a rush for the shops, hoping to get in and out before the crowds started pouring in. Only everyone had the same idea at the same time. Now we were all falling over each other.

'Mind me legs wit tha bleedin case a yours!'

'Sorry, missus,' I said to the aul one with a dying-looking face on her, after she sent me flying with a push because I bumped her legs.

She stopped to look down at her nylons. 'Looka! Yer after givin me a ladder in me new nylons,' she snorted, looking down at the ladder snaking itself up her right leg. 'The curse a Jaysus on yeh,' she muttered, fixing the brown mohair hat on her head, and looking at me with two crossed eyes.

'Well, pity about you and your nylons,' I snorted. 'It was an accident. You ran into me an that serves yeh right for pushing me,' I said. Giving her a dirty look and rushing into the GPO to ring about the job working in an Italian fish-and-chip shop I just saw in last night's paper. God, it was lucky I spotted that! It wasn't in the domestic section. It goes to show you. I should never take anything for granted. You have to go through the whole paper with a fine-tooth comb. Oh, dear God, grant that I may get the job. If I do, then that means I won't have to bother ringing Sister Eleanor and get the ear blasted offa me.

'Allo!'

'Yeah, hello. I'm ringing about the job you advertised, looking for a girl to work in the fish-and-chip café! Is the job still vacant?'

'You wait a minute. I get the wife to talk wit you. She know about dis.'

'Hellooo!'

'Yes, I'm ringing about the job. Is it still vacant?' I held me breath, squeezing the phone tight, waiting with me mouth open.

'Yes, I look for someone. Ave you got the experience working in a café before?'

'Yes, oh indeed I have. I'm very experienced!'

'You sound young! How old are you?'

'Me, no, I'm working for years. I'm sixteen.'

'How long you working?'

'Eh, three years. Straight after I left school.'

'You leave the school at thirteen?'

'Eh, yeah, well . . . I thought I was fourteen at the time.'

'OK, I don't care. I just want ta know you are not stupid. Can you count? You know how to work the cash register?'

'Yes, I'm very quick.'

'Do you have references? Where you work last?'

'Eh, can I come down and see you? It would be easier if you could meet me face to face.'

'OK, you can start today, I will give you a trial. If I don't like you, you go out the door. No messing! The job is live-in with the family. You free to do that?'

'Yes, that will suit me down to the ground,' I said.

'OK, see you around four o'clock. Goodbye.'

'Bye!' I roared as she hung up the phone. I got the job! Oh, my God! I have a job. And in a café! I just can't believe me good luck.

I hopped off the bus in Hangman's Wood, seeing the row of shops. Oh, there's the supermarket where I used to rob me butter. Bloody hell! I spent one time sitting half the night in a police station after getting picked up with a load a butter in me bag. The shop called the police after I made out the door with them chasing after me. The two aul fellas ran like the hammers of hell after me, but they didn't catch me. I ducked back later, and picked up the rest of me butter that I had hidden under the wheels of a car parked down a laneway. That's when I got picked up by the coppers. Walking along in the dark evening with me bag full of butter. They spent the time driving around trying to spot me. They struck lucky. I spent the rest of the night haggling with a lovely-looking copper with snow-white curly hair being very nice to me. Because he was trying to get me to admit I'd robbed the lot. I wouldn't give in, knowing they had no proof. Because most of the butter didn't belong to the shop that got me arrested. In the end, I admitted to robbing the butter only from that shop. I ended up in court for that anyway. But I managed to hold onto the sixteen other pounds of butter. Yer man kept telling me he had children too. He only wanted to help me! I didn't believe a word out of his mouth. He was a copper. They would sell their own mothers to make a case. But I liked him anyway! He was very nice to me. Yeah!

I gave a big sigh of contentment as I headed into the fish-and-chip shop with the café. Knowing that other life was all behind me, and here I was out on me own. Making me own way in the world, with no one to tell me what I can and can't do. Life is definitely a bowl of cherries!

I stood in front of the counter, waiting while the Italian fella with the jet-black wavy hair, slicked back with half a bottle of Brylcreem emptied on his head, finished serving a customer. 'Yes, what you want?' he said, throwing his head back, looking at me with big brown chocolate-drop eyes, then smacking a load of chips into the shelf under the window for everyone to see what they were getting.

'I'm looking for your mammy. She told me to start working here today.'

'Who? The boss? She not my mamma! You stupid? Do I looka like her? My mamma, she a saint,' he said mournfully. 'She back in Calabria,' he said, stabbing me with his eyes. Then whacking the hell out of the chips floating around in the boiling oil. Smacking the side of the metal handle of the spoon on the side of the fryer, trying to take lumps out of it.

Jaysus! I only asked him a civil question, I thought. Staring up at him, looking like he had the world on his shoulders. 'OK! No need to be so touchy,' I said quietly, wanting him to know I wasn't trying to annoy him on purpose. 'So, can you tell the boss I'm here? She's expecting me.'

He let out an unmerciful roar in me ear. Shouting in Italian at someone inside a room. Then went back to humping his cooked chips inside the hot shelf under the window.

'Si?' shouted a huge fat Italian mamma, coming to see what he wanted. She stood at the door into the back room, drying her hands on a dishcloth, listening to him sounding like he was giving out and throwing the head at me. I stood with me case in me hand and waited while she took me in from head to toe. Staring at me with an inquisitive look on her face. 'You the one about the job?'

'Yes, I rang you. I'm here now at four o'clock as you told me to be,' I said, smiling happily at her.

'Come on through,' she said, flipping her hand at the touchy fella to lift the counter and let me in. 'Come on, come in!' she roared, waving her head at me, with the eyes never leaving me for a minute. Then she waddled off with me trailing in behind her, banging me suitcase against the touchy fella's legs, with him standing there. Right in me way, gaping at me with his mouth open.

We headed into a sitting room that was a bit dark. I squinted around, trying to get me sight back after walking in from the bright lights in the shop. She pulled out a chair sitting under a big old table covered in a heavy wine tablecloth with tassels on the end, and a white linen lace cloth sat on top. 'Sit down,' she said, waving at me and heaving her huge heavy body into a chair that rocked and creaked. Then she steadied herself as she spread her arse, and lifted her big massive milkers, letting them drop and sink down onto the table. I watched as she leaned across with her tree-trunk arms to move a big red vase, stuffed with plastic roses covered in dust, so we could get a better look at each other across the table. I sat looking around at all the heavy old furniture. Two big armchairs sat, one each side of the fireplace, and two china dogs slobbered on the hearth. I looked around at the dark wine heavy flock wallpaper, with loads of pictures on the wall of the family. I suppose that's who they are.

I stared up at the big one hanging over the fireplace, of a granny and granddad sitting up straight on two chairs. With sons and daughters standing behind them, and grandchildren resting their elbows on the grandparents' laps. Everyone was looking very serious, like they didn't trust the fella taking the photograph. They stood up straight, staring at the camera, looking very uncomfortable in their best clothes. With the men wearing hats, and suits that were too big for them. The women and girls wore black frocks, and had sulky looks on their faces. Much as to say to the fella taking the photograph, 'I have to wear my best frock. I'm looking beautiful, but there is no one to admire me. No, I am cheated. I just stand here looking so good for this ugly little midget!'

The two little girls wore white frocks with white ribbons in their hair. They were tied up in a big bow that stood standing straight up on top of their heads. They looked like they wanted to smile, with the merriment dancing in their eyes, and their mouths ready to break out with all the laughing. But they didn't. They held their faces fast on the camera, because someone would only shout, 'Don't smile! This is serious business! We don't a want a make ourselves look like a the fools!'

They didn't look very well-off to me. The suits hung off their skinny bodies, making them get completely lost. All you could see was a head, a few fingers sticking out of the sleeves, and the toe of the shoes. Because the trousers landed in rolls, burying their feet. That made me think they must have got the stuff from some rich people. Maybe rich relatives living in America, who were in the Mafia. Yeah, that could be it. I leaned me head over for a better look. Yeah, them suits certainly do look American all right. But most certainly, whoever owned them suits, they were better fed than this lot. The younger ones stood with their thumbs stuck in their breeches, trying to make themselves look manly.

'So, how long you work in your last job?' said the aul one, making me jump and turn me head to land back on her. I was forgetting for a minute what I was supposed to be here for. After letting meself get carried away, trying to make out the family in the photograph. I blinked, trying to take her in. The room was getting darker suddenly, with the heavy old curtains pulled tight across, not letting in any light. I wonder why she doesn't bother to switch on the light. Maybe she's sparing the electricity. Jackser used to do that. Saying we'd be cut off if we didn't spare it.

'Eh, nearly two years.'

'You got references?' she said, holding out her hand.

Oh, fuck! Here we go. I thought she said on the phone I had the job. Think fast. Don't say you were fired. Suddenly, I heard meself saying, 'Ah, yeah, Mrs, eh, Lipstop.'

'Who?'

'Yeah, she was a Jewish woman. A lovely person altogether,' I said, shaking me head slowly, trying to think.

'Jewish!' she roared. 'Wha kinda shop?'

Eh, oh, God! Me mind's gone blank. Think, Martha! Fast! 'They sold everything, missus! Coal, bananas . . . I mean fruit—'

'Sì, sì, OK! But what about the references?'

'Oh, yeah! I'm just getting to that. Well, you see, her husband died suddenly, and she sold the shop and took off with Mister O'Brien.'

'Who ees dis mister? What you mean? They were no married?' she said, waving her hands slowly in the air, looking shocked.

'No,' I whispered, looking even more shocked.

'Sì! Continue,' she said quietly. Waving her hands at me and shaking her massive chest, settling herself in for more comfort to hear this shocking scandal.

God, this better be good, Martha. 'Yes, they were carrying on behind the poor husband's back,' I whispered, leaning meself across the table, giving a quick look around in case anyone was listening. Not wanting even the walls to hear the terrible goings-on. Then I paused, seeing her shocked face, and the eyes glittering with the excitement of hearing something shocking. She rattled her head up and down like mad, trying to get me to get on to the good bits. Then took a big swallow, pinning her eyes on me. Taking in every word I was saying.

'The two of them!' I puffed, drawing in me nostrils, and holding me breath with the shock of it all. 'They would be pretending to count the takings at the end of the night. But the husband found them rolling around under the counter when the shop was locked up for the night. And the whole lot of us only sleeping overhead on the next floor up,' I said, letting me voice and hand raise up to the ceiling. Looking up at it, with me face tortured, not able to take that part in.

'Rolling around?' she said, gripping her chest with her head leaning over to me with her eyes rolling around in her head. Looking like she was going into convulsions. Never having heard the like of such scandalous carryings on in her whole life.

'Oh, yeah,' I breathed. 'You see, O'Brien was the handyman. And he was, eh, young and the husband was old. He had grey hair.'

'But dis rolling around. Tell me about dis!'

'Oh, yeah. That was shocking,' I said, holding me hand to me chest. Still not the better of it. 'The husband went down to the shop unexpectedly and let an unmerciful roar outa him. We heard the screams. Me and the other girl who worked in the shop. We lived upstairs, we were—'

'Yes, yes! Go on. Dis rolling. I want to know about dis.'

'Oh yeah! I am still not over the shock of that.' I grabbed me hand to me chest again. Looking sick at the thought of it all coming back to me now. 'Well,' I said, slurping over me tongue. Enjoying meself no end, getting really carried away. 'We ran down when we heard the shouts. And the poor husband, Mister Lipman—'

'I thought you said it was Lipstop!'

I looked at her, confused for a minute.

'Oh, yeah! Of course it was. I get them foreign names mixed up. Anyway, when me and, eh, Maggie flew in the door to the shop . . . well, I am still having nightmares over it, missus,' I said, holding me head and closing me eyes. 'The two of them

. . . O'Brien and the missus . . . Lipstop . . . they were in their skin,' I whispered.

'No!' the mamma roared in a whisper. Slamming her fist on the table. 'You see all dis?' she roared, looking at me then sweeping her head around the room, nodding at the walls with her arms waving in the air, muttering in Italian and blessing herself, looking up to heaven. Then folding her arms and dropping her head to me. 'Sì, sì, sì,' she muttered, dying for me to get on to the next bit.

'Oh, yeah! The whole lot of us. Me an Maggie. And the world and his wife all heard about it, with the roarings outa the lot a them. Especially the husband. He was blue in the face with the shock of it, and went straight for the wife, grabbing her by the hair of the head. Then wrapped his hands around her neck, trying to strangle her. The handyman jumped in without a stitch a clothes on him! Oh my God! You should have seen what I seen!' I roared. Dropping me head into me hands.

'Sì, sì, sì! Keep telling!' she roared. Nearly losing the mind with the excitement of it all.

'Well, anyway, he jumped on the husband and tried to pull yer man offa her and the husband lost his mind altogether and picked up a bottle a milk sitting in a crate on the floor, with all the milk still in it,' I gasped, 'and landed it on yer man's head. Splitting it wide open. Oh, it was killings! Murder! We wondered if we should call the police because it looked like someone was going to get kilt! Then—' I stopped, pausing to get a breath. And think what might a happened next.

'So? Go on, go on! What?'

'Where was I?' I said, running outa steam.

'Tell me the rest! What happened then?'

'Eh, oh, yeah! Then she picked up a bottle and smashed the husband over the head with it. Then we definitely had to call an ambulance and everyone got themself carted off to the hospital, with the ambulance roaring away with the bells ringing, and the whole lot a them still stark naked as the day they were born. Only except for the husband. He was grand. He was wearing his pyjamas. But the other two were starkers! And blood was pouring everywhere. So then we were left minding the shop. The two of us. Me and the other one.'

'But the husband? You say he died! Did she kill him?' said the mamma, looking confused, trying to work out the story.

'Well, I don't know about that. But he died in the hospital. So then I called me mother straight away, from the phone box in the shop, and she told me to get the hell outa there. It was no place for a good Catholic Irish girl like me who was well-reared and brought up with the fear of God in her at that pagan way of carrying on. That's what me mother told me. So I rushed off and got the newspaper and here I am. Sitting here with you. Telling you the whole shocking story. I rang the mammy back to tell her I was now going to be working for an Italian family. She was delighted, missus. She said the good God is looking after me. Ending me up in a job with a good Christian God-fearing Italian family who would make sure I didn't go astray! So now you see why I don't have a reference, missus,' I said, waving me empty hands at her.

'Mamma mia!' breathed the mamma, holding onto her chest and breathing out heavily, not the better of hearing that lovely bit a juicy scandal. 'Si! Say no more. I ave the picture. You be a good girl. Keep outa trouble.' Then she came back to her senses, and sat staring at me, thinking. I sat trying to read whether she believed me or not.

Dear God, please let her give me the job. I'm sorry for telling lies. But I had to think up something quick. Or I had no chance at all. I sat quietly, waiting for her to make up her mind. Seeing her trying to read me and whether I was telling her a pack of lies. Then she snorted, giving me a dirty look, and huffed, shaking her head. Oh, oh! I could feel me heart sinking right down to the bottom of me belly. Here it comes. She's not going to give me the job. I listened anyway, dropping me head. Resting meself with me arms folded, waiting for me arse to get lifted straight out the door. Pity. I always wanted to work in a fish-and-chip shop. Then I could eat as much as I like, and all for free.

'OK, I give you one week on the trial. If you no work out, I let you go. Pssst! Out! We no mess here,' she said, as me eyes followed her hands slapping against each other, seeing the picture of me being sent flying out the door. 'You understand what I say?'

'Oh, indeed! Very well,' I said, lifting me head and looking at her with a big smile on me face. Not believing me good fortune at landing the job. 'Don't worry about a thing, missus. I'm a very good worker. As missus, eh,' – I was trying to remember – 'the Jewish woman from me last job used to say, she couldn't praise me enough. No, she couldn't,' I repeated meself, getting carried away with the excitement of getting the job and praising meself.

'OK, the money is one pound and ten shillings a week. You work and eat and live with the family. You good worker, I treat you right! We all happy. I have one other Irish girl here already. She is a good girl. Gives me no trouble. She is like a daughter to me. You watch and do what she do. You can keep your job. Now, you and she work in the café. That is it. I have no more to say. You start work right away. Come, follow me. I can't turn my back for one minute. Then they start the fighting.' We could hear the roaring before we hit the shop.

We walked into the bright lights of the shop. All I could hear was the noise, as I squinted, trying to get me sight back from the dark room. Two Italian fellas serving behind the counter were having a screaming match. The touchy one was shouting at the other fella because he was scratching his privates and staring out at the young ones, shouting and belting each other standing outside the shop. They were hoping to draw the attention of the young fellas who were doing the same. Milling each other around the counter, hoping to get served. The Italian fella wasn't taking a blind bit a notice of what was going on around him. The people were knee deep, all draped around the counter waiting to be served, and starving with the hunger. The gorgeous smell killing them as their eyes followed the lovely golden fish Touchy was humping around.

'Eh, Francesco!' he screamed in Italian, staggering with a load of steaming cooked golden-battered fish held in a big metal basket. He stopped, getting himself ready to aim. Then he hoisted the fish up, sending it flying to land under the hot shelf with the glass in front.

'Francesco!' he roared again, lifting his foot and giving Francesco an almighty kick right up the arse. Francesco leaped into the air with the fright and stared at Touchy while he rubbed the arse off himself, wondering what had happened to him. Then he lit into Touchy, giving him a smack across the head with the open palm of his hand. Touchy went mad and screamed into the face of Francesco, keeping his fists held tight down by his side and sticking his head into Dopey's face. Jaysus! All hell is breaking loose, I thought, staring at the two of them and enjoying the excitement of it all.

'Cut that out!' roared a little aul fella waiting to be served. 'Are yehs going to serve the paying customers or not? We want to get the grub and get the hell outa here. Youse can kill yerselves in your own time! I want me fucking fish and chips!' he roared.

'Yeah, we want chips! We want chips!' shouted the young fellas from the back. Jaysus! This is a mad house, I thought, looking at all the people shaking their heads up and down in disgust. Hopping from one foot to the other, getting very impatient. The young fellas started getting very rowdy, with their shouting and roaring. Looking like they were getting ready to jump over the counter and help themself. Dopey just looked at the aul fella and the rest of the people, with a dozy look coming back on his face, and just stared at everyone shouting and roaring and going mad. He went back to hanging onto himself. Scratching, like he had a bad itch and couldn't help himself, not even bothering to get moving.

Touchy lifted his voice, getting into an even worse rage. His face turned bright red as he stabbed at the metal bucket holding the raw white batter and the other bucket with the fish waiting to be dipped and battered. The aul one ran at Dopey, giving him an unmerciful shake, and dragged him by the shoulder, landing him over to the bucket, shouting and pointing at him to get on with the job. The touchy fella started cursing. It sounded like, 'Fucking this and fucking that.' 'Fungolase' or something. Then the aul one took off, satisfied the Francesco fella was now getting on with the job. But he was still looking a bit dopey to me.

I followed the mamma out through the counter and down the shop and into the café on the left side. There must be about twenty – well, maybe fifteen – tables I thought, trying to count them. Most of them were full. 'Saturday night is busy, always busy at the weekend,' the mamma said, watching the Irish girl rushing around, taking orders and clearing the tables as people left. 'Here! Take this,' she said, dipping into the pocket of her massive black-and-red-coloured flowery frock and handing me a little notebook with white sheets of paper, and the stub of a pencil. 'Take the order from the customers and write it all down on this, and write the table number. It starts at this first table up here. That is number one. Work your way back, then it goes to the next row. We have twelve tables. Now don't mix up the tables. Be sure you know what you are doing.'

'OK!' I said, getting all excited, dying to get cracking.

'Serve these people here,' she said, throwing her head at a couple waiting on the far side, staring over at us and watching the Irish girl serving.

I rushed over with me stub of pencil in one hand raised in the air, holding the notebook resting in the palm of me left hand. Hoping I looked like a waitress. 'What will you have?' I said. Slowly throwing me head from one side to the other, looking like the waitresses in Caffola's in O'Connell Street. You always look up to them. Because they feed you when you're dying for a bit of tasty grub.

'I can't make up me mind,' said the young one with the beehive dyed black hair, back-combed and sprayed with a whole can of hair lacquer. That ended up looking like a bird's nest sitting on top of her head. Anyway, that's what it looks like to me.

'What are you having?' she said to the fella. Flapping her false eyelashes and staring at him. With her two eyes covered in black pencil going all around the eye in a circle, making her eyes disappear into a black hole. She was hoping he had enough money for fish and chips, but was afraid to ask him, in case he thought she was mean. That she was only after him for his money. I could tell that by the way she was a bit shy with him, and he was saying, 'Go on, Joanie! Have what you like. I'm good for it. I'm flush this week. Go on, go on! I'm havin the big ray an a plate of chips,' he said, turning to me. 'Wit a pot a tea and give us a plate of bread an butter.'

'Yeah, I'll have the same,' she said, looking contented now that she knew where she stood and he was loaded with the money.

'Will we go on after this inta town an see a film or what?' he said, holding her hand across the table and dropping his neck inside his leather jacket. Trying to catch the whole bottle of hair oil dripping down the back of his neck.

'Yeah, that would be lovely,' she said, squeezing his hands and getting all lovey-dovey. 'There's a great one on at the Savoy. But the only thing is, it's all romance! An you mightn't like that,' she said, making her face look like she was going to burst into tears.

'Course I would! Anything for you. We can sit at the back in the dark, and get our own bit a romance goin,' he said, running his hand along the side of his greasy hair, and looking for somewhere to wipe it.

'Oh, go on, you! Yeh mean yer after a bit a courtin?'

'Now did I say tha?'

'No, but me ma said I'm to watch out for fellas like you!'

'Yeah? Do you want to hear wha my ma said?' he laughed. Grabbing her around the neck and leaning over the table, whispering into her ear. I took off, listening to the pair of them scream their hearts out laughing after taking me time clearing the table next to them and earwigging like mad. It sounded lovely. Coming in here with a nice fella, then going off to the pictures. It made me feel a bit lonely. Then I flew up to the counter and gave me order to Touchy. Feeling meself lift again just as quickly. This place is great, with the bright lights and people coming and going. But most of all, the best part is that I'm all a part of it.

I staggered out of the café, heading for the shop, trying to balance a load of dirty dishes stacked too high on the tray. 'Oh, mother a God,' I whined, watching them slip and slide. Jaysus! Ah! I took too many. I turned for the shop, then turned back again. Landing the tray on a couple's table trying to eat their dinner. I wrestled with the tumbling dishes, grabbing out at the plates, seeing them skid across and ending up in the man's lap. Some of the slops slid onto the man and woman's dinner.

'Hurry! I've been told to tell you your orders are ready,' the

Irish girl puffed, rushing past me carrying two plates of fish and chips. Looking all red in the face from trying to keep up with the rush, as she swept past me. Her eyes rolled to heaven, taking in me staring at the man's lap. While he jumped up, shaking off a load of beans stuck to his trousers!

'Ah! Oh, I'm very sorry,' I said, looking from the man to the woman with all the scraps from the dirty dishes sitting on top of their plates of dinner.

'For the luv a Jaysus! Can yeh not mind what you're doing?' he roared, shaking his trousers and wriggling his hips, trying to get the beans to drop off. Then he looked down at the big stain right in the middle of his legs, and started cursing like mad.

'I'll clean it up,' I said, trying to grab up the dishes and fix them properly on the table. Leaving him to clean himself up, taking the cloth off me.

'Gimme that!' he snarled, grabbing the wet dishcloth outa me hand.

'Jaysus! The service is getting worse in this place,' the woman moaned, throwing dirty looks at me and sweeping her eyes past her husband and landing them on the wall.

'Miss! Where's that fresh cod-and-chips we ordered, and a smoked cod-and-chips for her?' shouted an aul fella from the middle of the room.

'Yeah, coming. I'm just going to get it.'

I looked around, seeing people with empty tables in front of them, sitting patiently and looking hungry, staring over at me. The place was suddenly crowded. Bloody hell! How is this happening? Everything was going grand a minute ago, I thought, grabbing up the dishes and taking off to the crowded shop, with the man and woman screaming at me to come back and sort out the damage. I ignored them, shouting, 'Excuse me. Let me past.' I hiked the overflowing tray up onto the counter, letting a plate slip and smash to the floor.

'Hurrah!' shouted a gang of bleedin young fellas, delighted with the excitement of hearing something smashing and me making a fool out of meself.

'Here, Rosa!' shouted an Italian little aul fella with a brown weather-beaten face and little black beady eyes. He came out from behind the counter, wiping his hands on a long red-check apron, and waved me away. 'Go! Take your orders. Serve the customers.'

'Two large ray! Two chips! Tea, bread and butter!' shouted Touchy, slamming the two plates on the counter. I grabbed them and flew back into the café, making straight for hair oil.

'Jaysus, young one! Did yeh go back to Italy to catch the bleedin fish?' he said, following the plate of grub sliding over to him.

'Sorry about that! We're rushed off our feet tonight,' I said. Making it sound like I was here for years, instead of only a few minutes.

'Where's the tea?' he squeaked, his mouth hanging open, looking at the table seeing he didn't have everything.

'Coming.' I was off and grabbing up the tray with the pot of tea and bread and landing it back to hair-oil head. 'Enjoy your fish,' I said, smiling at the two of them. 'It's only just freshly battered!'

The girl paused her jaws that were slamming up and down, making short work of the fish and chips. She listened, then it hit her. Thinking I just said something funny. 'Did yeh hear that? Yer woman's just freshly battered the fish,' she said, with her eyes staring at him and her cheeks bulging with the grub. 'Looka! It's battered.' She pointed at his fish. There was a silence, while he stared at his fish. Then the pair of them burst out laughing.

She started choking and coughing so he leaned over the table, bashing her on the back, saying, 'Yeah, it's battered-lookin like herself!' he roared, looking at the girl, and pointing at me, trying to be funny. Then he grabbed up the knife and fork and attacked the grub. Stuffing his face with the fish and chips and half a slice of bread and butter and a big mouthful of tea.

I put me hands on me hips and was about to light into him when he saw me face ready to go mad. 'Ah, no, I'm only joking yeh! I didn't mean you,' he said. 'I meant meself. The fish is battered-looking like meself.'

'Ah, don't be saying that to the poor girl and she doing yeh no harm,' the girl said, looking disgusted.

I softened, and said, 'No, you're not battered-looking. Just a bit threadbare in the looks department. But I suppose you do have the kind of face only a mammy could love. But, then again, you must have something going for yeh. You got yourself a gorgeous-looking girlfriend.'

I saw her face turning red and yer man looking at her with his eyes starting to shine. 'Yeah, yeah, you're so right. She is an all. A lovely-looking bird,' he said. Leaning happily across the table to grab her neck, landing his greasy hands on the back of her beehive hairdo. Giving her a quick greasy smacking kiss on the side of her mouth, missing her lips.

'Get away, you,' she said, her face going bright beetroot. But loving the moment that just came out of the blue.

'Miss, where's me bleeding smoked cod and fresh cod-and-chips we ordered two hours ago?'

'Yeah, coming!' I shouted, waving at him.

I went flying out the door, roaring up for me order at Touchy. 'Si! Where you go? Dis order is now one week old,' he shouted, nearly spitting at me.

'Yeah, sorry! I'm run off me feet,' I panted, grabbing up the order and barrelling back in, carrying two hot plates. Then landing them down with the aul fella. 'Smoked cod and fresh cod and two chips,' I said, pushing the salt and vinegar in front of them.

'Yes, and about bloody time, too. The hunger is nearly gone offa me,' he moaned.

'Yeah, I'm very sorry about that. The place is crowded tonight!'

'Get us a pot of tea and bread and butter to go with this,' he said.

'Right!' I was about to rush off and suddenly stopped. Remembering to write down what they are getting and put the table number in me book. 'I won't be a minute.'

I took off, then felt a man grabbing hold of the sleeve of me cardigan. 'Excuse me, miss. We want something to eat.'

'Right!' I took out me notebook.

'Hey, young one! Get us our pot of tea and bread and butter, before we fall down here from the hunger.'

'Sorry! I'll be back,' I said. Rushing in to give the order to Touchy. People stood up at another table and I started counting the tables like mad to see if it was one of mine. I'm completely lost. I can't remember who is who and what I'm owed. Or even what I'm doing any more. The Irish one does that side of the room. The left side when you come in from the shop. Halfway down the middle. I look after the rest. Right, they're one of hers, I thought. Rushing to take the poor couple's order. The man and woman are looking desperate for a bit of grub.

'Are you serving us or not?' he roared, losing the rag after trying to hold onto me by the cardigan a minute ago.

'Sorry, sir!' I puffed, waiting with me hook gripped, and me pencil ready to fly, then dash and give in the order.

'Goodbye, now. Thank you very much,' I said. Taking the green pound note and giving the man his change. Happy now to say goodnight to the last of the customers. I watched as the man's wife struggled to put on her good red coat and wrap the scarf around her head, letting it slide down the back of her neck, and pulling up the collar. She grabbed it around the front to hold onto it as she followed the man out the door. The two of them heading off, out into the cold dark night. Making their way home, after the big Saturday night out. I put the money in me apron pocket, along with the pound note, wrapped up tightly in the other notes, and slid the notebook in. Seeing the Irish girl stacking the chairs up on top of the tables, I started to do the same.

'Sorry, we're closed!' shouted the aul fella out to more people looking in. Their mouths dropping down to their bellies at the thought of no grub.

'It won't take a minute. Just give us a quick bag of chips, and a fish!' shouted a fella, looking back at the woman who was shaking her shoulders, looking around at the miserably dark night, with eveything closed up hours ago. Then she looked back in, seeing the lights going off in the shop.

'Come on! Leave it. Let's get going and make our way home,' the woman said, sounding disgusted, and turned her back, digging her hands deep into her coat pockets, and lowered her neck down inside her coat. Then took off, heading away from the shops, making her own way home along the dark road.

'No, wait. Wait! Fuck yeh,' he shouted after her, waving his arm in the air. Then gave up and dug his hands into his trouser pockets and lowered his head, bending his back. Studying what was happening in the shop. He hung on for a minute. His mouth hanging open like he had too much to drink, and his eyes kept crossing. Then he gave up and staggered after the woman. Stopping to get the right foot going first, after taking a little dance to keep his balance, then he steadied himself, and he was off. Moving in a stagger, hurrying to catch up with the woman.

I followed the Irish girl up to the counter and handed in the last two customers' money along with the notebook. The little aul fella took it off me and checked the two receipts against the money I gave him. Then slammed open the cash register, taking out all the money to count it.

'You want fish-and-chips?' Touchy said to me, getting ready to grab up a plate.

'Yeah, give us, eh . . .' I was trying to think what I would like. 'Give us a fresh cod. A nice big one!'

'They are all big,' he moaned.

'And plenty of chips. Where do I get the pot of tea from? I want bread and butter, too.'

'OK, OK! You wait. I only have a the one pair a the hands,' he snorted. Letting his face lengthen with disgust.

'I'll have the same,' whispered the Irish girl. 'Here, I'll make us the tea,' she said, looking at me like someone had put the fear of God into her.

'Eh, Alfonso!' shouted Francesco, waking himself up at the thought all the day's work is over. He screamed something in Italian, then rushed back into the family's kitchen.

'Andeamo!' or something like that, the big fat mamma shouted out. Holding up a big metal basket with steaming spaghetti hanging out through the holes.

'SÌ! MOMENTO!' blasted Touchy right into me earhole.

'Fuck! Do they ever just speak to each other like normal people?' I muttered. Jumping out of the way, and taking the two plates of fish-and-chips he slammed down on the counter for me and the other girl.

'Come on! Do you want to eat in the café? I don't want to eat in with them. There's too many of them crowded in there,' she said. Rushing off to the café and putting the tray down on the table with the chairs underneath that she'd left free for us.

'We have no salt and vinegar,' I said, seeing all the stuff was gone inside to be filled by us tomorrow. I rushed in behind the counter, grabbing a bottle with vinegar left in it and a little bottle of salt. Then made to run back and decided to put me head into the family kitchen to get a look. They were all sitting on top of each other at a long table squashed into an alcove.

'Eh, eh, BASTA!' Touchy was shouting, slapping the hand of another fella I hadn't really noticed before. I think he was the one in the rubber apron peeling all the potatoes, and bringing in the buckets of batter and fish. They keep him in the back. Rubber-apron man roared because he couldn't get his hands on the big metal bowl with some sort of sauce and meat in it. Touchy was taking half the bowl for himself. The rest were helping themself to baskets of bread, and plates of tomatoes and cheese, and pouring wine out of a long glass jug.

'Papa!' shouted a big fat young one, about two or three years younger then meself. He took no notice of her, shaking the hell out of his arm. He was too busy shouting at a huge dopey woman helping the mamma to serve the lot of them. Jaysus! No way am I showing me nose in there, I thought. Shutting me gaping mouth and taking off for the café.

'It's like a mad house in there!' I said. Sitting meself down and cutting half the fish, trying to stuff it into me mouth.

'Yeah, there's an awful lot of them,' she said, staring at her grub and taking little mouthfuls.

'What's your name? Mine's Martha.'

'I know. I heard Alfonso call you Santa Martha.'

'You mean Touchy?'

'Who's he?'

'Oh, I call him that because you can't say anything to him. He's never happy-looking.'

'Yeah, he hates Ireland,' she said. Taking a little nibble of the bread. 'How long are you working here?'

'What did you say your name was?'

'Mary. I'm working here eight months.'

'Where are you from, Mary?'

'Sligo.'

'That's miles from Dublin, isn't it?'

'Yeah,' she said, looking at her plate and pushing it away.

'What's wrong with you? Why don't you eat your dinner?'

'I'm sick of the sight of fish and chips. I'd love a chop or something. I prefer Irish food. They only cook Italian stuff here. I wouldn't eat that.'

'No, me neither,' I said. 'I don't like the look of that spaghetti stuff. How old are you, Mary?'

'Twenty-three.'

'How long are you in Dublin?'

'Since I started working here. I saw the job advertised in a Dublin paper when I came up for the day to have a look around. I was working in a local hardware shop at home. Selling farm stuff to the local farmers.'

'Do you like working here, Mary?'

'Not really, it was good in the beginning. But now I want a change. I'm thinking of heading off to London. Me sister's over there working in a live-in job. It's a pub in Camden Town.'

'Oh, I might think of doing something like that,' I said, getting all excited at the idea of moving on. 'But I don't think I would like the idea of being around drunks all day. I'd be afraid I might get a liking for the stuff. No, I want to keep meself away from that kind of thing. There's no point in taking chances.'

'Well, we better get upstairs to bed,' she said. Taking up her plate and loading up the tray.

'Right, I'm just finished.' I finished the last of the bread, including hers, and drained the last drop of tea, and stacked the cups and saucers and plates on the tray. Letting her take off with it. 'Wait! I think I'll just sit here and have a cigarette first.' I'd forgot all about me smokes, even though customers were sitting here, puffing their hearts away.

'OK, I'll wait with you,' she said. 'Just let me drop these things off for Angelo, or Rosa. One of them can do the washing up,' she said, sounding tired. 'Oh, God! What a night. We were rushed off our feet. I'm just about ready for my bed,' she said, letting herself drop down into the chair, and rubbing her face with her two hands, then looking over at me and yawning.

She's very thin and pasty-faced, I thought, looking at her. Her mousey fair hair would be lovely if she put it up or something. It's too thin to be left hanging down around her shoulders. Gawd! She really is very quiet. She never says a word to anyone. Just keeps moving in and out of the tables, cleaning them and taking the orders and going quietly about her business. No one notices her with her shoulders humped and her eyes half-dead in her head, like she's got the weight of the world on her shoulders, and she wouldn't even care if she just dropped down dead, and that was the end of her.

'How many have you in your family, Mary?' I asked, seeing her mouth tighten, at the mention of her family.

'Nine. I'm the second-eldest,' she said, sounding like she didn't want to talk about them. I said nothing. Not wanting to ask her about her business. 'Me mother is dead!' she said after a while. Knowing I was not wanting to upset her.

'Oh, that's terrible! You must be lost without her.'

She shook her head, closing her eyes like she was trying to say, 'I'm used to it.' 'Yeah, she's dead these four years. I don't feel good about running off and leaving me younger sister to look after the lot of them.'

'What age is she, Mary?'

'Nineteen. Then the next one is fifteen. There were more in between us. But poor Mammy lost two after me when they were young. Teresa was only seven. Just coming up to Holy Communion. And Joseph who was five. Then we lost three more. They died when they were all little. The youngest is four now. He's me little brother, Alan.'

'But did you say your mammy died four years ago, Mary?' I whispered.

'Yeah, that's right. She had him at home and bled to death. By the time they got the ambulance and took her to hospital, she was gone. She was only forty-four. I blame me father,' she said. Letting the anger work its way up. She didn't raise her voice. Just said it, letting the last few words rise up, leaving the mention of her father hanging in the air. I shook me head, feeling the terrible loss she must carry around. Seeing her face turning to stone. Yet her eyes were half-dead from the pain of it all.

'I send them home a postal order for fifteen shillings a week. To my sister. I don't want that git of a father to get his hands on it, and drink it down his gullet. That's why I want to go to London. There's more money to be made over there. But I wanted to hang around in Dublin for a while. To keep an eye on the family. I send them a letter every week, asking them to let me know how things are going at home. The sister writes back. She wants to leave home, too. But she can't do that until Maeve gets a bit older. She's working now in my old job, in the hardware shop. The next one is just turned fourteen. She's started working for a local farmer. Helping the wife around the house and farm. So things are moving on. Getting a little easier on everyone. But the father has to be watched. He beats the hell out of the younger one, Maeve. Trying to get the wages off a her before she hands it up to Bernie. Bernie knocks the shite out a him. She's not afraid of him. Not like me poor mammy! She was too soft altogether. That's why she went to an early grave.'

'Yeah, she's right an all, Mary. I would split a man's head open if he lifted a hand to me.'

'Too bloody true!' Mary said, a spark of viciousness coming into her eyes at the mention of being hit by a man. 'You remind me of me sister Bernie,' she laughed, her eyes lighting up at the mention of her sister, making her face pretty. 'You're full a life, just like her. But you're younger. How old are you, Martha?'

'Sixteen,' I said, smiling at her.

'You're a Dublin girl,' she said, looking straight at me and thinking about this.

'Yeah,' I said.

'So . . . are you just out of a convent? Do you mind me asking?'

'No, no, you're right. I am,' I said, wanting to leave it at that. Not wanting to look back, and give much away.

'Them places can be fierce tough! I heard terrible stories about them.'

'Ah, no,' I said, thinking about it. 'I wasn't in the worst place. There are worse things that can happen to you,' I said. Thinking about the ma and the aul bastard, the Jackser fella. 'But I'm glad to be gone from it. They can be very lonely places at times,' I said. Remembering the cold empty passages, and rooms with nothing but young ones, tearing lumps out of each other. Everyone wanting to be noticed by the nuns. 'Oh, well! That's life,' I said. Wanting to turn away from all the bad times and be happy now.

'Turn outa da lights in there!' shouted the aul fella, roaring in at us from the counter.

'Come on, let's go up and hit the sack,' Mary said, standing up, waiting for me to put out the cigarette in the ashtray. I followed her out the door, seeing her switch off the light, and around the counter, heading out through a door into a little passage and up bare wooden stairs.

'I haven't seen where I'm sleeping, Mary! What about me case? I left that in the sitting room.'

'Come on! We're all in here together,' she said. Opening a door on a landing, hearing roars and banging and laughing coming from the room next door. 'We're in here,' she said, walking into a bedroom with two beds. One a double and a single pushed against the wall. The floorboards were bare, and a big old wardrobe sat against the far wall, at the end of the room just inside the door. I spotted my suitcase sitting behind it in the corner.

'There's only two beds!' I said, seeing the huge woman Rosa and the fat daughter heaving into the room after us, puffing and arguing. 'Are the four of us sleeping in two beds?' I shouted, not believing me eyes.

'Yes! You and me are in the single bed, and Rosa and Maria are in the big one,' the daughter said, pointing us to the single bed. We all looked at Rosa, peeling the big wide tent of a frock over her head, and heave herself into the double bed, wearing only big pink knickers and a long woolly vest, with a bunch of miraculous medals and purple scapulars swinging around her neck. I watched the mattress and the springs sink onto the floor.

I looked at the single bed as Mary started stripping, taking her nightdress out from under a pillow and pulling it over her head. The young one dived into her nightdress and sank herself into the single bed, moving into the wall, trying to make room for me.

'Fuck this! Not on yer nelly!' I roared, wanting me night's sleep. Raging at the thought I wasn't getting a bed to meself.

Mary had drawn her knees up and was hanging out of the edge of the bed when Rosa swung herself around, lying flat on her back, breathing 'Bene!' with a big sigh of contentment.

'Come on, out! What's your name?' I said, pointing at the young one and pulling the blankets down.

'Maria.'

'Right, Maria. You sleep with Rosa and, Mary, will you sleep in the single bed with me? We're a pair of skinnies. Leave the fatties with the big bed. Maria here is taking up the whole single bed to herself. Look at the size of her!' I was raging. The bleedin cheek of them Italians!

'Yeah, OK,' Mary said, swinging her legs out of the bed while I dragged Maria out of the single one.

'Go on! You'll be more comfortable sleeping in the big bed with Rosa.' She dived in happily beside Rosa, who grabbed her, laughing. The two of them snuggled up happily, laughing and tittering. Delighted with themselves at getting each other and the big bed. Mary and me squeezed into the single bed, and found our own space.

We had stopped coughing and shifting ourselves for more comfort, and were just dozing off when the fuckers next door started going mad. We listened as the gang of fellas chased and thumped each other. Throwing stuff and dragging the beds around, using them as a barricade to stop themselves getting caught. We listened, hoping it would stop. Then they got rowdier. The slaps and thumps were louder, and the screams of pain sounded like someone was being killed.

'Jaysus! Why does someone not go in and tell them to quieten down?' I huffed. Shouting at the wall, hoping they would hear me next door. 'It must be three o'clock in the morning,' I moaned, with nobody taking any notice of me.

A lone bird woke up, and started squawking like mad, screaming at his pals to wake up. I lifted one heavy eyelid, seeing the night getting pushed out by the grey dawn of a new day. 'Ah, Jaysus! Mammy! I'm banjacked. I'll never get up in the morning,' I croaked, feeling meself sinking down into a deep coma.

'Right, Mary, I'm off. Are you sure you won't change your mind and come with me for a ramble into town?'

'No! Sure everything will be all shut up. It's Sunday,' she said, standing there in her work clothes, looking all washed out.

'Ah, Mary! You should try getting out some time. This place would drive you mad, hanging around with them mad Italians day and night.'

'No,' she said, running her hands over her face then slamming them down by her side, making her eyes all red and her face even whiter. 'You go on and enjoy yourself. You look smashing.'

'Ah, thanks,' I said, looking down at me lovely clean frock. And the smell of the washing powder off me lovely trench coat. It came out lovely when I washed it and hung it out to dry on the line in the back garden. I even got Rosa to iron it for me. She's very good.

'Do yeh like the shine on me patent shoes? I clean them in Pond's Cold Cream! Don't they come up lovely?' I said, sticking out me foot for us to get a good look.

'Yeah, but I thought that was supposed to be for your face,' she laughed.

'Yeah, but people always look down at your shoes after they've seen your face,' I said. 'That's how they know if you have any taste or not.'

'Hmm, I hadn't thought about that,' she said. Shaking her head thinking about it.

'Right, I'm off.'

'Don't forget you're back at work at five o'clock this evening.'

'Yeah, I've plenty of time. I'm just taking the bus into town, get a look in the shop windows. I might have a cup of coffee in Caffola's. I love that place! Then back in time for work.'

'OK, go on then or you'll never get going.'

'Right, bye!' I flew out the door smack into Francesco, with Alfonso trailing behind him.

'Eh, eh, looka this! The little Santa Marta is ready for the town,' he roared, swinging his arms in the air and looking around at Touchy.

'Where you goin?' Touchy said. Looking me up and down, all dressed up himself. 'You want to come for a drive in my sports car?' he said. Flying ahead of me down the stairs in his black tight trousers with the little flare-outs at the end. Wearing black patent lace-up shoes, and a leather jacket with the collar pulled up. I got the whiff of aftershave lotion as he breezed past me.

'Eh, Alfonso, I come too! We all go, eh? Why no?'

'Fungolase!' shouted Touchy, roaring in Italian at Francesco tearing down the stairs after him. I think 'fungolase', or whatever it is, must mean fuck off. 'You want to come?' he shouted at me, holding his hand out in the air, waving his car keys.

'No, I don't trust youse Italian fellas. You're all too fast for my liking.'

'Sì!' shouted Francesco to me. 'He eat girls for breakfast. He very fast.'

'No me! I ham . . . how you say?' he said, kissing his fingers to his lips, giving them a smack. 'I ham beautiful,' he said, lowering himself to the ground. Half-sitting on his hunkers. 'Come with me. I show you the town.'

'Nah,' I said, wanting to go me own way.

We all ended up outside the family kitchen. With the mamma

shouting at Maria. Trying to tear her out of a short miniskirt.
'Papa!' screamed Maria, roaring for help and hanging onto the
skirt for all she was worth. While the mamma tried to drag it off
her, screaming and yanking, and blessing herself. Then she let go,
burying her face in her hands. Moaning and trying to cry. She
sniffed, giving a big sob, taking in huge sighs, sounding like her
heart was broken. Her eyes rolled from the state of Maria in the
miniskirt down to the lovely white frock she wouldn't wear.

'Gesù Cristo!' she implored. Whispering up at the ceiling and
crumpling the frock in her hand, wiping her face and blowing
her nose in it. Then she slapped her chest, grabbing onto it, and
started roaring at Maria again. 'MAMMA MIA! My Bambina!
She look like a . . . not a my bambina!' she puffed, running out of
words. This time I really could see a tear as she lifted her head,
looking like one a them tortured saints with the eyes rolling in
the back of her head. She lifted her eyes to heaven, holding up
handfuls of the frock, beseeching and moaning. 'Santa Maria! Give
me patience! Give me back my baby! I beg you!' she implored,
tearing lumps outa the frock with heartbreak and frustration.

Then the aul fella lost his patience. 'Basta!' shouted the papa.
Trying to squeeze himself past the two of them, and escape out
the door. The mamma thumped him on the arm and screamed
at him in Italian. Pushing the frock at him, holding it out in a
ball. Then pointed at what Maria was wearing. A short skirt up
to her arse. Showing off her big fat legs, and a tight skinny top
that showed nothing but her fat belly. The mamma sounded like
she was crying and raging at the same time.

He stopped and looked back at Maria, studying her, trying to
take her in. Then he gave up and slapped his forehead, giving
it a good smack with the open palm of his hand, and looked at
the ground, saying nothing. The mamma ran out of words and
stared at him with her mouth open, pointing her hand at the cut
of Maria. Then slowly swung her head down, looking mournfully
at the white frilly frock crumpled in her hand, and started wiping
her nose with it again.

'Jaysus! There's murder going on!' I muttered. Staring at the lot of them. 'Where did you get the get-up from, Maria?' I asked.

'My friend at school bought it for me in the new Rave Boutique in Clerys. I saved my pocket money,' she said, wiping her snots with the back of her hand. 'Do you like it? Mamma wants me to wear that childish thing,' she said, pointing at the white frilly communion-looking frock in the ma's hand.

'Eh . . .' I tried to think, looking at how short her skirt was, nearly showing up to her knickers. 'Eh, do you like it?'

'Yeah, I look really groovy,' she said happily, looking down at herself, not seeing what I'm seeing.

'Ciao!' shouted Touchy. 'Come on! We go in my sports car,' he said, yanking me behind him. 'You will ave the experience of your life,' he promised, blowing kisses with his hands. The mamma stared at me, then whipped her head at him, thinking there's more misfortune coming her way.

'No, you have to be a good girl if you want to marry a nice Italian boy!' she shouted, waving her finger at me. Looking shocked at the idea of him wanting to take me for a drive.

'I not asking to marry her!' shouted Alfonso. Looking at me with his mouth curling. 'I marry nice Italian girl when my mamma find one for me!' he shouted. Laughing and throwing his head back at the mamma. I looked at him, wondering if he was simple, or just joking. His mammy's looking for a wife for him? Nah, nobody's that stupid.

'Hey, come on!' shouted Alfonso, waving his car keys at me from the door. 'We will be back in time for work. Ciao!' he shouted, waving at them all gaping after us.

'OK,' I said. 'We can go out and do something nice,' thinking the mamma was making me mind up for me. The cheek a her, telling me I can't go out with an Italian fella. 'Right, I'm coming,' I said, heading after him out the door.

'He wants to kiss you!' shouted Maria, getting a slap in the gob from the mamma.

'Don't worry! Nobody's getting near me,' I said. Watching him screech up to the door in a little red car. It doesn't look like a sports car to me, I thought, staring at the colour of it. Red! Red for danger! Better watch meself with this fella.

I felt nervous getting into the car. This is me first time ever out with a fella. He revved the hell out of the engine, and before I could get the door shut he was off. Sending me flying back in me seat. 'Take it easy!'

'This car was made in Italy,' he said, stroking back his greasy hair. 'We likea the speed!'

'I don't,' I said, seeing all the other cars getting left behind us.

'This es nothin!' he said, staring straight ahead at the road flying up to meet us. Then he slammed down the gears, the engine roared like an animal in terrible pain, and we flew. Me eyes rolled in the back of me head, and I grabbed the seat, holding on with me fists, and me feet shot up in the air. I tried to look out, seeing only a blur of houses flashing by me, and me life going with it.

'Slow down! We're going to be killed stone dead,' I whined. Terrified to open me eyes in case it happened.

'This is good, eh, my little poodle?' he said, flicking his eyes over to me.

'Ahhhh! Look at the road! Don't be minding me! Stop the fucking car! Let me out!'

'Relax! I ham goin to show you the good life,' he purred, sounding like a kitten.

'Where we goin?' I screamed in a whisper. 'Dear God, don't lemme die. I'll never have anything to do ever again with another Italian fella. I promise, God. Just let me live in one piece!' I prayed like mad. Keeping me eyes shut.

I heard the blast of a horn, and opened me eyes just in time to see me last hour on earth. 'Ahhhh!' A car was heading straight towards us. 'We're in the middle of the bleedin road,' I moaned, terrified to scream. I could see the whites of drivers' eyes as we flew past. Trying to get in front of them, as the car coming straight towards us blared his horn. 'WE'RE DEAD!' I jammed me face in me hands. Waiting for the crash. Ohh, I never made it past sixteen! I felt the car whip around, and me stomach lurched, with me eyes clamped shut, and me body froze solid. Waiting for the terrible bang.

'Ha, ha! Irish drivers are like old women!' he roared, enjoying himself no end. I opened me eyes, seeing we were leaving everything behind us. All I could see now was a long narrow road with bogs flashing past, and sheep nosing around with their heads buried in the grass, taking life easy. Fuck! Now we're in the middle of nowhere!

'Where are we now?'

'In the mountains, cara mia,' he moaned. Trying to sound like a big film star. Then he suddenly braked, switched off the engine and pulled on the handbrake. 'Now we ave no one to disturb us,' he said. Looking at me for a split second before flinging himself on top of me, and grabbing something at the side of my seat. The pair of us went flying back, with him plastered on top of me.

'Help!' I couldn't get me breath with the shock.

'Oh, you are so beautiful, so fresh, so . . . Hmm, you smell lovely,' he moaned. Trying to eat me neck.

'Fuck off! Geroffa me!' I roared. Trying to peel meself from under him. 'I can't breathe!'

'No, it is the same for me,' he muttered, eating his way up around me face.

'Stop! Wait!' I shouted.

'What? What is wrong?' he said, lifting his head and looking at me, letting his hands stay on me hips.

'I don't want this!'

'Why? I ham great lover.'

'No, I don't care.'

'Yes, you will love me.' He grabbed me again. Spreading himself all over me like a rash. 'Give me a kiss,' he mumbled, trying to get his greasy mouth on me lips, licking the face off me.

'Are you going to stop or not?' I shouted from under him, managing to get me head up sideways for air.

'Ooh, you are too beautiful,' he moaned, grabbing his hand under me skirt, trying to work his way up to me knickers.

I grabbed his hand, clamping down on it, and said, making me voice go quiet, 'Alfonso, let me up for a minute.'

'No, we ave not much time to waste. You lie back an enjoy. This is good.' Then he was grabbing me chest.

Right! Fuck this! I could feel a rage flying up through me. 'Alfonso,' I said quietly.

'What?' he said, lifting his head to look at me.

'So, you won't stop even though I want you to?'

'Stop? We aven't even started!' he roared. Burying his head in me neck, snorting his way around to me lips again.

'Fuck! I've had enough of this,' I snorted to meself. 'Wait! Let me get me shoes off,' I puffed, trying to get me head up again for air.

'Why?' He leaped up, lifting his head up to stare at me in annoyance. He's not going to stop, I thought. Seeing the black eyes turn red, to match his beetroot face from all the excitement he was working himself up to. 'OK! You want to take your clothes off?' he said, leaping up from me and slamming himself down on his own seat and ripping off his leather jacket.

'I need air,' I said, opening the door, readying to spring meself out. Seeing him in the same instant reach across to shut it.

'No, you don't,' he muttered, sounding annoyed.

'Look, Alfonso.' He looked at me for a split second, seeing my hand come at him with two fingers pointed like arrows, sailing through the air, straight for his eyes.

'Ahhhh!' he screamed, grabbing his face, holding his eyes and twisting his head, trying to see and stop the pain. I could still feel his eyeballs shaking like jelly in me fingers. He lashed out, sending me a cracking smack on the side of me head, letting me see stars. I brought up me fist and smacked him under the chin, hearing the crunch of his jaw and the snap of his teeth.

'AHHHH!' he roared, cursing in Italian. Then he shot out of the car. Moaning and whining, reeling around, not knowing what hit him. I leaped out, screaming. The rage tearing itself around me body, wanting to kill him.

'You bastard! You think you can treat me like dirt! Why? Because I am only a girl and you are a man? You think because you are stronger than me it gives you the right to think you can piss on me if you want?'

He lifted his head, looking at me. I could see blood dribbling down his chin. He spat out a tooth, hanging out of his mouth on a string of blood. 'I will kill you!' he screamed, punching his fist at me and wiping his mouth. 'You will be buried in these mountains! You are loco!' he roared, stabbing his head with his finger.

'FUCK YOU, greasy Italian bastard! I will beat the shite outa yeh, if you lay another hand on me. Stupid skinny little runt had the cheek to think you could get the better of me!'

'I kill you,' he warned, waving his arm at me and looking at the blood on his hand. Trying to check how many teeth got knocked out.

'THAT'S IT!' I screamed, jumping up and down, with the rage nearly suffocating me. Seeing he still hadn't got the message that he was not going to best me. I whipped me head all around, looking for something to hurt him. Then me eyes lit on his car. I dived over and jumped in, wrestling off the hand brake, then leaped out and gave it a push. It started to roll, picking up speed, weaving its way towards the edge. Alfonso was still poking at his mouth, trying to find more loose teeth.

'ALFONSO! THE CAR'S GONE WALKIES!' I shouted.

He whirled his head in my direction, just in time to see the car skating past him. It took him a split second to take it in. 'MAMMA MIA!' he screamed, sounding like he was just being tortured. He took off so fast he couldn't get moving. His leather shoes skidded on the stony road, then he lifted his legs and took off. Flying like the hammers of hell. Skidding along the side of the car, trying to stop it then throwing himself in front. Slipping and sliding, holding it back from toppling down into the field.

Fuck! If he falls down over the edge, the car will land on top of him and he'll be killed. I raced down and dived in, grabbing a hold of the handbrake and tore it up with me two hands, feeling the car steady, and stopped it from going over the edge. Then everything suddenly went quiet. I rested meself on the steering wheel, hearing the sound of me heavy breathing, and feeling me heart flying like mad in me chest.

'Oh, my God!' I muttered, looking slowly around, seeing the desolation of the emptiness all around me. The white frost sitting on the empty bogs with the sheep now scattered in the distance and the sound of their bleating coming from far away. Then I landed me head on Alfonso. Seeing the whites of his eyes match the colour of his face. He was afraid to let go.

'I ham in trouble,' he moaned. His whole body shaking with the fright and his eyes locked on mine, then letting them peel slowly down the side of him. Still not trusting to let the car go. 'How do I get out of this?' he whispered, looking up at me. 'I need a push.'

'Right, we can wait for someone to come along and give us a push,' I said, slamming the door shut, feeling it rock and him slam himself against it, getting an awful fright. Then settling meself back, sitting for more comfort in the driver seat, and looking down through the window at him.

'We? Us? No, you can walk,' he snarled, with the rage whipping him up again. Forgetting himself still gripped tight under the car. 'I ham avin nothin more to do with loco Irish!'

'Fuck you! Then get yourself out of this!' I screamed, looking again to see what else I could do to him. I grabbed at the keys in the ignition, wriggling them like mad to get them out. Then leaped from the car, shouting. 'Hey, do you need these?' I said, swinging them in the air.

'No, no, I swear on my mamma's grave. I kill you, if you don't give my keys.' His face was now green.

'Right, here you are,' I said, throwing back me hand, sending the keys flying through the air, landing them somewhere next to the nosy sheep making their way over, looking up to see what all the fuss was about. Oh, the sheep are back! They had taken off, running for their lives when all the shouting started again.

He whirled his head, trying to spot the keys landing. Then dived at me, then changed his mind, taking off instead. Galloping after the spot where he thinks the keys landed. Screaming like a banshee he would kill me. Well, it sounds like that to me, because he's roaring in Italian.

I watched him throwing himself on his knees, tearing like mad at the weeds, trying to find the keys. So, the little skinny runt! He thought I was going to be an easy mark. Well, that's the end of him and me! I better tell the mamma not to start preparing the wedding. It looks like we won't be getting married after all. Fucking mad bastardin Italians.

I decided to make me own way back, and headed off down the long narrow road, with nothing on either side but bushes and fields and sheep. Jaysus! I hope I find me way back before that lunatic gets his hands on me. It's going to be a long walk back.

I must have walked for fucking miles, I thought, looking at the trees coming up beside me as I headed into a forest. Feeling happy now to leave the open desolation of the bogs behind me. Then I heard a droning noise in the distance. I stopped to listen, hearing it coming from back up the mountain. I could see the dust flying up behind the speck of a car, as I craned me eyes into the distance. It weaved its way through the narrow roads, bombing down the mountain, leaving a trail of dust flying into the air.

That looks like fuck face! Wonder if I should try to get a lift from him? The thought only hit me for a second. Not on yer nelly! I'm killed stone dead if he gets his hands on me. I flew, making for the trees, planting meself behind a huge thick one, waiting for the car to get close. Here it comes. It tore around a bend and came flying down the straight bit of road and thundered into the forest. I held me breath, watching as it flew past, sending out the smell of burning rubber. It looked like there was smoke coming out of the tyres as they tore over loose stones, flying them into the air. The car vanished for a minute, getting lost in the smoke coming out of the exhaust pipe.

Fuck! The speed a him, I thought. Getting a flash of him gripping the steering wheel, looking like he had murder on his mind. From now on I better watch meself with him. He's going to be out to get me. No, I'm not turning me back on him. Definitely not.

I took off, hoping I would make it back in time for work. It doesn't look like it now. Not at the distance I'm covering.

The curse a Jaysus on that bastard anyway! Ah, shut up, Martha! What did yeh think he was after? Hmm! Still an all. I thought I might strike lucky and end up having a lovely time, after he maybe taking me for a drive around the place. Then going for a coffee into town or something. That he might have been nice to me, driving nice and quiet, with the two of us having a lovely chat. No, there's nothing for nothing. There's always a price to pay for everything. Still, not everyone is as bad as that little weasel. Look at all the girls that get themself nice fellas! Ah, to hell with it! I wasn't looking for a boyfriend anyway.

OK, I better get a move on. Jaysus! I wonder what time it is? The aul one will kill me if I'm late. I started to really hurry. Running slowly through the forest. Right, nearly getting somewhere, I thought. Staring through the trees, seeing the light in the distance. But I was still walking half an hour later. 'That's what it feels like. How much time has really gone past?' I muttered, stopping to listen to the silence around me. I'm still no further on. It feels like I have been on this bleedin path before. I hope I'm not going around in circles. I stared at the ground, not wanting to break me neck over something, and I could feel the fear creeping up through me, seeing I was beginning to lose the light. I kept going, dragging me legs, feeling like they were two iron bars.

Bastards! I hate men. All they ever want to do is get their hands on you. Pity I didn't let that fucking car run over yer man and bleedin bury him in the mountains, like he threatened to do to me. I could feel meself beginning to cry with tiredness and the exhaustion of walking all day. I'm fucking starving, and freezing with the cold. No, he better watch out for me. I'll shove his ugly fucking face in that deep-fat fryer when I get me hands on him. 'AHHHH!' I threw back me head and screamed with the rage. 'Yer a stupid bastard!' Then I let out me breath and dropped me shoulders and carried on. Hearing me screams still echoing around the forest.

Then, suddenly, a clearing opened up in front of me, and I was back on the road again. 'I'M OUT! YEAH, YIPPEE!' At last. I made it! Me heart gladdened at the sight of the road running down the mountain, leading me back into Hangman's Wood. I'll be so happy to see people again. Get back at last to the café and eat a load of lovely grub. Oh, I can't wait. I'm definitely going to get to bed early. As soon as I finish work.

I stopped and took one last look back at the woods behind me, seeing how dark it got. I gave a shiver, thinking I could have been lost in there for the whole night. I moved on quickly, wanting to make tracks and get down the mountain as quickly as possible. I'm not out of trouble yet. I could still get stranded up here with all them fields around me, not knowing where I'm going in the dark.

I walked on, feeling the tar road jar up through me as I dragged me feet, lifting one foot after the other. Letting them fall back down again, feeling bone weary, like I'll never move again after this. The light kept fading very fast, and I was staring with me eyes wide open trying to see everything in the half-dark. 'Oh, God! I don't like where I've landed meself now. It's too quiet,' I muttered in a whisper to meself. I walked along the narrow road and kept looking up at the high stone walls. It feels like they are closing in on me and I'm afraid I'll run into something around the next bend. You never know what's waiting in hiding for you in this bleedin dark. Now it's all big trees and hedges. I stared up at the high hedges with big trees growing behind them. I could hear the wind blowing through them, making it sound like they were whispering in the dark and trying to reach out and grab me.

At last! I finally made it down the hill, leaving the dark road behind me, and came out onto a wide open road, and stopped for a minute to get me breath. I looked down the rest of the mountain at the city below. Seeing the lights twinkling in the distance. It really looks lovely from this height. Standing up here on this dark hill, with me breath turning to frost and the silence all around me. It feels like time is standing still. I could be without a worry in the world. Just standing looking at all the lights beginning to flicker on.

'Right, now I know I'm nearly there,' I puffed. The tiredness beginning to make me legs and back burn with the pain now seemed easier. I took off down the hill, half-running with the thought I'll soon get there. Then I heard a car coming up behind me. It slowed down as it went past me, then stopped. The driver said something to the elderly woman sitting beside him and the two of them stared out the back window at me.

I hesitated, seeing an old man and woman. They're OK. Maybe they want to give me a lift. I rushed up and the woman opened the window, rolling it down. 'Excuse me! I wonder would you mind please giving me a lift down to the village? I need to get there in a hurry!'

'Yes, of course, dear. What on earth are you doing at this time in the evening walking around up here?' she said, clucking her tongue.

'Hop in the back,' said the man, looking at me then looking in shock at the wife. 'Do you know anything can happen to you wandering around up here on your own?' said the old man, looking back at me and shaking his head like he never saw the like of it before in his life. 'Young ones have no sense.'

'No,' said the wife. 'The older they get, the worse they get. You nearly have to watch them twenty-four hours a day! What brought you up here?' said the woman, staring at me like I was her granddaughter and I better have a good excuse.

I just stared at her. Shaking me head, saying, 'I thought it was a good idea at the time.'

'Did you get lost?' the old man asked me, not taking his eyes off the road.

'Yeah, yeah, I did,' I said. Turning me head and looking back up the mountain at the trees, seeing it was really pitch black now. Jaysus! I just made it down in time, I thought. Letting meself fall back into the seat, wriggling and settling meself for more comfort. Oh, this is great. Here I am in out of the cold and getting a rest at last. I let me head fall back on the cushioned leather seat and stared out at more hedges and trees slowly going past. While this time all I had to do was just sit here feeling happy to be safe and sound, sitting in the back of the car with these really kind people, knowing they would do me no harm.

I closed me eyes, feeling a lovely sense of peace settle inside me as I listened to them muttering away contentedly to each other. The heat hummed out of the fan and washed over me, melting away the icy cold in me bones from being all day out in the frosty mountain. I felt meself beginning to doze off, with the seat gently rocking me. The rhythmic noise from the wheels

of the car under me was eating up the road, and all I had to do
was sit here, and I would be taken to where I'm going. Gawd,
cars are really marvellous things for getting you where you want.
Especially if you're in the right company, and you know you'll
be safe and sound when you get there. With nobody looking for
payment, like that mad bastard.

I stirred meself, seeing I was back at last. 'Will you just leave me
off down at the shops?' I said, leaning across the seat and pointing
at the shops ahead. 'Thank you very much for your kindness,' I
smiled, feeling very grateful to them. I could see we were nearly
passing them by.

'We can drop you home,' said the old lady, turning to me.

'No, this is it. The shops will be fine, thanks.' The old man
pulled over and stopped the car.

'Don't stay out too late now!' the old woman said. Staring at me
and looking at the chip shop with all the young ones and young
fellas hanging around outside.

'No, no, I won't. I really am very grateful to the two of you!
I'll say a little prayer for you before I go to bed tonight,' I said,
staring in at the two of them with their heads nearly together,
looking out at me.

'Yes! Good girl. You do that,' said the old woman, smiling at
me. The man nodded his head up and down, agreeing with his
wife, then he took off, driving slowly up the road.

I looked over at the shop, seeing the lights blazing inside, with
people sitting in the café, eating and drinking. With more people
standing around the counter, waiting to be served. The bright lights
from the café were throwing shadows on the footpath, lighting up
the darkness outside. My God! It's pitch black out! It really is dark
now, so that means it must be very late. I wonder what time it is?
Oh, dear God! I'm dead late. I hope I'm not in big trouble.

Me heart started to hammer like mad in me chest at the thought
of facing into the aul one because I knew I was late. Even worse,
Touchy will be there! Fuck him! I'll brain him, if he gives me
any more hardship!

I took in a deep breath and made for the shop. The aul fella saw me coming and rushed inside to the family kitchen. I clapped eyes on Touchy. Wearing his dirty white apron, over his old clothes. He stopped what he was doing, and held onto a basket of chips and watched me coming in the door. I said nothing, just stared back, watching him shake his head up and down, with his eyes half-closing, squinting at me like I was in for it now. Looking like he had been waiting for me. His face was white and the side of his jaw was swollen. I took in another deep breath and pushed past him, keeping me eyes steady, showing him I was ready for him. No, fuck face. I'm not afraid of a little squirt like you, I thought.

I was just heading through the door and up the stairs to get changed into me old clothes when I hear roars behind me. 'Momento! You wait! I wanta talk to you!' the mamma shouted, grabbing her frock and holding onto the banisters, puffing her way up the stairs after me. Trying to get up in a hurry. 'I am going to tell you to leave,' she snorted, dragging herself into the room and holding her chest, trying to get her breath back. I looked at her, not able to take in what she was saying. 'You go. Out of here. I no want trouble.'

'Why? What did I do?' I said, wondering what was wrong with her. I hadn't done anything wrong on her, I thought, staring at her. Trying to figure out why she was turning on me.

'You come back here late,' she said, holding up her hand and slapping her fingers one by one. 'You go gallivanting with the boys. No nice girl do that in my family. What you do is your business.'

'But I only went for a drive with Alfonso,' I said. Still not able to take in what was happening.

'No, no, I don't want to hear! It is not good, what you did.'

'What did I do?' I shouted, losing the rag.

'You upset Alfonso. His face. What did you do to him? He is a nice boy!'

'The bastard attacked me!' I shouted. She stared at me for a minute. Knowing full well what I was talking about.

I held me breath, waiting for her to say something. Hoping she might say, 'Well, you have learned your lesson. Don't go off in cars with men again. OK, go to work! Alfonso got what he deserved.

Maybe he won't be so quick to mess with girls again. Now, don't give me any more trouble.'

I waited. Me chest getting tighter. Please, God, don't let me lose me job. Then I heard her say . . . I lost the first few words, not able to take them in. I listened, while they flew around the room. Then I caught up with the words. 'Well, I am not having this in my home. First thing in the morning, I want you out of here. First thing!' she shouted, rushing her big fat body across the floorboards, making them thump and rock up and down. Then she was gone. Out the door and down the stairs. I heard her rush into the family kitchen and start shouting. Then it died away as she slammed the door shut.

I stood stock still. Hearing no more sounds. I was left with the sound of my breathing, and the feeling of pain as my heart hammered away in me chest. Not believing what just happened. I turned slowly around the room, taking in the wardrobe, the two beds against the wall, the curtains pulled closed. No one ever opens them, I thought. Then I stared down at my suitcase, thinking that's the only thing that ever stays with me. Everything else comes and goes. But it's just me and me suitcase! I felt somehow I had something that belonged to me. Me suitcase, carrying all me things. They belong to me. I have something that belongs to me. I'm not on me own really. I'm not down and out. No, a suitcase means I'm going somewhere.

Jaysus! I'm on the move again. Ah, well, it was nice while it lasted. I even picked up a bit of Italian. 'Fungolase!' 'Basta!' Fuck off, and stop! That should come in handy.

I woke up, seeing the light make its way in through the curtains. I looked around the room, hearing the sounds of snoring. Everyone was still fast asleep. They won't get up until later. I looked over, seeing Rosa plastered over the whole double bed. Lying on her back with her mouth wide open, huge snores blasting out of her mouth.

Maria is not there. She must be gone to school. Must be later then I thought. I better get up and get moving.

I moved gently, not wanting to wake Mary. Scrunched up in a

ball with her hands in a fist, and her head pushed into the wall. She's out for the count. Poor Mary! God love her. I wonder if she will ever get to be happy? I think she's carrying the worry of all her little brothers and sisters. I worry like that meself. But the ma and Jackser is holding onta them! Jaysus! Don't start, Martha. You have enough to worry you at the minute, to start finding another job. The kids will take off one by one, just like I did. Charlie has already done that, by the sound of things. Yeah, a hard life is about waiting. Just waiting for the time to come when yeh can start leading your own life. Well, that's what I'm able to do.

Pity I can't manage to stay in the one job, though. Whatever it is about me, no matter how hard I try. I even tell meself I'm going to be good. But I always end up getting into fights, losing me job. Getting bloody fired! How does that happen? I can't understand it. Other people . . . like Mary. She keeps quiet and nobody bothers her! Hmm, maybe I'm just not the quiet type! Some people say they can hear me before they see me. Fuck! Pity I'm not the quiet type! Even the ma's very quiet! No, thank God I'm not quiet after all! Look what kept happening to her! Right! I'm grand as I am. People can take me or leave me. Right, better get moving.

I grabbed me washbag from the end of the wardrobe, pushing all the others' stuff piled on top out of the way. Jaysus! There was never any room for anything here anyway. I had to keep all me stuff in me suitcase. I hurried out to the bathroom, and brushed me teeth and washed me face. Then combed me hair. No bath this morning. The water wouldn't be hot enough. Right, better get dressed. Yeah. And collect me wages from Saturday. That aul one owes me for one day. I wonder how much that is?

I came out of the bathroom and down onto me own landing, hearing the snores coming from the fellas' room. They're all still asleep in there. Then I had an idea. I turned the handle of their door quietly, making sure not to make it squeak. The door opened a little and I put me head in. Jaysus! Look at the state a the lot of them. They're filthy! The smell is disgusting. Rubber man, the fella that peels the potatoes and wears the rubber apron and Russian boots, was draped over Francesco. With his arm covering his head.

Francesco was breathing fast, trying to get air, because he was caught under rubber boots, with the blanket over his face and the big hand holding him down. Me eyes peeled to the single bed, with Touchy lying on his side, curled up in a ball, and the blankets wrapped up all around him. The only thing sticking out was his nose. Me eyes peeled all along the floor, then lit on Alfonso's clothes sitting in a heap, lying on the floor beside his bed where he'd dumped them last night. Fucker! You caused all the trouble! I even think you are too thick to get the message why you ended getting your teeth knocked out. I could feel me annoyance rising up again. Right!

I dropped me washbag on the landing and crept in quietly. Yeah, his work clothes. I grabbed the lot up in one go, seeing his shoes sitting under the bed and grabbed them, too. I crept off, holding me breath, and me face tight, and took off out the door on me tippy toes. What will I do with them? Yeah, the bathroom. I dumped them in the bath, smothering them in water until they were soaking to nothing. Then grabbed up the basin sitting on the shelf at the end of the bath and dumped them in it. Right, where will I hide them? Under the stuff in my bedroom. Well, Rosa's bedroom. Hee, hee! This is great!

I opened the wardrobe and pulled everything to one side and dumped the lot back over the basin. Then flew for me washbag and dived for me clothes. I better wear me work clothes. I'm definitely not ruining me one and only set of good clothes for nothing. I must have worn the soles of me good patent shoes with all that walking yesterday. Jaysus! I better make me escape before they wake up.

I put on me old coat and picked up me case and handbag and took off out the door and down the stairs. 'So, you are ready to go?' Fatty, the aul one said, coming out of the kitchen and wiping her hands on a tea towel. Lifting her head back and landing her fat arms on her hips, with her legs planted, watching to make sure I got the message.

'Yes, I'm going now. But first I want me wages.'

'You only worked one day. Saturday. Here is your money,' she said, diving her hand into her massive blue frock with the white dots and coming up with two half crowns. 'Here, take it. One day's work.'

'Thanks, missus. Goodbye,' I said, satisfied with the five shillings and making off out the side door.

I went out into the early morning, seeing the grey-blue light. It sounded quiet, with cars in the distance and the odd person walking down to get their shopping. Me breath hung around me face with the cold. Fuck! Winter. January. At least it's dry.

Right, I better get the bus into town and wait for the evening paper. Please, God, help me to find another job.

12

I stood in O'Connell Street, looking up and down the length of it. It's still too early to do anything. The few people hurrying through the streets kept their heads down, stuck inside their coats, with their scarves tied tight on their heads. Rushing to get what they had to do and get in out of the cold.

What will I do? It's bloody freezing. I started walking, carrying me case in one hand and me handbag held tight in my right hand, and headed off down towards the Parnell Street end. All the shops had their lights on, and very few had people in them. I stopped outside the Carlton picture house and looked up at the big poster, showing what was coming next week. *The Sound of Music*. I stared up at the woman flying over the mountain, her feet barely touching the ground. She had short straight fair hair, and her eyes were alive with excitement A big laugh was spread all over her face and she was dragging a load of happy laughing children behind her. That looks good. I'd like to see that. It's a pity I'm not settled in a job yet! Then I'd know what's happening, and I could make me plans to go to the pictures.

Jaysus! I don't know where I am at the minute. Everyone has somewhere to go. How the hell do they do it? How do you get to be settled in your own home, like everyone else? Do I have to have a husband first? No, God, no! I don't want that. There must be some way I can get a job that will pay me enough to get meself me own place! No, I'm too young. You have to be older, get plenty of experience working first, get trained, then you work your way up. Jesus! It all takes time. Everything comes down to time.

Or does it? All I need is the money. Ah, how would you get that, Martha? I could go to England. Look for a job in a pub. No, keep away from them. That's only bad news. What, then? Jaysus! I'll just have to get a job and hold onto it. I can go to night school. Learn to be a secretary. Yeah, that's definitely me best bet.

Right, where will I head off to now? What about Caffola's? That's me favourite spot. I haunt that place. Yeah, that's because it always makes me feel welcome. I can sit and look out at the world going by. Anyway, I always wanted to be able to go into these places. I promised meself as a child when I used to stand outside looking in. Yeah. I know now what it is. It makes me feel I'm just like everyone else, respectable. I have money in me pocket to go in. I'm not a pauper! No, I'm definitely not that any more. I'm clean and dressed respectable; well, even though me clothes are old, I thought. Looking down at me old green coat with the greasy sleeves that someone used to wear once when they were going to the secondary school. I wonder who that was and how did they get on? They're probably in a great job now, and working in London. That's where everyone goes. Yeah. I even have money in me pocket. So I'm really well-off. No, life is still a bowl of cherries! It just depends on how you look at it.

I picked up me suitcase and took off happily for me favourite haunting place. Seeing the lights and the red tables with the cushy benches behind your back. I like to listen to the waitresses talking. Complaining and giving out about everything, even about the customers, and having no money. Then cheering up at the mention of what they had to look forward to. I like that. It makes me feel like one a them. That we all have the same worries.

No, nothing in the damn paper. Jaysus! What am I going to do? The time is moving on. I have nowhere to stay, never mind no job! Fuck this! I better run over to the GPO and ring Sister Eleanor.

I dumped the newspaper on the table and grabbed up me stuff, making out the door, and headed across the road into the post office. 'Right, here we are,' I puffed, getting outa breath. I could smell the ink, and dust and chalk, and especially the stale smell of people that lay around the building from years of nobody bothering to open the windows and give the place a good airing, or even a good cleaning. Still and all, I like this place. The world and his wife come in here. With people wanting to make important phone calls home to the country, or Dubliners phoning relations in England to tell them they have the money saved and they are coming over. Yeah, you can see lots of people with suitcases getting lost around the place. So I don't stand out here. Right, better get moving.

I checked to see I had enough pennies for the phone. Yeah, I have enough coppers. I made me way along the rows of phone boxes, looking for an empty one. Here we are. The second-last one. I pulled open the door and put me suitcase down on the floor, shutting the door after me to keep out the noise. Right, I don't need the phone book. I know the number off by heart. I dropped in the tuppence and dialled the number. It's ringing! I held me breath, hearing me heart flying in me chest. Dear God, grant that she won't eat the head off me and will be able to get me a job.

'Good afternoon. Holy Redeemer Convent.' Me eye flew to the A button and I pressed it.

'Hello, could I speak to Sister Eleanor, please?'

'Who is this?'

'Martha, sister. Martha Long.'

'Oh, just a minute, Martha. I think she's in the recreation room.' I held me breath, afraid to breathe with the nerves. Dear God, please make sure she has a job for me. Maybe I should have gone down. It might have been better that way. Face to face. Then if she hasn't a job, she might let me stay for a few nights. Hmm, pity I gave me name to the nun. Then I could have hung up the phone once I knew she was there. Ah, that's a pity. I never think before I act. I could have galloped down to see her. Making meself look desperate enough so she'd have to let me stay. Ah well, it's too late now.

'Hello, Martha. What is it?' she said, sounding worn out.

'Eh, how are yeh, Sister Eleanor? It's me, Martha.'

'Yes, Martha, I know that. Look, I hope you're not ringing to tell me you have gone and lost your job! This is the . . . how many jobs have you had since you left here?'

'Whadeyehmean? I haven't lost any jobs!' I roared, getting annoyed because she was blaming me in the wrong.

'Good girl, because I can tell you now, I can't be still running after you and letting you waltz back here when it suits you,' she puffed.

'Eh, I didn't mean, eh . . .' I was trying to think of the best way of putting it. 'No, I'm definitely not asking to come back,' I said, letting out me breath.

'Good girl. I'm delighted to hear you are doing very well. Now I must hurry, Martha. I can hear sister calling me to go out on the cloister walk to get my prayers,' she whispered, sounding delighted to get rid of me so fast.

'No, wait! Just a minute, sister. Don't go. I have something important to ask you.' I could hear her catch her breath.

'Yes, what is it?'

'Eh, sister . . .'

'Quickly, Martha. Say what it is you want!'

'I lost me job, sister,' I whispered, feeling ashamed.

'WHAT? But you just told me this minute—'

'Yes, sister! You misunderstood me. What I wanted to say was I'm not asking to come back. I just need another job. I've been looking now since early morning. This is only Monday. So there won't be any more new jobs advertised until Wednesday. There's nothing in the papers, sister! I need to get a job, otherwise I have nowhere to go,' I whispered, then pulled the phone away from me ear. There was a silence. I waited, then put the phone to me ear again.

'Well, really!' she roared, losing the rag when it hit her what I just said. 'You are so irresponsible! I told you, Martha. You are not rushing to me every time you feel free to lose your job. No, no, I am not having it!'

'But, sister, please!'

'No, Martha! There has to be an end to it.'

'Right, I'm coming down there and I'm going to sit on the

convent doorstep and freeze to death,' I snorted, losing me rag at the unfairness of her. She lets everyone else back when they lose their jobs, why not me? I'm thinking, the rage boiling up in me.

'I'm going to hang up this minute. You are trying to browbeat me into giving in to your demands,' she snorted, looking for an excuse to hang up the phone on me.

'No, don't go, Sister Eleanor. Please! I'm sorry for speaking to you like that. This is the last time I'll ever ask you for anything. I promise,' I said, feeling desperate to hang onto her.

'Right. I shall have to go and see if there are any calls in looking for a girl.'

'Oh, thanks, sister! I really appreciate it!'

'This is the last time now, Martha!'

'Yes, sister,' I said, feeling down because she was annoyed with me, and raging because she has her pets, and I'm not one of them.

'Ring me back in an hour. I will have to go and get my prayers first. Then I will check that out for you. Goodbye now.'

'Bye, sister!' I roared, before she hung up the phone.

I opened the phone box for air, and looked at the long line of boxes with people shouting down the phones, and wondered if they had big worries too. Jaysus! I felt let down and really fed up. It pains me when I feel I can't go to her when I have trouble. It would be lovely if she was nice to me. I just want her to care about me. But she's always in a hurry, and has no time for me.

I stood with me back resting against the windowsill, not bothering to go out into the street again. I didn't feel like putting one foot in front of the other. I lit up a cigarette and glared at a fella making for my phone box. 'Excuse me, that's engaged! I'm waiting for a phone call.'

'I don't see anybody in here, do you?' he asked me, looking in the phone box, and whipping his big red-neck culchie head back at me.

'Ger outa me way,' I said, pushing him back, and sending him staggering, after taking him unawares. I rushed back into the box, banging me case in behind me, and slammed the door shut in his face. Taking a big suck on me cigarette, and stared out at him. Watching him staring back in at me with his mouth gaping open. Trying to think. Wanting to say something really smart that would annoy me, and he would be able to get his own back.

'Yar only a thick jackeen!' he roared, shaking his head and moving off. I opened the door, feeling meself suffocating with the smoke in the little box, and stared out after him. Watching him walking up and down the row, looking for an empty phone box. Then my phone rang.

'Hello,' a man's voice whispered. I listened, wondering what was going on. 'What colour knickers are yeh wearin?' the voice whispered. I was shocked, then wondered how he got this number.

'Green!' I shouted. 'What colour are yours, yeh fuckin eejit?' Then it dawned on me. I left the phone down on top of the phone book, and opened the door quietly, shutting it, leaving me suitcase inside. Then I looked down the row of phone boxes, spying the culchie with the big red neck talking with his back bent, definitely looking very shifty. 'That fella's up to no good,' I muttered to meself. I wandered over quietly and listened outside the door.

'Are yeh dere? Hello,' he whispered, nearly resting his head on the phone book. 'Would yeh like a good ride?' Me face dropped, listening to every word. I could see his red face, with the mouth hanging open, and watch him trying to get his breath. He was breathing like someone with a chest complaint.

'Yeh fucking bastard!' I shot at the door, whipping it open, shouting, 'HELP! This man is molesting me!'

'WHA?' He dropped the phone, whipping his head around at me, with the eyes staring out of his head.

'Yes, you! Yeh dirty aul bastard! I have the coppers waiting outside the door for yeh. I'm going to get you arrested!' I roared, pointing me finger at him as people put their heads out of the boxes to see what all the fuss was about.

'Yeh mad fuckin bitch! I never laid a hand on yeh,' he moaned, pushing past me to fly out the door. I grabbed a hold of his heavy overcoat. Hanging onto it, not wanting to let him off that easy.

'Get the man in charge!' I shouted, 'You were asking me what colour knickers I'm wearing and saying all the dirty disgusting things yeh were going to do to me.'

'Gesh away outa dat!' he screamed. Tugging like mad at the coat, trying to get free a me. 'Help!' he screamed, looking and seeing all the people staring. I could see he was nearly crying with the shock. 'Let go a me coash outa dat!' he screamed, sounding like a woman singing opera.

I was dragging him and he was pulling. Then, finally, he managed to tear himself loose from me fists, tearing the end of his coat outa me hand, and flew for all he was worth out the door. I whipped me head from staring after him, disappearing like greased lightning. Then me eyes peeled back to everyone looking at me. 'Yer man,' I said. 'The cheek a him. Trying teh molest me, he was,' I puffed. Blowing out me cheeks. They stared for a few minutes, trying to make this out, with their eyeballs pinned on me, then stared at the door where your man had just shot out, leaving a draught behind him. Then they saw nothing else was happening and everyone disappeared back to their own business.

'Right!' I muttered to meself, heading back to me phone box and waiting for the phone call. It will be a long time before he tries anything like that again, I thought, laughing to meself. Bleedin hell! I've had enough of dirty aul men trying to molest me! Well, even if it was only on the phone! I wasn't expecting that.

The phone rang just as I lit up another cigarette. Me nerves are gone with all this waiting, I thought, feeling meself shiver with worry as I picked up the phone. 'Hello, Martha, is that you?'

'Yes, sister, I'm here.'

'Wait until I tell you. I have a lady looking for a girl to do housework and mind a ten-year-old girl. She wants someone to live-in. I have just given her a ring this very minute and you can start right away. Now,' she said happily, whispering in her quiet voice, 'have you a pen handy?'

'Yes, yes, sister, I have. Hang on a minute, I just want to get it out of my handbag.' I dropped the phone and wrestled with me handbag, trying to open the catch, and dipped to the bottom, bringing up me Biro. Paper! Where's me little notebook I bought in Woolworths? I opened the pocket in the middle and took out me little red notebook. 'Right, I'm ready, sister. Just give me the address, yeah?'

'It's thirty-two Millers Field, just off Old Court Road.'

'Grand! I have that. It's just up off the Old Court Road. Is that what you just said?'

'Yes! You can start straight away. She's a national school teacher and she finishes school at three o'clock. She collects the child herself. They are in the same school. So make your way out there straight away. Now, remember, Martha, keep out of trouble! I don't want you to lose this job. If you do . . . be it on your own head. I can't help you.'

'Oh no, sister! This is it. No more trouble for me. I'm definitely going to last in this job. That I can promise you. Have no fear about that, sister!'

'Good girl. Go, now. The lady's name is Mrs Purcell.'

'OK, sister. Thank you very, very much. I'm delighted to get a job at last, before the day ended. Goodbye now, sister, and thanks again.'

'Goodbye, Martha. Be a good girl.'

'Yes, sister. I'm off.' Then I put the phone down and grabbed me suitcase, flying meself out the door. I could feel me heart going like the clappers. Oh, thank you, God, for being so good to me. I'm so happy at getting a job at last. The best bit as well is Sister Eleanor was very nice to me. Maybe she does like me after all. Right, I better make for the bus.

I shot across the road, making for the side of Clerys. Heading meself down to the Pro-Cathedral, to hurry in and light a penny candle and say a little prayer to God for being so good to me. As I neared the church, I passed a woman sitting on the freezing cold ground at the side of the church. She was wrapped up in a red plaid shawl with a little baby snuggled inside. God help that poor woman. She's going to get pneumonia sitting on that cold ground. She's probably been sitting there all day and has nothing to show for it.

I crept into the chapel quietly, smelling the incense and smoke from the burning candles, and looked at all the little lights burning around the huge church. It's lovely and peaceful and warm in here. No harm can ever come to you when you're in a place like this, I thought, looking around at all the statues and making me way over to the one of the Sacred Heart. I took out me purse and rooted for a penny, putting it in the brass box, and lit a little white candle. I stared at the flickering light, watching it catch, then flare into life. Then I leaned over, putting it with all the other candles burning for people's intentions. I blessed meself as I knelt down on the soft cushion on the kneeler and looked up at the statue. A lovely red lamp was glowing, giving out a cosy warm heat.

Dear God! Thank you so much for looking after me. I know I can never go far wrong when you are always there to watch over me. I will try to be good and do my best at everything I do. Please keep me safe and, above all, help me to stay out of trouble. Because you know, Sacred Heart, I can't afford to lose this job. Thank you for everything you do for me, and please, God, look after me ma and all me sisters and brothers. But especially for Charlie! He's on his own, too! Thank you, God.

I lowered me head, closing me eyes, and paused for a minute. Letting the warmth of the Sacred Heart's little alcove, with the statue looking down at me, and the red lamp glowing, and all the little white candles burning in their brass holders. Making me feel safe and warm and peaceful. I sat on, letting it sink into me.

I have more to say, God. Today was a very worrying one. I felt a bit lost and lonely wandering up and down, feeling different from all the rest of the people. Especially when it was so cold out. That makes you feel worse. I really wanted someone I could sit down with and have a talk. Tell them all me worries. But I can't tell me business to anyone. I mean, to people I don't know. Even though I don't know many people, just Sister Eleanor, really. Now, you know she doesn't really know anything about me business. Yeah, she knows we are poor. She saw me little brothers and sisters when they came that time to the convent. But that's all she knows. She doesn't know I'm a bastard, and I don't belong to Jackser! Yeah, thanks, God, for that. I'm very grateful to you for small mercies!

Well, that's a big mercy! Anyway, God, nobody knows nothing about me and I intend it stays that way. So I have to hide all that. You know how shocked people would be if they heard that kind of thing about me. They would run a mile. Definitely they would look down on me. I could even see Sister Eleanor's face dropping if I told her any of the things that went on with me ma and Jackser.

They knew I was different in the convent. I wasn't one a them. They saw me as a street kid. So can you imagine what people would have said if they knew what I really came from? But it still pains me, God, when I'm down and out like today. That's when it really hits me. Anyway, God, what am I talking about that for? Sure that doesn't matter any more. So what am I on about? Oh, yeah! What I really mean to say is, all them things about me makes me feel different. No . . . that's not what I'm trying to say. Look, God, I just felt different. I wanted to have someone for meself. Someone I belonged to, to have somewhere to go. In other words, God, if I could turn up somewhere and knock on the door. Even if they didn't like me. That would be OK. Because I'd know when they open that door they would have to let me in because I belong to them. That's my home, God. Not go wandering in the cold looking for somewhere to sit in and get a bit of heat. Hoping to meet someone to pass the time with and have a bit of company and a little chat. So I won't feel so lonely and take me mind off me worries. You know, about having no job. Worrying about finding another one.

Sorry, I'm moaning, God. No, I know what I want to say but I can't work it out. But this is what I want to tell you. I know when everything else is gone, and I'm left with nobody, I'm still not alone in the world. I can always come here and sit with you, and tell you about me worries. You will never let me down. You are always listening to me, because I know you really care about me. You have helped me all through my life in my hours of need. I know even when I walk out of here, you will stay with me. So, God, I need never be afraid as long as I have you. You are the greatest power on this earth. So how could I ever be afraid? No, you love me as I am. I know that because you know everything. So you know what I'm thinking and what I'm really like, who I really am. Yet you still love me. That makes me feel I am somebody. I'm not dirt. Even though I have no home of me own to go to. Or a family I can talk about. You know, dear God, what people are like if they knew what I was really like and what kind of life I've had. They would look down on me, think I'm only dirt! But you know I'm not. I will become somebody one day. I will have me own place to go to. Everything will work out in the end. Thanks, God, for listening to me. Goodbye now.

No, not really goodbye! Sure aren't you coming with me? I mean, you can be everywhere at the same time! But this is where you live. In the quiet here. The chapel, in this house of prayer. I heard somebody call it that once. It must have been a nun. Yeah, I like that – house of prayer. Holy God's house. Me ma used to always call it that. I miss her, God, me old ma, the one I had before she met Jackser! That pains me now, God. Just remembering her face back then. Oh, I'm off again. Wanting to cry. No, I'm fine now. I'm all grown up. I don't really need a mammy any more. I can take care of meself. Yeah, life's a bowl of cherries! I'm all grown up. Right, I better get moving.

I gently lifted me head, and took up me suitcase, and made me way quietly out of the church, feeling at peace with meself and the world. Making me feel lovely and warm inside meself. The cold hit me straight away as I stood on the steps buttoning up the top of me coat and took off, heading for the bus. I saw the woman was still sitting there and I paused to look at her. 'Fer the love a God, daughter, would yeh ever have a few coppers teh get a sup a milk for the babby?' she implored me, stretching out her hand. I dropped me suitcase and left me handbag down on the ground and took the purse out of me pocket.

'Here, will that do you?' I said, handing her a shilling.

'Oh, God bless yeh, and may yeh be rewarded in heaven for yer bit a kindness,' she said, blessing me.

'Can you not get up out of the cold and go home now?' I asked her, hoping she had made her few bob and could move herself off home and maybe get a few messages and have a bit of heat.

'Ah, I think I will, daughter! Sure there's no day left in it anyways,' she said, looking up at the cold clear sky.

'OK, goodbye now,' I said, grabbing up me suitcase, and took off heading for the bus.

'Fares now, please.' I heard the conductor rattling his money bag and muttering at people for the money. Where's me bag? I shot me head down, looking at me suitcase sitting on the floor beside me on the seat. Bag? Where's me handbag? Me heart leaped. No bag! Oh, Jesus, don't say I've lost it.

I jumped up, grabbing the suitcase out of the way, putting it in the aisle, looking down on the floor and all round the seat. Nothing. It's gone. Then it hit me. I left it on the ground when I stopped to give the poor woman the shilling. I had the distinct picture of putting the suitcase down and the handbag. Or where did I put the handbag? On the ground beside the suitcase, I suppose. It will be well gone by now. All me savings, everything I had, was in that bag.

I sank down in the seat, feeling the colour drain out of me, and slipped me hand into me pocket, taking out me purse. Two shillings and ninepence left. That's all the money I have left in the whole world to keep me going, I thought. Feeling a terrible weakness draining me. The woman would have picked that up. Now she might have fifteen pounds and the shilling I gave her.

'Fares, please!' I handed the conductor tuppence and took the ticket. Just as well I'm starting a new job. At least I won't have to worry about eating and finding somewhere to sleep. Well, so that's that then! I will just have to start saving all over again. It took me a whole year to save that money. I hardly spent any of me wages. Oh, well! Serves me right for being so stupid. I'll be more careful next time.

I got off the bus and headed into a cul-de-sac with rows of modern houses all looking the same. The houses look like they were built by the Corporation! No, maybe not. These are private houses, but very cheap-looking. I heard that builders were now putting up all new houses for the people getting married. I hear and see mention of these things in the newspaper. But, then again, these are not very new-looking. So Missus Purcell is not really well-off. I thought teachers were well-paid.

These houses look like the ones me ma and the Jackser fella live in, out in Finglas. I don't think much of them, judging by the look of the pebble-dashing on the walls. Only maybe these are bigger than the houses out where me ma is. Jaysus, Martha! Yer getting very uppity with your 'BIG HOUSES' and 'SMALL HOUSES'! You haven't even got a cardboard box to live in, so look who's talking! Still, you would think that a person who can afford to have someone live-in and do their housework for them would be well-off! Right, where's number thirty-two?

I looked from one side of the road to the other. Down further, over there, is seventeen. The even numbers are on this side. Thirty-two! I stopped for a minute, with me jaw hanging down to me belly, gaping at it. Oh, holy Jesus! The state of it. Me eyeballs nearly fell out a the back of me head staring. Seeing the dirty net curtains and the heavy ones were drawn halfway across the side, with the middle hanging down. Nobody has bothered to open them properly and stand up on a chair and fix the one pulled down. Jaysus! Look at the state of the garden. It's full of holes, with rubbish blown in from the road. The garden looks like it has never seen a blade of grass. Not with all them holes in it, and the few tufts of grass are only weeds. I stared at the sweet wrappers and Tayto crisp bags lying around in the muddy garden. The mud was dragged all along the path. Right up to the front door. Jaysus! It's plain to see they don't look after this place.

I rang the doorbell, seeing the shape of a woman through the foggy glass in the door. I could hear her big culchie voice talking on the telephone. 'Just a minute, Katie. I hear someone at the door.' The door was whipped open by a big aul one built like a bus, looking frostbitten in a long, well-worn aul brown overcoat with the buttons missing in the middle. Jaysus! That coat has definitely seen better days. I looked up at her with the big red culchie face and the mop of dyed-brown wiry permed hair that stood up on top of her head. The dye and the perm had grown out, and the grey was showing like mad.

'Yes?' she huffed, barely moving her lips to get the words out.

'Eh . . .' I said, hesitating, not liking the look of her.

'What do you want?' she barked, staring at me with her hungry-looking, muddy-green bloodshot eyes. I watched them narrowing. Taking me in from head to toe, sizing me up. Judging to see if I was what she wanted.

'Are you Missus Purcell?'

'Yes! Who are you? Are you the one the nuns sent me from the convent?'

'Yes, mam, I'm the one,' I said, acting the fool, annoyed at being insulted.

'Come in,' she said, whipping her head at me and aiming it down the hall. I stopped beside her, not knowing what she wanted. 'Wait in there for me!' she roared, throwing her hand and whipping her head again, pointing me down the hall. I looked, seeing a long narrow hall into what looked like a kitchen. I walked into a big kitchen that looked like two rooms made into one. With a window looking out onto a back garden and a stainless-steel sink underneath, overflowing with dirty dishes. The kitchen smelled of grease and dust and years of cooking. Dirty brown filth was covering the kitchen units, and the worktop was covered with more dirty dishes. A loaf of bread was cut and dumped without being covered on the bread board. I could see a half-bottle of milk turned sour, with lumps floating in it. It was left sitting and forgotten, down in the corner of the worktop. Opened packets of biscuits spilled out around the worktop and a packet of cheese was left sitting, ripped out of the packet and the rest left dumped to the open air, and all sorts of germs.

Bleedin hell! It's the fumigation man this aul one needs, not the likes of me, to come in and help her, I thought, throwing me head around the place. Taking in the crumbs and bits of food walked into the dirty brown, well-worn-out lino. Jaysus! The floor is maggoty dirty.

The doors of the kitchen presses were left hanging open on the wall and the smell of the place would knock you out. The cooker had dirty pots stacked inside each other, and the frying pan was full of dirty brown grease. Oh, my God! What have I walked meself into? I thought, looking at the kitchen table covered in dirty plates and dishes from the last night's dinner. They didn't even bother to clear the table, never mind do the washing up. Underneath the table was filthy. With bits of carrot and food dropped off the plates and walked into the floor. I could feel meself getting very annoyed and worried. This aul one is off her head. She's bleedin filthy.

I could see a packet of open margarine with the knife still plastered in butter thrown beside it, getting butter mashed into the table. I turned around, looking to the left at the rest of the room. An alcove with an ironing board was left standing, with the iron sitting on the floor, and a white shirt still waiting to be ironed. I stared at the yellow plastic laundry basket thrown in the corner, piled high with dirty washing. Some of it was spilling onto the floor. With even more dirty clothes piled in a heap, climbing the wall in the corner.

That must be the dining area. It looked like it was two separate rooms at one time. But now they were all one. With the walls knocked out in the middle, making it the dining room one side and the kitchen all in one. It looked very bare, with no furniture. Except for the washing and the ironing board and a small dirty battered aul sofa with the springs sinking in the middle. It's smothered now, with clean washing dumped all over it waiting to be ironed, and the middle has collapsed onto the floor.

'What's your name?'

I whirled around, hearing the voice of a child, and stared into the white pasty face of a fat little girl wearing dispensary eye-glasses. Her brown-black hair was thick and wiry like the ma's. It stood out on her head with no direction. Some bits were nearly cut to the scalp, chopped to nothing. Bloody hell! Someone got loose at that head with a knife and fork. She could be mistaken for a boy, it's so short.

'Martha. What's yours?'

'Grainne,' she said, staring me up and down, then resting herself with her hands behind her back, leaning against the wall. 'We had a girl called Brigid. Mammy had to get rid of her because Mammy says she was always telling lies!'

'Is that right, now?' I said, smiling at her.

'You better not tell lies or Mammy will get rid of you, too. And you better not be lazy. Mammy hates girls who are lazy.'

'Well, she won't have to worry about me. I'm not lazy, and I don't tell lies.'

'Yes, but that's what Brigid said, and she told lies and she was shocking lazy. So you better not be lazy!' Grainne said. Staring me up and down, not believing a word I was telling her.

Oh, Jaysus! I'm going to go mental in this place. Now I've gone and got meself stuck with a load of loonies. And not even a penny in me pocket! God, I want me savings back. How could you let me be so stupid? Me whole life fucking savings! I need them to get outa here. 'Oh, fuck!' I snorted again, this time muttering, not caring if the young one heard me. I feel like screaming at you, God! I'm telling you this, it will be a long time before you get any more penny candles outa me. I definitely bleedin mean that. I could have gotten meself inta this mess without you. So if this is your idea of helping me, then FUCK OFF! But if you weren't helping me, I thought, worried I might be going too far at the idea of cursing God. I started to think about this then got meself all confused and I lost me rag again. Ah, fuck off with yourself, God! I don't care. I just don't know anything any more.

I could feel meself beginning to go mad with the rage. I stopped and took in a deep breath, then let it out slowly, thinking, right, it's a job. I'm still lucky! But I can't seem to stop meself feeling the terrible loss of me money. Without that, I'm now trapped here. At the mercy of the lunatics living in this kip!

I stood in the middle of the floor, waiting on the aul one, feeling me heart sinking, and an empty feeling of being lost inside meself. This place is cold and miserable. There's no life here, and that aul one looks like she's one very mean culchie aul cow. She's definitely going to be looking for trouble. Well, I'll just have to make the most of it.

I'm stuck here until I can find something better. I won't give her any excuse to get rid of me. I'll just work hard and keep her satisfied.

'So!' she said, coming slowly into the room, watching me, and wrapping the coat around her to keep out the cold. Then she folded her arms and slowly let herself drop against the wall, crossing her ankles, and studied me. 'What's your name?'

'Martha Long.'

'What age are you?'

'Sixteen.'

'Hmm!' she said, studying me, with her eyes narrowing, flicking up and down the length of me. Working out what I'm made of. I stared back, taking her in. She's an aul one thinking I'm an eejit, just let out of a convent after being reared by nuns and I don't know me arse from me elbow. She's definitely going to milk me for all I'm worth. Well, maybe for the short while, missus, I promised meself. Yeah, it's no wonder the other one left.

'Did the nuns train you?'

'Sorry? Train me in what?'

'Domestic science!'

'Science? Eh, what do you mean?'

'I thought so,' she said, looking at the young one and shaking her head, with a satisfied look on her face, and a sneer lifting her mouth. 'Can you clean? Look after a house? Did they teach you to cook?'

'No!'

'What?' she snapped, wrapping the coat tighter around her. 'What did they teach you?'

'I know how to clean but I can't cook!'

She shook her head up and down, looking satisfied at the mention I can clean.

'Well, it's not cooking really. I only want you to prepare the potatoes and vegetables for the evening meal. I can cook the dinner myself when I come back in the evenings.'

'But I can't cook. Sorry, but I'm not going to be doing any cooking. I can clean,' I said, looking around the filthy, smelly kitchen.

'Don't make a fuss,' she said, waving her hand at me and walking off to put on the kettle. 'I will leave the potatoes and the rest of the vegetables out for you to peel. You can do that much, surely! Any fool can peel vegetables,' she snorted, grabbing hold of the kettle and slamming dishes out of the way to get the kettle under the tap.

'I suppose so,' I said, feeling really fed up before I even had a chance to get started in the job. I stood waiting, looking at me suitcase, hoping she would tell me I can take it up to me room.

'Here, get started straight away on these dishes. I'm going to put the dinner on.' I looked at me suitcase sitting on the floor and lifted it up, wondering what I should do with it. 'Where are you planning on going with that?' she said, looking down at me case.

'Sorry, eh, could I put it in me room?'

'Just leave it there and get started. I've wasted enough time,' she snapped.

I took off me coat and left it on me suitcase, sitting it in the alcove against the wall. Then I rolled up the sleeves of me cardigan and made for the sink. 'Where's the rubbish bin, please, missus?'

'Under the sink! Where else would you expect to find it?'

I opened the press underneath the sink and took out a metal bucket with tea leaves and potato peelings and all sorts of rubbish. It smelled to high heaven. Then started to clear the draining board and put the stuff on the table, trying to make room, and scrape and stack the plates and dishes, trying to make order. When the sink was empty, I turned on the hot tap and waited for it to get hot. 'The water's cold,' I said, turning to her taking vegetables out of the plastic racks sitting against the wall.

'Use the water from the kettle when it boils,' she muttered, not looking at me because she was busy examining the vegetables that had turned rotten in the racks and was trying to find some that had not gone off. Jaysus! Don't tell me she's going to eat that rotten stuff! Fuck! Not even hot water.

'Grainne, go and turn on the immersion in the hot press. They will be wanting hot water for their baths this evening,' she shouted to the young one sitting on top of the mound of washing on the sofa and reading a book.

'OK, Mammy,' the young one said, looking over at me like she was making sure I was doing me job.

I finished all the washing and drying up, then opened up all the presses to find where everything went. I had to take out most of the stuff, because half of the pots were years old and had been dumped on top of each other, with some of them so burned the bottoms were black and only fit for the bin. I made room and put them all back in order. Then cleaned the filthy, greasy sink, scrubbing the hell out of it with Vim from the press under the sink, and wiped down the table. Giving it a good wash with soapy water in a plastic basin. Then cleaned the worktops and started to sweep the floor. I had to get the dustpan and handbrush first or the food would be dragged around the floor and mashed in. Jesus! There's no wallpaper on the walls, nothing but the bare plaster, and the grey was covered in grease. This place reminds me a bit of the ma and Jackser's. They were pure filthy as well.

'Right,' I said, putting the brush and dustpan away in the long corner press. 'I'm finished,' I said, looking over at her taking thick slices of already-cooked ham out of a plastic packet. There were two slices in each packet. She put them in the clean frying pan with margarine turning brown and smoking away like mad.

'Start on that ironing,' she said, nodding her head over at the mountain of washing on the sofa. Fuck! I never ironed a thing in me life. I hesitated, wondering if I should tell her. 'Go on! What are yeh waiting for?' she barked, throwing her head at me. Right, I'll just do them, I thought, making for the iron and looking around to see where the plug goes. 'The socket's right behind you on the wall,' she said, seeing me looking around. 'Fasten all the buttons on the shirts. Then fold them up as you press them and put the shirts in individual piles!' she shouted over, without looking at me.

'OK,' I said, grabbing hold of the shirt and starting to button it.

She whipped herself over, muttering. 'No, no, no! Don't be so stupid. You iron the sleeves first, then the back and sides. *Then* you button it and fold it into shape,' she moaned. Showing me with her hands slapping at each place.

'OK, I've got that,' I said, picking up the iron with smoke coming out of it.

'Holy mother of God,' she whined, grabbing the iron off me. 'You can't iron at that high temperature. You will scorch a hole in the shirt. Look! Test it first on the table cover! Test it with your hand,' she said, slapping the iron and snapping her arm back, burning the hand off herself. 'Plug it out of the socket if it gets too hot,' she said, whipping out the cord from the wall. Working herself up into a nervous collapse. 'Don't leave it plugged in too long.'

'OK,' I said, starting to iron the sleeves, looking up into her purple face. Then she was gone. Back to serving up the dinner.

'Hi, Mam! Is dinner ready?' A long skinny one, wearing black-framed glasses, and a long, thin face with a pointy nose and straight black stringy hair hanging down around her face, came flying in and dropped her books at the kitchen door, landing them smack on the floor. Sending loose pages scattering everywhere. 'Oh, you managed to get another one,' she said, waving her head in my direction, and looking at the ma.

'Oh, she's here well enough,' the ma muttered. 'The last convent I rang had someone. They said she was a good worker.'

'Yeah, that's what they said about the last one,' the young one muttered, staring me up and down, muttering out of the corner of her mouth, still keeping an eye on me. 'Is she any good?' the young one whispered, standing beside the ma and nodding her head in my direction.

'That remains to be seen,' the ma mumbled, flicking her eye over at me and lowering her head to the frying pan.

Jaysus! They're all ugly in this family, by the looks a that one, I snorted to meself, feeling annoyed at the way your woman was talking about me as if I wasn't a person. Just a fucking nobody to skivvy for them.

'Sinead, you're back!' shouted Grainne, flying down the stairs and into the kitchen. 'Did you spend the day in the library, like Mammy told you to?' she asked, sounding like her aul ma.

'Yes, yes, I did! Go on back to your room, you little trouble maker,' laughed Sinead, playfully hitting Grainne in the shoulder.

I heard the front door opening and banging shut. 'I'm home, Mam!' shouted some fella running up the stairs.

'Come down now, Padraig! Dinner's ready!' shouted the ma, the hair dropping down over her eye, and her face getting even redder from the heat and smoke pouring out of the frying pan. I watched her slapping the burned, greasy-looking ham down on the plate. One for each person.

I looked back at me shirt, seeing a bit of brown scorch right on the front. I stared at it. Jaysus! She'll go mad. I'll have to hide it at the bottom of the pile when I get going on the rest of the stuff.

The front door opened again and I could hear someone coming in and the young fella belting down the stairs. 'How're yeh, Dad? How's it going in the old civil service?' said the young fella, rushing into the room, looking at the plates of dinner stacked on top of the cooker.

'Don't grab at them plates. You'll send the lot crashing to the floor!' the mammy roared, watching him and the plates, all balancing against each other sitting on top of the grill, and more on the very top.

'I'm starved. Jaysus! I could eat a scabby babby,' he moaned, wringing his hands and bending his neck, following the ma's hands landing the plates of dinner on the table.

'Pat, come in out of the hall and have the dinner while it's hot! I'm not switching on that oven to heat it up if it gets cold,' she shouted to an aul fella coming in the door. He stopped, and dropped his brown leather office case that looked like a school bag, dumping it on top of all the other books and papers scattered at the kitchen door. Then whipped open his evening newspaper, before he even sat down at the top of the table.

'Hello, Dad!'

'Hello,' he muttered to Sinead. Shaking open his newspaper and burying his head in it.

'Mammy got another domestic from a convent. Look! She's over there,' shouted Grainne, shaking his shoulder and pointing him in my direction.

'Good,' he muttered. Flicking one eye over at me, then smothering his head back in the newspaper.

'Come on, Grainne. Sit down and start eating. I'm telling you! If the dinner is cold, you can eat it. I'm not stirring myself to heat it up again for you!'

'Have you the immersion on, Mammy?' Sinead muffled through a mouthful of grub. Dropping half of it back onto the plate, trying to hang onto a piece of ham sticking out of her mouth.

'Yes! Go up straight away. I'm only leaving it on for an hour. That can do the lot of you. The electricity bill was sky high this month.'

'Yes, you can get yourselves a job, if I get any more bills like the last one,' the daddy barked. Lifting his head and looking over the glasses sitting on his nose, dropping the newspaper to get a better look down the table at the two big ones.

'Don't blame me, Daddy! I never go near the shagging immersion. It's Sinead who spends all her time in there, primping herself for that fat fool from college! What's his name? Fatty Arbuckle!' laughed Padraig, sounding like a horse neighing.

'Shut up, you! At least I have a boyfriend. No girl would even give you a second look, never mind go out with you!'

'Shut up, the pair of you! I want some peace when I'm trying to eat my dinner!' roared the dad. Dropping his head back to the reading and shovelling the fork into the dinner from behind the newspaper. Not bothering to see what he was doing, and just aiming it for his mouth. Half of it ended up on his lap and some on the floor. The rest managed to find his mouth.

Dirty fuckers, I thought, knowing now how the food ends up on the floor. Who would believe a school teacher could have a family like this? She doesn't even teach them manners. Not even a hello to me. Ah, fuck them, the shower a culchies!

'Would you ever start on that washing-up?' the ma shouted over at me, as everyone was starting to get up and leave the kitchen.

'OK,' I said, pulling out the plug from the wall and leaving the da's trousers half-ironed. I can finish them another day, I thought, staring at the pile of nice ironed stuff I'd done. Feeling very satisfied with me work. Then I started to clear the table and empty the slops into the bucket.

'Put on the kettle and boil the water for the washing-up. Don't dare touch that hot-water tap. I want that for the baths!' she shouted at me like I was slow in the head.

'Right,' I muttered, filling the kettle.

I had neared the end of the washing-up when Sinead came wandering into the kitchen in her dressing gown and slippers, with her hair wrapped in a towel. I watched her dragging open the presses and pulling out plates and a mug and started making herself sandwiches. Then took out the frying pan and made herself fried eggs and fried bread. Dropping the egg lifter on the cooker, not even bothering to put it beside me on the sink.

'What's cooking, Sinead?' shouted the Padraig fella, peeling in and grabbing at the fridge to take out more eggs and making for the cooker. 'Where's the cheese? Did you leave any ham? Make us one of them. An omelette,' he said, scratching his arse and hopping from one foot to the other. Dying to get his jaws into the grub.

'No, make it yourself. I'm not your servant,' she said, sitting herself down at the table, splashing tomato sauce on the eggs and the other half on the table.

'Hey, miss! Young one! What's your name? Will yeh make us an omelette? Hurry!' he said to me, laughing, and throwing his eye at the Sinead one, who laughed, thinking this was very funny, with him trying to make dirt out of me. 'Come on! Hey, I'm speaking to yeh!' I ignored him and went on with the washing-up. I dried the last of the pots, slamming them in the press under the sink. 'Christ, Sinead! She's deaf as a post!' he laughed. 'I'm telling yeh!'

'Shut up, you!' laughed Sinead, throwing a piece of bread at him.

'Excuse me,' I said, turning around to face Sinead. 'Do you have a dog?'

'Wha? What did she say?' laughed Padraig.

'No, why?' said Sinead, with her big marble eyes staring out of her head, shining with the laughter and leaning forward to hear why.

'Well, either you have a dog that will eat that bread off the floor or you can get down and shovel it up yourself! Lick it up, for all I care. Another reason,' I said, looking at the long string of misery Padraig fella, 'that moron has either been talking to the wall or calling his dog. Surely he wasn't talking to me? I don't waste me time on fools! Would you?' The two of them gaped at me, with their heads leaning forward waiting for me to finish, then screamed the house down laughing.

'Now, fuck faces,' I said quietly, turning back to them, 'if you want to live in a clean and tidy house like ordinary decent people, then you better watch how you speak to me. Otherwise, you can go back to living like pigs in this kip. Because I'm walking out that door. Now, which is it?'

'Get Mammy,' Sinead said quietly to Padraig.

'What? She'll kill us!' he roared, swinging his head from me to her. She stared at me, clamping her lips together, weighing up the odds of calling the mammy and maybe seeing me walk out and they're all left in their own bleedin mess again.

While she was thinking about this, I said, 'You can start by washing up your own dishes, the pair of you. And clean that cooker. I'm going to bed. It must be after nine o'clock and I didn't even get offered a cup of tea, never mind a dinner.' Then I threw down the dishcloth and grabbed me suitcase and walked out the door.

'Where are you going?' shouted Sinead, running after me.

'Well, I might stay on, if I know there's a bed for me to sleep in.'

'Wait there. I'll get Mammy.'

The ma came out of the sitting room. I could hear the television blaring out behind her. 'What?' she said, looking down at my suitcase then up at Sinead.

'She wants her room, Mam! Will I take her up to the spare room?'

'Yes! Where else would I be putting her? Is that what you called me out for? I am missing the news!' Then she tore back into the sitting room, banging the door in me face.

'Come on, I'll show you where you are sleeping.' I followed her up the narrow stairs, watching out for the carpet not fitted in properly. Somebody will break their bleedin neck on these stairs, I thought, looking at the filthy stair carpet. 'In here,' she said, opening the door off a small landing, with three other rooms and the bathroom with the door open and water spilled onto the lino!

'Jesus wept!' I heard meself saying, repeating what Sister Eleanor used to say when things got too much for her. I walked into a room with mounds of curtains and shoes and coats and boxes stacked in every corner, and more piled high under the window. There was only room for a small, two-foot-wide bed and a chair.

'This is your bed. We mostly use this as a junk room,' she said in a half-hearted laugh, seeing my face getting very annoyed looking around at the state of the room. It was freezing.

'Do you not have any heat in this house, Sinead?'

'Yeah, we have fires in every room. Oh, you better clean out mine in the morning and set it for the evening. Before I get in from college. Around half-four get it going. Then it should be blazing by the time I get in around five, half-five,' she said, swinging her head around the room and giving me a final look, then taking off out the door.

I looked at the bed. Someone had slept in it and the sheets were not changed. I pulled down the blankets, seeing blood stains, and the sheets were grey with the want of a wash. Jaysus! I can't sleep in that! It's bleedin manky! That's it!

I marched out the door and down the stairs and knocked on the sitting-room door. The television was blaring. No answer. I went into the kitchen, looking for Sinead. I was nearly crying with the rage boiling up in me. I stood looking around the empty room. No one here! I looked around, seeing the kettle and filled it, deciding to have a cup of tea and think about me next move. There's no point in causing a row unless I'm pushed.

I went back upstairs and decided to look in the hot press on the landing. Ah, good. Just what I'm looking for. Sheets. Clean ones. I took out two, and two clean towels. Now, what else is there? I opened the top press, seeing two spare pillows. Just what the doctor ordered. I rushed into the spare room. It's not mine. I'm not calling it that because I'm not bleedin staying long enough in this kip. I grabbed hold of the chair and stood up on it to get at the pillows. Ah, that looks like a clean bedspread. I took the green nylon bedspread down and grabbed two pillowcases from the bottom after rooting around. Then I took off, carrying the lot on the chair and back into the room. Now, that's better, I thought, standing back to admire my nice clean bed, all made up. Right, where's me cigarettes?

I dipped into me coat pocket and came up with the ten-cigarette box of Major and the box of matches. Now for a cup of tea. Oh, I can fill me hot-water bottle while I'm at it. Then I'll have a few comforts. Lovely. I opened me suitcase, taking out me nightdress and washbag and the hot-water bottle and locked the case again. I'm leaving me stuff in the case. There's nowhere to put anything, and anyway I'm getting out of here as soon as I can get another job. I know what I can do. I'll look through the aul fella's newspaper, and use the aul one's phone to ring up about any jobs going.

Right, now for me hot-water bottle, and a nice hot cup of tea and a cigarette. Then get to bed and read me book. I got nothing to eat, but I'm not bothered now. It's too late. The miserable aul bastards. You wouldn't treat a dog the way they carry on with me. Fuck them. They're only an ignorant bunch of bastards. I managed to get through today. Maybe I will be out of here when I get me first week's wages. Jaysus! I better find out about that. She never mentioned a word about how much she was going to pay me.

'Come on, wake up!' My head shot up from the pillow before I knew what was happening. 'Out of the bed. Quickly. Move!' I stared at the red face with the red eyes boring into me, trying to make out what was happening. Then I rubbed me eyes squinting, making out the shape of the aul one roaring at me to get up. 'It's ten to seven already. You were supposed to be up and out of that bed by half-past six!' she roared, throwing her head to me with the rest of her already out the door. 'UP! NOW! It's late in the morning and we all have to be out of the house by eight o'clock!' she roared like a bull, wrapping the aul granddad's dressing gown tight around her neck from the freezing cold. 'Get downstairs now and put on the porridge!' she shouted back from the landing.

Oh, Jaysus! Another day in this madhouse! I stretched, trying to get the stiffness out of me bones from the cold and the mattress sinking down in the middle. Then I whipped the two thin blankets back, threw meself out of the bed, diving into me clothes, and made me way down the stairs and into the kitchen.

I switched on the cooker and got a spoon to start stirring the Odlums porridge. She leaves it soaking overnight, so it won't take too long to cook, she says. The aul one and aul fella like this for their breakfast and they make the big ones eat it, too. They hate it and go mad. Hmm, I wonder! Maybe I will put too much salt in by mistake. I hesitated, thinking about it. No, I don't want to lose me job! Ah, go on. Fuck it! Just look stupid and play the eejit. I grabbed the packet of salt and dumped in half the packet. Maybe I should put in sugar as well. Yeah, good idea! Why not? It might sweeten them up after they get over the shock of the salt. I put in nearly the whole packet of sugar. I couldn't stop me hand from pouring. Though I wanted to stop, me body kept going. Then I put the nearly empty packet in the bin.

Right, what's next? The kettle for the tea. I filled it and put it on the cooker to boil and took down the bowls for the porridge. The aul ones like a boiled egg as well, so the big ones have the same. Right! I grabbed the eggs out of the fridge and put six in a pot. One for me when they're gone. I learned me lesson after the first night when they wouldn't feed me any dinner. So now I just help meself.

I set the table and turned off the porridge, all stuck to the end of the pot now. Jaysus! I better serve it quick then dump the pot under the water.

I could hear the roar up the stairs for the bathroom. 'Come outa there this minute, Sinead! Your father is waiting to get in for a shave!' I cocked me ear to listen. That's the aul one!

Right, that's the kettle boiled. I poured the boiled water into the pot with the eggs and put them on to boil. Then poured a drop of water into the teapot to heat it up. I learned that one from Sister

Mercy in the convent. Mind you, it was the hard way after a couple of digs in the snot! I have to learn everything from scratch when it comes to anything other then cleaning. The ma never did anything. No, not even cooking. Anyway, if there was grub to cook, she didn't know how to bleedin cook it. Pity about the convent, though. I might have learned something about the cooking there, if I hadn't gotten meself barred straight away the first day I set foot in the kitchen. Right, stick on the grill for the toast.

I put four slices of bread under the grill and switched it on. I better not forget to watch that. Last time it all went up in smoke! The aul one said I was trying to burn the house down.

I could hear doors slamming and the thump of feet hammering down the stairs. 'Hurry! Jesus, I'm late! Is the breakfast ready?' The aul one came marching into the kitchen, throwing a dirty eye at me and one at the eggs hopping around like mad in the pot. 'How long have these been on?' she roared, grabbing the pot.

'Not long, I just put them on now.'

'Hmm, we all like them soft! I keep telling you that!'

'Mammy, where's me red polo-neck jumper? Is it washed?' Sinead roared, rooting through the ironed stuff I'd left sitting there all nice and neat next to the rags still waiting for me to iron.

'Sit down! Have your breakfast while it's hot!' shouted the mammy. 'Oh, the grill is on fire!' She whipped the grill tray down, with the toast smoking and turning black, and blew like mad to put out the little fire on one of the slices of bread. 'Jesus Christ! Them blasted nuns churn out idiots!' she roared, throwing an evil eye at me. I kept me head down, concentrating on washing out me burned pot with the porridge still stuck to the bottom.

'Hurry up, everyone, if you want a lift into the city! The traffic is bad this morning,' the aul fella moaned, rushing in smelling of Lifebuoy soap. That's what they have in the bathroom. Then he planted himself at the top of the table and grabbed the spoon to start on the porridge. No one else touched theirs. The mammy looked at hers, seeing the bit of rusty colour from the burned bits sitting on top. Then the aul fella took one mighty spoonful, and halfway to his mouth he stopped. 'Eat up that good food, you lot!' he shouted, roaring the head off himself. 'Come on, eat that porridge. It will keep you going for the rest of the day.' Then he shovelled it into his mouth. I held me breath, waiting, and lowered me head into the sink to examine me pot. 'AAAAAAAHHHHHHHH! Jesuschristalmighty! Wha in hell is this?'

'What? What's wrong with yeh?' shouted the mammy, looking at him and staring at his porridge.

'Who made this?' he shouted, slamming down the spoon. The mammy tasted it.

'Aaahhh, it's pure poison!' she screamed, with her face turning all colours, and letting her tongue hang out of her mouth, trying to get rid of the porridge still sitting there. 'WHAT DID YOU DO TO THIS, YOU IMBECILE?'

'Who, me?' I said, putting me fist to me chest and pointing me finger at meself. 'Nothin, missus! I did just as you asked.'

'YOU DID NO SUCH THING!'

'Why could yeh not have made the porridge yourself?' shouted the daddy, with the eyes bulging out of his head and his nostrils flaring, making heavy breathing sounds, the rage killing him at the loss of his porridge.

'Oh well, that's it. Nobody can eat that,' said Sinead, pushing the bowl away and smirking over at me. 'I'll just have the egg and a bit of toast. Any toast, Mammy?'

'No! The fool burned that as well.'

'You should get somebody in who can cook,' said the aul fella, lathering margarine on the bread and making short work of the egg.

'Is there any cheese, Mammy?' said the young fella. 'Hey, you! Get some cheese out of the fridge! I'm starving here.'

'Did you hear him?' the aul one shouted at me.

'Who, me?' I said, standing and staring, not moving meself.

'Jesus Christ almighty! Do I have to do everything myself?' she snorted, slamming back her chair and making for the fridge with her back bent and her head trailing the floor ready to land it in the fridge. 'Here! Does anyone want that?' she said, slamming a little box of cheese down on the table.

'I hate cheese,' moaned Grainne, lifting her shoulders under her neck and wrinkling her nose. 'I want another egg. Is there any left, Mammy?'

'How many did you cook?' the aul one roared at me, then she leapt up and grabbed the pot with the egg left for me. 'Here! Take that and hurry up! We are going to be late. I'm going to get my bag ready. The rest of you get a move on.'

'You can all make your own way into the city,' said the aul fella, looking at his watch and threatening them. Then he pushed back his chair and made out the door.

'Mammy, what about me jumper?' the Sinead one roared, blasting the ears off me as I came up behind her to clear the table. 'Listen you! Wash my jumper. It's the red polo-neck. It has to be hand-washed. Don't dare put it in the machine or it will shrink.'

'Hey you,' I said, as she made for the door. 'I don't know how to use the washing machine. I think your mother can look after the washing.'

'Did you just be rude to me?' she said, not hearing a word I said, just the 'Hey, you' bit. With the shock still hitting her, she just stared, waiting for my answer.

'Rude? What do yeh mean?'

'Don't speak to me in that fashion, miss! You better learn your place or Mammy will have you out that door faster then you can think with that little feeble mind of yours!'

'Nah,' I said, shouting after her flying out the door. 'It's just a misunderstanding between you culchies and us Dubliners!' She came to a standstill in the hall, listening, letting the words sink in, then came back in slowly.

'What are you saying to me now?' she said, cocking her ear to me and her head facing away, trying to make me afraid.

'No, you culchies and us Dubliners speak differently. It's not your fault. We know when you come up from the bog. You're all confused when you hit the city because you're not used to being around people that make fools of you. But not me! I always feel sorry for you poor culchies!'

'MAMMY!' she screamed, looking up at the ceiling. 'That's it! You're gone!' She took the stairs two at a time, roaring for the mammy. 'That young one has just given me the most almighty cheek, Mammy! Get rid of her now. She's worse then the last one. She's trouble, Mammy. Mark my words, that one is nothing but trouble.'

'Oh, what are you talking about at this hour of the morning? Get ready for college, if you don't want to take the bus, Sinead. Leave that young one to me! That's my place to deal with her. Now get moving, the lot of you.'

'I'm off!' shouted the aul fella, coming down the stairs.

'Just a minute, Pat. I'm coming. Grainne, where are yeh? I am going to cut the legs off you, if you don't get moving this minute.'

'But, Mammy, I haven't finished my homework yet,' I could hear the young one moan.

'It's too late now! I told you yesterday evening you were to start on the homework straight after we get home from school. Every evening I tell you the same thing. But do you listen to a word I say? No, indeed you do not! Now you can just go in and tell Mrs Taylor she has my permission to cane the hands off you.'

'Will you all come on? I'm giving the final warning!' shouted the aul fella, coming back into the hall and shouting up the stairs. I heard the stampede of feet down the stairs, making the house rattle and shake. Even the windows shook with the noise across the ceiling, as everyone raced to get down the stairs.

'Now, listen carefully,' the aul one said, coming into the kitchen wearing a fawn three-quarter-length coat that wouldn't button in the middle because she was too fat. 'I want all that dirty washing over there . . .' she said, pointing to the corner. I looked to see the big mountain she was talking about. '. . . in the washing machine and hanging out to dry on the clothesline this morning. Check to see when they are dry and take them in. There's lovely drying weather,' she said, looking out at the watery sun trying to make its way seen in the icy-cold morning. 'Make all the beds, and you'll find the hoover under the stairs in the press out there. Hoover all the bedrooms, the landing, the stairs and the sitting room. Clean out the fireplaces in the rooms upstairs and the sitting room. Then set them for this evening. You can start lighting them around four o'clock. The weather is turning even colder today so we need to get the heat going for everyone coming in. Bring down any dirty washing from the bedrooms, and put them with that pile over there and wash them. You can go out to the coal shed for the coal, the tin bucket is in there. When you've finished setting the fires, leave the bucket in the shed. You may have to make a few trips up and down. Oh, the bundle of sticks for lighting the fire is in there, too. Now, I have left all the potatoes and a head of cabbage sitting there in that low shelf for you to prepare.'

'What? I'm to peel the cabbage and put it in the pot?'

'Yes,' she said slowly, watching me. 'Don't be such a fool. You cut it up and wash it. Use the big pot. Peel the potatoes and cut them up. I want them mashed for tonight's dinner. I'll cook the chops when I get in. Now, have you got all that?' she said, looking at me.

'I'm gone!' roared the aul fella, coming into the hall then out again, banging the door shut after him. We heard the car start up.

'Wait! Oh, that bloody man has no patience,' she said to the wall as she flew out the door on her brown wedgie high heels.

'Jaysus! Only a culchie would wear the likes a them,' I sniffed. Watching her trying to hurry, hoping she would break her neck. I listened, hearing the muffled sound of the aul fella saying, 'I'm gone! I'm tellin yeh now, I'm gone outa here!'

'Whist! Stop yer aul carrying on!' she barked, with the noise of the shouting coming from the rest of them. Then the car door slammed and they were off. The car took off at a great lick, and roared off down the road, making the engine sound like it was screaming for mercy. Then I heard the gears tearing, with the aul fella trying to get up speed. The noise carried until they were halfway out of the estate, then they were gone. Taking the noise and confusion and madness with them. Leaving me with only the peace and quiet behind. I let out me breath in a long sigh, not realising I was forgetting to breathe.

That's better, I thought, looking around at the filthy mess of the kitchen. Now, what's first? My breakfast. Feed meself! I'll have toast, for a start. I looked in the bread bin. Nothing! There's nothing bloody left! Not even a crust left on the table. Fuck! I opened the fridge, seeing a half-opened packet of margarine. That's it. Empty! Bare! I looked in the little pot, knowing there would be nothing there either. Grainne got the last egg. Mine! That makes two the little fucker got. No wonder she's so fat. Jaysus! There isn't a scrap left to eat. The no-good hungry miserable shower a red-neck bleedin culchies! They left me nothing! Right, that's it. Tomorrow's Friday. I get me first week's wages, then that's it! I'm taking off out of here as fast as me arse will move me.

I snorted in disgust, not able to get over it. The meanness a them culchies! OK, at least I can have a cup of tea, I thought, eyeing the milk bottle with the drop of milk left sitting in the bottom. I puffed me cigarette, trying to blow out rings. How do they do that? I wondered, trying to amuse meself.

Right, I better get going. Now, where will I start first? Kitchen, bedrooms, washing machine? I hope that thing is easy to work, I thought, throwing me eye over at the washing machine sitting at the end of the worktop. Go on, have a go now. Get the clothes washing then start on the kitchen.

Right! Now, I wonder how you work it, I thought, examining it from top to bottom. Lift off the lid. Ah, there's the knobs. And you put the clothes in this drum thing. Right, that looks easy enough. This is really the first time in me life I ever got a look at one. I barely ever set foot in the laundry if I could help it. Not unless Sister Eleanor was there. Then we were all herded in on a Monday to help with the pressing of the sheets. Two of us stood at each end, three girls and one nun to supervise us. That was always Sister Eleanor. She would feed the sheets in under the roller, and guide them through the huge mangle, and we would catch them coming out the other end while sister slammed her foot up and down like mad on the long thick running board to get it going. That was great gas! Eleanor would turn all colours from the heat, tearing like mad at the white collar around her neck and dripping with the sweat in her long heavy black habit while the lot of us got covered in steam from the wet sheets. But we didn't have washing machines like this. Only huge things that I kept well away from. I had enough to be doing with me own work, but I always liked to help Sister Eleanor. Yeah, I would do anything for a bit of attention. Hmm, I was only a kid then. Nowadays I demand me weight in gold! No more paying for a smidgen of attention with the sweat off me brow. No, getting attention and a bit of praise won't put a roof over my head or food in me belly. Yeah, and neither will working in this godforsaken dump! Jaysus, if I stayed here any length of time, I'd end up looking like a skeleton! Right, keep moving.

I rushed over, grabbing up a pile of washing from the corner, and dumped the lot on top of the already full plastic washing basket, carrying the lot over to the machine. Right! I picked up handfuls, dropping them down inside the machine and kept going until it was full. I looked from the machine to the basket. Damn! I still have loads left. It won't all fit in. She wants it all done in a hurry! Right! I squeezed like mad, pushing and packing them as hard as I could. Then I spotted the red polo-neck belonging to Sinead. I better put that in, too! She wants that in a hurry, otherwise there will be ructions. She will only have a blue fit if I don't get it washed. I squeezed it in, pushing like mad until it was well down on the inside. I wanted to make sure it got a good wash because the stuff was all piled high on the top, bursting out and now I will have to squeeze the lid down to get it all in.

Jaysus! The bleedin lid won't close. Now what am I going to do? I stared at it, thinking. Then I had an idea. I got a chair and stood up on it and sat on the lid to make it go down. It still won't go down. Right! I bounced up and down for all I was worth until I felt a dinge coming in the middle. Fuck! I lifted the lid and gave it a good bang and it popped back into shape again. Grand! At last.

Now, what do you do next? Powder! I need washing powder. Right, I know where that is. Under the sink. Perfect. Omo washing powder. Jaysus! I have to lift the lid again! Hmm, I need to get the powder down in the middle of the wash. Right, here we go again. I dumped out half the clothes and emptied half the packet in. I don't suppose you use the whole packet. No, I might need that for another wash. Right, got them all in at last. Now twist the knob to get it going. Right, that's that done. I'm now flying with the washing. What's next?

I filled the kettle for the washing up and started to clear the table, then stacked the dishes on the side of the draining board for washing.

I'm finished at last. That's everything washed and put away and the kitchen's looking nice and clean. I just have to sweep the floor and I have me kitchen out of the way. I heard water running, then saw it pooling around me feet. Jaysus! Help! Mammy! What's happening? Then a hose shot around from the back of the washing machine with water pumping out. Aaaaahhhhh, help! I grabbed hold of it, wondering what to do. It won't stretch! I need to put that in the sink. I pulled like mad and the rest of it appeared and I dumped it in the sink. Right, the washing is now rinsing. I better dry up the bleedin floor. It's completely flooded. That's more work for meself.

At last, the floor is dry. I squeezed out the mop under the tap and admired me floor. I didn't know it was that colour, a sort of burnt orange. It looks grand. That must be the first time in years that floor has seen a drop of water!

The washing machine had stopped growling, and thumping, and trying to throw itself around the kitchen, and it was quiet now. I didn't know it was supposed to do that kind of thing. I thought it must be broken when I grabbed it earlier, trying to stop it lepping into the air. Jaysus! Everything in this house is crazy! Even the washing machine is in on the act.

Right, now to get the clothes out on the line. I lifted up the lid and stuff started bursting out. I got the top stuff out but now the rest won't move. I heaved and pulled because everything was wedged tight, tangled and stuck underneath. Aaaahhh! Jaysus Christ almighty! This is pulling the heart outa me. I can't get the stuff out!

I lost the head and started yanking, holding onta the leg of a pair of trousers and had a tug of war. Digging me feet in and tearing meself across the kitchen. I felt a heave then a pop and the stuff . . . no, it's the drum started to come up with the clothes. I stopped to look. I don't think it's supposed to do that! I pulled the clothes and the drum rocked loose. Oh, Mammy! I think it's broken. Wha'll I do? I *told* that dyed-haired grey-haired aul cow I can't do washing! 'I don't know how to use a washing machine,' I whispered, staring at the stuff looking back at me.

I stood thinking for a minute, holding onta the leg of the trousers. Right, get the stuff out and close the lid and say nothing. What she won't know won't hurt her. I dug me hands in, trying to get a grip on the middle stuff, getting it a little bit loose. Then I pulled hard on the trousers, seeing the rest of it appear, taking a load of other stuff with it. Lovely! I'm getting somewhere. I pulled the trousers, black ones, then heard a ripping sound. Oh, Gawd! What have I done now? I looked at the trousers, seeing the huge tear right down the middle. Ah, mother a God, the arse is gone out of the trousers! How can anyone be as stupid as me?

I felt like crying. 'She will go stark-staring raving mad! The only good thing is she won't ask me to do any more washing. That's a good thing. I'll just let her go mad, and keep saying sorry,' I heard meself whispering, getting outa breath. What else can she do, Martha? Yeah, it will work out grand when she gets over the terrible news I'm even more stupid then she thinks. Yeah, that's what will happen.

I went back to me pulling, and finally got a huge bundle coming up, but I had to stand each side of the drum to stop it coming up with the stuff every time I tried to pull. Maybe I could get a job in a circus doing a balancing act! Oh, Mammy! What's the worst thing she can do to me? I felt me nerves rattling. I lifted the clothes out in a heap, seeing more and more coming. Oh, thank God! At last, I'm getting somewhere. But they don't look right. I stared at the clothes and dumped them all on the sink and started to untangle the lot. Oh, no! This definitely doesn't look right. They all look the same colour! A reddish pink. Oh, Mammy! That's the aul fella's shirt. I'm sure that was white going in.

I lifted them up one by one, putting them in the yellow basket. Everything is looking the same colour. All the white stuff is now pink, with a mixture of red and blue. The coloured sheets have even gone grey. Well, with bits of different colours. Fuck! That must be from the jeans. Oh, no! The woollen jumpers have shrunk. I held up one that looked like Grainne's. It wouldn't fit a sixpenny doll. All the woollen stuff is shrunk, even Sinead's good red polo-neck. It's gone smaller then the size of a hankie. Me heart leaped with the fright. What am I going to do? Jaysus! I'm definitely dead.

I put all the stuff in the basket and carried it out to the line, half dragging it. This weight would pull the heart out of a horse. Dear God, what will she say? How am I going to get out of this? I started to hang the clothes on the line, trying to keep everything away from the full view of the kitchen window. I know what I'll do! I'll try to get the lot dry as soon as possible, and stuff it down underneath the stuff still waiting to be ironed. Yeah, OK. That's all I can do.

I rushed in with the empty basket and looked over at the clock sitting on the windowsill. Bloody hell, it's after two o'clock! Where did the time go to? I haven't done the rest of the house yet! I still have the hoovering and beds to do and the fires to clean and get ready for lighting. Right, move fast. The vegetables have to be done as well. I dumped the rest of the dirty washing in the basket and left it sitting back where it belonged in the corner of the so-called dining room. There's not even enough room on the line for the stuff I already put out. I had to squeeze in the stuff, putting some things on top of each other. Right, now for upstairs.

I cleaned out the fire in the aul fella and aul one's room, then rushed down and out to the coal shed. Maybe I should clean all the fires out first then set them for lighting all at the same time. That would make more sense. Right, I might as well dump these cinders. Where does she put them? Not in the shed. That's full of coal. I looked around the garden, seeing a dump at the end of the wall behind an old tree that was on its last legs. It never even really got growing before it started to die. Hmm, this place is going to put years on me. Oh, I can't wait to get the hell out.

I just need to wait until tomorrow when I get me wages. I felt meself beginning to cheer up at that thought.

I rushed back up with the bucket, leaving it on the landing, and started on the bed. I stripped off all the blankets and the eiderdown and made up the bed, with the mattress sagging in the middle. They must have bought that when they were first married. That was probably about fifty years ago! You would think they would go out and buy a new one. Miserable aul sods! There's two of them working. I wonder what they do with their money? Right, that's that done.

I dragged the bucket and started in the Sinead one's room. Oh, holy Jaysus! What a filthy pig. Me eyes travelled around the room, taking in the kip of a dump. She has dirty clothes and knickers, shoes, bags and magazines, cups with mouldy tea festering away, a dinner plate with the remains of a fried egg cementing itself to it, and tons of rubbish all thrown in every direction. Every bit of the floor is covered in filth. Jaysus! She's definitely mental. They're all fucking mental. Right, get on with it. I better start on the fire.

Jesus! Am I glad that room is finished? I dragged the hoover, leaving it on the landing, and went into Padraig's room. This is too much. The place is stinking to high heavens! Oh, just keep moving.

OK, that's all done! Now, let me see. Where am I now? The fires are set, the beds are made, the rooms are cleaned and the carpets are hoovered. It must have taken me the whole day. I just have to do this landing and the stairs then I can start on the sitting room. That only leaves me with the vegetables to do.

Me back aches from all that stooping and bending up and down. This is as bad, if not worse, than the work I was doing in the convent. At least in the convent you could see what you were cleaning and it didn't smell like this place. Gawd! I would just love to sit down now and have a rest with a lovely cup of tea. Yeah, I really need a cup of tea and something to eat. I'm starving with the hunger. Jaysus! I'm working all day and I got no breakfast! Oh, just leave it. Get on with the job and get finished. Thinking like that won't do any good or get the job done. It must be late. God knows what time it is. I'm afraid to look at the clock.

OK, that's the last of the stairs. Now for the sitting room. 'Oh, that's great! I'm finished at last,' I puffed, letting out me breath with the exhaustion and making me way out of the sitting room, dragging the hoover with me. Right, that's everything done. The house is now spic and span. All I have to do now is the vegetables.

I was just making me way into the kitchen when the hall door opened. 'It's home again! Mammy, can I phone Betty Norton, the girl from my class at school? I promised I would. I want to borrow that Enid Blyton book she said I could borrow.'

'No, you are not allowed to make any phone calls, and well you know it, so stop bothering me about such nonsense!'

'But, Mammy!'

'No, go upstairs now and start doing your homework!' roared the aul one, losing the rag. She whipped her head around, seeing me head into the kitchen. 'Have you got them potatoes on yet, with the head of cabbage I told you to prepare?'

'I'm just about to start peeling them now,' I said, looking down the hall at her, seeing the red face and the eyes blazing out of her head. Jaysus! She really is in bad form.

'You are completely useless!' she roared, flying down the hall and whipping the scarf from around her neck and dumping it on the table. 'What's this? You have nothing ready?' I stood looking at her, trying to take in what she was talking about.

'Excuse me, missus!'

'Don't you give me any of your aul excuses!' she roared. 'You are bone idle! The lot of you from these convents. The nuns should be ashamed of themselves, letting people like you free when you can't even tie your own shoelaces.'

'What? I have been cleaning this house since early morning!' I started to roar, losing me rag. 'Fuck this!' I muttered to meself. 'Listen, missus! No one could have worked harder then me, you know?'

'I want no more cheek from you!' she barked, going purple in the face and tearing open the press and slamming down the pots. 'Now, get started on them vegetables straight away or you'll be looking for another job quicker than you know!'

'Listen . . .' I started to say, trying to keep me head and not let the fear and temper get the better of me. I felt trapped in this place. There was something about that aul one that reminded me of Jackser. But I didn't have to put up with it.

'Mammy, can I call up to her house then? I won't be long!'

'No! How many times do I have to tell you? Get up them stairs this minute and start on your homework.'

I lifted the head of cabbage out of the rack, feeling meself shaking inside with the nerves. I feel pulled between telling her to stick her job up her arse and wanting to hang on just one more day to collect me wages. I have barely enough money to buy meself a cup of coffee, never mind buying something to eat! Yeah, there is definitely a bit of the feeling of Jackser in this house. I can sense it around that woman.

'I'm home, Mammy! Is dinner on?' Sinead roared, rushing into the kitchen and throwing down her coat in the corner of the hall then letting her books and bag land on top of it. 'I will be going out around nine tonight. Clem is picking me up in his mother's Mini,' she said, talking to the ma and watching me wrestling with the head of cabbage.

Do I cut it or wash it first? I looked at the head, wondering if I should take off the leaves one by one. 'Did you light the fire in my room?' Sinead said, suddenly shouting at me. I whipped me head away from the head of cabbage and looked over at her standing with her hands on her hips.

'Oh, sorry! I knew there was something I should do. But your mammy and me have to do the dinner,' I said, showing her the head of cabbage.

'Mammy, is there no fire lit in my room? The bloody house is freezing. It's nearly as cold in here as it is outside! How can I be expected to study in my room without heat?' she screamed, looking at her mother and roaring at me. Then she was gone, flying out the door and up the stairs.

I went back to me head of cabbage. She was no sooner up the stairs than I heard a roar coming from up on the landing. 'Where's my red polo-neck sweater I told you to wash? Did you hand-wash it, like I asked you to?'

Me heart leaped with the fright. Then a key turned in the front door and a voice said, 'Hello, everybody, I'M HOME!' I looked, seeing it was the Padraig fella, shouting and laughing as he put his head in the door. Then he got knocked sideways by Sinead flying back into the room and heading straight over to the wash basket. I turned me head slightly, holding me breath and watched her leaning her head in and pulling all the dirty clothes from the basket, sending them flying in all directions.

Oh, dear God! Here it comes. I was afraid to breathe. Then the ma whipped her head up, looking out to the clothes line at the mention of washing. 'What happened to the clothes?' asked the mammy, looking out the window, not able to believe her eyesight. I felt meself getting weak. I have been on the go all day and have nothing in me stomach and now I feel like I'm living with fucking Jackser all over again. 'What have you done to the washing?' screamed the aul one, rushing to the back door and yanking it open.

'What? What's going on?' said Sinead, lifting her head to get a look out, then taking off to the back door to see what's happened to the washing.

'The clothes are destroyed,' the ma said quietly, muttering to herself. 'That imbecile of a girl has destroyed everything. Everything!' moaned the aul one. I could hear her voice and guessed she must be walking up and down the line, taking in all the dyed clothes. 'The shirts. Your father's shirts. He needs them for work.'

'MY GOOD POLO-NECK!' screamed Sinead.

Right, that's it. I've taken enough, I thought, feeling the rage make its way around me chest and down into me belly. I didn't feel like screaming. I just knew when enough was enough. I'm not staying here one more minute around these people. I may be desperate, but I'm not that desperate. I left down the head of cabbage and walked off up the stairs and into the dog box they had a cheek to call a bedroom. I picked up me suitcase and put it down on the bed, taking me nightdress from under the pillow and me hot-water bottle from under the blankets. I never even got the time today to make me own bed.

I picked up me washbag off the chair and packed everything in. 'Where is she?' screamed the aul one from the hall. I could hear the two of them rushing up the stairs.

'What did you do to my clothes? The jumper is ruined!' Sinead roared, holding it up in the air. 'Look at the rest of my stuff, Mammy!'

'Where is that fool?' screamed the mammy, rushing into the room. Then stopped dead, her red bloodshot eyes flying from me putting on me coat to me suitcase sitting packed on the bed. 'You are not getting one penny in wages from me,' she snorted. 'Not until you have discharged every last penny for destroying the whole household's clothes. Where do you think you are going, miss?' she whipped, throwing her head at me suitcase, seeing me button me coat and lift me case off the bed. 'You can put that suitcase back, for a start! Give me that case.'

'Get your hands off my property, missus!' I said, looking straight into her face and holding the case in both me hands.

'Take that case off her, Sinead. If she attempts to leave this house, we will have the guards after her. I'm going to phone the nuns. She has destroyed our personal property! We will see what the nuns have to say about this. In any case, you can't just walk out the door when it suits you, madam. You have to give me one month's notice!'

'Give me that case!' Sinead said, standing in front of me and slamming out her hand. I stared up at her, seeing her eyes cold as ice, with her face made of stone. I've seen that look many times before. It's the look of someone who thinks they are so far above you they can do what they like with you. The idea of even crossing this one hasn't entered her mind. She thinks she knows me. I'm a fucking nobody from a convent, used to doing what I'm told. She leaned down, making to take the case off me.

'We'll lock it away!' shouted the aul one, standing by the door with her arms folded and her lips clamped together, with her red eyes spitting venom. 'It can stay locked up until we can get a replacement for her. But I certainly intend reporting her to the Garda! In fact, I'm going to phone the convent straight away. Get that case, Sinead.'

I could feel a fire running through me veins but the funny thing is I feel icy cold at the same time! It feels like I'm taking on Jackser at his own game, someone thinking they can own me! 'Missus, get outa me way before you regret ever clapping eyes on me. Outa the way, hatchet face,' I said quietly, gritting me teeth at Sinead. She hesitated, taken unawares at the way I acted. I took off out the door, taking the stairs quickly but yet slowly. Like I wasn't really in a big hurry.

I whipped the front door open wide, leaving me suitcase down on the ground, sitting it well away from the door, further down the path. 'Come back here, you! How dare you behave in this fashion.'

'Don't worry, missus. I'm not going anywhere in a hurry! Not until I get what's due to me,' I said, holding out me hand for me money.

'You are out of your mind. Me, owe you money?' she said, curling her hand into a fist and pointing one finger at her chest, her eyes bulging outa her head with what she was hearing. A car slowed down and the aul fella drove up, parking the car outside.

'What's going on here?' he barked, slamming the car door shut and wrapping the newspaper under his arm, trying to lock the car and keep his eyes on what was happening.

'Pat, this little guttersnipe is attempting to walk out without so much as a by-your-leave! Can you believe it? After all the damage she has done! She has ruined all the clothes in the washing machine, including your best shirts. Your trousers are in shreds.'

'What are you talking about?' he said, looking at her with his face twisted then bringing his head back down to look at me, trying to make sense of what is going on.

'Aren't I after telling you? She has just destroyed every stitch of clothes we have in the house. All the jumpers are ruined. Shrunk! They are only fit for throwing out. Your good black trousers, the one belonging to the suit, is ripped beyond repair. Now she thinks she can just waltz out of here without paying any recompense!'

'Get in out of the street! Go inside, the lot of you!' he shouted, throwing his head at everyone, waving his rolled-up newspaper to whoosh everyone in the door.

I picked up my suitcase. 'I'm not going anywhere until I get me money!' I said, raising my voice enough for them to get the message without shouting.

'Well, if it's true what my wife says,' he laughed, making a jeering sound, 'you won't be going far until this matter is settled. Now, get inside.'

'Pat, I'm going to call the guards,' she said, her eyes flying to the phone.

'Listen, missus! Cut the fucking game out!'

'Don't you dare use that kind of language in my house,' he barked, curling his fists, jabbing them down by his side and making for me.

'Listen, you pair of gobshites! This might've worked for you up until now, frightening the shite out of poor young ones straight out of a convent, getting them to work day and night, slaving away for nothing. But the pair of you fuckers have no idea who you're up against. This is not Victorian times! Now, do I get me wages for slaving away for the last four days or do I have to show you I mean business? You have all met your fucking match!'

'Get the police, Irene!' shouted the aul fella, waving himself in the door then screwing up his newspaper and slamming it against his open palm, swinging himself back to look out at me, like he was watching to make sure I was not going anywhere until the police arrived. 'You will be locked up for threatening behaviour,' he said, getting very white in the face from the rage in him. 'We are all witnesses here!'

'Hurry up, then, because I hope they arrest me. I am going to sing like a canary to anyone that listens. Certainly the judge! Yeah, I can't wait to tell him how you threw a poor orphan girl out onto the street into the freezing cold dark night without a penny in her pocket after slaving for you lot for over a week without even being given proper food to eat. I had to scrape around for the leftovers you lot left in the pots. Oh, yes! You have no idea just how I can talk, missus! Now, are we getting the coppers or not?' I said to them, standing there looking at each other, trying to work out their next move. 'Because yeh see, hatchet faces. I intend going next door, to ask the neighbour of yours to ring the nuns from the convent where you got me from, and ask them to come and collect me from the street where you heartless bastards threw me. I'm starting to cry me eyes out now at the thought of it all. The terrible injustice you fuckers are doing to me. The whole thing is making me nerves go bad. Here you all are,' I sniffed, 'supposed to be a pair of Christians, and a civil servant and a teacher no less. But what are you doing? THROWING ME, THE POOR ORPHAN, OUT ONTA THE STREET TO DIE IN THE FREEZING COLD! Now, do I get me money?' I said quietly, holding out me hand, 'or do I have to start knocking on doors until someone listens to me plight? Oh, yeah, I intend telling them everything there is to know about the lot of youse! From Sinead's dirty filthy knickers on the bedroom floor to how you have rats running around the house because you live in filth and dirt! They know that anyway. They can see that from the outside of the house, the way the house is falling down around your bleedin ears. Now, gimme me bleedin money! I'll tell them as well what you have for your dinner, that you eat only margarine, either because you can't afford it or you are too fucking mean to buy butter. Maybe the pair of you are in debt right up to your eyeballs! That's why you can't afford to buy a bit of heat in the house. Now, you know neighbours like nothing better then a good aul gossip—'

'Get out! Shut the door, Pat!' The aul fella stood staring at me. I could see the fat on his chin shaking and the eyes sinking into the back of his head with shock and rage, with him not able to believe what was happening. They didn't want to let the likes of me best them. I could feel the rage inside meself. Well, I'm not letting go either. These bastards are not getting the better of me. The fuckers think they are better then I am. The shower of culchie ignorant bastards need to learn they are wrong.

I watched her as she stood beside him. Her eyes are dancing in her head, with the rage and fear and the worry of what I might do running through her mind all at the same time. 'So, you're not as foolish as you look,' she said, walking over to me and grabbing her coat around her, smirking at me. Her sleevin eyes were saying, 'Yeah, we understand each other very well!' I gave her the same smirk back, letting her see I could read her very well. Her bullying ways didn't worry me in the slightest. Nor did her tricks about the coppers, using that one to hold me a bleedin prisoner, her very own free special slave, working away in her house until I either ran off or she managed to get another poor eejit before she was left stranded.

'Listen, missus! You're not as smart as you think yeh are. You have been playing this game long enough. Why don't you pay someone the wages they are owed? You said yourself, you've run out of convents to get girls to slave for you! By the way, I know the school you work in. I might just turn up there and cry me eyes out looking for you, begging to get me money and pleading with you to let me go free. I'll start with all the mothers outside the gate and work me way in to the head teacher! Wha deh yeh think about tha, missus? Another thing. I want to let you inta a secret, missus. Not too many people know this. I was making me way on them streets when you were still getting yer arse wiped. Yeah, I'm only sixteen but if you live to be a hundred, missus, you'll never be able to outsmart the likes of me! Now, give me me money. I want the full amount! Thirty bob. If you keep me standing here any longer, I can promise you it will go up to three quid!'

She kept smirking at me, like there was something inside of her enjoyed bringing out the worst in me, the street fighter! She really likes trying to get the better of people. I was right. She is another Jackser!

I met another teacher like her once. She was the very same. She beat the hell outa me just to get me to knuckle down under her, all because she couldn't stand the sight of a child who was half-naked, bare-foot and had lice crawling in her hair. They saw us as an easy mark to vent their madness on. Well, not any more. I am more then a match for anyone who thinks they can best me.

'I'll give you no more then ten shillings,' she said, walking off.

'No, you can wipe your arse with that. I want what I'm entitled to.'

'You didn't work a full week,' she said, walking in and closing the door. I walked up to the front door and rang the bell. 'Wait there,' she said, opening the door then getting ready to shut it again.

'No, listen, missus! You better listen carefully. I am going to make it my business to get my full amount of money from you. I don't care what it takes. Never fear! I'm not going to start shouting and making trouble for meself. No, I'm going in next door to cry me eyes out and ask them to ring the nuns.'

She stared at me. I stared back, wanting her to meet me halfway, because I knew I wouldn't be able to give in. The cold was biting into me, along with the hunger. I just wanted to get away. But that won't happen if she thinks she can get the better of me. 'I'm nobody's fool,' I said, shaking me head and looking into her eyes, wanting her to understand she was not going to win.

'Stay there!' she snapped. I waited. 'Here! There's a pound,' she said, putting a green pound note into me hand and waiting for a second to see would I refuse it. I turned away, making for the gate, and she slammed the door shut. I felt a great weight lifting off me shoulders, like I was getting rid of Jackser for the second time in me life.

13

I hurried on out through the estate, wanting to put as much distance between them and me. I walked past houses, seeing the lights on and the curtains pulled across. They're all lovely and cosy in there now, well in out of this freezing cold.

A door suddenly opened and a man came out. I could hear shouting. 'Daddy, I want to come!' A little fella of about three came flying out the door in his pyjamas and slippers with his hands in the air, wanting to be lifted up and carried.

'No, no! In you go.' The daddy picked him up and flew him back into the hall.

'Bring me back sweets, Daddy. I want a bar of chocolate!' shouted a little girl of about five, standing in the kitchen staring out with her finger wrapped around her hair, curling it and holding a doll under the other arm. She was wearing a little red dressing gown with a long nightie hanging underneath. The mammy suddenly appeared and stopped next to her, looking out to see what was going on. She stared out watching, with a very annoyed look on her face, drying a pot in her hand. Then, suddenly, she gave an almighty roar, losing the rag. 'Carl! Come in here this minute, Phillip! Will you ever go about your business and shut the bloody door? You are letting out all the heat, not to mention tormenting the kids.'

'OK, I'm off!' shouted the daddy, making to shut the door.

'Kiss, kiss!' screamed the little boy, putting up his mouth for a kiss.

'Me! I want a kiss, too, Daddy!' shouted the little girl, running down the hall.

'Shut the door!' screamed the mammy. The daddy flew in and shut the door then came flying back out again and headed for his car. I could hear the screams behind him.

Well, not everybody's happy, judging by the looks of that mammy! I wonder when we ever know how well off we are? Here I am, running for me life away from them bleeding lunatics, and now I have to find meself somewhere to stay for the night. Jaysus! I hope it's only for tonight! Please, God, help me to find a job as soon as possible, because right now, this very minute, I'm banjacksed! I would love to swap places with that woman. Well, maybe not! Then I would have to be her, ending up with a sour face on me and feeling very fed up by the looks of her! Anyway, there's probably people out there this very minute who would give their eye teeth to be me right now. I'm young and healthy and have me whole life just starting off. Yeah, this is really just an adventure.

Yeah, I thought, trying to fool meself into thinking life is a bowl of cherries as I felt the freezing cold go right up through me. Right, I'm going to catch that bus into town then see what happens. I need to get in somewhere and get a bit of heat and something to eat then find me bearings. I still feel a bit shook up after me run-in with them bastards, not to mention the hunger. That's not doing me much good at the minute. I feel a bit run-down from me week of starvation. Mad fucking bastards! They didn't even bother to feed me. Jaysus! What did they think I was? A mangy fucking dog that could scrape around looking for a few scraps for meself? Yeah, that's what I was doing. Jaysus! The world is full of madness! Oh, just let me get on that bus quick. I want to get out of this freezing cold and it really is getting pitch black out.

Me eyes peeled ahead past the fields covered in the white frost, making it look like snow. I could see the main road ahead and the street lamps lighting up the trees all along the road. I hurried on, wanting to get down to the bus stop.

Oh, this cold would put years on you. I stamped me feet up and down, slapping me arms to keep the heat in me. I don't like it around here, I thought, looking along the dark road with the trees looking very bare hanging over the high walls. It's very desolate. There's nothing to see but the long road heading into the city, with walls on both sides and broken footpaths. This is really all country, except for the new estate over there. I'll be glad to see the back of it.

Suddenly, me eyes landed on the bus flying towards me in the distance. Me heart gladdened. I grabbed up me suitcase and stood ready to stretch me hand out. I don't want that bus flying past without me. Them drivers can be in a hurry and race past pretending they don't see you. I watched it like a hawk, making sure to see if it was slowing down. Otherwise I'm getting ready to throw meself out into the middle of the road and make him stop!

I climbed on, making me way down the bus to the long seat. 'Bus fares!' the conductor shouted after me, putting his hand out, not wanting to walk down the empty bus after me. I turned and came back, sitting meself down on the long seat next to him, and pulled out me purse.

'Tuppence, please, mister, into O'Connell Street.' He rolled off the ticket out of the machine and handed it to me, letting it drop on the ground. I watched him sitting himself down on the seat opposite me and start counting his money. Aul fucker, I thought as I stooped down picking it up, not getting over the idea of him doing that. Walking off, letting me stoop down to pick it up without even saying a word of sorry. I was tempted to say something. No, save your breath. It's just been one long day of putting up with ignorant people. I would be better to move away from him and have the bit of peace and quiet.

I lifted up me case and carried on down the empty bus, sitting meself on the last seat, and put me case up in front of me on the long seat. Right, I better put me pound note at the bottom of the case. Hide it there just in case I lose it. That money has to do me until I get another job. Right, how much have I got altogether? One pound two shillings and sevenpence. Jaysus! How long will that last me? I certainly can't afford to pay for somewhere to stay, like a bed and breakfast. This money's going to have to keep me going for food and newspapers and bus fares while I'm looking for a job. Right, I better spare it. I'm not going to break on that until I have to.

OK, here we are. I stood up, waiting for the bus to stop. Just as it pulled to a halt, I hesitated on the platform and looked up at the ugly mug of the aul fella, the conductor, who looked like he hated the whole world. He gave me a dirty look when he saw I was watching him, then walked halfway down to the platform and took a big snort of snot, and shot it out from the back of his throat, sending it flying out the door. Aaah, dirty aul sod! Me stomach turned, hearing the sound of him dragging it from his nose then back from behind his throat.

I watched, waiting for the bus to slow down, then said, seeing the bus coming to a stop, 'Jaysus, mister! With that face a yours, I'd say you've been miserable from the day you were born. What happened? Did yer aul one not succeed in drowning yeh at birth? You're the ugliest-looking fucker I ever met!'

'Geroff me bus outa tha, yeh whore's melt, yeh!' he screamed, banging hell outa the bell, sending the bus flying off, with me cackling like a hyena and taking a flying leap onta the footpath with me case sailing through the air. I roared laughing, seeing the face on him snarling with the rage as he whipped his fist after me. Ha, the look of surprise on his face was worth it! He wasn't expecting me to insult him. He thought he was getting away with making a fool outa me. Gobshite! I enjoyed that!

Oh, it's nice to be back. I looked up and down O'Connell Street, seeing all the lights looking dim in the foggy night, with the icy-cold mist hanging around the air. It looked a bit deserted, with not too many people around. The shops were all closed up and the only lights showing were coming from the picture houses and the cafés. Gawd! It's great to be free again, with no worries of living with people who don't like you and are ready to eat the head offa yeh at the drop of a hat!

Right, what's first? I think I'll go around to the café and get a bag of chips to take away. That will be cheaper. I need to take it easy on me money. That should keep me going. Then I can come back here and be good to meself. I'll go into Caffola's and have a cup of coffee. That way I can eat me chips there in comfort, providing they don't catch me.

I hurried up O'Connell Street with the hot chips under me arm. Gawd! I'm dying with the cold and hunger. I wonder where I'm going to go after this? Never mind. Get in out of the cold and have something to eat. I hurried on and flew in the door of Caffola's. The place is half-empty! I could see only a few people sitting at the tables. Lovely! The table behind the door in the corner is empty. I rushed over and sat down, putting me case safe behind me in the corner, and waited for the girl to serve me. I better keep these chips hidden under the table until she's gone. I can't afford to get meself kicked outa here.

'Yeah, eh, will you give me a white creamy coffee, please?'

'Anythin else, love?' she said, sticking the pencil back behind her ear.

'No,' I said, staring at it sitting there. I love the way they do that. It makes them look somehow important and very busy.

'There yeh go,' she said, coming back and landing a lovely cup of white frothy coffee in front of me.

'Thanks, miss,' I said, smiling up at her. I watched her making her way down to stand behind the counter again and stare out at the street. Lovely! I whipped up me chips and opened the paper, seeing them all soft and mashed-looking, with the vinegar dried in. It poured up me nostrils, making me belly rumble and me mouth water with the hunger. I dived on the chips and took a little sip of the coffee, wanting to spare it.

Oh, nobody could ask for more, the way I'm feeling so happy at the minute. Here I am eating at last and back in me favourite haunt, looking out at the world passing by and nobody to bother me. I gave a shiver with the delight and the lovely heat running through me.

Ah, that's the last of them. I stared at the empty white paper with the little bits of fat sitting in the corners and dipped me finger in, catching them up and crackling them between me teeth, tasting the salt and vinegar. Pity! I'm still starving. I could eat another bag. But that's me lot for tonight. I sipped on me coffee, making it last, and lit up a cigarette. Now what? Where am I going to go tonight? Who do I know that will take me in for just the one night? Dear God, help me to find a job tomorrow. I'm desperate now, God! I will have nowhere to sleep and no money in me pocket soon. Please, God, don't let that happen to me.

Who can I go to? Sister Eleanor is definitely out for a start. Number one, she won't hear of getting me another job after losing this one that was me last. When she says something, she means it. Anyway, even if she did get me a job, which she won't, I wouldn't ask her. Not on yer nelly!

That last job proved I was right all along. When aul ones hear you came out of a convent, they try to make an eejit outa you. They think you don't know any better and they can do what they like with you because they know you have no one to back you up. No, I'm just going to have to get me own jobs from now on and not say a word about ever being in a convent. That's too dangerous. That aul one and aul fella tonight tried to pull the wool over me eyes by threatening to get the police for me when I tried to leave. Another young one might have been frightened outa her life, but not me. I'm well-used to the police. God knows, I was in enough trouble with them, not to mention I know the law. You can't get someone arrested for destroying their washing. On the other hand, that bastard the husband was on the right track with his I'm-making-threatening-behaviour. Yeah, they would listen to them saying that all right! They would question me, hear I'm from a convent, know I haven't a hope in hell of having any comeback at them. They could even take me down to the station and make life difficult for me. Keep me there for hours. Maybe even ring the nuns saying I was in trouble. Or even charge me with threatening people. Them bastards could say what they like and be believed. He's a civil servant and she's a school teacher. Decent, respectable and law-abiding citizens . . . how are yeh? Respectable, me bleedin eye!

No, you don't have to do anything to get into trouble. Just not come from a respectable background or just be let out of a convent! They know you have no one behind you. That's all it takes.

Right, I was lucky to escape them. It won't happen again. No more nuns! But I better watch meself. That was a warning. It is too easy for me to land in a trap at the minute. I'm still only sixteen. The world still thinks I am an easy mark. So, I better keep wide awake from now on.

I must have dozed off without realising. Me head shot up from the table with the noise around me. I had fallen asleep, plastered on the table with me head lying on me arms. I stared into the face of a fella with dirty black greasy hair, slicked back with olive oil. A woman with long black wavy thin hair was sitting next to him. 'Were yeh asleep?' he grinned, staring at me with shifty, sleevin little grey eyes that reminded me of a ferret watching me every move. I shot up in the seat, sitting up straight, and shook me head, trying to get me senses back. 'What happened to yeh? Yeh look worn out! Have yeh no place teh stay?' he said, flicking his head over to me suitcase, taking in I'm on the move.

I shook me head slightly, muttering, 'I'm fine,' then looked away, not wanting to make any conversation with him.

'Listen, if yeh have nowhere teh stay, yeh can come back teh our place. We have plenty a room. Yeh can stay wit us!'

I looked across him, muttering, 'I'm fine.'

'No, honestly,' he said, pushing to get me to come with them, 'yer more then welcome. Come on, we don't live far from here. Come on! Get yer case. Yeh can come with us now.' He made a move, standing up and moving over towards me to pick up me case and get me moving.

'No, it's all right,' I said. 'I'm fine. I have somewhere to stay.'

'Listen, you'll be safe with us,' he said. Totally ignoring what I'm saying, then sitting back down again and leaning across the table to talk into me face. I stared at him, seeing the desperate pleading in his eyes, not wanting to let go. 'Won't she, Mary?' he shot at the woman, whipping his head around to demand she agree with him.

I looked at the woman, seeing her flick her eyes at me then turn away like she was saying, 'That's the last thing I want.' Then she lowered her head, keeping her eyes down, much as to say, 'But there's nothing I can do about it. I have to accept it.' She reminded me of my ma. That same beaten look. The look that said, 'There's nothing in this life for me. I just have to go along with this fella and do what I'm told. Otherwise, I really will have nothing. He's better than nothing. Anyway, he owns me.'

'No thanks!' I said, standing up and looking him straight in the eye. 'I'm OK. What gave you the idea I needed somewhere to stay? I'm off home now.'

'Right,' he said, jumping up, knowing I was trying to pull the wool over his eyes. 'We're leavin, too. Come on, Mary! We'll walk this young girl to wherever she's goin.' I watched the way he said that to the woman. He said it like it was a threat, that she better buck herself up. He was going to get his hands on me and she better help, if she knew what was good for her. Oh, here we go! This bastard is not only shifty but he's a dangerous shifty bastard. He's not going to let me get out of his clutches, no matter where I walk now. He has me.

I walked off, heading down to the toilets, and lit up a cigarette, thinking if I walk out that door now, he's going to follow me. Where can I run to? I have nowhere to go to. Even if I tell the waitresses here, what can they do? He will just lie in wait, watching to see where I go. Jesus! That suitcase is a dead giveaway. It tells people straight away at this hour of the night I am homeless.

Think! Right, I know what to do. I marched out and there they were, sitting at the table waiting for me with their coats on. 'Right, are we ready?' the little weasel said, taking it for granted I was just going to follow him. He was already acting like I belonged to him. Jaysus! The world is full of Jacksers. I know his game now. I have him worked out. He uses the woman as a blind, to put you at your ease that he's a respectable married man, sitting with his wife. The pair of them are offering me, out of the kindness of their hearts, a bed for the night. So he can't possibly do me any harm. What could be wrong with that? Yeah, plenty, mister. She does what she's told. She's a beaten woman. But he has plenty of uses for her. I recognise their type straight away. Yeah, I had more then me share of them as a child. He's a fucking pimp. I have been around bad bastards long enough to recognise one when I see one. I am going to have to play cute.

'You still here?' I said, hauling meself back inta the seat and grinning at him.

'Are yeh coming? Come on, it's getting late out,' he said, looking at me like he was losing patience with me.

'Wha? Wha are yeh on about? Go where? Jaysus! Where did you come out of? Was I fuckin asleep?' I said, staring at him waiting for an answer. He stared back at me, trying to make out the change in me. He hadn't really heard me talk.

'Yeah, yeh were,' he said slowly, his mouth hanging open, trying to make out what was happening.

'Where do yeh live?' I asked him.

'In Gardiner Street. It's not too far from here,' he said, looking confused. 'We can walk it in five minutes.'

'Listen, did yeh see a big fella with short blond mousey hair and a crooked nose,' I laughed, 'comin in here looking for anyone?'

'No! Why?'

'It's me bleedin bruther! Me ma will fuckin be dug outa him when I tell her the poxy bastard left me sittin stranded here for the whole fuckin night. He left me here with a plate a bleedin fish and chips and tha was the last I saw a him. "I'm ony goin down teh Mooney's pub for a quick one,"' I mimicked. 'We just got back from England in the early hours a the mornin. He took me over there fer a weddin. Me sister just got married, she's livin in Birmingham, an we've been doin the fuckin rounds all day! We've only been missin fer a week. But the carry on a him, goin around meetin up wit all the pals. Yeh would think the eejit was gone outa the country for years! Can yeh credit tha?' I asked him, staring with me mouth hanging open. 'I've probably missed the last bus back home now so the fucker is goin to have teh pay for a taxi. So tha should shut him up! Yeah, tha will put a stop teh his gallop, wit all the bleedin excuses that's bound teh come pourin outa him. I'm ragin, I am! Wha deh yeh think about bleedin tha?' I asked him again, staring with me eyes boring into him and me lips clamped together, breathing heavily through me nose, waiting for an answer.

I sat staring, watching his eyes staring out of his head then blinking like mad, trying to figure how he could have been so wrong about me. I looked so nice and innocent and all respectable, and stupid. Definitely fair game, with me sitting here with the suitcase, looking like a lamb waiting to go to the slaughter. Then along comes the likes of him, springing on me and trying to claim me for himself. No fucking chance, you little toerag. I'm going to eat you alive. Jaysus! He must have thought all his birthdays came on the one day when he clapped eyes on me. I can't get over the cheek a him, picking on me!

'Did you say Gardiner Street?' I suddenly roared, interrupting him shaking his head, trying to agree me bruther was a bastard. 'I know that place like the back of me hand. Do yeh know anyone livin in the buildins or Foley Street? Maybe me bruthers know yeh! Wha did yeh say yer name was?' I asked him.

'Listen,' he suddenly said, wrapping his hand across his mouth like he just remembered something. 'We have teh hurry, don't we, Mary?'

'Wha?' she said, looking up at him with a glint in her eye, beginning to enjoy herself now I was no longer trouble for her and delighted he had made a fool of himself.

'Come on, will yeh? Let's get moving, for fuck's sake,' he growled, grabbing a handful of her coat by the shoulder and slapping her with his other hand to get her moving.

'Ah, Jaysus! Are youse off, too?' I moaned. 'Will I tell Lasher, me bruther, yeh were askin after him?' I roared, looking up at them wit me mouth hanging open, making meself look disappointed to see them going.

'Nah, yer all right,' he said, waving at me and rushing Mary out the door.

I waited a few minutes, giving them enough time to put distance between us. Then I got up, taking me suitcase, and walked slowly to the door. I opened it, looking out to see what he was up to. I watched the pair of them make their way along the street with their shoulders hunched and him with his hands pushed into his pockets. He wriggled his neck, trying to keep it from getting exposed to the icy-cold wind, letting it drop and get buried deep inside the collar of his overcoat. He rushed ahead of her, turning himself right down Talbot Street, leaving her to trail behind, taking little steps, rushing to catch up with him.

I walked on until I hit the corner and stopped to watch where he was going. He flew, rushing himself like mad and half drew his head back, telling her to hurry. He looked like he was worried someone might come after him. Accusing him of trying to molest the little sister of some hard men from the city centre.

Ah, that's the last I'll see of him. That little runt is in too much of a hurry to get himself home to Gardiner Street. He wants to get back while he's still in one piece. No, he's not going to hang around bothering me. I watched him flying off down the road. Yeah, that's right, you little snot rag! Run back to your rats' nest! You're not getting an easy life at my expense. Fucker!

I turned back, heading across the road, and took off in the opposite direction. Hurrying down through the long empty streets, seeing the Liffey lying just in the distance. I turned right and the wind coming across the Liffey whipped me clean off me feet. Fuck! Jaysus! I caught me breath, whipping hold of me coat collar, and bent me head inta the wind. I pushed on, making me way down the quays along Bachelors Walk.

Jaysus! Everything is locked up, I thought. Staring around, looking at the empty dark old Georgian houses that sold second-hand furniture alongside the old bookshops. It's very lonely down this way. It's even darker, with no lights from anywhere. The street lamps are far too wide apart from each other. Some of them are not even working. Where am I going to sit in for the night and get a bit of sleep?

Sleep? Forget that! I need to get in off the streets fast, before someone else tries to land their hands on me. Who would believe it? Here I am, walking along here in the dead of night with me suitcase in me hand. Looking like a lost culchie searching for me way back to the bog. Fer the lovin Jaysus, Martha! How thick can yeh get? Oh, I'm raging with meself. Imagine getting caught out like this! And the bloody freezing cold would rip yeh in two!

I could feel the icy wind whipping across from the river and running straight up through me. A car came towards me and started to slow down. I saw the driver lean his head down to get a look out at me. Help! Mammy! He's stopping. I hurried past, leaving him stopped. Ah, no! Now he's reversing.

'Are you all right?' an aul fella said, leaning across to whip down the window on the passenger side and leer out at me. I could see by the way his eyes was dancing up and down in his head, he wanted to get his hands on me. I gave a quick look straight at his eyes. No, run! He's not offering charity! I said nothing, just flew meself over to the other side of the road and took off along the river. I heard the squealing of tyres and he shot across the road after me. I stopped dead to meet him head-on, and see what he was about.

'Are you lost?' he said, smiling. Looking at me like he would love to have me for his dinner!

'Nah,' I said easily. 'Me bleedin bruther dumped me outa the car because he thought the coppers were followin him for havin no insurance on the car. He's hidin down the road, waitin on me. He put me outa the car in case he got lagged! Nice a him, huh? Doesn't want his little sister in any trouble! Me ma would only kill him, big an all as he is. I'm just back after me holidays! They had me in Mountjoy Prison for attemptin teh knife me aul fella. I was bunged up for threatening behaviour! That's wha the coppers called it. Usin a lethal weapon, or somethin like tha, the charges was. But it was his word against mine. Me bruthers had a little word wit him, and he dropped the charges pronto! So they had teh let me go. Anyways, they couldn't keep me there cos I'm only a minor! Do yeh want teh give us a lift in outa the cold, an we can go down an see if he's still waitin on me? He's goin teh be . . .'

Ah! He didn't let me finish what I was going to say. I watched him whip the car back around the way he just came. The eyes were turning in the back of his head with the shock he just got.

'Eh, mister! Where're yeh runnin?' I watched him burning the rubbers on the tyres of the car, he was in such a hurry to get back about his business.

'He didn't even bother teh say goodbye!' I snorted to meself. Taking in icy-cold air right up through me nostrils. That was great gas! I laughed to meself, getting the picture again of your man's face turning all colours in the dark. I stood, still staring after him, watching the car vanish into the distance over the Liffey on O'Connell Bridge. I felt like I could handle anything.

Right, that's it! Enough of this, Martha. You can run outa luck, if you meet the wrong kind of bastard. So far you've been lucky. Them fellas are only chancers!

I took off running for all I was worth, looking for a place where I could sit in out of the cold and hide until the night was over. I flew on, trying to warm meself. But me legs feel like lead and I'm freezing to the bone. Jaysus! There's nothing! No place I can hide. I need to sit down in a bit of heat and comfort and think up something.

More cars were driving slowly along the road, coming towards me then slowing down. Bleedin hell! I'll just have to keep ducking and diving, flying from one side of the road to the other. I ran, running like a blue-arsed fly, trying to keep in the wrong direction to the way the cars were coming. 'Where the fuck are they all coming out of?' I puffed, slowing down to get me breath.

I stopped rushing altogether when I came towards the Four Courts. I stared at the great big columns and the high steps up to the inside, where the High Court is held. I looked up at the height of it as I hurried for the steps. Seeing the great big dome sitting on the top. Gawd! Mammy! I have somewhere to sit down at last. I dashed up the steps and hid meself behind one of the great big columns. Oh, that's better. No one can see me here. But I can see who's coming when I put me head around the corner. I shivered and pulled the collar of me coat tight, trying to wrap it across me neck.

Bloody hell! Why didn't I think of something better than this before I fell asleep in that café? I think I had a plan! What was it? I don't even remember falling asleep. Bloody gobshite! Imagine letting meself lie there, sleeping away, stretched across the table, making a holy show of meself! No wonder that crackpot thought you were an easy mark!

Oh, bloody hell! I can't think straight when this cold is going right up through me. Even me nerves are gone on edge. I'm thinking any minute now someone is going to jump out at me from behind that flower pot with the big bush sticking out. What am I going to do? What about a church? There's plenty of them further down. Even Adam and Eve's is just across the road . . .

No, they're all well locked up by now! But I can't stay on here. This stone-cold ground is making an ice block outa me arse. It's cutting right up through me. I'm beginning to turn inta a stone statue, like the ones draped around this place. Ah, Jaysus! I feel like I'm a criminal on the run, with all this keeping ahead a the posse! Bleedin men! They're good for nothing!

It feels like I'm in the jungle, running for me life because I'm the dinner. I started to think about the story of the big wolf blowing down the house on the little pigs. I might as well have had the same thing happen to me. Did the poor pigs get eaten or were they just left without a roof over their head? A cold fear started to fly through me at that sudden thought. That's it. Now even the fairy tales I read as a child are beginning to picture in me head. I used to frighten the life outa meself looking at them pictures and trying to work out what was happening. Now they're all coming back to haunt me.

Will yeh stop it? For the love a Jaysus! I'm frightening meself to death. Oh, Mammy! No, think of something good, yeah. Like I want to cry! No, cut out the snivelling. Some people love to see you crying! It makes them feel big. Some fella could come creeping along here any minute and catch me crying. He may well decide straight away I'm a stupid little softie. Then there's no getting outa that.

OK, definitely no crying. So think of something else. The dome sitting on top of the building. It's very high up! Come to think of it, I think they blew this place up during the War of Independence, them culchie eejits from the country! They came up here blowing up the place, saying they were having a war against the English! Yeah, that's right. They blew this place up. And the only thing left standing was the dome sitting on the top. My Gawd! Imagine that. And it still stands here today. Right, if that thing up there can stay standing, so can I. It won't kill me. The cold won't either and I'm definitely not worried about some man coming and dragging me off and killing me! No, I can outrun most people. I'm very fast on me feet. I had to be when Jackser was always making his way to kill me. Yeah, I'm definitely very nippy on me pins. And usually I'm always wide awake. I can spot trouble coming a mile away!

Right, so! Just get through tonight. Then in the morning I can have a wash somewhere. I might just take meself down to the Gresham Hotel and wash in the toilets. Grand! Then go somewhere and have a lovely hot breakfast! Yeah, I'll go up to Woolworths. That's a great idea! Then I can look for a job. I'll get the newspaper.

But if all else fails, where will I sleep tomorrow night? I'll go down to the buildings. I could always ask someone down there to put me up for a few nights. Couldn't I do that? No, I tried that years ago when me and the ma took off, leaving Jackser to mind himself, and we went to England. No, the poor people down there barely have enough room to swing a cat, never mind take in two more bodies!

So what then? A church! I can hide in the confessional box until they lock up the church. I wonder if that's a good idea, hiding in a church for the night? The statues would be all staring down at me in the pitch black! I wonder if they leave the lights on? I could light the candles. Yeah, but then I would have to pay for them. It would be robbing God, if I didn't pay up. So, as I'm not spending the last of me money on candles, where will I go? Jaysus! I'll work that one out when I get a bit of heat into me and a bit of hot grub. Right, that's settled.

I pulled the packet of cigarettes out of me pocket and lit one up. 'Excuse me!' I looked up, jumping with the fright at the voice coming out of nowhere. 'Have yeh gor a light, love?' I looked up into the face of a woman wearing a short mini-frock, with black knee boots and a white fun-fur jacket. Her dyed-black hair was standing three feet up in the air, it got so much back-combing.

'Jaysus! You frightened the life outa me,' I said, laughing. Handing her me cigarette to take a light because I wanted to spare the rest of me matches.

'Wha are yeh doin here, sittin in the freezin cold?' she said, leaning back her head and dragging the smoke all the way deep down inta her lungs. Then she sucked air up through her nose and looked at me. Waiting for me answer.

'I have nowhere to go,' I said, knowing I could trust her.

'Aren't you like meself? A Dubliner?' she said, letting the last word rise inta the air.

'Yeah, but I still have nowhere to go.'

'Jaysus! That's terrible. On a night like tonight of all nights. They say it's goin teh snow.'

'Is it?' I asked her, seeing her slapping her arms to get a bit of heat, thinking snow would make things even worse. Now I would have to worry about leaving me footprints in the snow when I might have to run for me life, trying to escape some aul fella chasing me down the road. I could very easily be tracked to me hiding place. I was trying to picture that, with me nerves really beginning to get the better of me again.

'Gawd! Do you know, I have been chased down that bleedin road by aul fellas in cars trying to pick me up!' I said, looking at her, shocked.

'Yeah, they see you as fresh! The fuckers are not coming around me at all tonight,' she said, looking very sour and whipping her head up and down the road. I stared at her. It was just dawning on me now. Oh, Mammy! Your woman must be on the game! Now look what I'm after getting meself inta. Here I am, drawing even more attention to meself when they come looking for her! There are bound to be lines and lines of cars, all stopping to pick the pair of us up!

Mammy! Jaysus! God! Help! Oh, fuck! I felt me heart lepping in me chest with the sudden fright. I could feel the legs going from under me. Right, that's it. I'm off. Jaysus! Just let me outa here!

'Listen, goodbye now. I have to run. I just thought of something,' I said, feeling me heart flying as I whipped up me suitcase and took off, taking the steps two at a time.

'Here, wait!' she said, waving at me. I looked back and waved, smiling back at her. 'Go up to the bus station. You can kip down on the buses,' she said.

'Oh, yeah! Thanks very much. That's a great idea,' I said. Feeling delighted at the thought of getting in somewhere safe and warm. Then I felt bad at the idea of making her think I thought she was dirt. That's not what worried me at all. I felt sorry for her. God help her. 'Listen,' I said, stopping to shout back at her, wanting her to know I thought she was very good. 'Thanks very much, missus. I'm very grateful to you.'

'No worry! You mind yerself now. An don't stop teh talk teh any a them fellas in the cars,' she shouted, giving me a warning, waving her finger at me.

'Yeah, I knew that full already. Yeah, thanks very much again,' I shouted, flying for all I was worth back up the road and heading for the bus depot.

I dragged me feet along the ground with the heavy suitcase pulling the arm outa me. That hill looks like it's going to kill me. I dropped me head and pushed me legs, one foot in front of the other, and stopped on the bridge. I collapsed me arms, letting them fall with the exhaustion, leaning on the railings resting meself. Then stood, looking down into the canal. I stared at the brown, muddy-looking water, surrounded by all the old red-brick warehouses looking into it. I wonder what it would be like if I was to stand up here on the top and just let meself drop down? I could feel me head going under the water and not being able to get me breath. It would be suffocating for a few minutes. I wonder how long it takes before you die? I hate water! I'm afraid of me life of it, because I can't swim.

Me head turned slowly around, landing on the big old building of the glass-bottle factory. I wonder how many people have come and gone through that factory. It's been there for hundreds of years. At least one hundred anyway. Them people who first worked there long, long ago, they're all now well dead and gone. I suppose they had their worries, too. I bet if they were given the chance to come back, they would probably take it. Even with all the fear and worry. All these old buildings were here long before I was born. Imagine life was going on before I got here! But these have seen their last days. Everything around here is lying idle, all run down. Just like meself.

Snowflakes started to fall, landing on me eyelashes. Jaysus! I hate this snow. It's nothing like you see in the fancy photographs of long ago. With people wrapped up in scarves and hats and long coats with warm boots. All laughing and throwing snowballs at each other. This turns to slush, then freezes hard on the ground, until you have to take it easy walking or you slip on your back and break your bleedin neck.

It started to get heavier. I looked up at the sky turning all shades of blue, grey, and now black. All before me eyes as I watched it. Heavy white snowflakes was suffocating the air, making its way to land softly on the ground, covering it like a white sheet. There's nothing to be seen but white. The air and ground is covered in it, including meself. Jaysus! I look like a moving snowman. And I'm covered in it.

I looked down at meself, seeing it sit on me shoulders and coat and brown bokety shoes. Me hair hung around me like a white stringy hat. Ah, what next? I'm plastered in white snow. Now I'm going to get me coat and shoes wet again. Fuck!

I walked on, making me way down the hill, heading for the bus depot. I hope nobody's hanging around tonight. I want to get straight into a bus and try to get a bit of sleep. This snow is going to stick even heavier tonight. Maybe they won't be moving the buses tomorrow. That means I won't get run out by the cleaners when they start coming in the early hours of the morning to clean the buses.

God, where are you? Please help me to find a way to get back on me feet before it's too late. I'm worried because the heart is going outa me. It feels like I'm going to be stuck walking the streets for ever. I'm not looking like meself. I know I'm looking worn out from the hunger, because I can't buy much to eat and I hardly have any money left. Then, on top of that, I'm not getting much sleep and the terrible cold is killing me.

This is me second week now, walking the streets searching for work. You know yourself I've been looking very hard. Walking the feet offa meself, tramping the length and breadth of everywhere, but it's all for nothing. I even banged on the doors of the bed and breakfasts, asking them will they give me food and a bed in exchange for me work. That didn't bloody do any good! They took one look at the desperation on me face, seeing how rough I looked from all that sleeping out. Well, that was enough for them. They had all the information they needed to decide something must be wrong with me and slammed the door shut straight inta me face. One aul one stared at me for a few minutes. I held me breath, hoping I was getting somewhere. I gaped as she stared, letting her think about it. I could see her head flying with the thinking, the eyes hopping and blinking like mad, working on the lovely idea of getting me free. All for a bit of grub and a bed that wouldn't a been used anyway.

'No!' she finally said, with her eyes closing down, pulling herself back from the door, getting ready to bang it. 'No, you wouldn't do me. I won't bother. Goodbye now!'

I stood, not believing me ears. No? Not even for nothing? I went straight inta shock. The heart left me and sank right down inta me belly. Then I shouted. 'No, wait, missus! Why not? I'm a hard worker!' I ended up shouting at the door, as it slammed with a bang in me face. I stood staring at it for a few seconds while the information got through to me brain. Then I banged on the door again. 'I'm not ready to give in,' I muttered, straightening meself up, getting ready to talk her into it.

'What do yeh want? I told you already I have no need of your sort!'

'What sort is that, missus?' I asked, with me voice squeaking at the insult she just gave me. The bleeding cheek a her, I thought, forgetting now I had been readying meself to try and talk her inta changing her mind. Instead, the rage and fear working itself up through me was making me lose the run of meself. Then I felt meself dropping, with the air going outa me. I could feel me heart sinking with the disappointment and fear of getting nothing. I just wanted to know where I was going wrong.

'What's wrong with me, missus? I'm nearly offering me work free! Missus, can't you just tell me why?' I asked her quietly, looking up at her.

'It's . . . you're too young!' she burst out, trying to work out why she didn't want to take me. 'Young ones are more trouble then they're worth! I'm sorry,' she snapped, 'but me mind is made up! Now, I'm busy. I've wasted enough time.' Then she was gone, slamming the door shut for the second time.

'Aul fucker!' I shouted at the door, nearly crying at the rage starting to fly around me chest. Then she opened the door again, and me heart leapt with the hope.

'Now,' she roared, 'you just went and proved me right! Foul language and plenty of cheek, that's all your sort has to offer. Now, get away from me door or I'll call the police.'

'Fucking aul hag! Stick yer poxy aul flea-ridden bed and breakfast up yer fat arse!' I screamed, letting fly at the door. She didn't come out again so I couldn't really tell her what I thought about her. I looked around me with the rage, wanting to do something – make a holy show of her.

'What's wrong with the place?'

I looked up inta the face of a red-necked culchie appearing outa nowhere. He stopped next to me, and stood looking down at me from about six feet up inta the air. He looks like a long string of misery, I thought sourly, staring up and down the length of him, with the bony face and the dirty brown-pink nylon shirt that was too big for his red skinny neck. The red clashed with the pink. 'Did ya just get hefted outa the place?' he said, swinging his brown suitcase at the door then looking down at me with such a look on his face that told me everything I was going to tell him would be taken as gospel. In other words, a right gobshite.

'Oh, my God!' I gasped. 'Whatever you do, don't go in there. That aul one has a houseful of cats. She insists yeh let them sleep in the bed wit yeh! They run riot. Then, first thing in the morning, they even get to your plate of rashers before you do! That's why we were having a shouting match. She threw me out after I complained about it. Not to mention the damp cold bed I had to sleep in last night,' I huffed. Snorting out me disgust.

'Shockin!' he breathed, with the eyes hangin out of his head, listening to me every word.

'Oh, yeah!' I carried on, encouraged by his two ears wigging, taking in everything I was telling him. 'And another thing! She charges seventeen shillings and sixpence!'

'What? Not at all! Sure I'm just after turning down nine and six back up yonder!' he gasped, waving his suitcase back up the road.

'There yeh go!' I shouted, waving me hands at him. 'She's a daylight robber!' I roared, wagging me finger at the door.

''Tis true for yeh! The Dublin people would rob yeh blind, if yeh didn't hang onta deh shirt tails hangin outa yeh. Deh brother warned me right enough dis would happen. "Mick," he said, "cow tail it outa dat city as fast as yeh can. Mind out for dem city young ones. Dey'll rob the shirt offa yer back."'

I hope he's not including me. Maybe I can get him to buy me a nice hot meal, if I play me cards right. I shook me head, agreeing. With him shaking the side of his head like mad, not able to take in all the daylight robbery that was going on. Then sniffing air up through his nostrils like he was getting a bad smell. 'Be Gawd! He was right, sure enough there,' he said, thinking his brother very smart altogether, getting lost with a far-away look in his eye of sheer admiration for the brother. 'On the other hand,' he muttered, staring at me with the eyes hanging outa the back of his head, getting outa breath from all the bad news, 'I'm told this one was good an aisey on the money,' he said, looking confused, with a different thought entering his head.

Then he whipped out a dirty piece of paper and squinted at it. I had a look with him. It was written in pencil and I couldn't make out the writing. 'I writ all this back home. It's a list of the clean an chaipe places dat are handy in Dublin,' he said, looking down at me as the two of us gaped at the bit of paper.

'Well, whoever it was that told you about this place was leading yeh astray. I'm telling you, you go in that door at yer peril! For sure, once that aul one gets her hands on your pockets yer done for! She will even charge yeh half a crown for the hot water. So you may as well forget about having your shave in the morning,' I said, looking disgusted, craning me head up to look at him. 'That aul one will lighten your pockets. Make no mistake about that,' I said, shaking me head, feeling very satisfied I had done a good hatchet job on yer woman.

'Oh, right so! I'll give dat a miss,' he said, picking up his suitcase, making to move off. 'Well, it's plenty more I have teh look at. I only want somewhere teh kip down for the one night and the bit of grub in the morning. Anything will do me,' he said, nodding his head and setting his sights further down the road. 'I suppose I'm looking teh make a bargain. I want teh pay as little as passable,' he said, dropping his long skinny red neck inside his overcoat. He took off, letting his arse stick out, heading himself off down the road. I stared after him, thinking it's not worth me while trying to butter him up to buy me something to eat. I'd love a plate of fish and chips but that fella is so mean he probably thinks he owes himself money, judging by that hungry look on his culchie mug.

Jaysus! If only I could land a job. But I'm too desperate-looking. It's putting them off. They think I must be on the run from something or someone. Right, I better get a move on and start trying to find somewhere to get in out of the cold for the night.

Yeah, that was today, God. Now look at the state of me! I'm up the creek without a paddle! Will you please let me luck change? I need something to turn up for me soon. I have no one I can turn to. Do you know that? Is this your idea of a joke? In a way, I'm blaming you! Yeah, if I hadn't gone down to the church to light a penny candle and have a little word with you, I wouldn't a lost me money!

You know I only have the one shilling and thruppence left to keep me going. What will I do then? I'm not going back to robbing.

I'm definitely not even thinking about that terrible idea. I can't ask Sister Eleanor for help. She would only run me out the door. I'm left the convent now and that's that! I can hear her saying, nearly crying with the torment she thinks I'm putting her through.

I even thought about going back to the ma. Just for a little while. That mad idea only lasted me a few seconds. I would sooner start robbing for meself then for them. So, as there doesn't seem to be much left open to me, what am I going to do? Please tell me, God! Don't let me down now, in me hour of need. I can even get meself picked up by the police. Yes, God! I'm getting very annoyed about this whole thing. You started it in the first place.

I could really begin to feel meself getting worked up, now that I knew who to blame. They could say I'm a vagrant because I'm beginning to look a bit in threadbare order. God, you know that could happen. They could easily get me bunged into a home, locked away, for being on the streets! They would say it's for me own protection because I'm too young, yeah.

I was thinking about meself being called a vagrant. No, I'm not going to let that happen. I would really have to be one complete gobshite. I'm just really, really tired, that's all. Me nerves are just running away with me. I'm only letting me mind wander, thinking of the worst things that can happen.

Then I had a thought. I have gone through much, much worse then this in me days on this earth. I'm still here now. Nothing that ever really frightened the life outa me or all the worry I had or all the terrible beatings I got, none of it killed me! No, I'm still here and it will get better. Just like before! I had happy times and hard times. That's just the way life is. So I have happy times to look forward to. It always gets worse before it gets better, Martha. Doesn't it, God?

To be honest, the only reason I'm still talking to you, God, is because I have no one else to talk to. I'm beginning to think a heart-to-heart talk with you only lands me in trouble. If only I had gone on about me business.

Anyway, where was I? Oh, yeah! Of course things are going to get better. 'Yeah, they will,' I whispered, staring at nothing. I could feel a terrible tiredness come over me again. 'Course it does,' I mumbled to meself, moving on again. 'So now, take it easy. Yeah. Take it easy,' I whispered, wanting to cheer meself up.

Suddenly, without warning, I felt a hot flush flying up me chest and I burst out crying. 'Ma, I wish I had a mammy. I'm still not really grown up at all. I still want a mammy!' I croaked, hearing the same voice I heard when I was only little and life got too much for me. I walked on, feeling the same as I did then, somehow like a little child again, lost and lonely.

I cried to meself as I made me way through the heavy snowflakes, smothering me from head to toe, making me feel cold and wet and miserable. Only God knows what I am going to do now or what will happen to me.

Please, God, stay with me. Don't desert me now. That's all I ask. I don't really mean to be giving out to you. But I'm so worn out. I walked on, trying to hurry, watching me steps on the icy path, seeing it getting covered in thick snow. I feel like I'm rushing but I'm really going very slow. Ah, Mammy, I can hardly see with this snow. Gawd, it's getting very heavy. It really is beginning to come down now.

I stared ahead, trying to judge the distance to the bus depot. I can hardly see where I'm going. Everything looks blacker, except for this thick snow swirling down around me. 'Jaysus! Let me get in outa this!' I snorted. This is madness. It feels like even the weather is out to get me.

I can't believe I got meself into this mess. And worst of all, I haven't even managed to get meself outa it! How in the name of Jaysus could anyone be so stupid? How could I have let this happen? To me of all people? I should have known better. Stupid cow! Martha, you are one bleedin thick eejit, make no mistake about that. No, I definitely haven't been thinking this last while. Now look what you have done to yourself, wandering the streets like a lost fucking soul. Ah, fuck!

I felt a sudden hot rage flying through me. It shot up through me belly and surged through me chest, exploding itself inta me head, making me see all colours. I looked around me in an awful fury, seeing the heavy thick snow swirling and descending on me in buckets. Me head swung back, seeing I was the only one out in this godforsaken weather. Then, without warning, I threw back me head and took in an almighty lungful of air. I could hear it hissing up through me chest, rising itself right up to me neck. Then, not even thinking, I let go of me suitcase, letting it drop to the ground, and slowly threw back me shoulders and let rip, giving an unmerciful roar outa me.

'FUCK OFFFFFF! FUCK THE WEATHER! FUCK THE NUNS, FUCK THEIR AUL DOMESTIC JOBS AND FUCK EVERYBODY! AND AUL ONES! ESPECIALLY THEM! AND AUL FELLAS! OH, YEAH, ESPECIALLY THEM AS WELL! I DON'T NEED ANY OF YOUSE! I'LL MAKE ME OWN WAY! GO TO HELL, THE LOT OF YEHS. AS FOR YOU, GOD, I DON'T NEED YOUR IDEA OF LOOKING AFTER ME. I'M FINISHED WITH YOU! IT'S OVER! I'M NEVER SPEAKING TO YOU EVER AGAIN! SO THERE! STICK THE WORLD RIGHT UP YOUR ARSE!' Then I remembered one more. 'I HOPE A BOMB DROPS ON THE HEADS OF ALL YOU FUCKIN ITALIANS!'

I stood dead still, watching and waiting. Nothing happened. I'm not struck stone dead. 'Right, so that's telling youse,' I muttered, wondering if I left anyone out. Then I let meself go and listened, waiting just in case to see if anything really would happen. No, I'm still here. Nobody is rushing to get me locked up, either. I let out a huge sigh, feeling meself go limp.

'Right, now, that's telling them all! Yeah, I feel better after that,' I muttered to meself, feeling me face starting to smile. I felt meself loosen all over and me shoulders drop. Then me head started to clear. I paused, holding me breath to take in all around me, hearing only the silence. Me eyes wandered over to the line of little cottages all snuggled together with the lights on and the curtains drawn, looking lovely and cosy with the roofs covered in snow. I stared up and down the deserted street, looking through a curtain of swirling snow. I could see flashes of dark blue and grey, dancing in and out with the warm yellow from the street lamps. Everywhere I looked was covered in snow. Then me eyes peeled up ahead to the bus garage, waiting, with the buses gone to bed for the night.

Everything is so quiet, so still, I thought, whispering to meself. It feels like the world is holding its breath, like I'm the only one out here wandering around. Then I started to laugh, seeing the state of meself. Here I am, standing out in the middle of a snowstorm in the pitch black night, soaking to the bloody skin, complete with me suitcase standing right beside me on the ground. Then, to cap it all, I'm roaring me head off like a mad woman. Yes, me little dew drop, this is where you have landed yourself up! No one could ever accuse you of not being stupid! Oh, no! And mad! I must take after me aunt Nelly. She was always throwing herself inta mad fits, too. Oh, Jaysus! You sure don't do anything by halves. That's for sure, Martha.

Well, that feels better, I sniffed to meself. I had done something mad, yeah, shouting at the weather like it was meant specially for me and roaring into thin air. That should get me locked up fast enough. Right, but I'm OK now. That did me good. It woke me up.

I need to think to get meself outa this mess. OK, start thinking for a change, because the older yer getting, the more stupid yer becoming. I walked on, coming into the yard of the bus station, and stopped at the entrance. I looked around to make sure no one was hanging around. Grand! It's all deserted. Anyway, who would be thick enough to show their nose out on a night like tonight? You would, Martha. I felt a laugh coming up me at that thought. Yeah, I'm not fit to be let loose. I had one last look around before making a move for the buses. Good, there's nobody around, not a sinner. Right, me luck's in.

I could see the buses all standing beside each other, parked for the night. They were all covered in snow. Me heart lifted at the sight of them. OK, get moving. I hurried over before someone came out of the depot and ran me out. Me heart was clapping away, trying to hurry before I got caught. I passed by the first one, and made me way heading to the very back, where no one would catch me when they started to move out the buses in the morning or the cleaners started arriving. I could be up and gone as soon as I heard them making noise. Jaysus! They make enough noise to wake the dead, them cleaners, with their roaring and shouting at each other.

'Come on, Mary!'

'We'll be in and out before we know where we are!'

'How did the daughter's weddin go?'

Jaysus! I don't know where they get the energy that hour of the morning.

Here we are. I stepped up onta the platform, leaving the snow behind me. This bus will do me lovely. It's grand and protected, with the other buses sheltering it. I staggered down the aisle and landed me suitcase on the floor, happy to get rid of the weight of it. Oh, this is grand. I could feel the comfort of having a roof over me head and all the warm, soft-looking seats making it nice and cosy.

I took off me wet coat, leaving it to dry on the seat in front of me, and opened me suitcase. Right, where's me towel? I dried me hair and took off me wet shoes and tights and dried me feet. It's a pity I haven't got a blanket. I could always wander up to one of the hospitals and help meself to one! No, no robbing. Anyway, that's all I would need to turn meself into a tramp, carrying me bleedin bed around with me! Stop your messing, Martha. This is the last time you end up sleeping like this.

I took out me good trench coat and lay down on the long seat, pulling it over me. Oh, my God, this is heaven. I sat up again and threw off me wet frock and pulled me feet under the coat then collapsed back down. Still not satisfied, I jumped up to grab the towel and put it under me head. I closed me eyes, feeling the exhaustion sink down along me body and curl out through me toes. Me eyes felt very heavy and I could feel meself sinking.

'I better have a plan for tomorrow,' I muttered, trying to work something out before I went out cold. First thing is, I have to get something to eat. That's what has been the problem for the last two days. I haven't eaten or had anything to drink. No wonder I'm banjacked and weak from the hunger, then wandering aimlessly around all day, ending up going nowhere. Right, tomorrow morning first thing I'm taking meself into Bewley's café and sitting meself down where they serve you, in the toffs' part. I'll eat meself stupid by ordering everything they have on the menu. Then when she comes with the bill, I'll say . . . eh, what will I say? I'll say, 'Missus, I forgot to bring me money. I'm very sorry about that but I'll make it up to you. I'll do all the washing up for the day, if you throw in dinner as well!'

Will that work? Of course, I could always nip out the door when they're not looking! No, that's taking me straight back where I started in the first place. I'm definitely not robbing. It's too easy to go down that road, but there's no way back. No, I'll just face them head-on! I have no money and that's that! Once I get a good sleep tonight, and I have a belly full of grub in me, I should start using me head again. I'll be able to start thinking more clearly.

Sister Eleanor used to say I was very cunning, like a fox. But she wasn't throwing bouquets at me. No, that was usually when I managed to pull the wool over her eyes. Then when she found out, that's when she went mad. So, I better start being foxy again, using me noodle. I'm only hurting meself with all this truth I'm telling. For a start, I'm going to raise me age, say I'm eighteen. Hmm, I don't think that's any good. Some people accuse me of only looking twelve, because I'm a bit small for me age, I suppose.

Anyway, no more messing. This is serious business. I have to get meself off the streets! I need to find a job and that's that. So that is exactly what I'm going to do. Of course there's something for me out there! For the love a Jaysus, Martha, just go out and find it. Stop this dozy carry-on out of yeh. OK. Right!

I could feel the heat in me belly at the thought I was going to get somewhere. Yeah, lovely! I'm having a good sleep now and in the morning I'll be up early, ripping and roaring to get going. I just needed to have a good talk with meself. I wasn't getting anywhere because me heart and soul wasn't in it. Now I'm ready to take on the world.

I took in a big sigh of contentment, letting meself drop off to sleep, knowing I can get anywhere I want in this life. Now that I have made me mind up that I'm definitely going to get a job, then I will get one. All I have to do now is go after it with a vengeance. Yeah, this world belongs to me, too!

Martha Long

Ma, Now I'm Goin Up in the World

A MEMOIR OF DUBLIN
IN THE 1960s

THE IRISH TIMES #1 BESTSELLER BY THE AUTHOR OF MA, HE SOLD ME FOR A FEW CIGARETTES AND OTHER MEMOIRS OF DUBLIN

I

I sat in the bath up to me neck in hot water. Ooh, lovely! That's one of the great things about this place – they never spare the hot water. No, I would be lost without it. I grabbed up the big bar of carbolic soap slipping around the bath. Got it! Pity, I thought, holding it up to examine it. It's only really for scrubbing the floors. That will take half me skin off! I managed to rob that out of the cleaner's bucket when she wasn't looking.

Right! Beggars can't be choosers! I rubbed it into me washcloth until I was satisfied, then lifted me leg to give it a good wash. 'Ohhhh! Grafton Street's a wonderland! DERE'S MAGIC IN DE AIR!'

I suddenly felt a draught and whipped me head around. An old woman came wandering in, looking at me confused.

'Where's Dickie? Where's me husband?' she moaned, sounding like she was near to crying.

'Eh? Oh, he's gone next door. Close the door quick, Missus! I'm getting an awful draught here.'

'Wha? I want Dickie!'

'Mrs Kelly! What are you doing out of bed? Get back quickly before Sister catches you.'

'Nooo! Let me go!'

The nurse tried wrestling the old woman out the door, but she was having none of it.

'You have to stay in bed! Now come on like a good girl . . . Who are you?' she suddenly asked, letting go of the woman's arm and coming at me.

Oh, Jaysus! I'm done for. I hid me face, ducking me head under the water. Then lifted it back, nearly suffocating. I let the wet hair streel around me face, hoping to hide it. I couldn't hear her right with all the water rolling around in me ears.

'What's this?' she roared, whipping me head around and pointing at me suitcase standing up against the wall. 'Are you a new patient?'

'Eh, yeah.'

'What's going on here? Wait a minute! You're that young one going around eating up all the patients' dinners, causing mayhem!'

'No, I most certainly am not!' I snorted, lifting me face and looking at her squarely in the eyes. 'I'm a hospital visitor. I come here visiting the poor patients who have no visitors whatsoever. And furthermore, they are always delighted to see me!'

'Yes! At lunchtime, when they are having their dinner, which you sit eating!'

'EXCUSE ME! I'm only helping them out! They don't want it, and it's a sin to be wasting good food.'

'I . . . this . . .' she said, lost for words, with her head whipped around making her hat spin, and her eyes crossed in her head. She was outa breath from trying to understand all the confusion.

'Look!' I said, snorting air up through me nose, hoping the bit of air would make me brain think, then getting on with me washing, playing for time.

'How did you get in past the porters' desk?' she asked, trying to keep her voice calm. Then she suddenly let rip, before I could get a word out, 'You know full well you are barred from entering this hospital, Miss! Your antics are well recorded. You even had the cheek to make yourself right at home one night in an empty annexe right next door to the morgue! The porter went down with a corpse and had to hunt you out! You gave the poor man the fright of his life!'

'Well, the dead don't need it!' I shouted. 'But I did!' I said, thumping me chest.

'This is preposterous! It is an absolute outrage!'

'Excuse me! I did no such thi—' I said, getting ready to deny everything else, before she opened her mouth again.

'This is not a hotel,' she interrupted.

'Well, really!' I gasped, sounding just like Sister Eleanor. Hoping to make meself sound respectable.

'Not to mention it is not even visiting time!' she spluttered, gasping for the want of a bit of air, with her face turning purple from all her outrage, as she calls it.

Suddenly I heard a man's voice whistling. I looked over, seeing a porter stopping his whistling, leaning his head down to get a good look at me through the open door. His mouth looked like he was blowing something and his eyes leapt outa the back of his head he was so intent at getting a good look at me. He even forgot about the patient moaning on the trolley that he was supposed to be pushing.

I let out a scream, grabbing me washcloth to hide meself. 'Aaaahhh! Nurse! Ye're lettin that man look in at me!'

'What?' she screamed, sending the door flying shut with a bang.

'Ooooh!' a voice moaned. Then the door whipped open again.

'Staff Nurse! Have you seen Mrs Kelly? She's gone missing.' Then the young nurse's eyes peeled on me, hoping to see I might be Missus Kelly. 'Doctor's on his rounds!' she gasped.

'What?' Staff Nurse puffed, whipping her head around in even more confusion. 'She was here a minute ago! Ohhhh! This is too much, Nurse! Can you not keep your eye on the patients even for one minute?'

'But, Staff Nurse, I was taking temperatures!'

'Stop prattling, girl, and go and find her! Quickly!'

I watched as they flew out the door with their heads going in one direction and their bodies in another, not able to decide which way to go first. Then they crashed into each other as the staff nurse made back in for me.

'Oh, for heaven's sake, Nurse! Pull yourself together! Go that way!' she pointed, waving her arm down the passage. Then she leapt back into me. 'Out, you! And if I see sight or hair of you again you will be in major trouble. Very big trouble,' she snorted, rattling her head like mad, making the cap shake as if she was having some kind of a fit.

'Certainly! I have no intention of staying here to be insulted!' I snorted back.

I shuffled me way down O'Connell Street, then stopped, trying to get a look at meself in a big plate-glass shop window. Me hair was standing up in all directions. Jaysus! The state of me! I thought, gaping at meself. I plastered it down with me two hands, yawning the face offa meself. Ohhh! Me neck. Me bloody neck! I have a crick in it. I walked on, rubbing it. That's the last time I am ever sleeping in a confessional box. I woke up in the middle of the night gasping for me life. The bloody air was all gone! I nearly suffocated meself. Then when I pushed open the door, crawling out of the box, I got an awful, terrible fright. I even started screaming me head off for all I was worth. It was the sudden shock of seeing all them statues staring down at me, an me still half asleep. I didn't recognise them for a minute, with their faces all lit up and their eyes glowing red in the dark. Jaysus! I didn't know what I was looking at! There they were, all standing up in the dark corners of the church, with the little red lights burning underneath, making me think they were a load of ghosts coming to get me. Gawd, Mammy! I'm still not the better of that! I thought, giving a shiver at the memory. That must have come outa me sleeping in the empty room next to the morgue. Never again!

I looked back, throwing me eye up at Cleary's clock, seeing the time was ten to eleven. Right! Just in nice time. I turned left, heading down Abbey Street, then crossed the road to the hotel. I peeked in the door, seeing the aul fella, the porter. He was stretched in his chair at the desk, scratching himself. Then he picked his nose, looking at his finger to see what he got. Ah, bloody hell! I have no chance getting past him! Think, Martha.

I straightened meself, getting ready, then moseyed in, sliding past the desk. I held me breath and kept one eye on him. I had just made it to the stairs, with one foot on the step, when I heard the roar.

'Eh! EXCUSE ME! Where do you think you're goin?'

I took in a big breath, letting it out, saying, 'Oh, I'm all right thanks, Mister! I'm, eh, just heading up the stairs!'

'I can see that! But wha business have ye in comin in here?' he barked, waving his hand around the place and landing it on his hips. 'You're no payin guest! I don't know wha yer game is, but ye can take yerself and yer bloody suitcase!' he said, waving his finger down at me suitcase and twisting his nose outa shape like he was getting a bad smell from it.

'Eh, excuse me, Mister! You are barking up the wrong tree if you think I'm only here to get up to no good! I'll have you know I am looking for me granny. Where is she?' I roared.

'Wha in the name a Jaysus are ye on about? There's no granny of yours staying here!' he said, slamming his fists on his hips.

'What! Then you must be blind, Mister! She came in here to use the toilet an she hasn't come back. So would ye mind goin an lookin for her!' I snorted, losing me rag.

'Listen!' he barked, shaking his head, with the pockmarked face on him turning red. 'Don't come in here tellin me my job! I am sittin at tha desk since half past eight this mornin!' he roared, bending his back and head, pointing in at the desk like he was bowing to it. 'An nobody, but NOBODY, has got past me fittin tha description. Now get out before I call the manager. You have no rights te be comin in here unless ye're a payin patron!'

'Right! But at least go and check the toilet! She could be lying in there now, dead. Dead as a stone corpse!'

'I will do no such thing. Eh, wha are ye talkin about? Stone corpse?! Wha the hell is tha, I ask you?'

I thought for a minute, hearing the words again. Then roared, 'You know what I mean! Stone dead!' I shouted, annoyed at making a fool outa meself.

He let a big breath outa his nose, shaking his head at me, then asked me patiently, 'Now, are ye goin to leave peacefully, or do I have to call the guards to remove you?'

'Huh! Bloody aul culchie! Only an aul culchie would be fond a callin the coppers!' I roared, knowing that insult would get a rise outa him.

'Get out! Before I raise me boot and send you flyin out tha door!' he roared, making to grab a hold of me.

I ducked under his arm, making to fly out the door, and went headlong straight into a man coming in wearing a long check apron, carrying a big tray of sausages and black and white puddings and chops. The lot went up into the air, and as I skated over the sausages, me eye lit on them for a minute! No good. They're raw! Then I was out the door like greased lightning.

'You whore's melt!' the sausage man roared.

'I'll fuckin brain you if I ever get me hands on ye again!' roared the porter as I looked back.

Then I shot me head forward just in time to see the bus barrelling down on me. I stopped dead, frozen for one second, doing a see-saw, rocking on me feet. Back? No! I leapt forward, tearing for the footpath. Made it! Phew! Nearly got me last gasp there!

The bus driver lashed open his little side window, roaring his head off at me, 'Get off the road, you stupid, dirty-looking pile a shite!'

'Ah, go on now,' I said, grinning and lifting me chin slowly. 'Ye're just jealous cos ye look like the back a yer bus! But that's a grand horn ye have there. Did you gerrit for yer birthday?' Then I turned tail and headed back up to Cleary's, making me getaway.

I better get meself a squirt of scent. It doesn't look like I'm going to be getting a bath today. Pity! I liked that place. The hotel bathrooms were nice and handy to get at. Just up the stairs and along the corridor. And it even had a thing on the bath for holding me soap and washcloth and Palmolive shampoo. Yeah! And I could take hours if I wanted, with nobody to bother me. Hmm, I had all me comfort there. Pity I couldn't get in today. I was looking forward to using me nice clean fresh towels I managed to grab off the nurse's trolley before I got thrown out.

I wandered back out of Cleary's smelling of Lavender Water. I sniffed the air, that's a bit strong. I put too much on. You can smell me a mile away. I stood looking up and down. It was drizzling down with the rain. And the wind blew me coat up around me legs. I pulled the collar of me coat up. Brrr! It's bloody freezing. I looked up at the clock. Half past twelve. Time for din-dins up at the hospital. Wonder what they're getting to eat for the dinner today? Never mind. I better keep me nose outa there for a while. Pity! Poor Arabella, Lady Arabella. She will miss me today. The poor thing gets no visitors. Imagine! Ending up in a paupers' hospital, left lying, dumped in a ward with no one to care whether she lived or died, and she the daughter of an 'aristocrat', as she called it. Her family owned half of the best parts of Dublin city in the old days!

I met her on me travels around the hospital. I do wander around, stopping to smile and chat to the patients, especially the old ones, when there's no one bothered with them at visiting time. It can be very lonely watching other people getting fussed over, and you lying there like a spare part. I know what that's like meself. Anyway, it's a grand way to pass the time.

The first time I wandered into the ward, I made straight for her because she was looking at me very intently with a big smile on her face. 'Hello! How are you?' I said. 'Would you like me to sit down for a chat? I'm a hospital visitor.'

That's what I call meself, I thought.

'I visit people for a chat,' I said to her. 'Me name's Martha. What's yours?'

'Arabella, Lady Arabella. How do you do, Martha? What a wonderful idea! Oh, how lovely, you are so kind! Yes, please, do sit down, dear,' she beamed up at me, patting the chair beside her bed, wanting me to sit down.

We talked for hours, with me listening to all the great balls, parties, dinners and dances they had in the big house over on the south side of the Liffey. She even got to meet the King and Queen of England – the old one, not the new one – when she was eighteen, for her 'Coming Out', she called it.

But the other patients are very good to her. 'Here, Missus!' – they call every woman that, even though she's not married. 'Have them few aul biscuits.' 'Would you like a bit of that cake?' 'Take them aul oranges. I have too much stuff.' 'Them relations of mine are tryin to start me up in me own sweet shop judgin by the amount of stuff they're bringin me in.'

Then they clap eyes on me, too. 'Ah, it's too much for me. Here, love, come over to me, an I'll give you a bit of stuff for yourself. I want to clear out some of this stuff! Me locker's collapsin wit the weight!'

Yeah, they're very good to me, too. There's eating and drinking in the place and all the entertainment I could want.

Right, I'm starving. So, what have I got left for eating? Hmm. Two oranges and a couple of custard-cream biscuits. That won't get me far. And I need to save them for later. By tonight, when it gets really cold, I may be falling off me feet with the hunger!

I could get the lovely smell of chips pouring out of Caffolla's café up the street. Pity I have no money. I would love to get me jaws into a big plate a chips! So, what now? Think! A big bowl of steaming hot soup would be even better. Bewley's! I'm desperate. I better get moving. I want to get there before the dinner-hour rush starts or I won't get a seat.

2

I could smell the lovely scent of coffee before I even hit the place. I rushed in the door, getting the lovely blast of heat straight away. I stopped to look. Self-service downstairs? No! You need money for that. Waitress service upstairs? Me eyes peeled into the women busy rushing around carrying trays held high in the air. They were piled up with plates of steaming grub. Me belly rumbled and me mouth watered. They were wearing white frilly aprons over black skirts, with matching white-and-black striped caps on their heads. They had pencils stuck behind their ears and notebooks hanging out of their pockets. Waitress service! That's better.

I rushed in, then stopped, looking for the best spot to sit.

'Are you looking for a table, dear?'

'Yes, please, I am,' I said quietly to the grey haired woman with the hair coming out of her chin. I could feel meself rattling inside but hoping for the best.

She walked me over to a table and chairs against the wall beside the stairs leading down to the other eating place and the toilets. Good! I will be able to make me escape that way!

She handed me a white piece of paper showing what today's grub was. 'I'll be back for your order in a few minutes, love. OK?'

'Oh, yeah. Thanks very much, Missus.' Me eyes landed on the big silver thing sitting in the middle of the table. It was weighed down with cakes. You can help yerself to as many as you like then tell them how many you had. Gawd! Poor aul Mister Bewley! He's very trusting! Yeah, everyone talks about him. Mister Victor Bewley is a very good man they say. He does an awful lot for charity. He even gave all his workers a share in all the cafés! Whatever that means. I suppose everyone owns a bit of the place they work in. I heard he was a Quaker. I read about them down in the library. They believe in peace. They have nothing to do with rowdy people or get involved in wars. They used to shake at the mention of someone threatening them in the old days. Quake, shake – that's what it means! I read up all about it.

Hmm! Me eyes whipped back to what's on offer for the dinner.

'Are you ready to order?'

Me head shot up, seeing the waitress whipping out her notebook and grabbing the pencil from behind her ear. I took in a deep breath. 'Yeah, thanks. I'll have the kidney soup and rolls with plenty a butter. Then I'll have the, eh, shepherd's pie. No! Give me the lamb chops and peas and mash potatoes and gravy. Then after that—'

'Right! That will do to be getting on with!' she puffed, losing patience with me, snapping the notebook shut. 'I'll get you your soup,' she said, giving me half a smile.

'Thanks very much,' I said.

I pushed the plate away feeling I couldn't eat another cake even if I got paid for it. Me belly felt like a cement bloke.

'Everything OK?' the waitress asked, appearing back beside me, whipping out her notebook. 'Now let's see,' she said, tapping the list in her notebook with the pencil. 'Soup, rolls, butter, lamb chops, peas, mash, two helpings of apple tart and ice cream! Did you have any cakes?' she asked, letting her eyes light on the empty silver cake holder. Then she whipped them over to the old woman sitting in front of me. She was wearing a big hat with a fancy scarf wrapped around her shoulders. The face on her was so painted and powdered she must have put the stuff on with a shovel. Me and the waitress watched, waiting for her answer. She put down her knife after using it for the last half hour to cut her cake into tiny little bits, then chewing for so long I was blue in the face watching. I wanted to see when and if she would ever swallow it.

She kept us waiting as she wiped an imaginary crumb off her mouth with the linen napkin. Then she lifted her baldy eyebrows.

They were marked in with a brown pencil. That was to show where they used to be. Then she stretched her eyeballs and curled down her mouth, flicking her eyes shut, much as to say, No! I would not be so common as to make such a glutton of meself! Then she finally opened her mouth and we held our breath.

'I have partaken of one, my dear,' she announced, making my Lady Arabella sound common.

'Oh, yeah, thanks very much,' I said. 'That was lovely altogether. I, eh, had the rest a them.'

'How many was that?' the waitress said, looking down at me belly bulging outa me skirt. I had to open the zip!

'Eh, I think it was five.'

'Let me see,' she said, thinking. 'We generally put out a dozen. I think that cake stand was just put out when you sat down.'

'Was it?' I puffed, feeling shocked I had eaten so many.

She peeled off the bill and plastered it down on the table. 'Glad you enjoyed yourself!' she said, smiling. 'Now! Here's the bill,' then took off to serve more customers.

The place was filling up fast. People were crowding in, looking hungry and wanting somewhere to sit. Jaysus! How am I going to get outa here? I picked up the bill without looking at it. Me eyes were flying around the room, watching and waiting. I was looking to see if the aul fella, the manager in the suit, was standing outside the door. He watches like a hawk, seeing everything that goes on. His sharp eyes took everything in at once, missing nothing. He was busy rushing in and out, leading people by the arm then pointing them to a vacant seat. Fuck! He's looking over at me, seeing the two free chairs next to me. I kept me eyes down, pretending to be busy examining the batch of new cakes that just appeared on the table.

'Are you all right, dear?' the waitress asked, wanting me to get going.

'Oh, I'm grand, thanks,' I muttered, me insides rattled with the nerves.

Two women made for my table. I watched the waitress head over to take an order in the far corner, then me eyes flew to the aul fella in the suit. He was watching me and the two people heading over to the free chairs beside me. Then his head was out the door again, making to ask the next batch of people to wait for a seat.

Suddenly I was up standing on me feet and lifting me suitcase from under the table and making me way over for the back stairs. I walked down without rushing, then past the toilets and the self-service and up the other stairs. I stopped before I got to the top, then lifted me head to see where the aul fella in the suit was. The cash desk was just to me left. I would have to pass that. But the aul fella was over to me right, standing just outside the dining room. He was keeping the people on the queue moving in as soon as someone left and, more importantly, making sure they went to the cash desk to pay the bill.

I held me breath, moving back down the stairs again. He only has to catch one sight of me and I'm done for! I wouldn't be able to turn back. I would have to go to the cash desk and then the game would be up! Jaysus! Pity I ate so much! When they see the bill . . . Wonder how much it is? Oh, bloody hell! Me nerves are gone! I moved up again, seeing him disappear into the dining room.

Right! Now's the time to move. I was up the stairs, turning the corner, then walking past the cash desk with the woman looking out at me through her glass box. I kept me eyes peeled ahead like I hadn't a care in the world, and walked on, looking into the distance, feeling me back prickle. I was waiting for the shout and the tap on the shoulder. I was out the door, turning left down Grafton Street, walking quickly now, trying to get lost in the dinner-hour rush. I turned left on to Wicklow Street and sat meself down on the side entrance to Switzer's, managing at last to be able to let me breath out, knowing I was free and clear, for the moment.

Jaysus! Enough of that! I may be starving be times, maybe even most of the time, but that is pure stupidity! I got carried away and nearly ate them outa the place. My intention by going there was only to get meself a hot bowl of soup. That way, if I was caught, they might have let me go. But, oh no! I had to go and lose the run of meself. Jaysus! It goes to show, Martha, if you give yourself an inch, you take a mile. Hunger is one thing but that is bleedin sheer madness! Imagine the bill if I ended up in court! *Two pounds ten shillings, your honour! That is what the bill came to for the amount of food she ate!* Well, it must have been near it anyway. That place is very dear. No, let that be the end of it. One more time doing that, I would be right back where I started. No, better to starve than that. Robbing is only for mugs. I'm at rock bottom now, just living on me wits, with no money, no job, no place to live and not one soul in the world to turn to. So, there's only one place I can go now and that's up!

'Would you move, please!'

I stood up, grabbing me suitcase outa the way, looking at the woman standing well back, waiting for me to give her plenty a room.

'Sorry, Missus,' I muttered, giving her a bit of a smile. She ignored me, just lifted her face and turned away, then started sniffing air up through the two narrow slits punched into the middle of her hatchet face. Then she rushed past, pulling her big fur coat well away from me, giving me a smack in the face with the big black leather handbag swinging on her arm. I rubbed me cheek, waiting for her to say sorry. But she was gone! Straight through the door leaving it swinging open. Then she stopped dead in the middle of the shop, making the big fur hat on her mallet head fly in all directions because she was so worked up about buying herself something she didn't know where to start first.

I could still feel the stinging in me cheek. Suddenly I put me head in the door, letting out a roar. 'Dyin lookin, aul cow! I hope you die roarin! Yeah!' I muttered. 'An I hope the pickpockets get their hands on all yer money!' I sniffed, rubbing me cheek. Bleedin hell! The cheek a her treating me like dirt. You wait, Missus! One day I will have the likes of you rushing and gushing all over me, wanting to know me. I will be somebody then. Because I am going to make it right to the bleedin top! I'll be the best at whatever I do. I don't care how long it takes me. But one day I am going to walk through this door here wearing a fur coat and a matching fur hat, then have them carry all me boxes over to Brown Thomas for another spot a shopping. Then they can deliver all me parcels to me mansion in its own grounds! It may take me years and years, I may starve, but I will get there. 'Yeah! So fuck off!' I muttered, nearly crying with the rage as I stood just inside the door, watching them all rushing around, trying to outdo each other spending money. One thinking they are better than the next.

Then I spotted the store detective flying her head in my direction. She stood watching, with her little beady eyes taking me in from head to toe. I moved back. Fuck! Them aul fuckers are still on the mooch. I remember that one. But she never got her hands on me! I was always too wide awake for her. But they're great gas to watch. Sneaking around the shop holding tight to their handbags, pretending to be shoppers. Then when they get the sniff of a robber, the chase is on, with you flying ahead, then stopping to see where they are before dropping something into your shopping bag then pretending to be intent on looking at something. They do the same thing. The pair of us giving sneaky looks to see what the other one is doing. I used to double back on them then come up behind them when they were peeping around the corner, intent on trying to spot where you'd gone without them being seen themself.

Yeah! These days that's great gas. I can have many happy hours giving them the run around, knowing I don't have to rob any more. Bleedin gobshites. They're not that good at the job. I can spot a robber a mile away just by seeing the shifty look on their face. You can smell the fear! Only last week up in Dunnes Stores, I came face to face with an aul one after wrapping half the shop around her body. She got an awful fright when our eyes locked on each other. There she was, hiding herself under all the coats in the back corner of the shop. I felt sorry for her. She probably had ten kids waiting at home, starving with the hunger. The husband was probably drinking all the money and wouldn't work in a good fit! I could tell by looking at her she was desperate.

'The store detective is on my tail,' I muttered.

The poor woman's eyes nearly leapt outa her head, whipping it around so fast, trying to spot them. I gave a big wink to the detective, grinning like mad, then headed meself over in her direction. The detective got such a fright I was on to her, she turned her back, pretending to be examining the ladies' jumpers. The poor aul woman spotted her too and took off in an awful hurry, shuffling like mad, desperate to make it out the door but getting herself slowed up with the amount of stuff weighing her down. Meanwhile the detective was raging! Now she knew she wouldn't get the glory of catching me robbing because I was on to her. While the real robbers had been cleaning the place out! Yeah, culchie eejits! They're not wide enough for us Dubliners.

Right! I looked around, shaking meself, then let out a big breath, thinking it's getting late. It's definitely time I got moving. Now, where will I go to get meself changed into me good clothes? I better wash me face and clean meself up. But I'm not too bad. I had that grand bath yesterday over in the hospital. OK! I'll head down to the quays. There's a nice hotel there just opposite the bus I need to take. Bus? I haven't got the fare! Never mind. They can't throw you off if you give them your name and address. Any address. I'll make up one. Now, what will I tell this aul one looking for the mother's help? Ah, play it by ear, let her do the talking. Lucky for me I spotted it in that newspaper dumped on the ground. I even managed to get tuppence for the phone call outa that culchie in the GPO. 'Ah, here, keep the thruppence,' he said after getting fed up waiting for me rooting in me coat pocket looking for the thruppenny bit I didn't have.

'Are you sure, Mister?' I said, pushing me luck! Sometimes I can be a right gobshite!